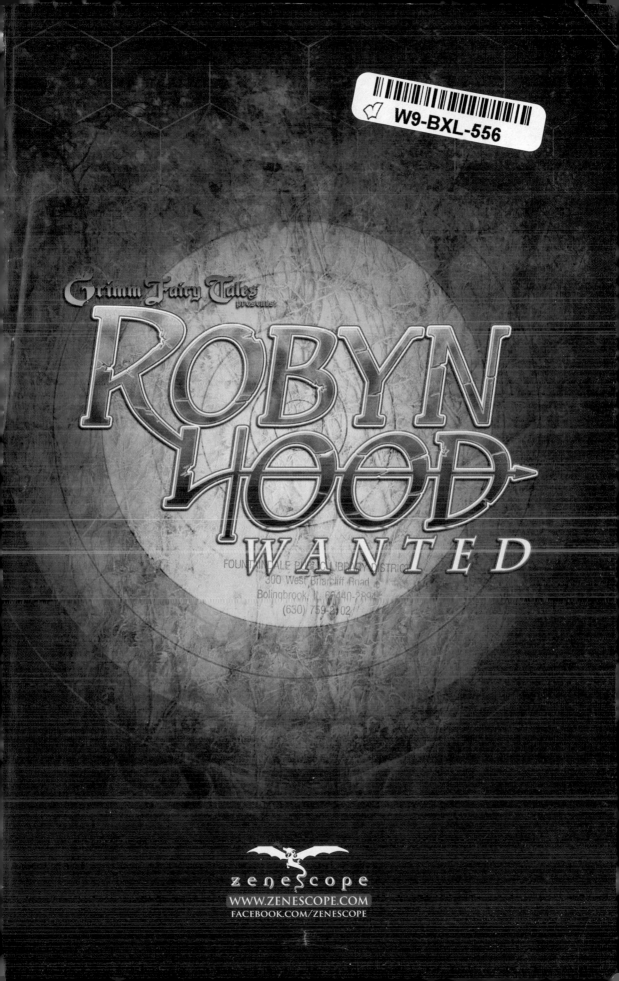

Grimm Fairy Tales presents:

# ROBYN HOOD
# WANTED

zene/cope
WWW.ZENESCOPE.COM
FACEBOOK.COM/ZENESCOPE

GRIMM FAIRY TALES CREATED BY
JOE BRUSHA AND RALPH TEDESCO

Grimm Fairy Tales

# ROBYN HOOD
## WANTED

STORY
**JOE BRUSHA
RAVEN GREGORY
RALPH TEDESCO
PAT SHAND**

WRITER
**PAT SHAND**

ART DIRECTOR
**ANTHONY SPAY**

TRADE DESIGN
**CHRISTOPHER COTE**

EDITOR
**RALPH TEDESCO**

THIS VOLUME REPRINTS THE COMIC SERIES
GRIMM FAIRY TALES PRESENTS ROBYN
HOOD: WANTED #1-5 PUBLISHED BY
ZENESCOPE ENTERTAINMENT.

WWW.ZENESCOPE.COM

FIRST EDITION, OCTOBER 2013
ISBN: 978-1-939683-04-5

zenescope
WWW.ZENESCOPE.COM
FACEBOOK.COM/ZENESCOPE

**ZENESCOPE ENTERTAINMENT, INC.**
**Joe Brusha** • President & Chief Creative Officer
**Ralph Tedesco** • Editor-in-Chief
**Jennifer Bermel** • Director of Licensing & Business Development
**Raven Gregory** • Executive Editor
**Anthony Spay** • Art Director
**Christopher Cote** • Senior Designer/Production Manager
**Dave Franchini** • Direct Market Sales & Customer Service
**Stephen Haberman** • Marketing Manager

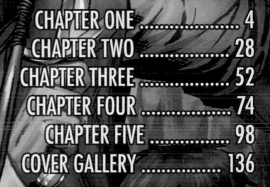

Grimm Fairy Tales presents

# ROBYN HOOD
## WANTED

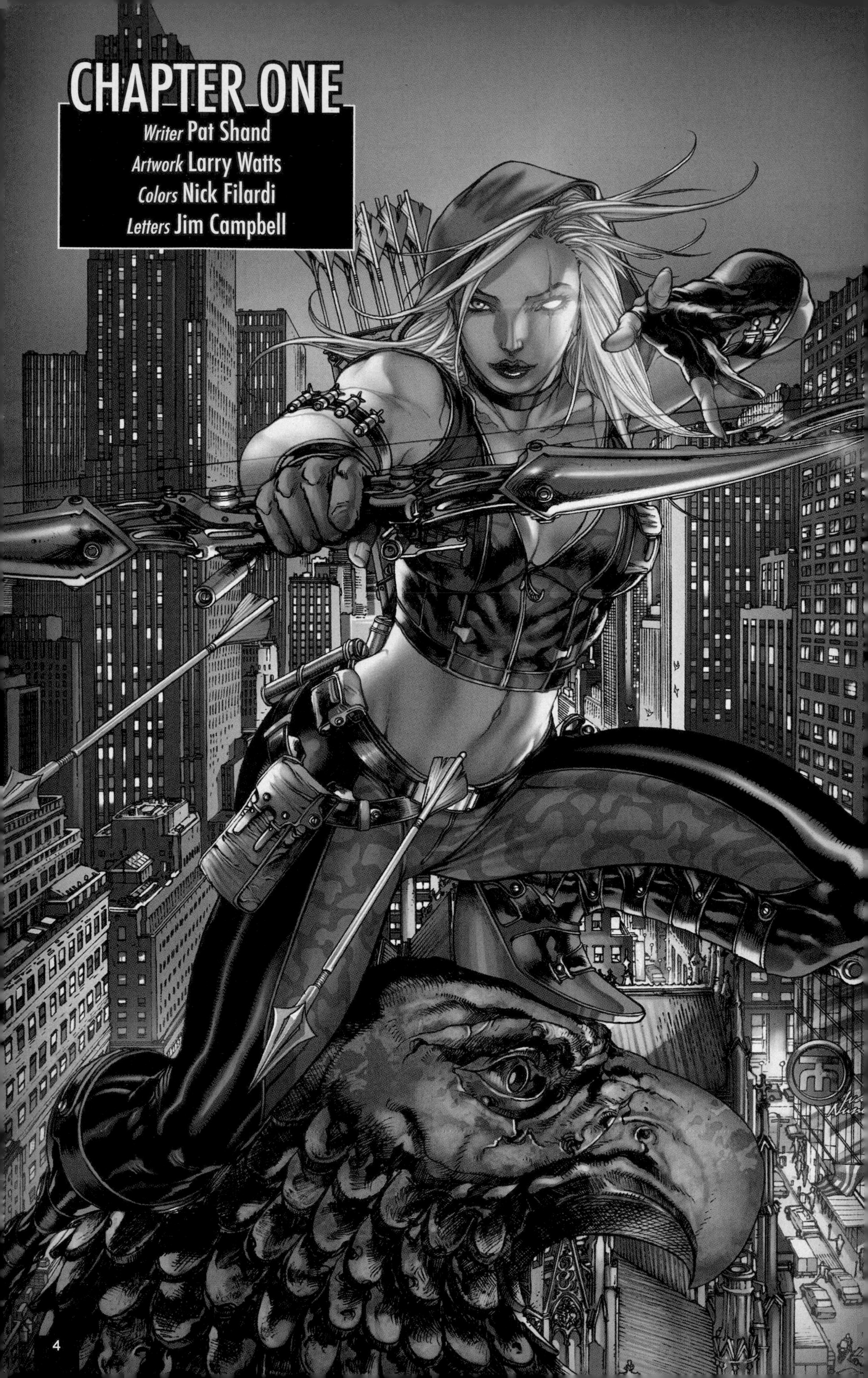
CHAPTER ONE
Writer Pat Shand
Artwork Larry Watts
Colors Nick Filardi
Letters Jim Campbell

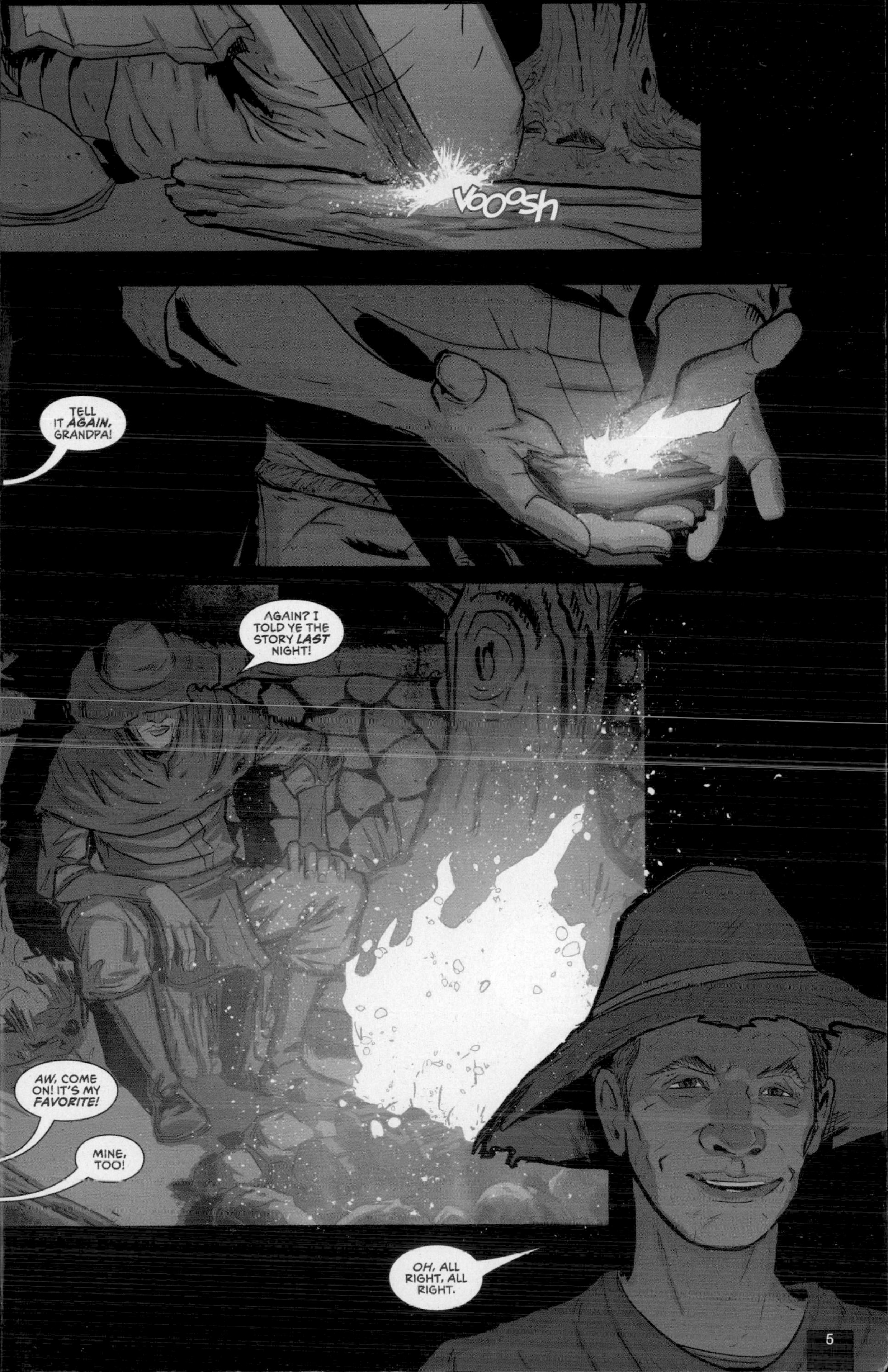
VOOOSH
TELL IT AGAIN, GRANDPA!
AGAIN? I TOLD YE THE STORY LAST NIGHT!
AW, COME ON! IT'S MY FAVORITE!
MINE, TOO!
OH, ALL RIGHT, ALL RIGHT.

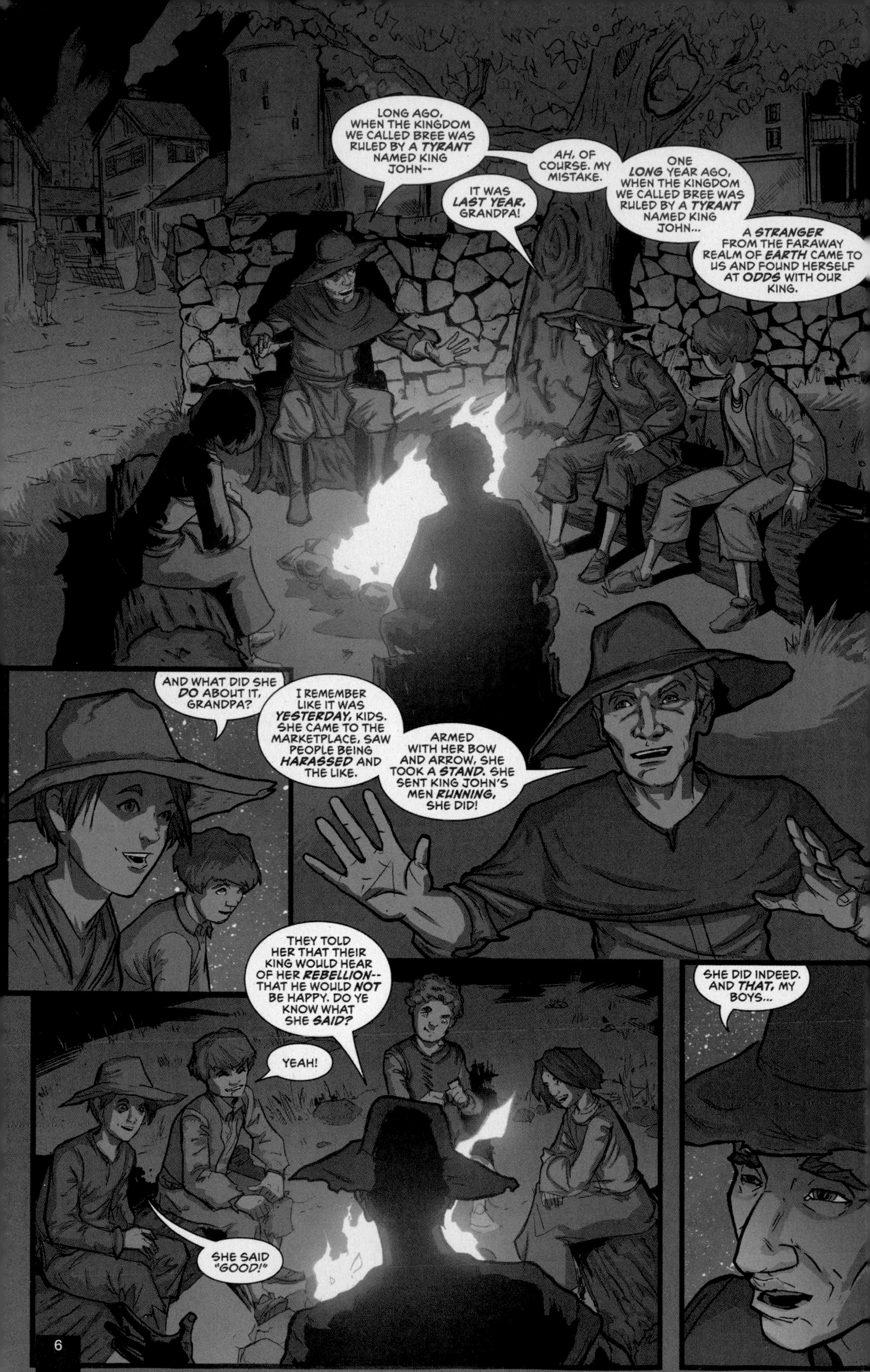

LONG AGO, WHEN THE KINGDOM WE CALLED BREE WAS RULED BY A TYRANT NAMED KING JOHN--
IT WAS LAST YEAR, GRANDPA!
AH, OF COURSE. MY MISTAKE.
ONE LONG YEAR AGO, WHEN THE KINGDOM WE CALLED BREE WAS RULED BY A TYRANT NAMED KING JOHN...
A STRANGER FROM THE FARAWAY REALM OF EARTH CAME TO US AND FOUND HERSELF AT ODDS WITH OUR KING.
AND WHAT DID SHE DO ABOUT IT, GRANDPA?
I REMEMBER LIKE IT WAS YESTERDAY, KIDS. SHE CAME TO THE MARKETPLACE, SAW PEOPLE BEING HARASSED AND THE LIKE.
ARMED WITH HER BOW AND ARROW, SHE TOOK A STAND. SHE SENT KING JOHN'S MEN RUNNING, SHE DID!
THEY TOLD HER THAT THEIR KING WOULD HEAR OF HER REBELLION--THAT HE WOULD NOT BE HAPPY. DO YE KNOW WHAT SHE SAID?
YEAH!
SHE SAID "GOOD!"
SHE DID INDEED. AND THAT, MY BOYS...

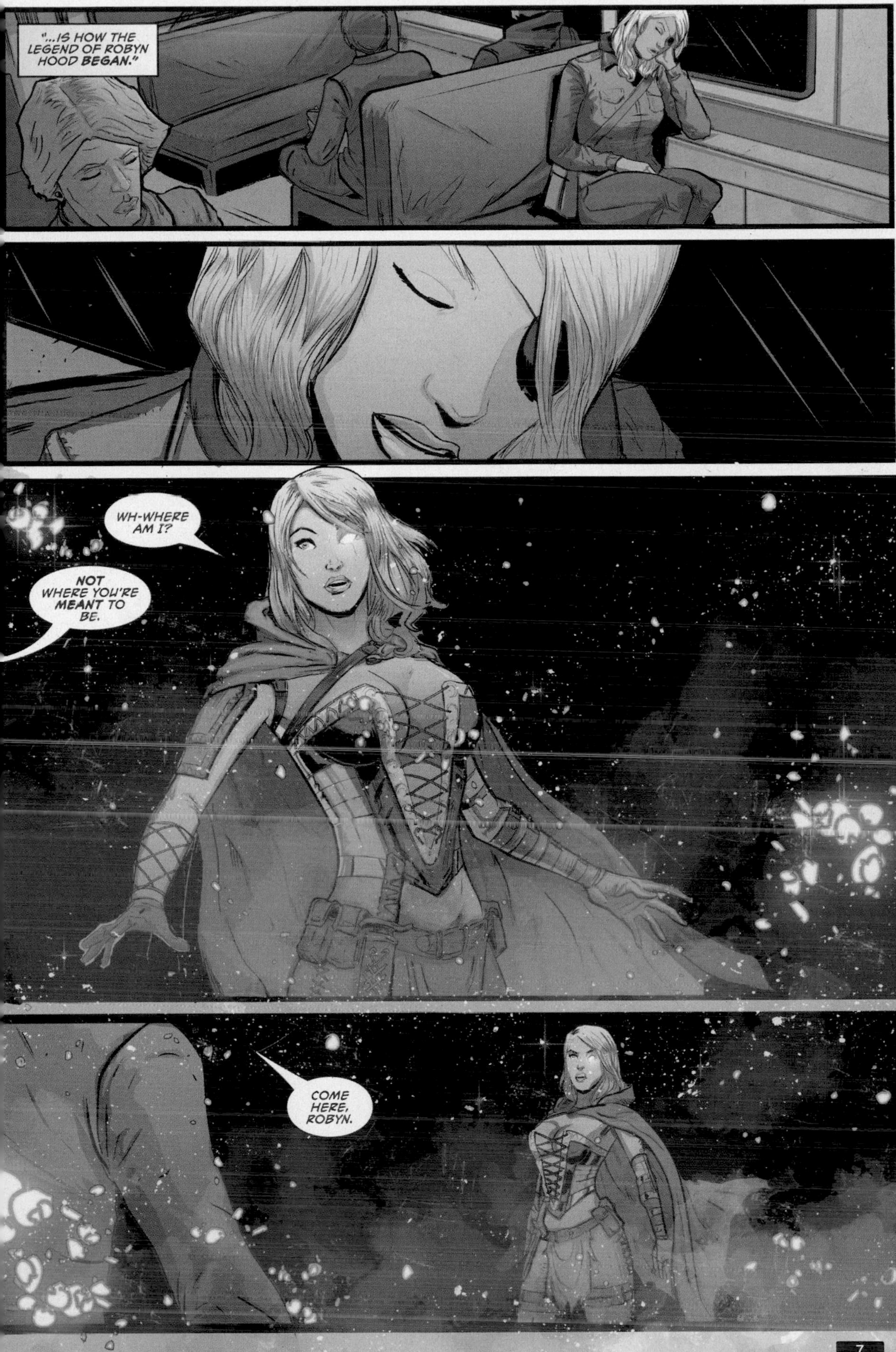
"...IS HOW THE LEGEND OF ROBYN HOOD BEGAN."
WH-WHERE AM I?
NOT WHERE YOU'RE MEANT TO BE.
COME HERE, ROBYN.

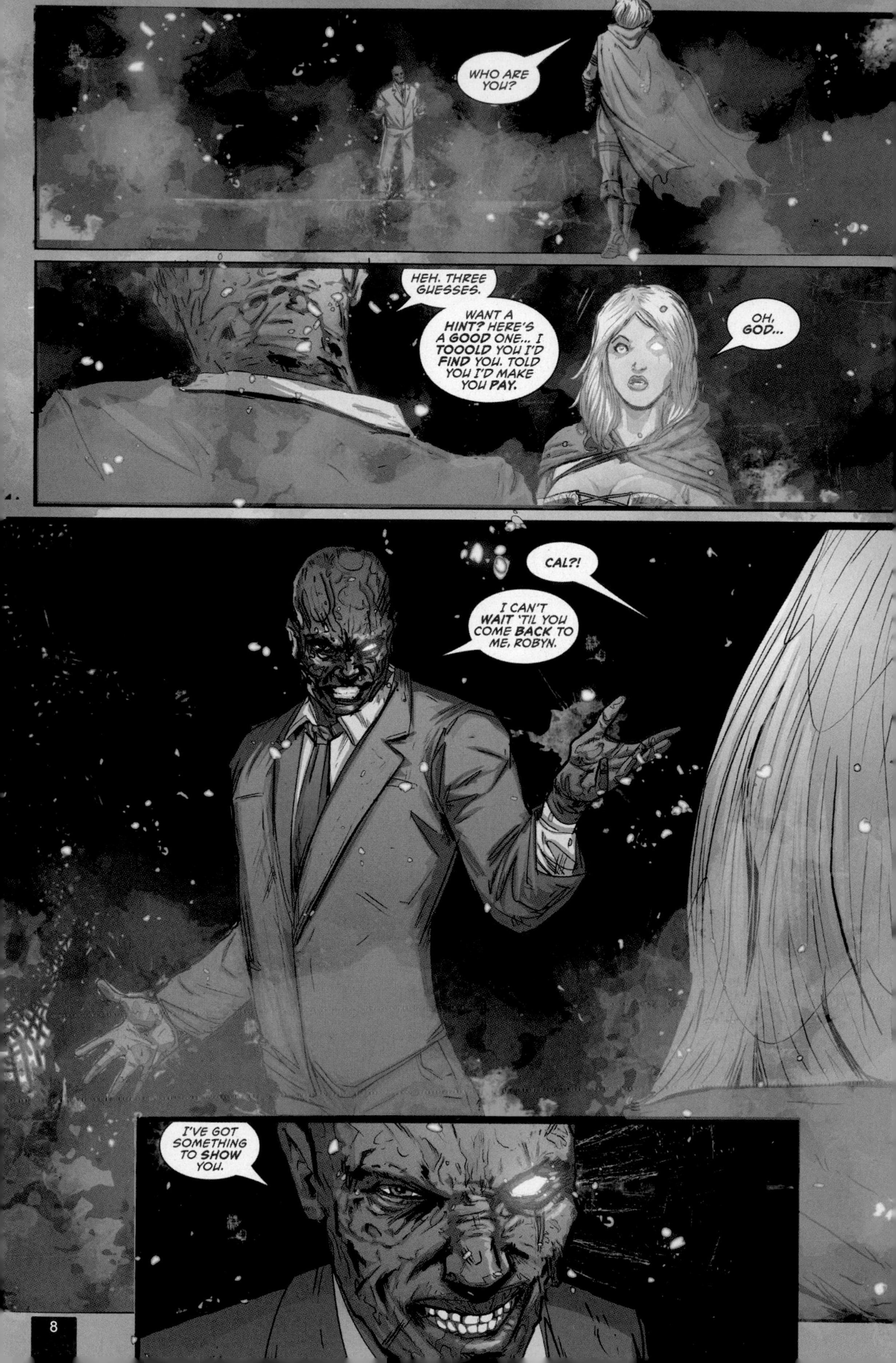
WHO ARE YOU?
HEH. THREE GUESSES.
WANT A HINT? HERE'S A GOOD ONE... I TOOOLD YOU I'D FIND YOU. TOLD YOU I'D MAKE YOU PAY.
OH, GOD...
CAL?!
I CAN'T WAIT 'TIL YOU COME BACK TO ME, ROBYN.
I'VE GOT SOMETHING TO SHOW YOU.

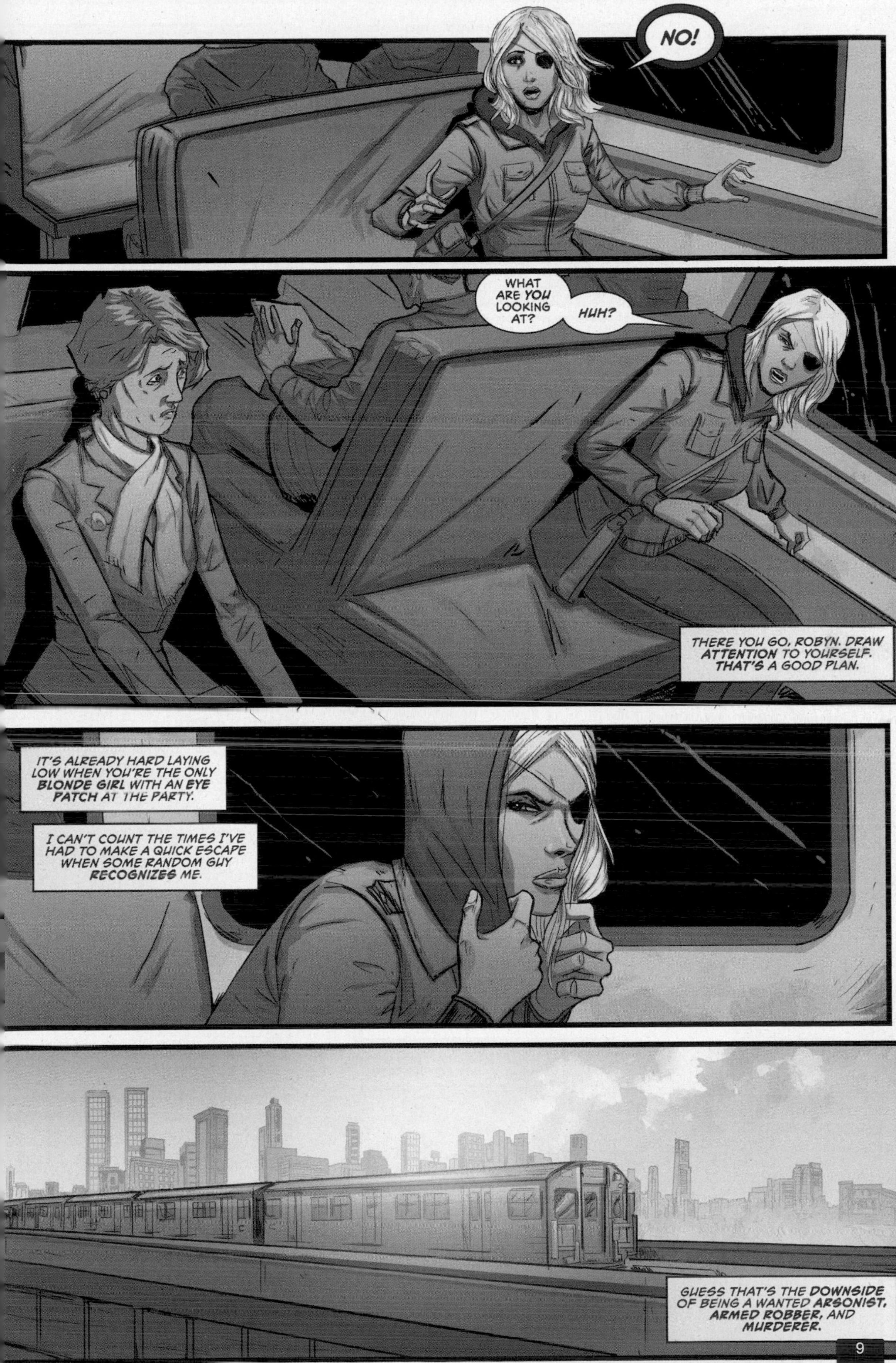
NO!
WHAT ARE YOU LOOKING AT?
HUH?
THERE YOU GO, ROBYN. DRAW ATTENTION TO YOURSELF. THAT'S A GOOD PLAN.
IT'S ALREADY HARD LAYING LOW WHEN YOU'RE THE ONLY BLONDE GIRL WITH AN EYE PATCH AT THE PARTY.
I CAN'T COUNT THE TIMES I'VE HAD TO MAKE A QUICK ESCAPE WHEN SOME RANDOM GUY RECOGNIZES ME.
GUESS THAT'S THE DOWNSIDE OF BEING A WANTED ARSONIST, ARMED ROBBER, AND MURDERER.

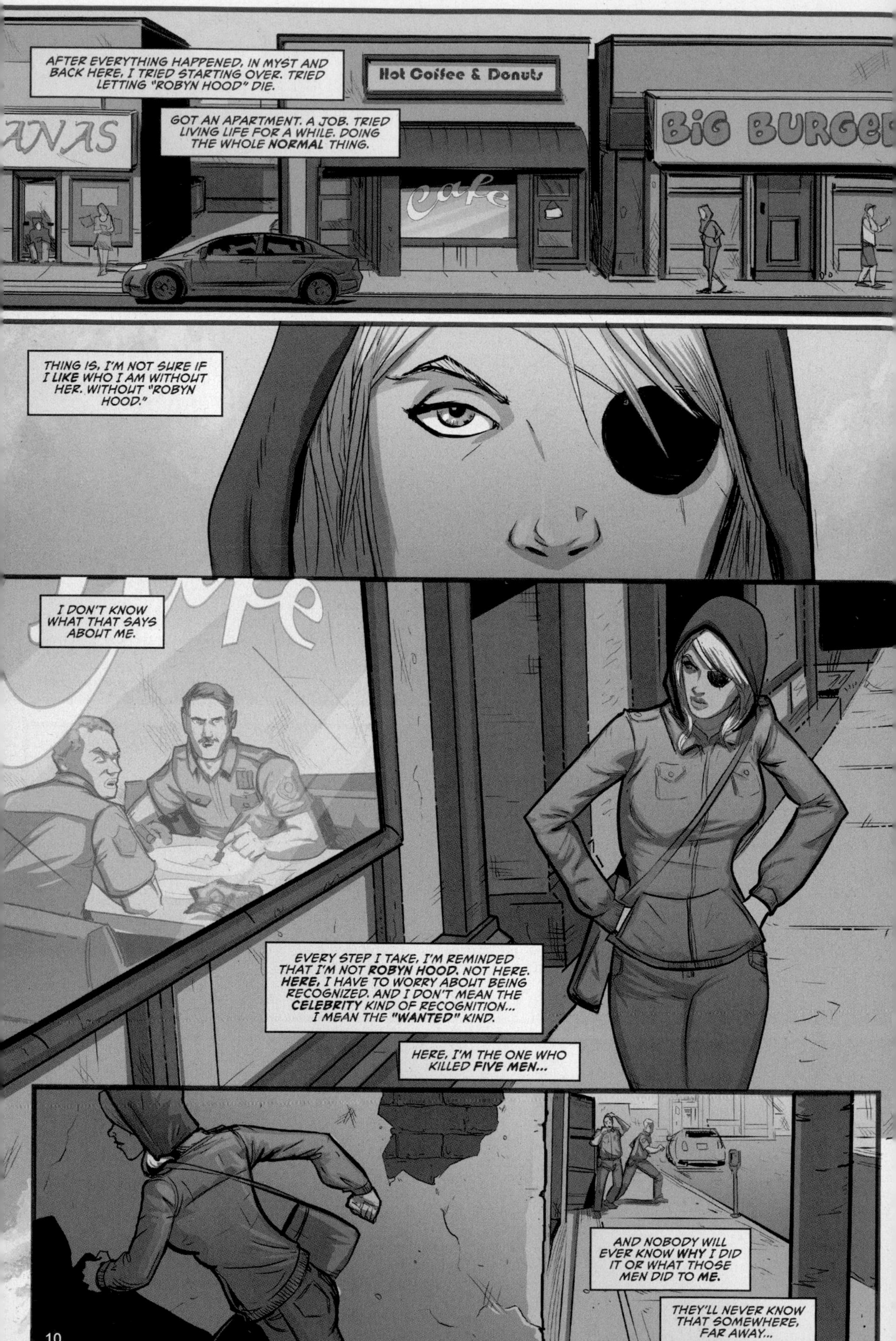
AFTER EVERYTHING HAPPENED, IN MYST AND BACK HERE, I TRIED STARTING OVER. TRIED LETTING "ROBYN HOOD" DIE.
Hot Coffee & Donuts
ANAS
GOT AN APARTMENT. A JOB. TRIED LIVING LIFE FOR A WHILE. DOING THE WHOLE NORMAL THING.
BiG BURGER
Cafe
THING IS, I'M NOT SURE IF I LIKE WHO I AM WITHOUT HER. WITHOUT "ROBYN HOOD."
I DON'T KNOW WHAT THAT SAYS ABOUT ME.
EVERY STEP I TAKE, I'M REMINDED THAT I'M NOT ROBYN HOOD. NOT HERE. HERE, I HAVE TO WORRY ABOUT BEING RECOGNIZED. AND I DON'T MEAN THE CELEBRITY KIND OF RECOGNITION... I MEAN THE "WANTED" KIND.
HERE, I'M THE ONE WHO KILLED FIVE MEN...
AND NOBODY WILL EVER KNOW WHY I DID IT OR WHAT THOSE MEN DID TO ME.
THEY'LL NEVER KNOW THAT SOMEWHERE, FAR AWAY...

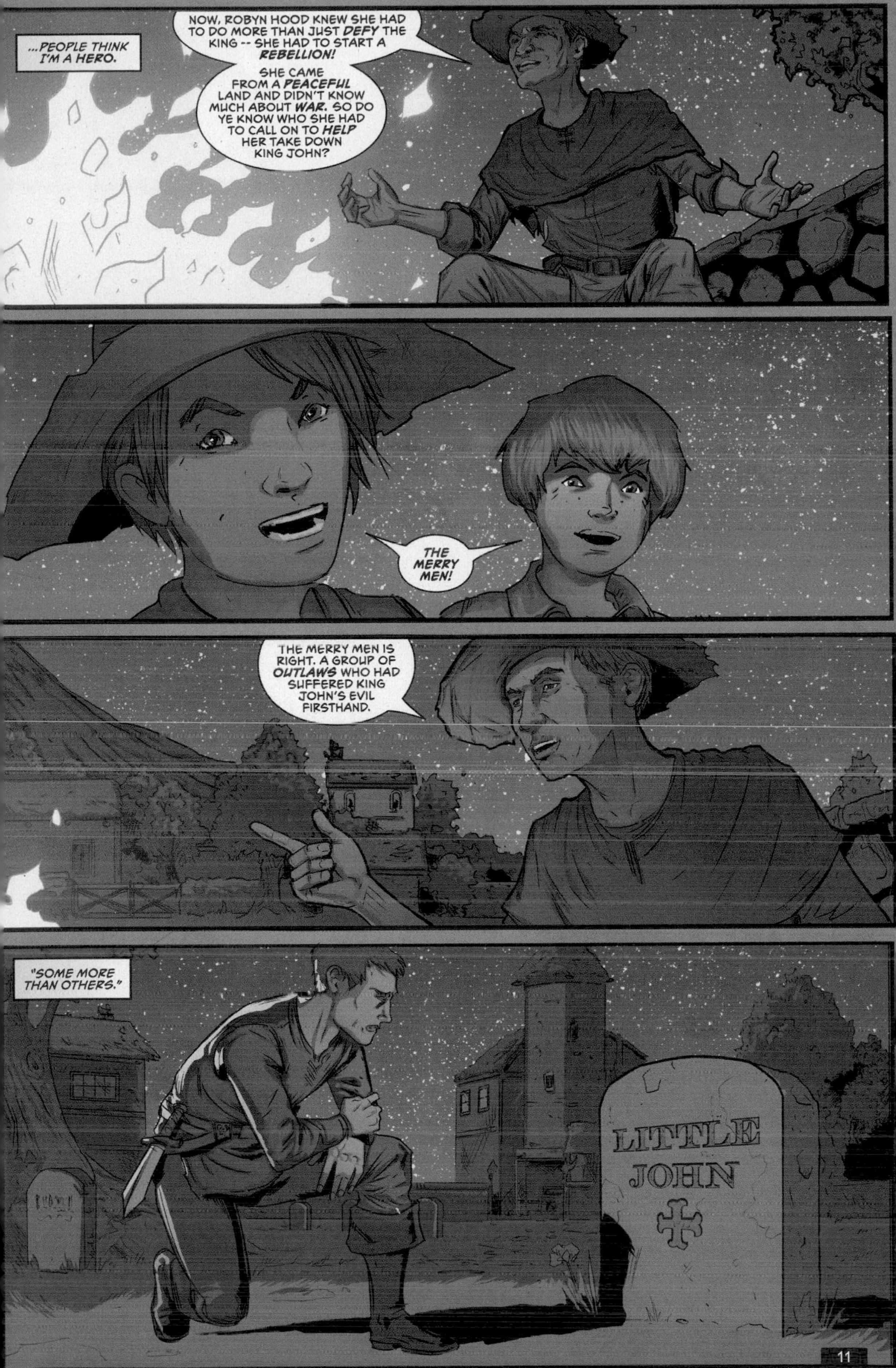

...PEOPLE THINK I'M A HERO.
NOW, ROBYN HOOD KNEW SHE HAD TO DO MORE THAN JUST DEFY THE KING -- SHE HAD TO START A REBELLION!
SHE CAME FROM A PEACEFUL LAND AND DIDN'T KNOW MUCH ABOUT WAR. SO DO YE KNOW WHO SHE HAD TO CALL ON TO HELP HER TAKE DOWN KING JOHN?
THE MERRY MEN!
THE MERRY MEN IS RIGHT. A GROUP OF OUTLAWS WHO HAD SUFFERED KING JOHN'S EVIL FIRSTHAND.
"SOME MORE THAN OTHERS."
LITTLE JOHN

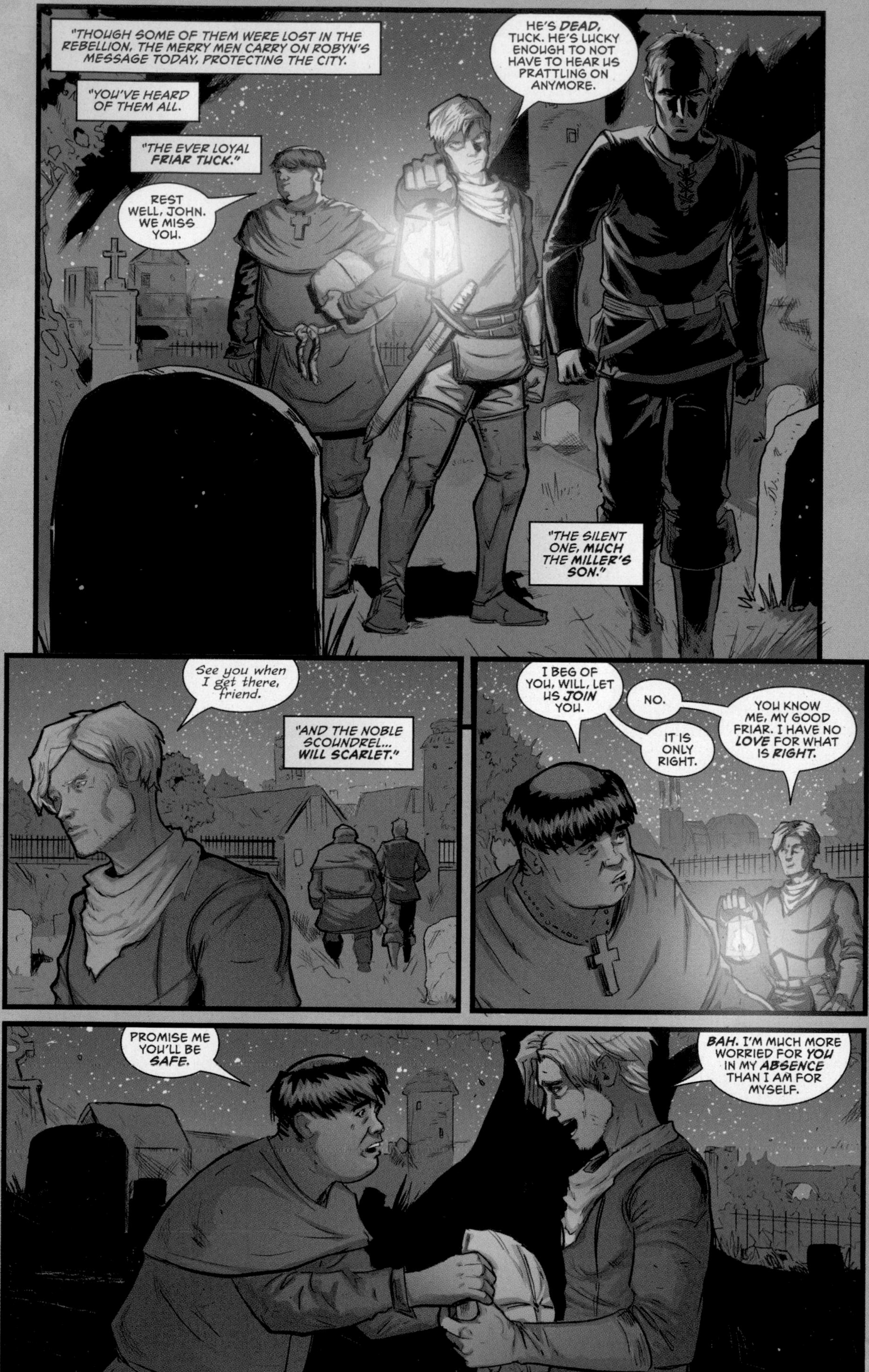
"THOUGH SOME OF THEM WERE LOST IN THE REBELLION, THE MERRY MEN CARRY ON ROBYN'S MESSAGE TODAY, PROTECTING THE CITY.
"YOU'VE HEARD OF THEM ALL.
"THE EVER LOYAL FRIAR TUCK."
REST WELL, JOHN. WE MISS YOU.
HE'S DEAD, TUCK. HE'S LUCKY ENOUGH TO NOT HAVE TO HEAR US PRATTLING ON ANYMORE.
"THE SILENT ONE, MUCH THE MILLER'S SON."
See you when I get there, friend.
"AND THE NOBLE SCOUNDREL... WILL SCARLET."
I BEG OF YOU, WILL, LET US JOIN YOU.
NO.
IT IS ONLY RIGHT.
YOU KNOW ME, MY GOOD FRIAR. I HAVE NO LOVE FOR WHAT IS RIGHT.
PROMISE ME YOU'LL BE SAFE.
BAH. I'M MUCH MORE WORRIED FOR YOU IN MY ABSENCE THAN I AM FOR MYSELF.

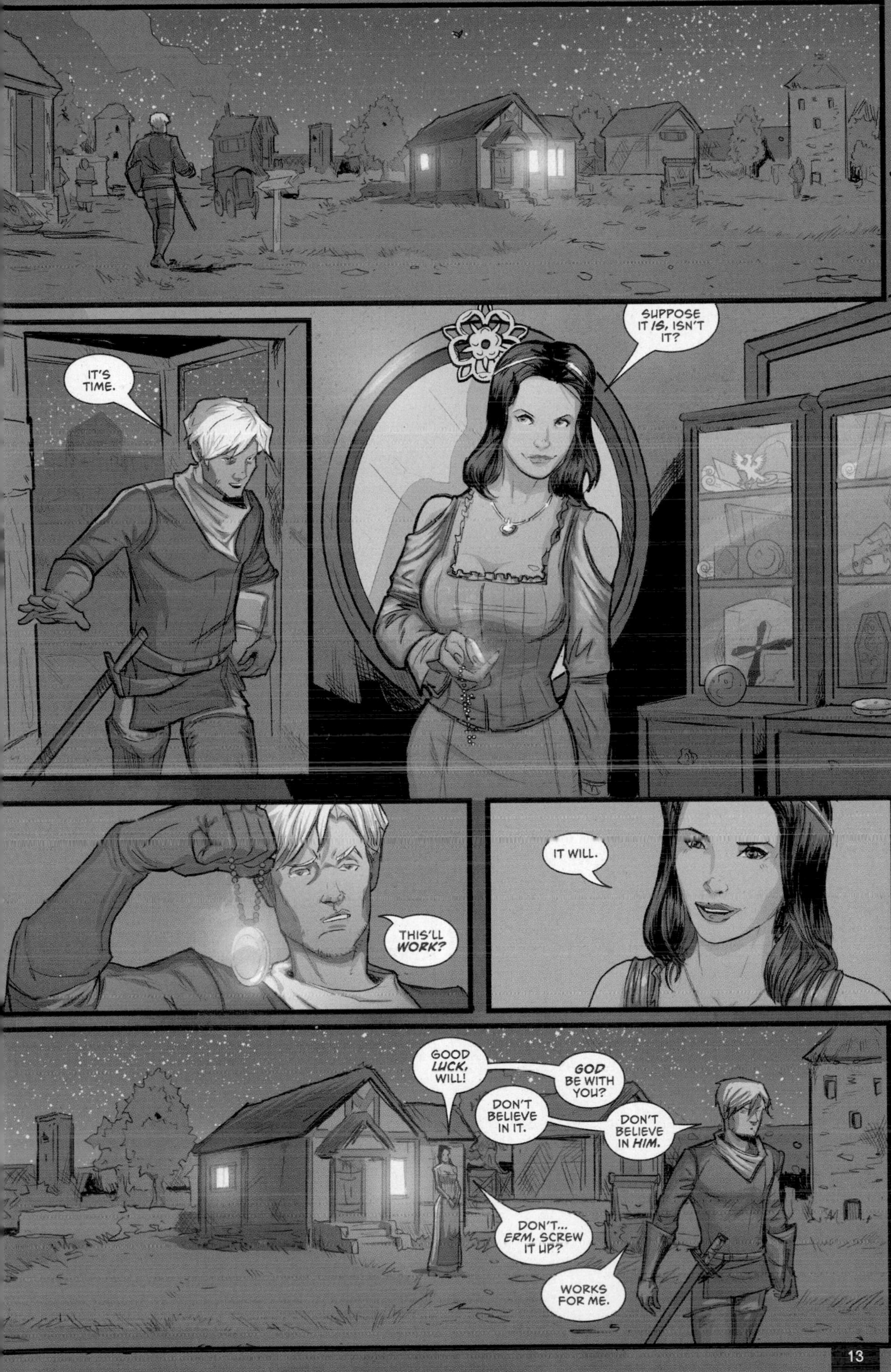
IT'S TIME.
SUPPOSE IT IS, ISN'T IT?
THIS'LL WORK?
IT WILL.
GOOD LUCK, WILL!
GOD BE WITH YOU?
DON'T BELIEVE IN IT.
DON'T BELIEVE IN HIM.
DON'T... ERM, SCREW IT UP?
WORKS FOR ME.

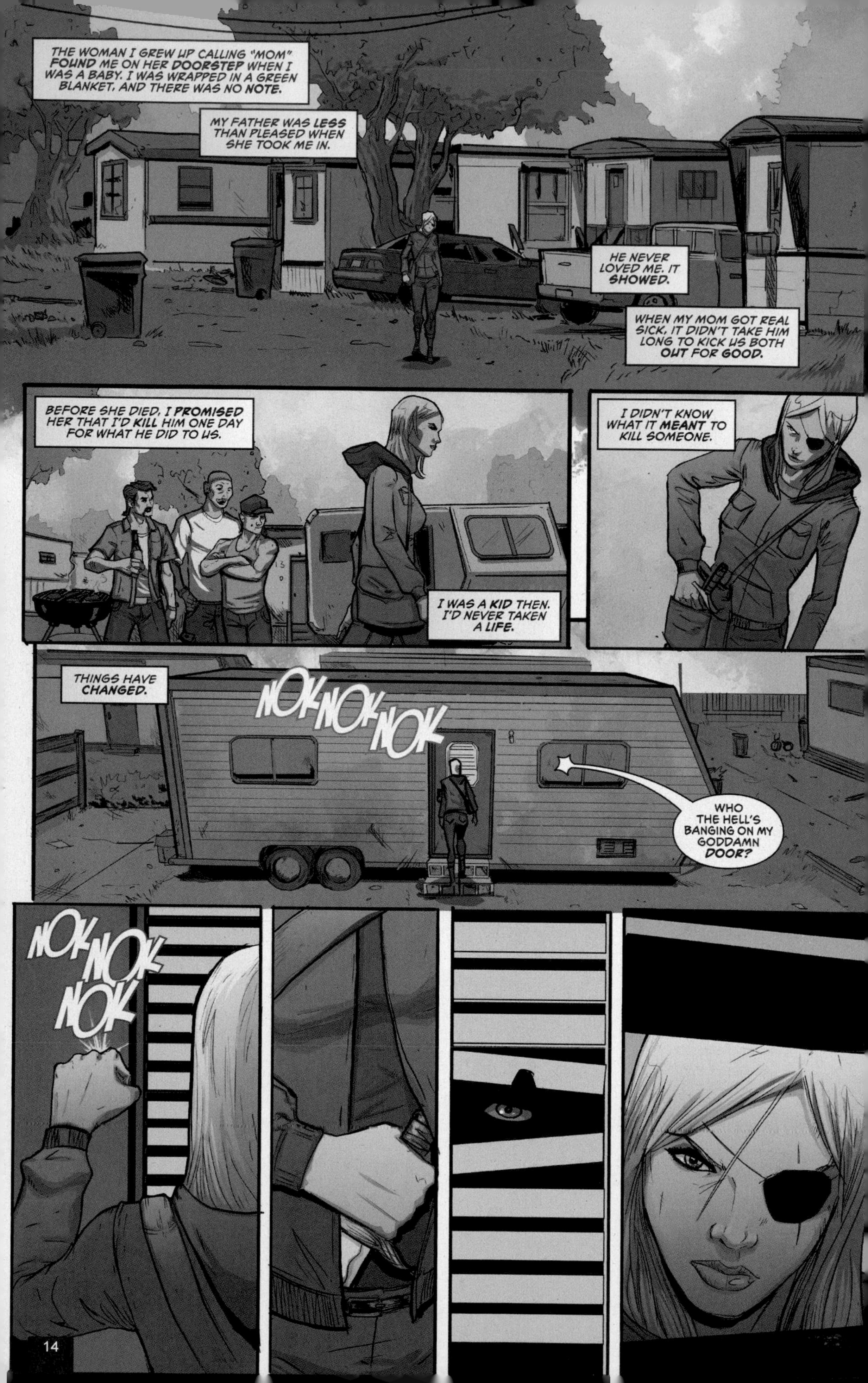
THE WOMAN I GREW UP CALLING "MOM" FOUND ME ON HER DOORSTEP WHEN I WAS A BABY. I WAS WRAPPED IN A GREEN BLANKET, AND THERE WAS NO NOTE.
MY FATHER WAS LESS THAN PLEASED WHEN SHE TOOK ME IN.
HE NEVER LOVED ME. IT SHOWED.
WHEN MY MOM GOT REAL SICK, IT DIDN'T TAKE HIM LONG TO KICK US BOTH OUT FOR GOOD.
BEFORE SHE DIED, I PROMISED HER THAT I'D KILL HIM ONE DAY FOR WHAT HE DID TO US.
I WAS A KID THEN. I'D NEVER TAKEN A LIFE.
I DIDN'T KNOW WHAT IT MEANT TO KILL SOMEONE.
THINGS HAVE CHANGED.
NOK NOK NOK
WHO THE HELL'S BANGING ON MY GODDAMN DOOR?
NOK NOK NOK

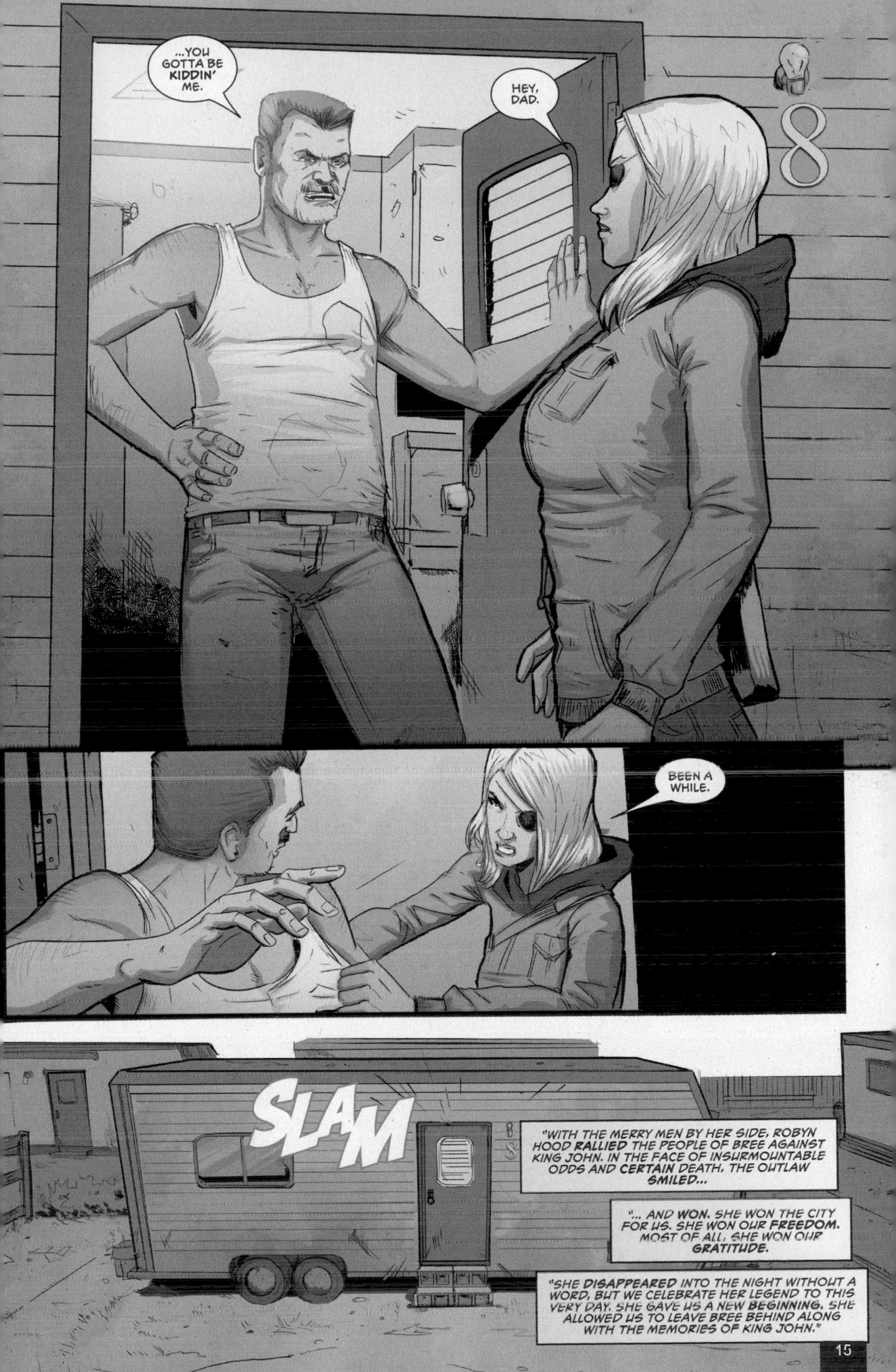
...YOU GOTTA BE KIDDIN' ME.
HEY, DAD.
8
BEEN A WHILE.
SLAM
8
"WITH THE MERRY MEN BY HER SIDE, ROBYN HOOD RALLIED THE PEOPLE OF BREE AGAINST KING JOHN. IN THE FACE OF INSURMOUNTABLE ODDS AND CERTAIN DEATH, THE OUTLAW SMILED...
"... AND WON. SHE WON THE CITY FOR US. SHE WON OUR FREEDOM. MOST OF ALL, SHE WON OUR GRATITUDE.
"SHE DISAPPEARED INTO THE NIGHT WITHOUT A WORD, BUT WE CELEBRATE HER LEGEND TO THIS VERY DAY. SHE GAVE US A NEW BEGINNING. SHE ALLOWED US TO LEAVE BREE BEHIND ALONG WITH THE MEMORIES OF KING JOHN."

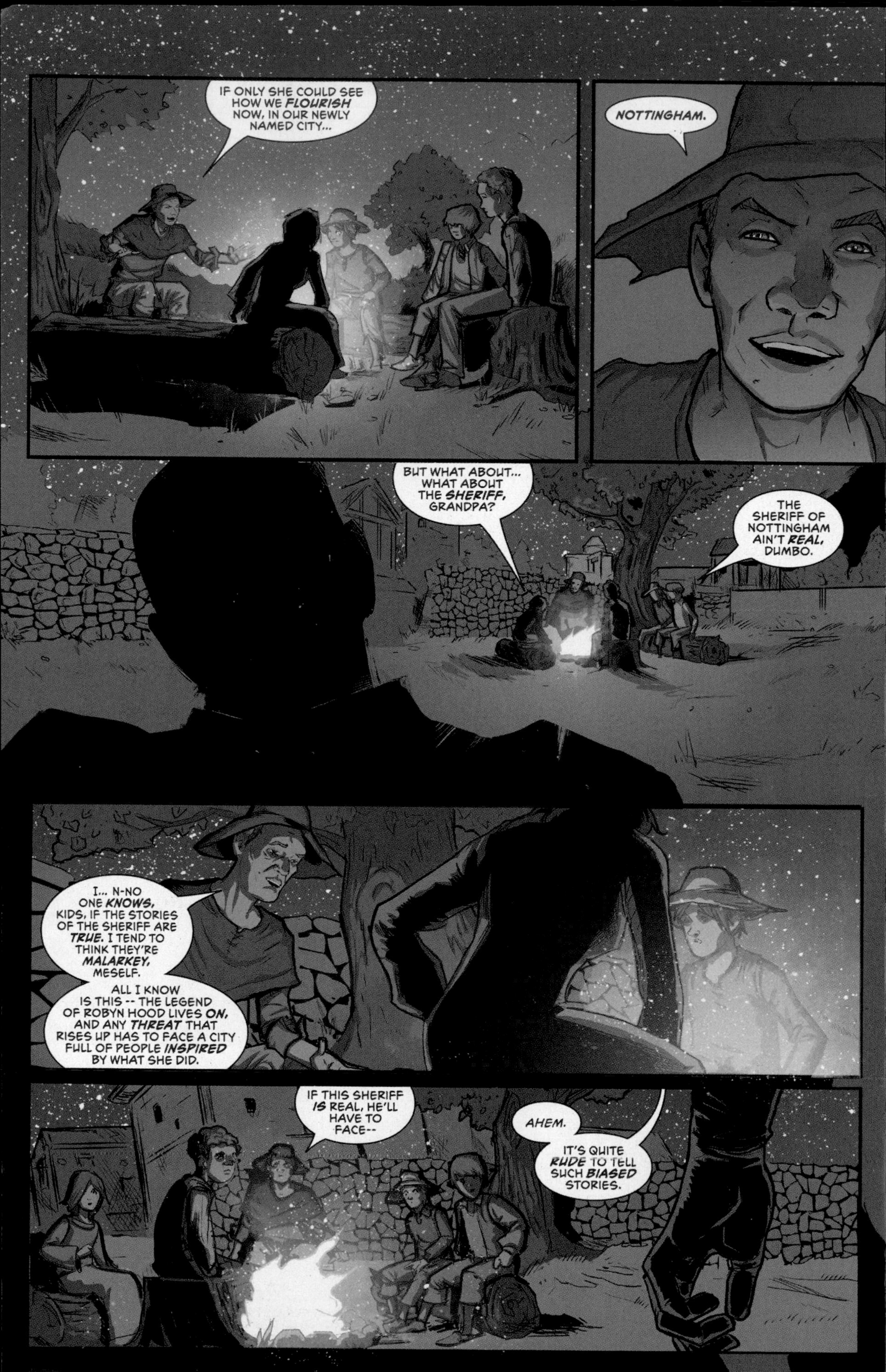
IF ONLY SHE COULD SEE HOW WE FLOURISH NOW, IN OUR NEWLY NAMED CITY...
NOTTINGHAM.
BUT WHAT ABOUT... WHAT ABOUT THE SHERIFF, GRANDPA?
THE SHERIFF OF NOTTINGHAM AIN'T REAL, DUMBO.
I... N-NO ONE KNOWS, KIDS, IF THE STORIES OF THE SHERIFF ARE TRUE. I TEND TO THINK THEY'RE MALARKEY, MESELF.
ALL I KNOW IS THIS -- THE LEGEND OF ROBYN HOOD LIVES ON, AND ANY THREAT THAT RISES UP HAS TO FACE A CITY FULL OF PEOPLE INSPIRED BY WHAT SHE DID.
IF THIS SHERIFF IS REAL, HE'LL HAVE TO FACE--
AHEM.
IT'S QUITE RUDE TO TELL SUCH BIASED STORIES.

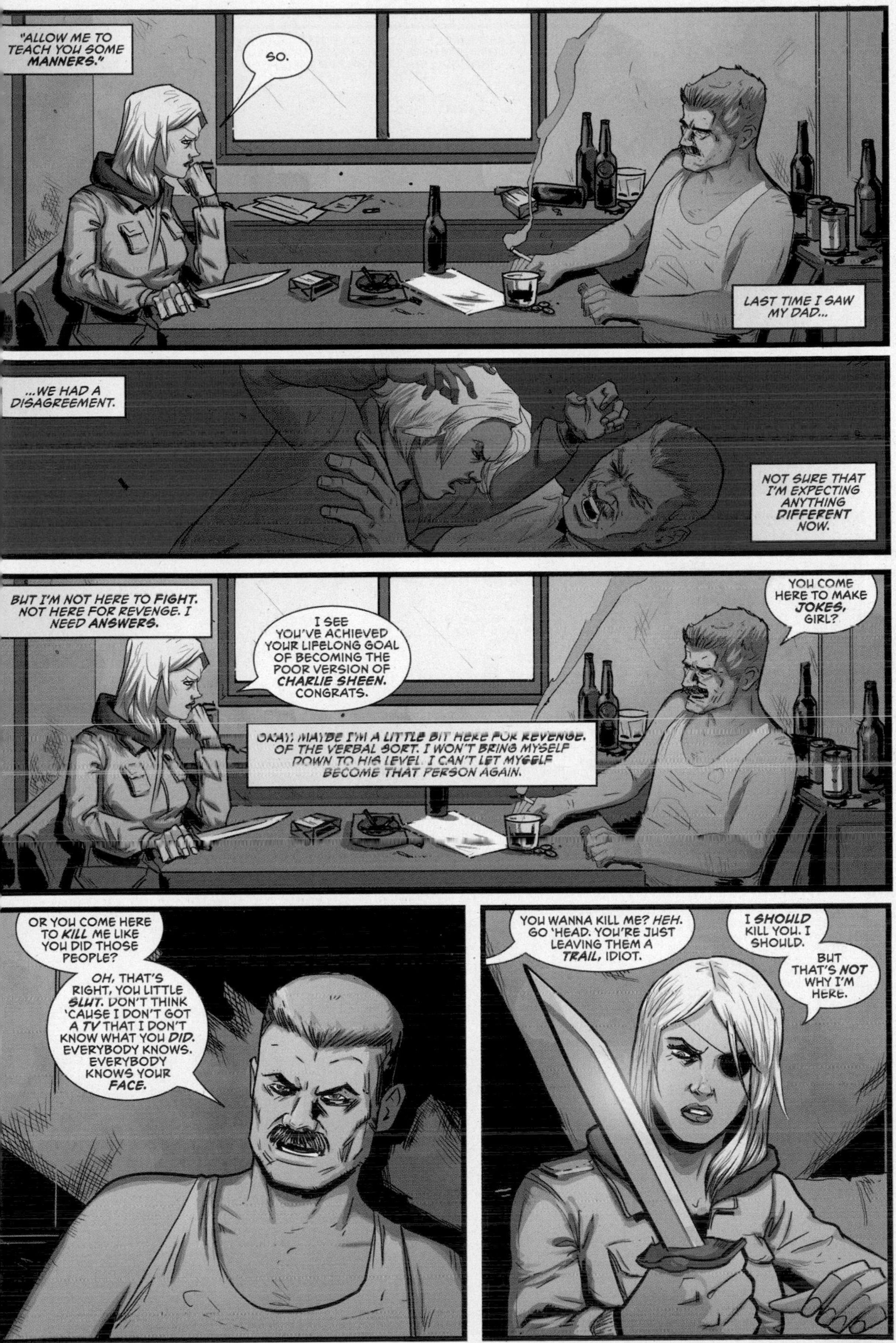
"ALLOW ME TO TEACH YOU SOME MANNERS."
SO.
LAST TIME I SAW MY DAD...
...WE HAD A DISAGREEMENT.
NOT SURE THAT I'M EXPECTING ANYTHING DIFFERENT NOW.
BUT I'M NOT HERE TO FIGHT. NOT HERE FOR REVENGE. I NEED ANSWERS.
I SEE YOU'VE ACHIEVED YOUR LIFELONG GOAL OF BECOMING THE POOR VERSION OF CHARLIE SHEEN. CONGRATS.
YOU COME HERE TO MAKE JOKES, GIRL?
OKAY, MAYBE I'M A LITTLE BIT HERE FOR REVENGE. OF THE VERBAL SORT. I WON'T BRING MYSELF DOWN TO HIS LEVEL. I CAN'T LET MYSELF BECOME THAT PERSON AGAIN.
OR YOU COME HERE TO KILL ME LIKE YOU DID THOSE PEOPLE?
OH, THAT'S RIGHT, YOU LITTLE SLUT. DON'T THINK 'CAUSE I DON'T GOT A TV THAT I DON'T KNOW WHAT YOU DID. EVERYBODY KNOWS. EVERYBODY KNOWS YOUR FACE.
YOU WANNA KILL ME? HEH. GO 'HEAD. YOU'RE JUST LEAVING THEM A TRAIL, IDIOT.
I SHOULD KILL YOU. I SHOULD.
BUT THAT'S NOT WHY I'M HERE.

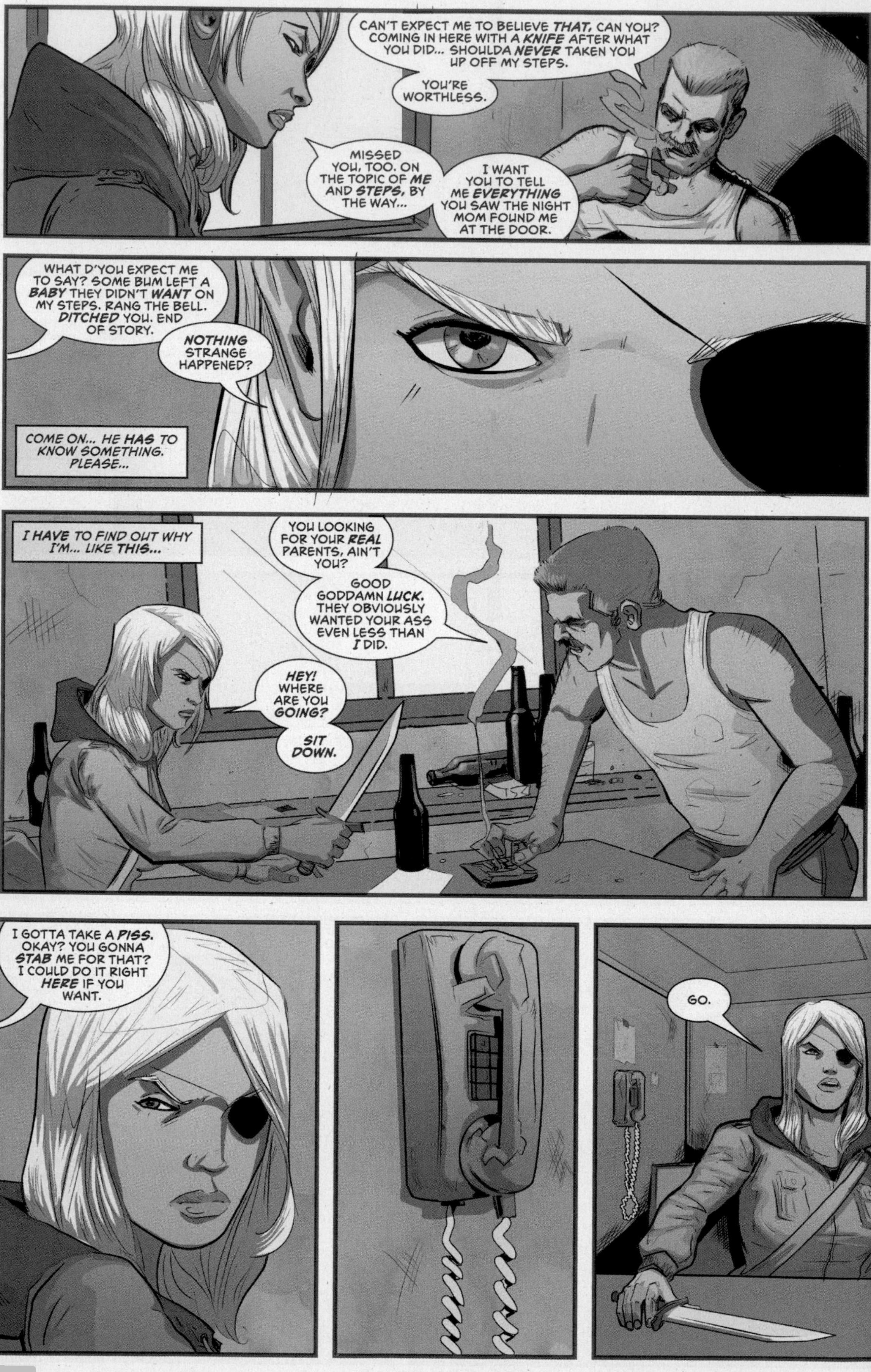

CAN'T EXPECT ME TO BELIEVE THAT, CAN YOU? COMING IN HERE WITH A KNIFE AFTER WHAT YOU DID... SHOULDA NEVER TAKEN YOU UP OFF MY STEPS.
YOU'RE WORTHLESS.
MISSED YOU, TOO. ON THE TOPIC OF ME AND STEPS, BY THE WAY...
I WANT YOU TO TELL ME EVERYTHING YOU SAW THE NIGHT MOM FOUND ME AT THE DOOR.
WHAT D'YOU EXPECT ME TO SAY? SOME BUM LEFT A BABY THEY DIDN'T WANT ON MY STEPS. RANG THE BELL. DITCHED YOU. END OF STORY.
NOTHING STRANGE HAPPENED?
COME ON... HE HAS TO KNOW SOMETHING. PLEASE...
I HAVE TO FIND OUT WHY I'M... LIKE THIS...
YOU LOOKING FOR YOUR REAL PARENTS, AIN'T YOU?
GOOD GODDAMN LUCK. THEY OBVIOUSLY WANTED YOUR ASS EVEN LESS THAN I DID.
HEY! WHERE ARE YOU GOING?
SIT DOWN.
I GOTTA TAKE A PISS. OKAY? YOU GONNA STAB ME FOR THAT? I COULD DO IT RIGHT HERE IF YOU WANT.
GO.

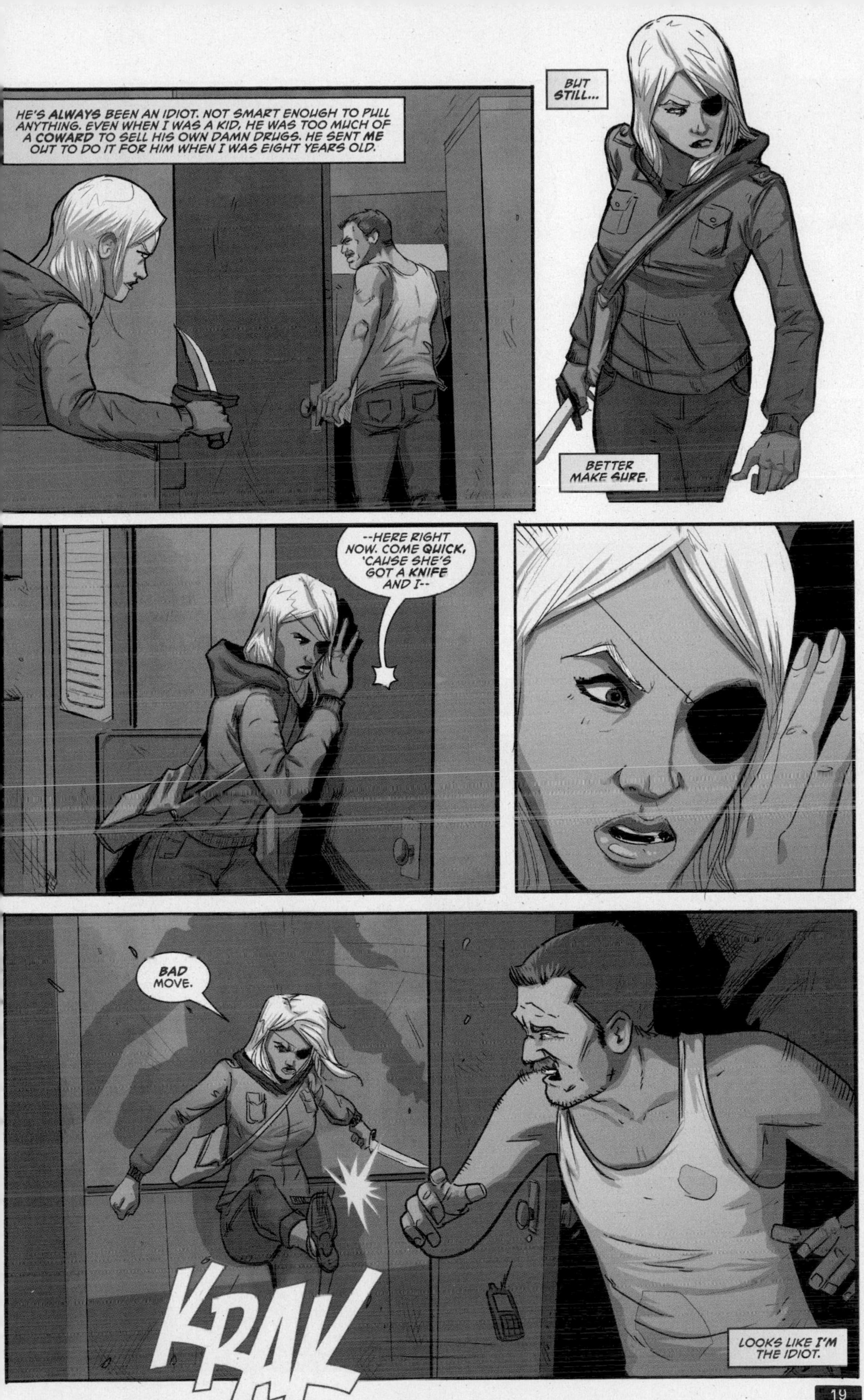

HE'S ALWAYS BEEN AN IDIOT. NOT SMART ENOUGH TO PULL ANYTHING. EVEN WHEN I WAS A KID, HE WAS TOO MUCH OF A COWARD TO SELL HIS OWN DAMN DRUGS. HE SENT ME OUT TO DO IT FOR HIM WHEN I WAS EIGHT YEARS OLD.
BUT STILL...
BETTER MAKE SURE.
--HERE RIGHT NOW. COME QUICK, 'CAUSE SHE'S GOT A KNIFE AND I--
BAD MOVE.
KRAK
LOOKS LIKE I'M THE IDIOT.

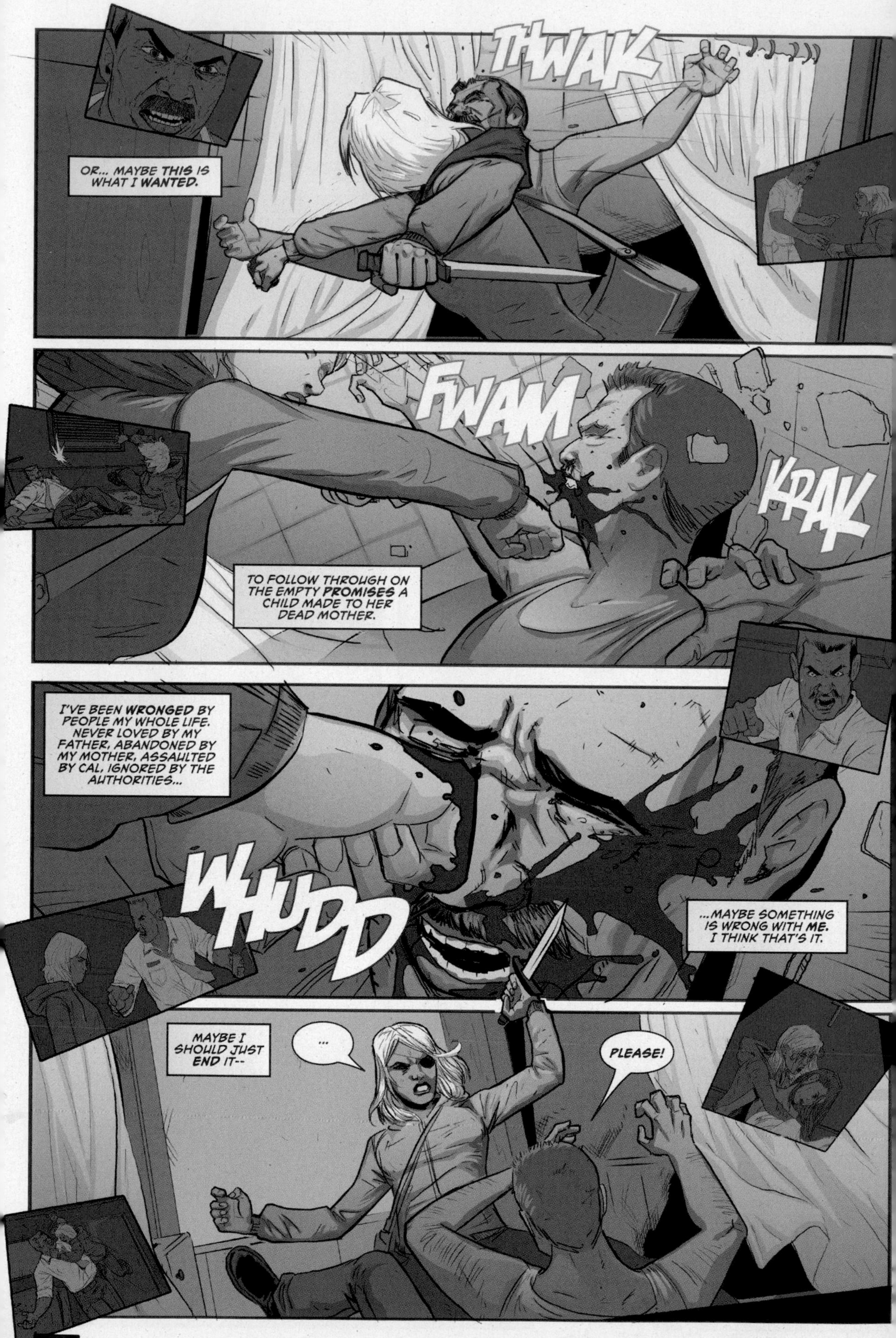

THWAK
OR... MAYBE THIS IS WHAT I WANTED.
FWAM
KRAK
TO FOLLOW THROUGH ON THE EMPTY PROMISES A CHILD MADE TO HER DEAD MOTHER.
I'VE BEEN WRONGED BY PEOPLE MY WHOLE LIFE. NEVER LOVED BY MY FATHER, ABANDONED BY MY MOTHER, ASSAULTED BY CAL, IGNORED BY THE AUTHORITIES...
WHUDD
...MAYBE SOMETHING IS WRONG WITH ME. I THINK THAT'S IT.
MAYBE I SHOULD JUST END IT--
...
PLEASE!

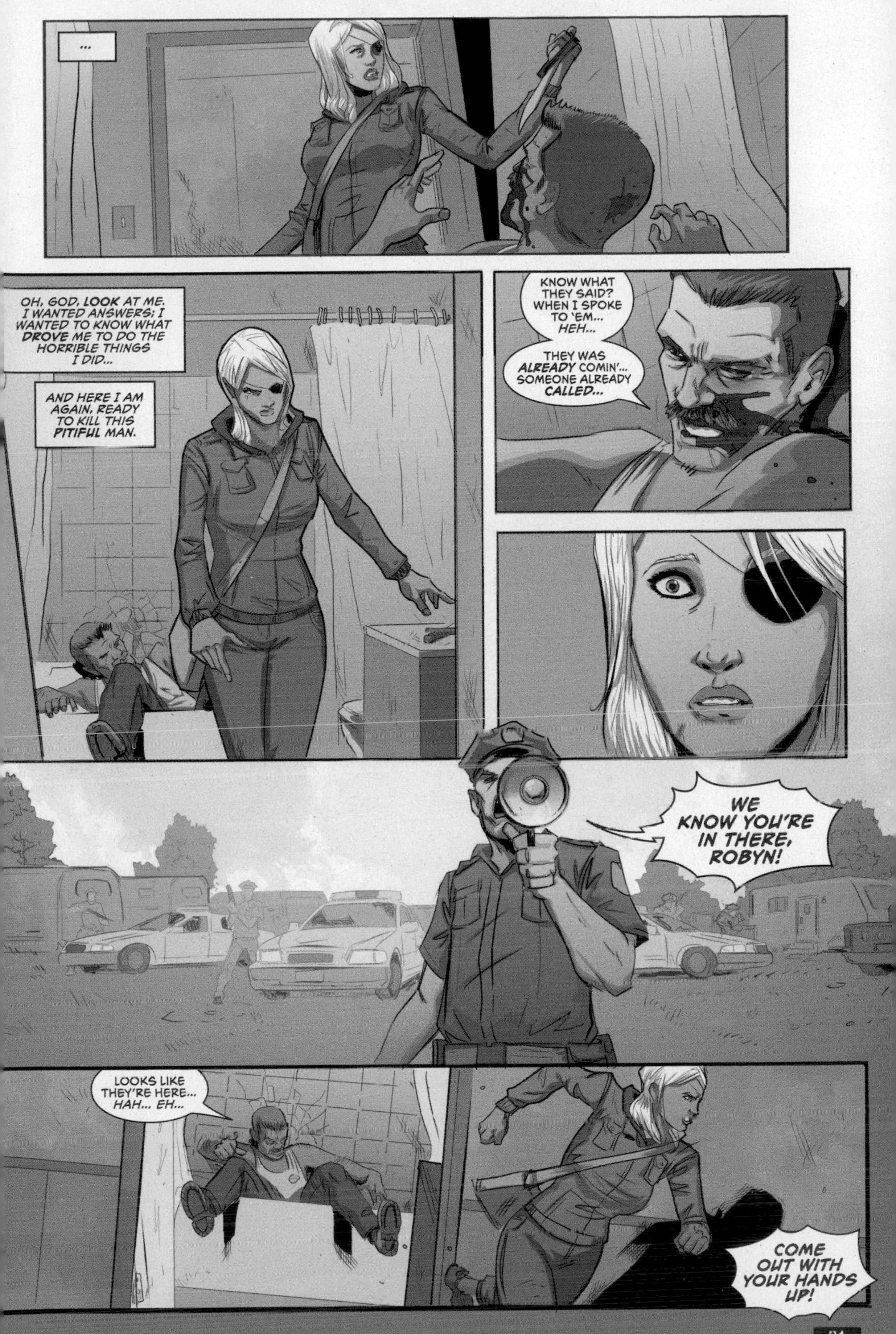
...
OH, GOD, LOOK AT ME. I WANTED ANSWERS; I WANTED TO KNOW WHAT DROVE ME TO DO THE HORRIBLE THINGS I DID...
AND HERE I AM AGAIN, READY TO KILL THIS PITIFUL MAN.
KNOW WHAT THEY SAID? WHEN I SPOKE TO 'EM... HEH...
THEY WAS ALREADY COMIN'... SOMEONE ALREADY CALLED...
WE KNOW YOU'RE IN THERE, ROBYN!
LOOKS LIKE THEY'RE HERE... HAH... EH...
COME OUT WITH YOUR HANDS UP!

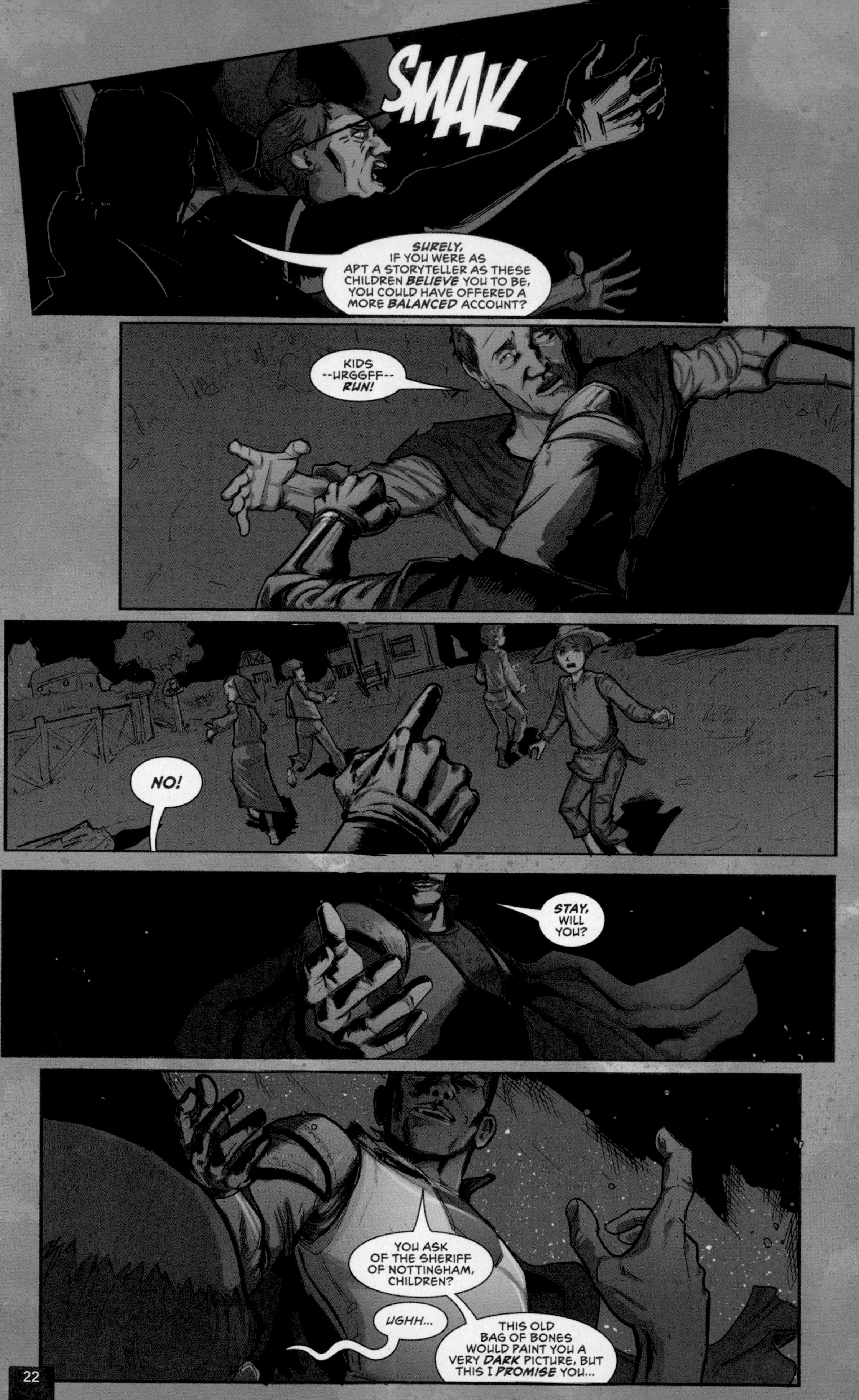
SMAK
SURELY, IF YOU WERE AS APT A STORYTELLER AS THESE CHILDREN BELIEVE YOU TO BE, YOU COULD HAVE OFFERED A MORE BALANCED ACCOUNT?
KIDS --URGGFF-- RUN!
NO!
STAY, WILL YOU?
YOU ASK OF THE SHERIFF OF NOTTINGHAM, CHILDREN?
UGHH...
THIS OLD BAG OF BONES WOULD PAINT YOU A VERY DARK PICTURE, BUT THIS I PROMISE YOU...

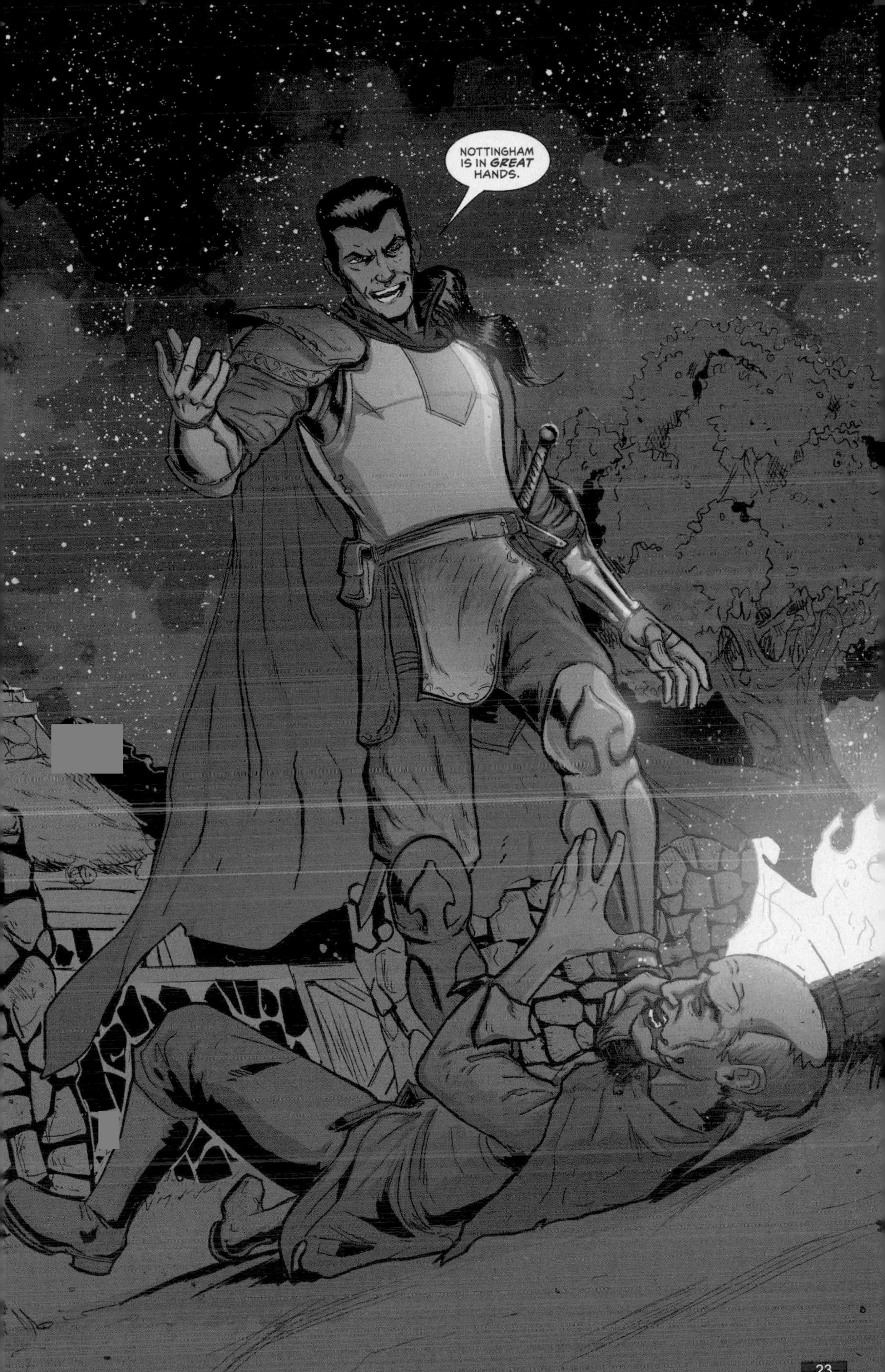
NOTTINGHAM IS IN GREAT HANDS.

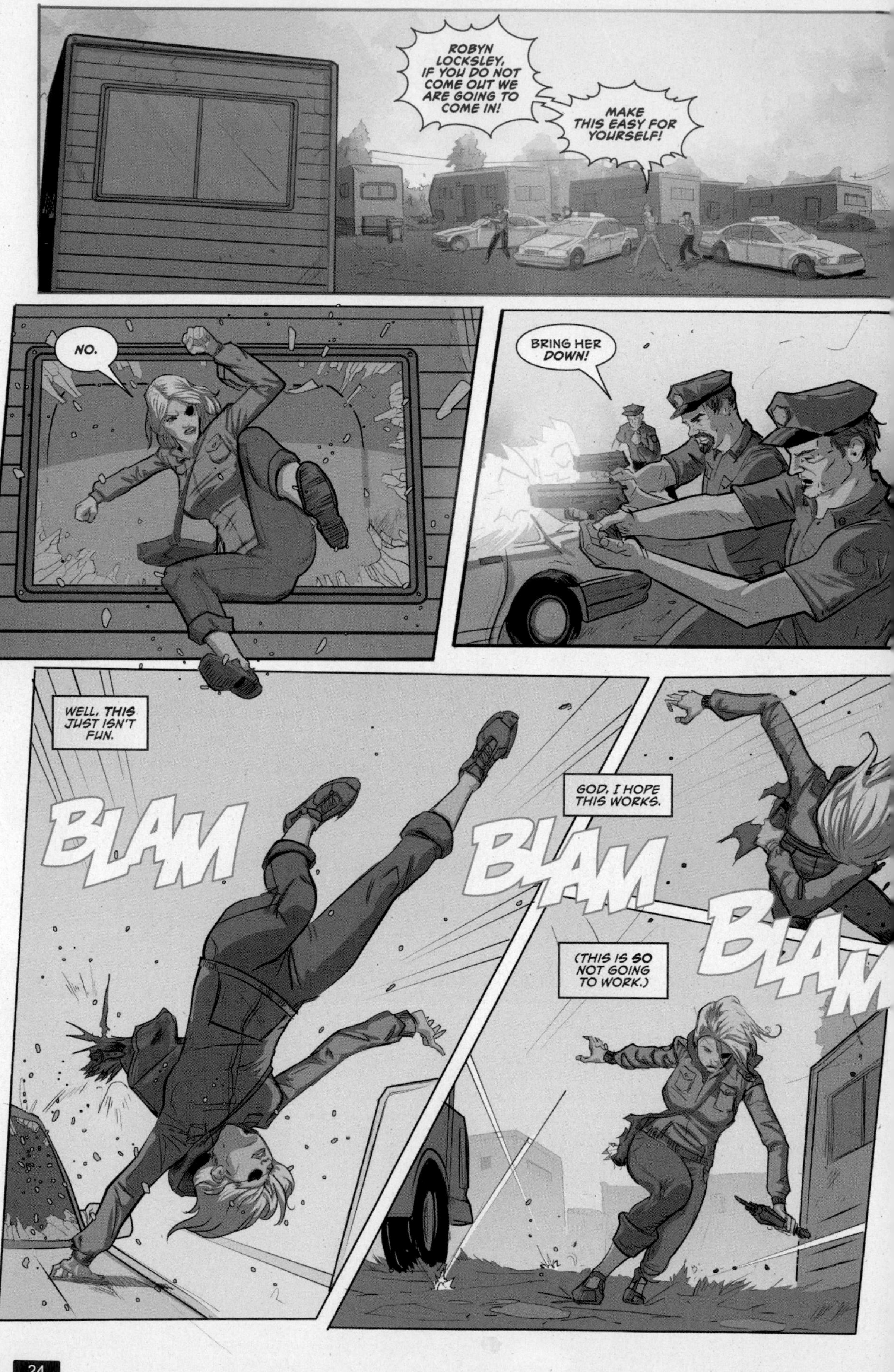
ROBYN LOCKSLEY, IF YOU DO NOT COME OUT WE ARE GOING TO COME IN!
MAKE THIS EASY FOR YOURSELF!
NO.
BRING HER DOWN!
WELL, THIS JUST ISN'T FUN.
BLAM
GOD, I HOPE THIS WORKS.
BLAM
BLAM
(THIS IS SO NOT GOING TO WORK.)

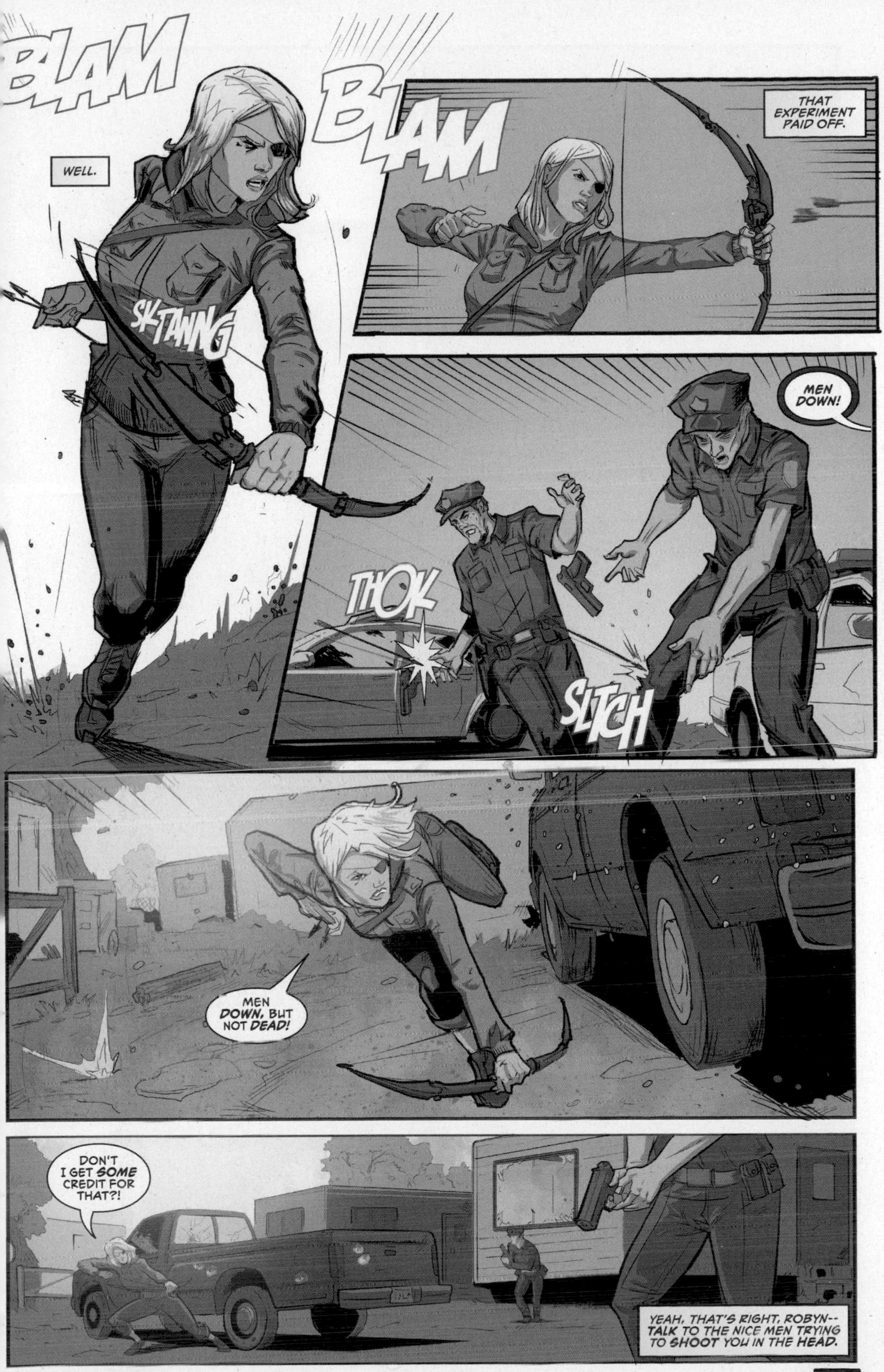

BLAM
WELL.
BLAM
THAT EXPERIMENT PAID OFF.
SK-TANNG
MEN DOWN!
THOK
SLTCH
MEN DOWN, BUT NOT DEAD!
DON'T I GET SOME CREDIT FOR THAT?!
YEAH, THAT'S RIGHT, ROBYN-- TALK TO THE NICE MEN TRYING TO SHOOT YOU IN THE HEAD.

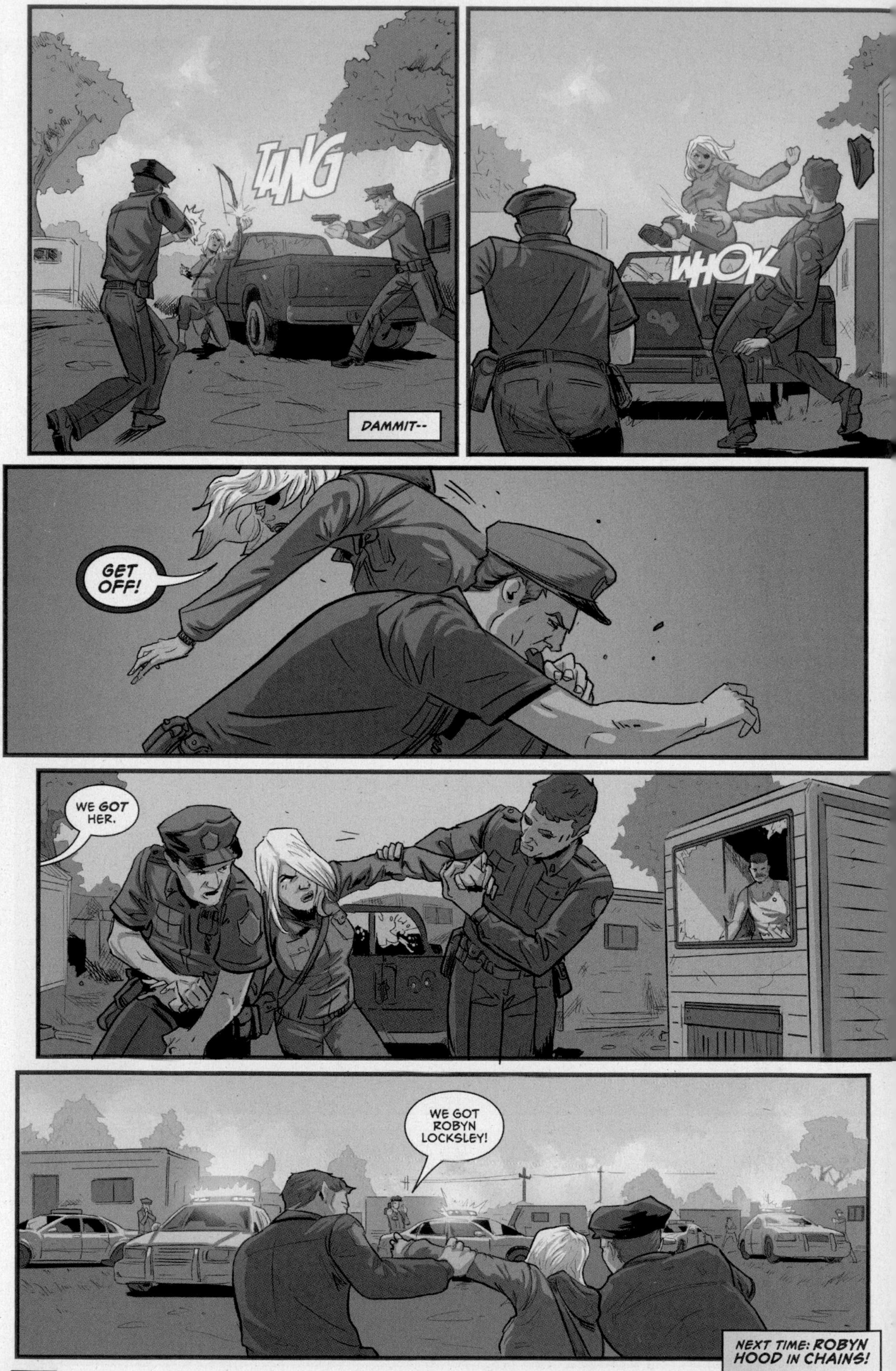
TANG
DAMMIT--
WHOK
GET OFF!
WE GOT HER.
WE GOT ROBYN LOCKSLEY!
NEXT TIME: ROBYN HOOD IN CHAINS!

Grimm Fairy Tales presents:

# Robyn Hood

## Wanted

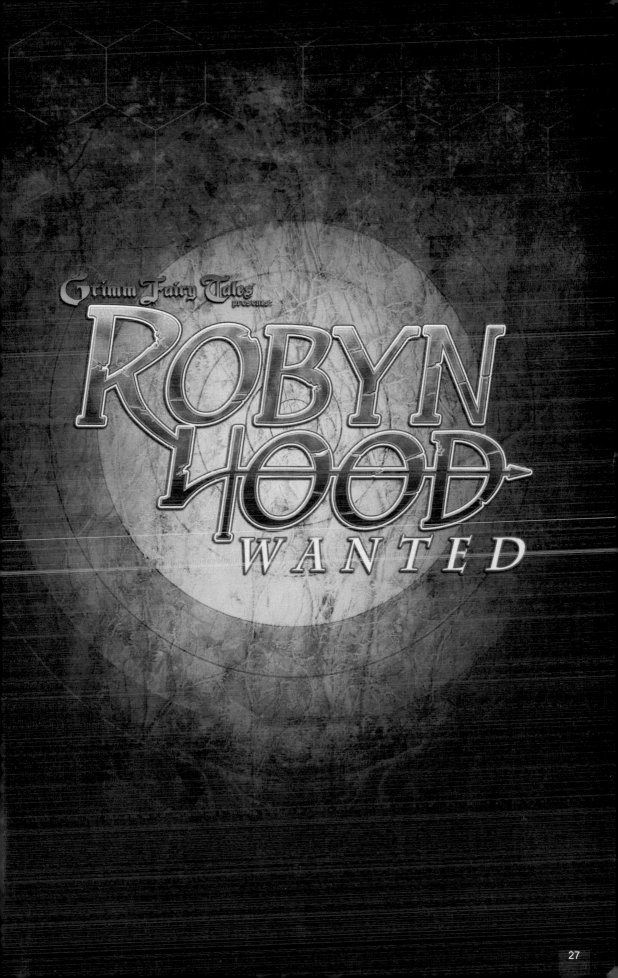

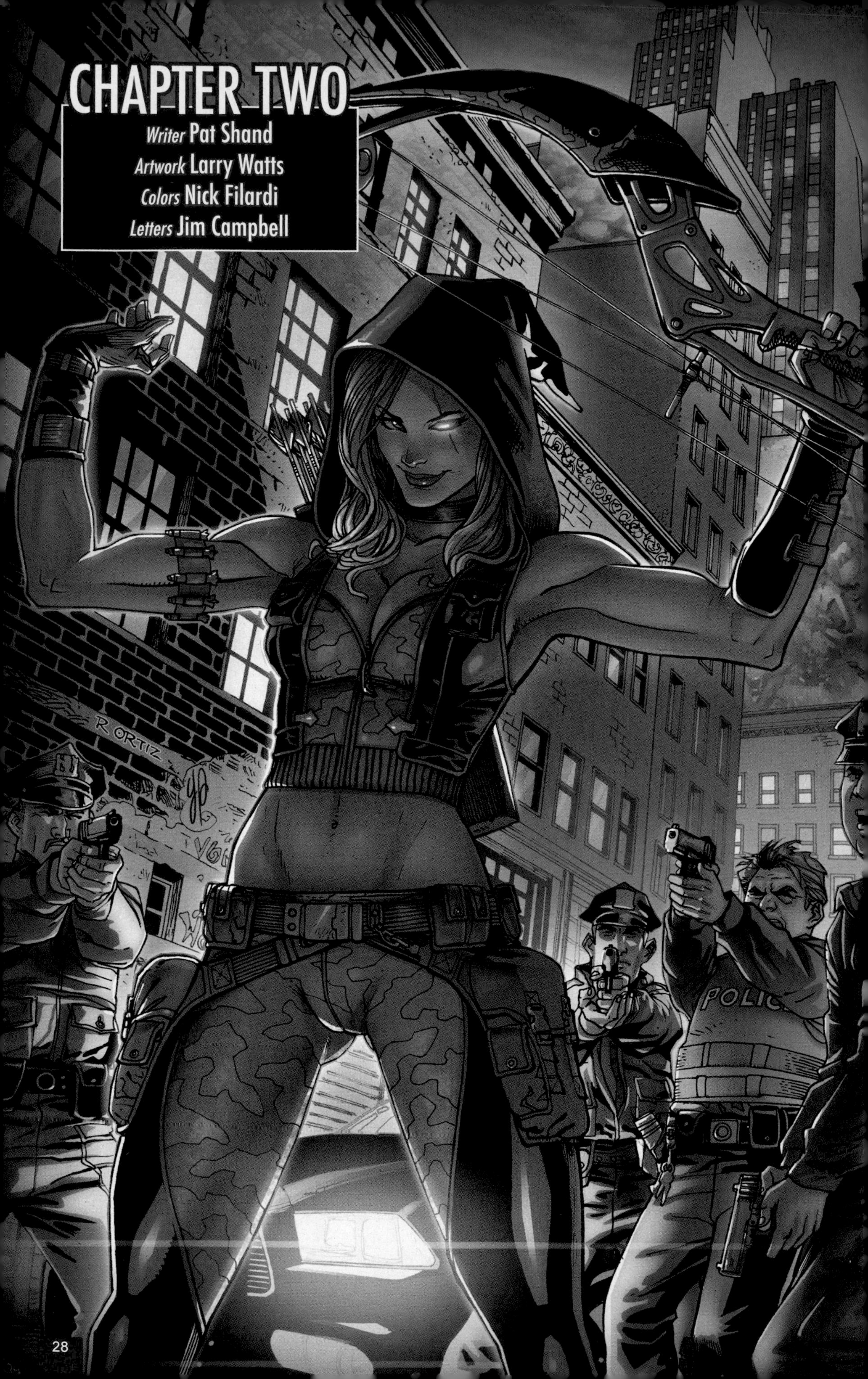
CHAPTER TWO
Writer Pat Shand
Artwork Larry Watts
Colors Nick Filardi
Letters Jim Campbell
R ORTIZ

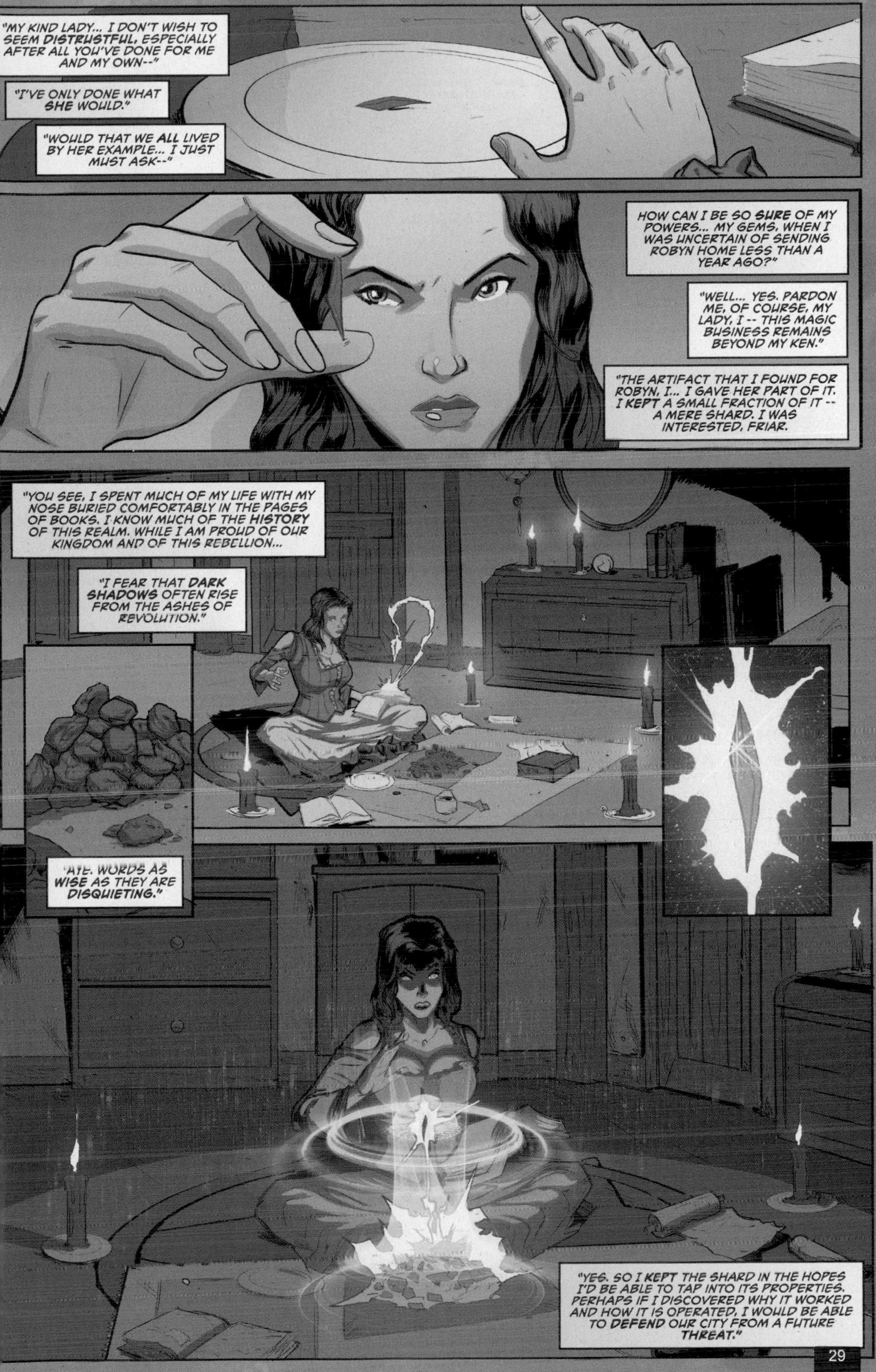
"MY KIND LADY... I DON'T WISH TO SEEM DISTRUSTFUL, ESPECIALLY AFTER ALL YOU'VE DONE FOR ME AND MY OWN--"
"I'VE ONLY DONE WHAT SHE WOULD."
"WOULD THAT WE ALL LIVED BY HER EXAMPLE... I JUST MUST ASK--"
HOW CAN I BE SO SURE OF MY POWERS... MY GEMS, WHEN I WAS UNCERTAIN OF SENDING ROBYN HOME LESS THAN A YEAR AGO?"
"WELL... YES. PARDON ME, OF COURSE, MY LADY, I -- THIS MAGIC BUSINESS REMAINS BEYOND MY KEN."
"THE ARTIFACT THAT I FOUND FOR ROBYN, I... I GAVE HER PART OF IT. I KEPT A SMALL FRACTION OF IT -- A MERE SHARD. I WAS INTERESTED, FRIAR.
"YOU SEE, I SPENT MUCH OF MY LIFE WITH MY NOSE BURIED COMFORTABLY IN THE PAGES OF BOOKS. I KNOW MUCH OF THE HISTORY OF THIS REALM. WHILE I AM PROUD OF OUR KINGDOM AND OF THIS REBELLION...
"I FEAR THAT DARK SHADOWS OFTEN RISE FROM THE ASHES OF REVOLUTION."
"AYE. WORDS AS WISE AS THEY ARE DISQUIETING."
"YES. SO I KEPT THE SHARD IN THE HOPES I'D BE ABLE TO TAP INTO ITS PROPERTIES. PERHAPS IF I DISCOVERED WHY IT WORKED AND HOW IT IS OPERATED, I WOULD BE ABLE TO DEFEND OUR CITY FROM A FUTURE THREAT."

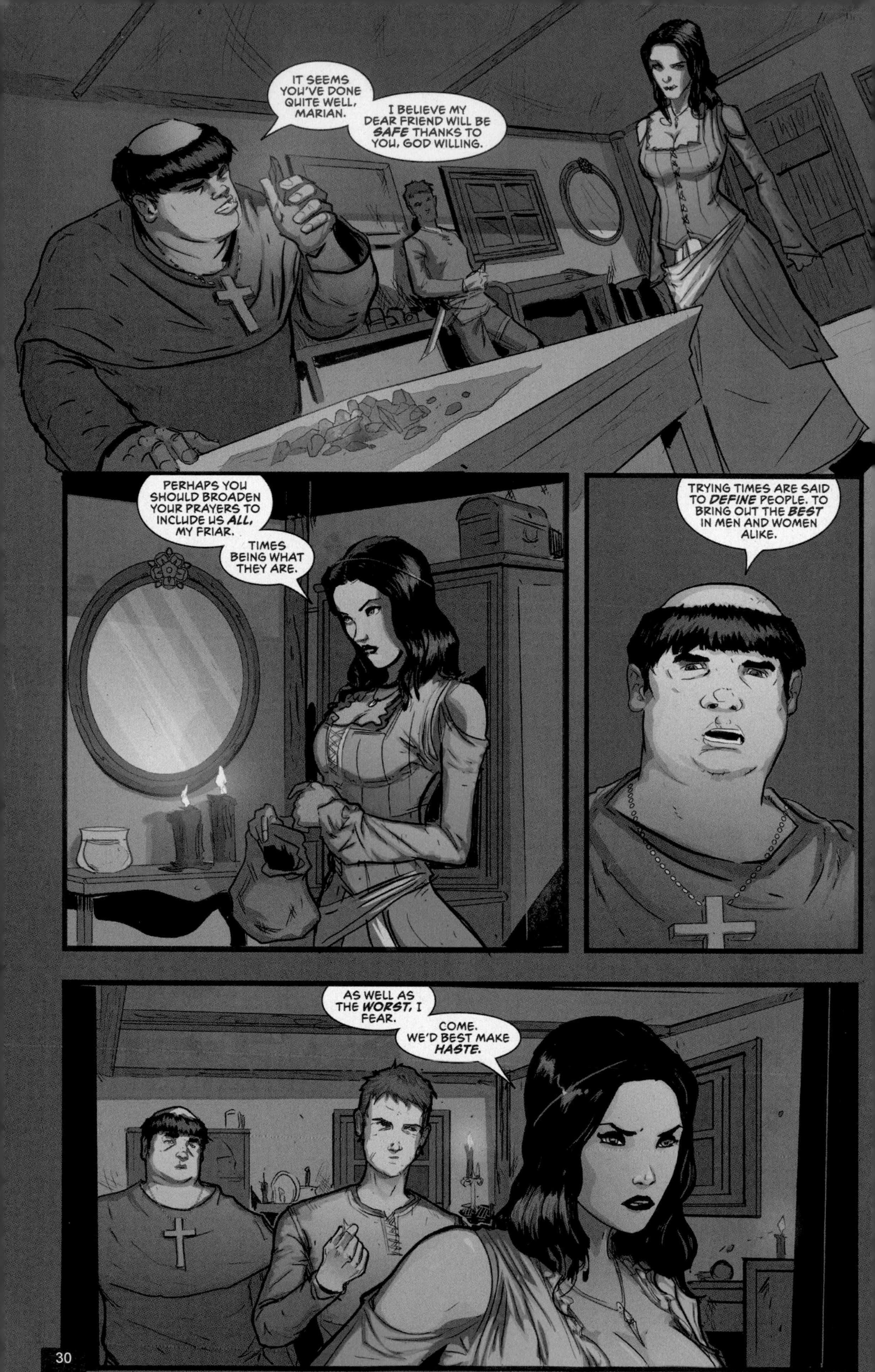

IT SEEMS YOU'VE DONE QUITE WELL, MARIAN.
I BELIEVE MY DEAR FRIEND WILL BE *SAFE* THANKS TO YOU, GOD WILLING.
PERHAPS YOU SHOULD BROADEN YOUR PRAYERS TO INCLUDE US *ALL,* MY FRIAR.
TIMES BEING WHAT THEY ARE.
TRYING TIMES ARE SAID TO *DEFINE* PEOPLE. TO BRING OUT THE *BEST* IN MEN AND WOMEN ALIKE.
AS WELL AS THE *WORST,* I FEAR.
COME. WE'D BEST MAKE *HASTE.*

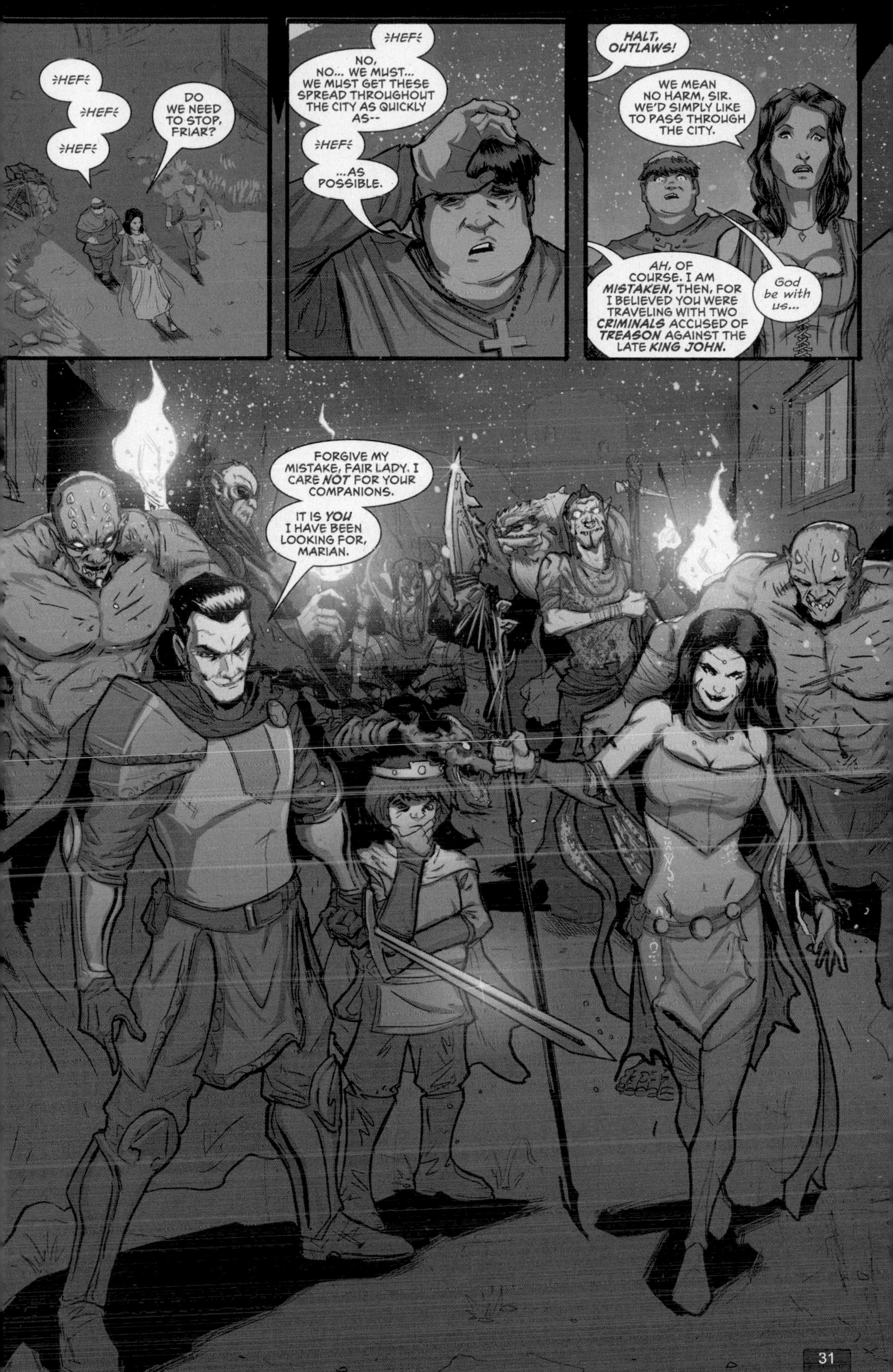
HEF
HEF
HEF
DO WE NEED TO STOP, FRIAR?
HEF
NO, NO... WE MUST... WE MUST GET THESE SPREAD THROUGHOUT THE CITY AS QUICKLY AS--
HEF
...AS POSSIBLE.
HALT, OUTLAWS!
WE MEAN NO HARM, SIR. WE'D SIMPLY LIKE TO PASS THROUGH THE CITY.
AH, OF COURSE. I AM MISTAKEN, THEN, FOR I BELIEVED YOU WERE TRAVELING WITH TWO CRIMINALS ACCUSED OF TREASON AGAINST THE LATE KING JOHN.
God be with us...
FORGIVE MY MISTAKE, FAIR LADY. I CARE NOT FOR YOUR COMPANIONS.
IT IS YOU I HAVE BEEN LOOKING FOR, MARIAN.

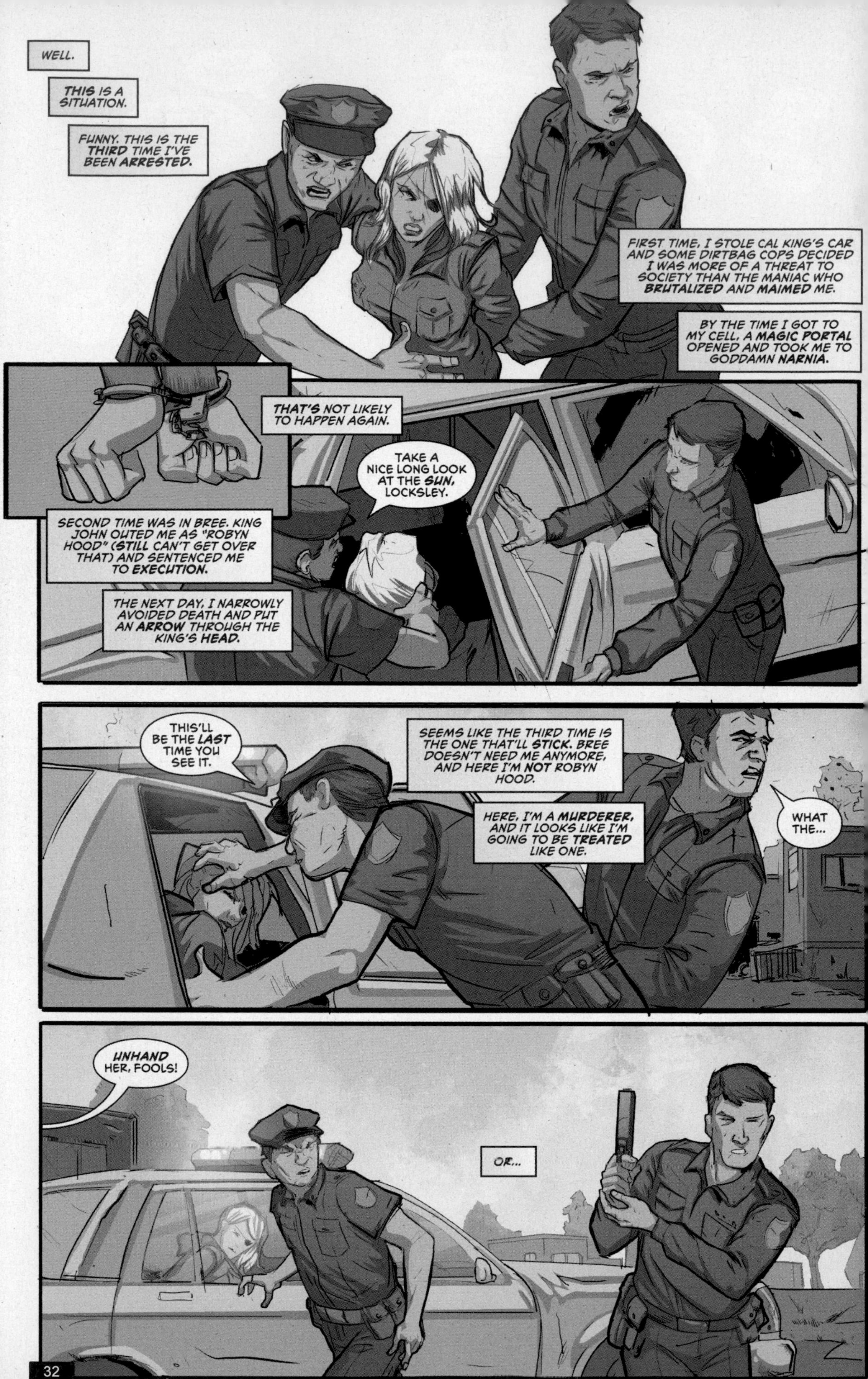
WELL.
THIS IS A SITUATION.
FUNNY. THIS IS THE THIRD TIME I'VE BEEN ARRESTED.
FIRST TIME, I STOLE CAL KING'S CAR AND SOME DIRTBAG COPS DECIDED I WAS MORE OF A THREAT TO SOCIETY THAN THE MANIAC WHO BRUTALIZED AND MAIMED ME.
BY THE TIME I GOT TO MY CELL, A MAGIC PORTAL OPENED AND TOOK ME TO GODDAMN NARNIA.
THAT'S NOT LIKELY TO HAPPEN AGAIN.
TAKE A NICE LONG LOOK AT THE SUN, LOCKSLEY.
SECOND TIME WAS IN BREE. KING JOHN OUTED ME AS "ROBYN HOOD" (STILL CAN'T GET OVER THAT) AND SENTENCED ME TO EXECUTION.
THE NEXT DAY, I NARROWLY AVOIDED DEATH AND PUT AN ARROW THROUGH THE KING'S HEAD.
THIS'LL BE THE LAST TIME YOU SEE IT.
SEEMS LIKE THE THIRD TIME IS THE ONE THAT'LL STICK. BREE DOESN'T NEED ME ANYMORE, AND HERE I'M NOT ROBYN HOOD.
HERE, I'M A MURDERER, AND IT LOOKS LIKE I'M GOING TO BE TREATED LIKE ONE.
WHAT THE...
UNHAND HER, FOOLS!
OR...

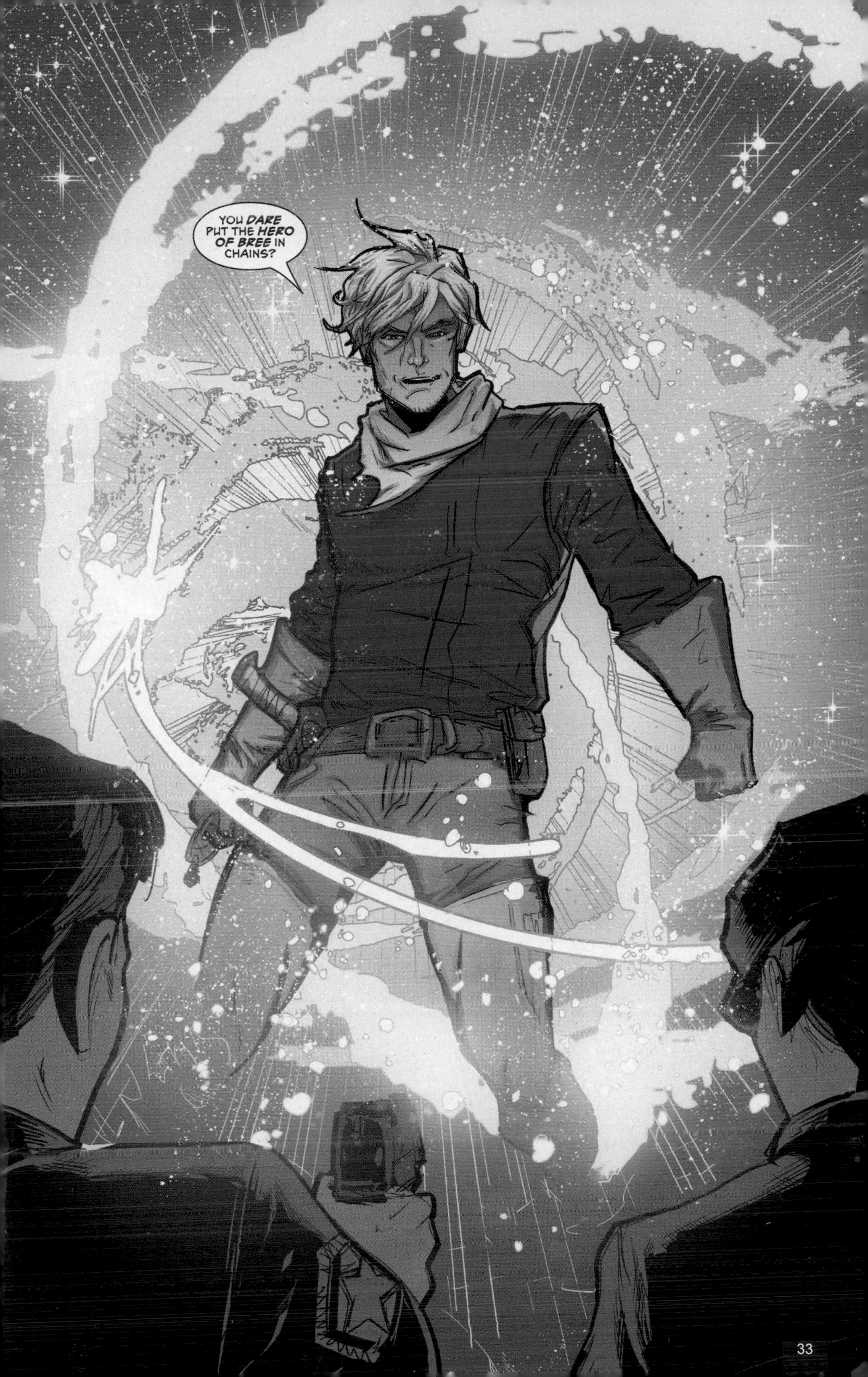
YOU DARE PUT THE HERO OF BREE IN CHAINS?

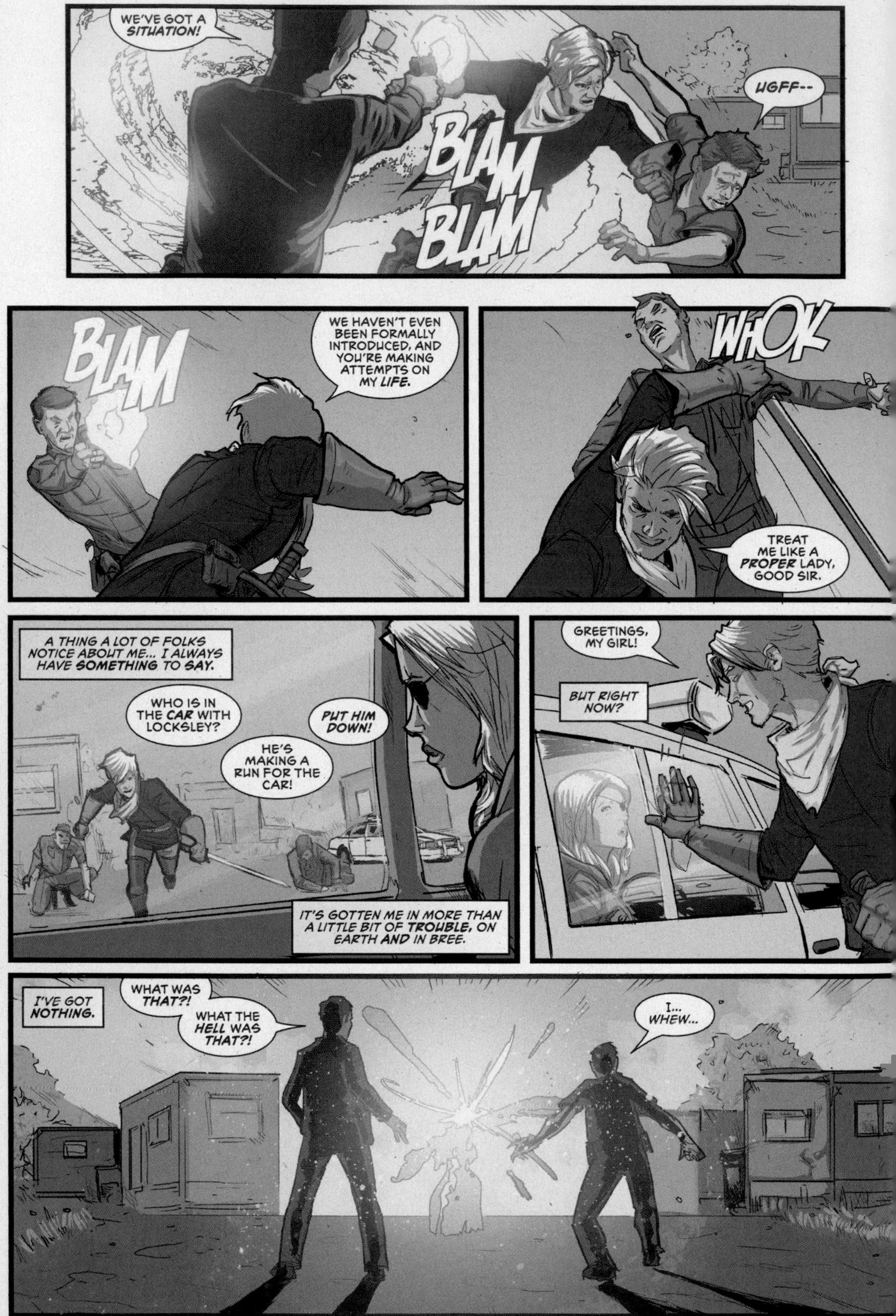
WE'VE GOT A SITUATION!
BLAM
BLAM
UGFF--
BLAM
WE HAVEN'T EVEN BEEN FORMALLY INTRODUCED, AND YOU'RE MAKING ATTEMPTS ON MY LIFE.
WHOK
TREAT ME LIKE A PROPER LADY, GOOD SIR.
A THING A LOT OF FOLKS NOTICE ABOUT ME... I ALWAYS HAVE SOMETHING TO SAY.
WHO IS IN THE CAR WITH LOCKSLEY?
PUT HIM DOWN!
HE'S MAKING A RUN FOR THE CAR!
IT'S GOTTEN ME IN MORE THAN A LITTLE BIT OF TROUBLE, ON EARTH AND IN BREE.
GREETINGS, MY GIRL!
BUT RIGHT NOW?
I'VE GOT NOTHING.
WHAT WAS THAT?!
WHAT THE HELL WAS THAT?!
I... WHEW...

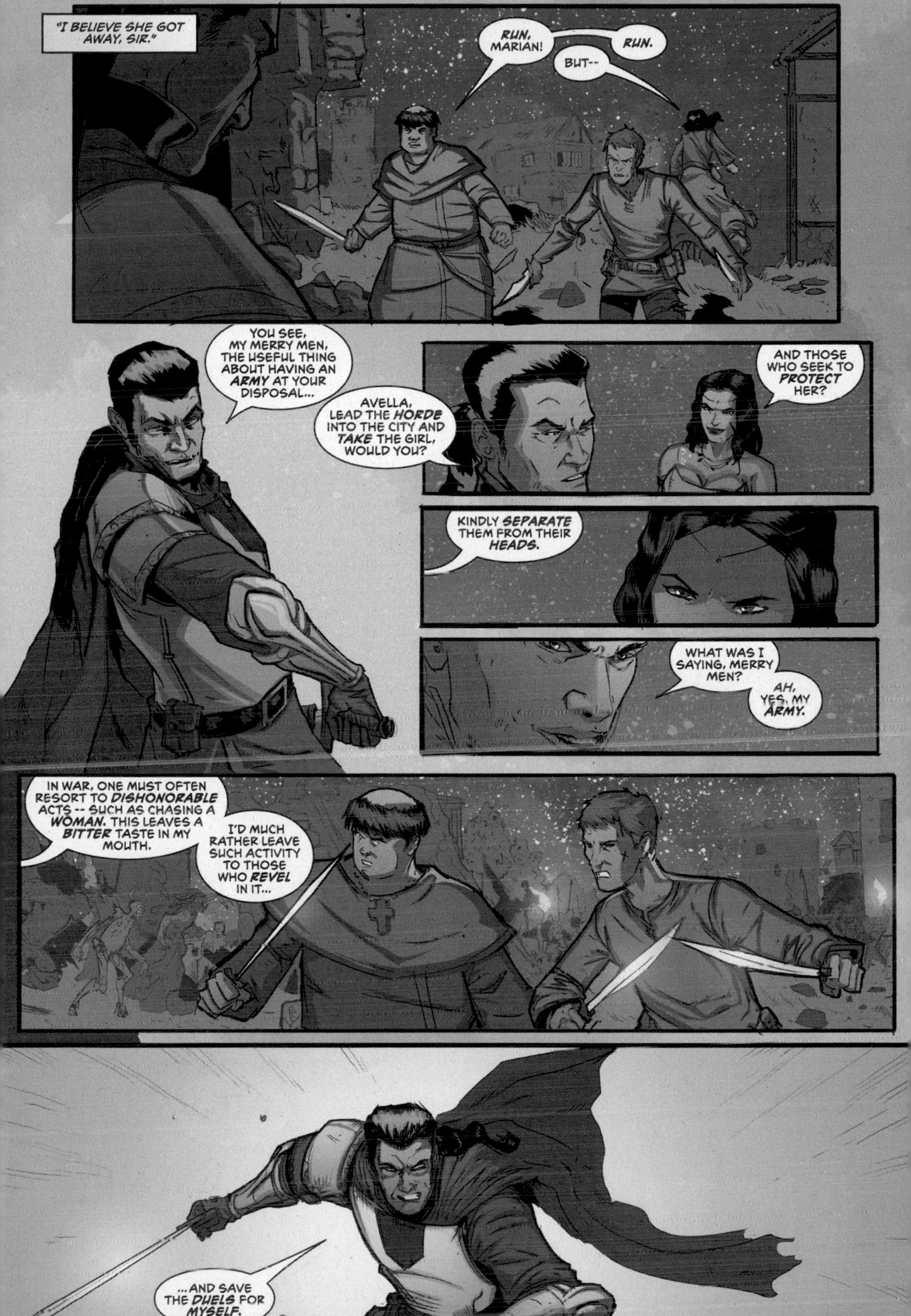
"I BELIEVE SHE GOT AWAY, SIR."
RUN, MARIAN!
BUT--
RUN.
YOU SEE, MY MERRY MEN, THE USEFUL THING ABOUT HAVING AN ARMY AT YOUR DISPOSAL...
AVELLA, LEAD THE HORDE INTO THE CITY AND TAKE THE GIRL, WOULD YOU?
AND THOSE WHO SEEK TO PROTECT HER?
KINDLY SEPARATE THEM FROM THEIR HEADS.
WHAT WAS I SAYING, MERRY MEN?
AH, YES, MY ARMY.
IN WAR, ONE MUST OFTEN RESORT TO DISHONORABLE ACTS -- SUCH AS CHASING A WOMAN. THIS LEAVES A BITTER TASTE IN MY MOUTH.
I'D MUCH RATHER LEAVE SUCH ACTIVITY TO THOSE WHO REVEL IN IT...
...AND SAVE THE DUELS FOR MYSELF.

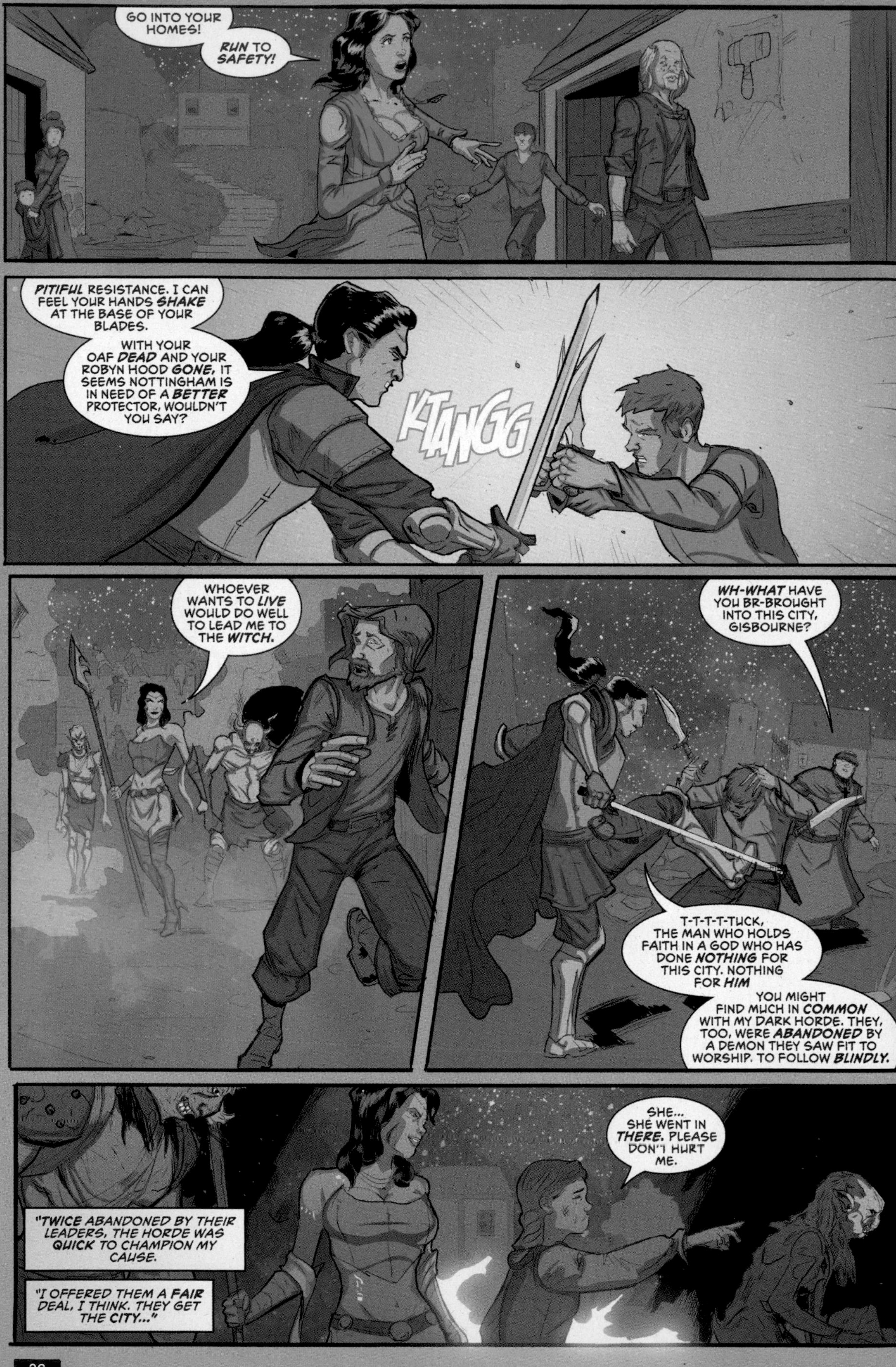
GO INTO YOUR HOMES!
RUN TO SAFETY!
PITIFUL RESISTANCE. I CAN FEEL YOUR HANDS SHAKE AT THE BASE OF YOUR BLADES.
WITH YOUR OAF DEAD AND YOUR ROBYN HOOD GONE, IT SEEMS NOTTINGHAM IS IN NEED OF A BETTER PROTECTOR, WOULDN'T YOU SAY?
KLTANGG
WHOEVER WANTS TO LIVE WOULD DO WELL TO LEAD ME TO THE WITCH.
WH-WHAT HAVE YOU BR-BROUGHT INTO THIS CITY, GISBOURNE?
T-T-T-T-TUCK, THE MAN WHO HOLDS FAITH IN A GOD WHO HAS DONE NOTHING FOR THIS CITY. NOTHING FOR HIM
YOU MIGHT FIND MUCH IN COMMON WITH MY DARK HORDE. THEY, TOO, WERE ABANDONED BY A DEMON THEY SAW FIT TO WORSHIP. TO FOLLOW BLINDLY.
"TWICE ABANDONED BY THEIR LEADERS, THE HORDE WAS QUICK TO CHAMPION MY CAUSE.
SHE... SHE WENT IN THERE. PLEASE DON'T HURT ME.
"I OFFERED THEM A FAIR DEAL, I THINK. THEY GET THE CITY..."

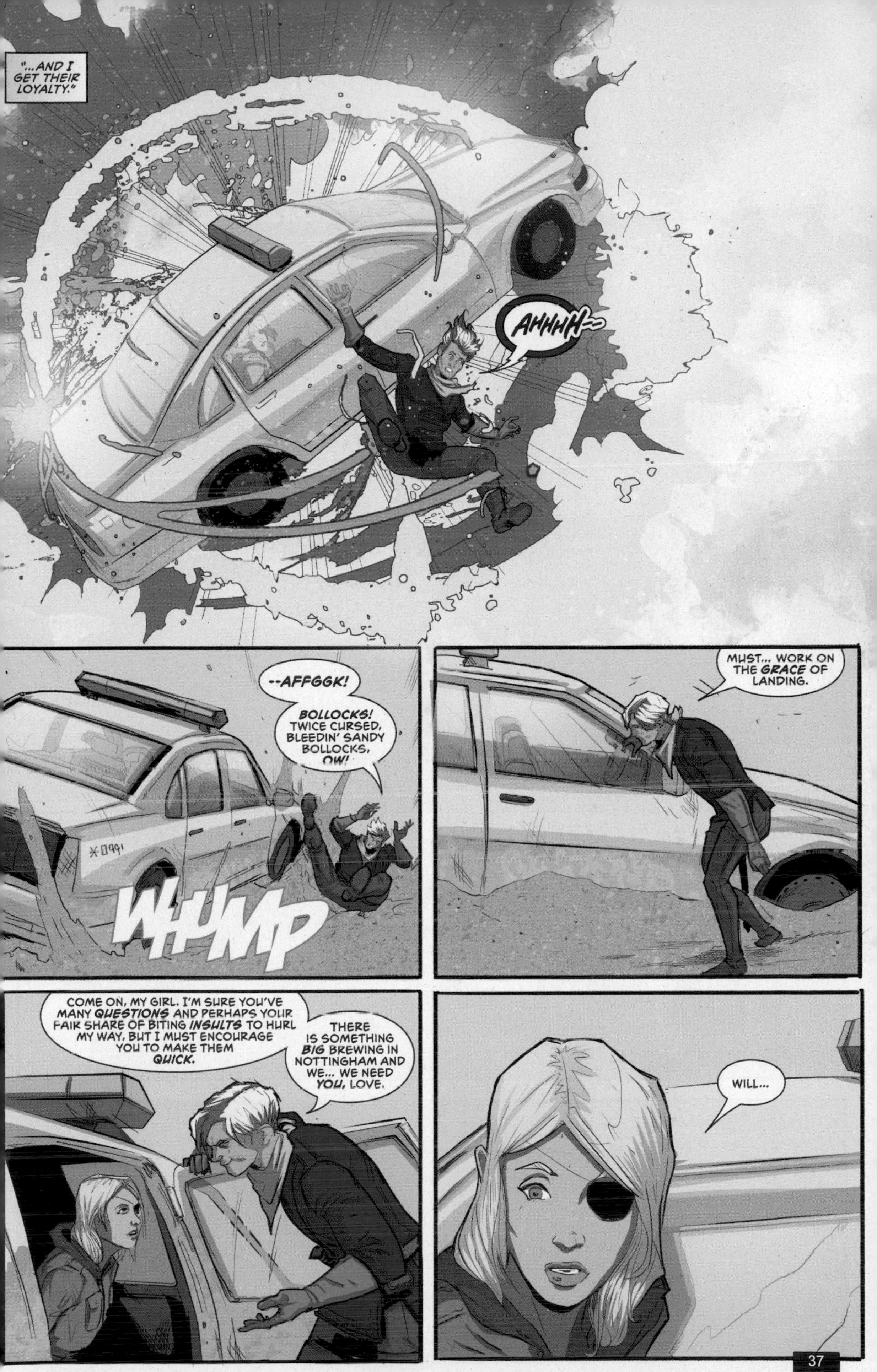
"...AND I GET THEIR LOYALTY."
AHHHH--
--AFFGGK!
BOLLOCKS! TWICE CURSED, BLEEDIN' SANDY BOLLOCKS, OW!
WHUMP
MUST... WORK ON THE GRACE OF LANDING.
COME ON, MY GIRL. I'M SURE YOU'VE MANY QUESTIONS AND PERHAPS YOUR FAIR SHARE OF BITING INSULTS TO HURL MY WAY, BUT I MUST ENCOURAGE YOU TO MAKE THEM QUICK.
THERE IS SOMETHING BIG BREWING IN NOTTINGHAM AND WE... WE NEED YOU, LOVE.
WILL...

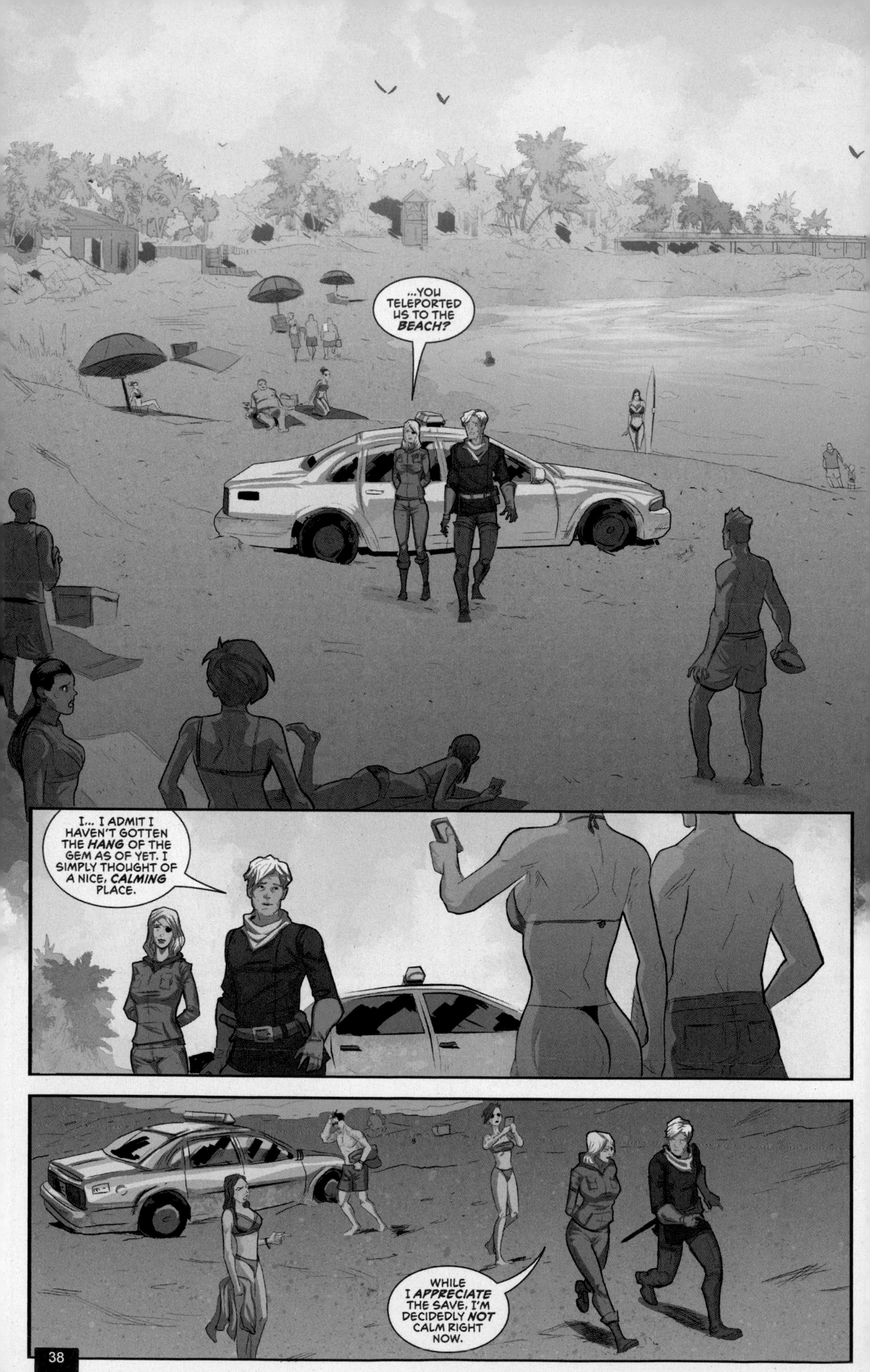
...YOU TELEPORTED US TO THE BEACH?
I... I ADMIT I HAVEN'T GOTTEN THE HANG OF THE GEM AS OF YET. I SIMPLY THOUGHT OF A NICE, CALMING PLACE.
WHILE I APPRECIATE THE SAVE, I'M DECIDEDLY NOT CALM RIGHT NOW.

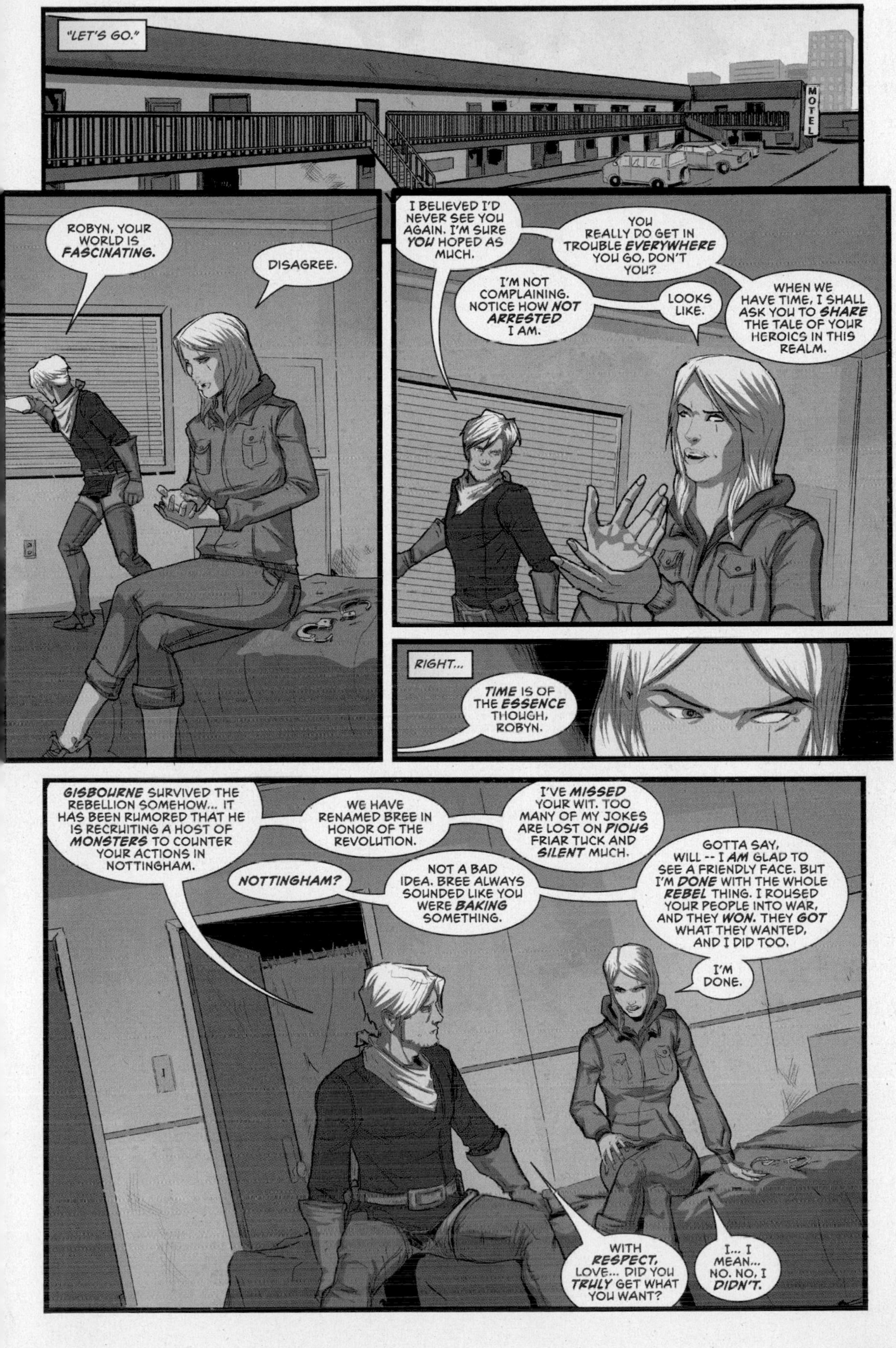
"LET'S GO."
ROBYN, YOUR WORLD IS FASCINATING.
DISAGREE.
I BELIEVED I'D NEVER SEE YOU AGAIN. I'M SURE YOU HOPED AS MUCH.
YOU REALLY DO GET IN TROUBLE EVERYWHERE YOU GO, DON'T YOU?
I'M NOT COMPLAINING. NOTICE HOW NOT ARRESTED I AM.
LOOKS LIKE.
WHEN WE HAVE TIME, I SHALL ASK YOU TO SHARE THE TALE OF YOUR HEROICS IN THIS REALM.
RIGHT...
TIME IS OF THE ESSENCE THOUGH, ROBYN.
GISBOURNE SURVIVED THE REBELLION SOMEHOW... IT HAS BEEN RUMORED THAT HE IS RECRUITING A HOST OF MONSTERS TO COUNTER YOUR ACTIONS IN NOTTINGHAM.
NOTTINGHAM?
WE HAVE RENAMED BREE IN HONOR OF THE REVOLUTION.
NOT A BAD IDEA. BREE ALWAYS SOUNDED LIKE YOU WERE BAKING SOMETHING.
I'VE MISSED YOUR WIT. TOO MANY OF MY JOKES ARE LOST ON PIOUS FRIAR TUCK AND SILENT MUCH.
GOTTA SAY, WILL -- I AM GLAD TO SEE A FRIENDLY FACE. BUT I'M DONE WITH THE WHOLE REBEL THING. I ROUSED YOUR PEOPLE INTO WAR, AND THEY WON. THEY GOT WHAT THEY WANTED, AND I DID TOO.
I'M DONE.
WITH RESPECT, LOVE... DID YOU TRULY GET WHAT YOU WANT?
I... I MEAN... NO. NO, I DIDN'T.

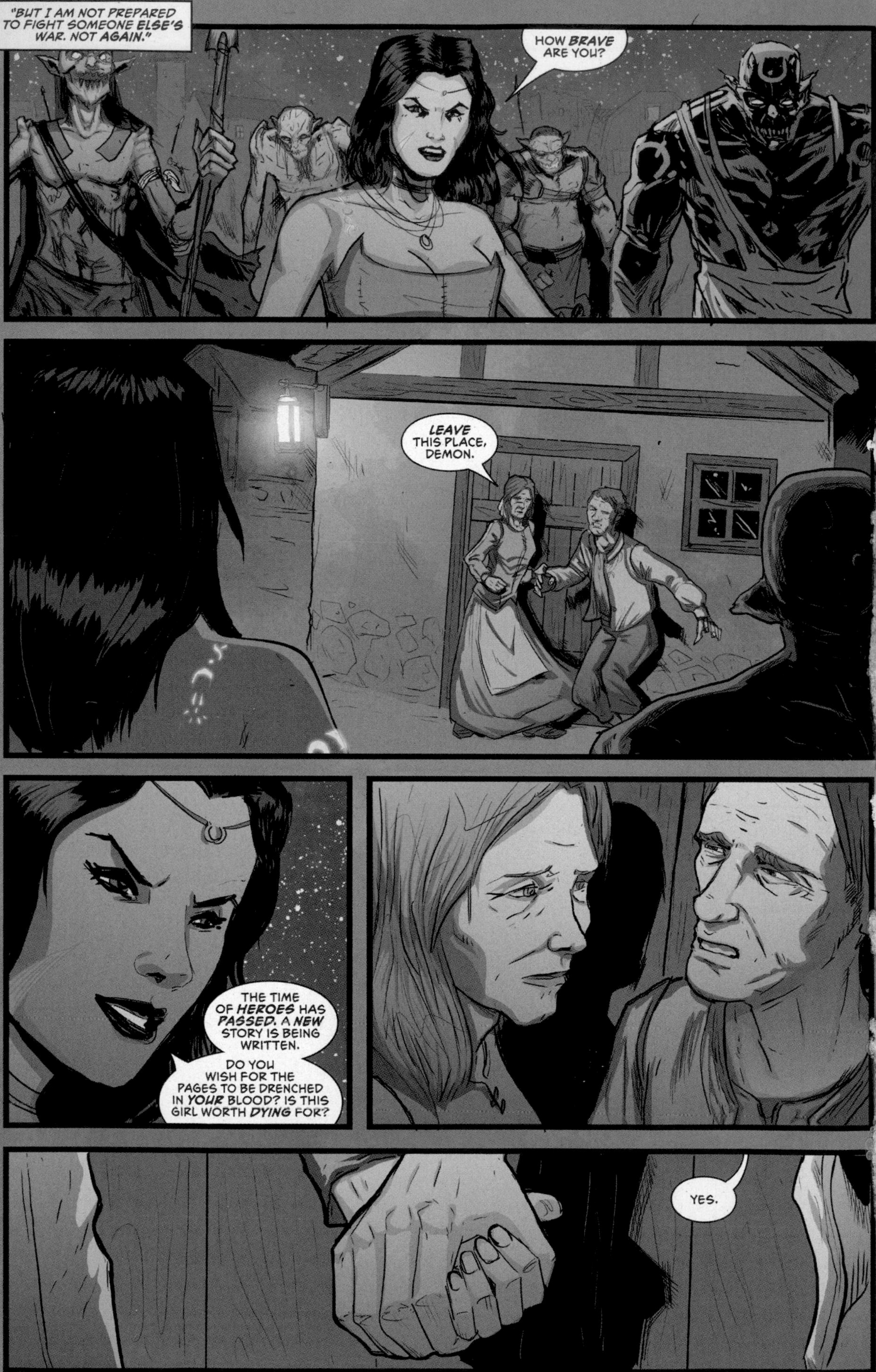
"BUT I AM NOT PREPARED TO FIGHT SOMEONE ELSE'S WAR. NOT AGAIN."
HOW BRAVE ARE YOU?
LEAVE THIS PLACE, DEMON.
THE TIME OF HEROES HAS PASSED. A NEW STORY IS BEING WRITTEN.
DO YOU WISH FOR THE PAGES TO BE DRENCHED IN YOUR BLOOD? IS THIS GIRL WORTH DYING FOR?
YES.

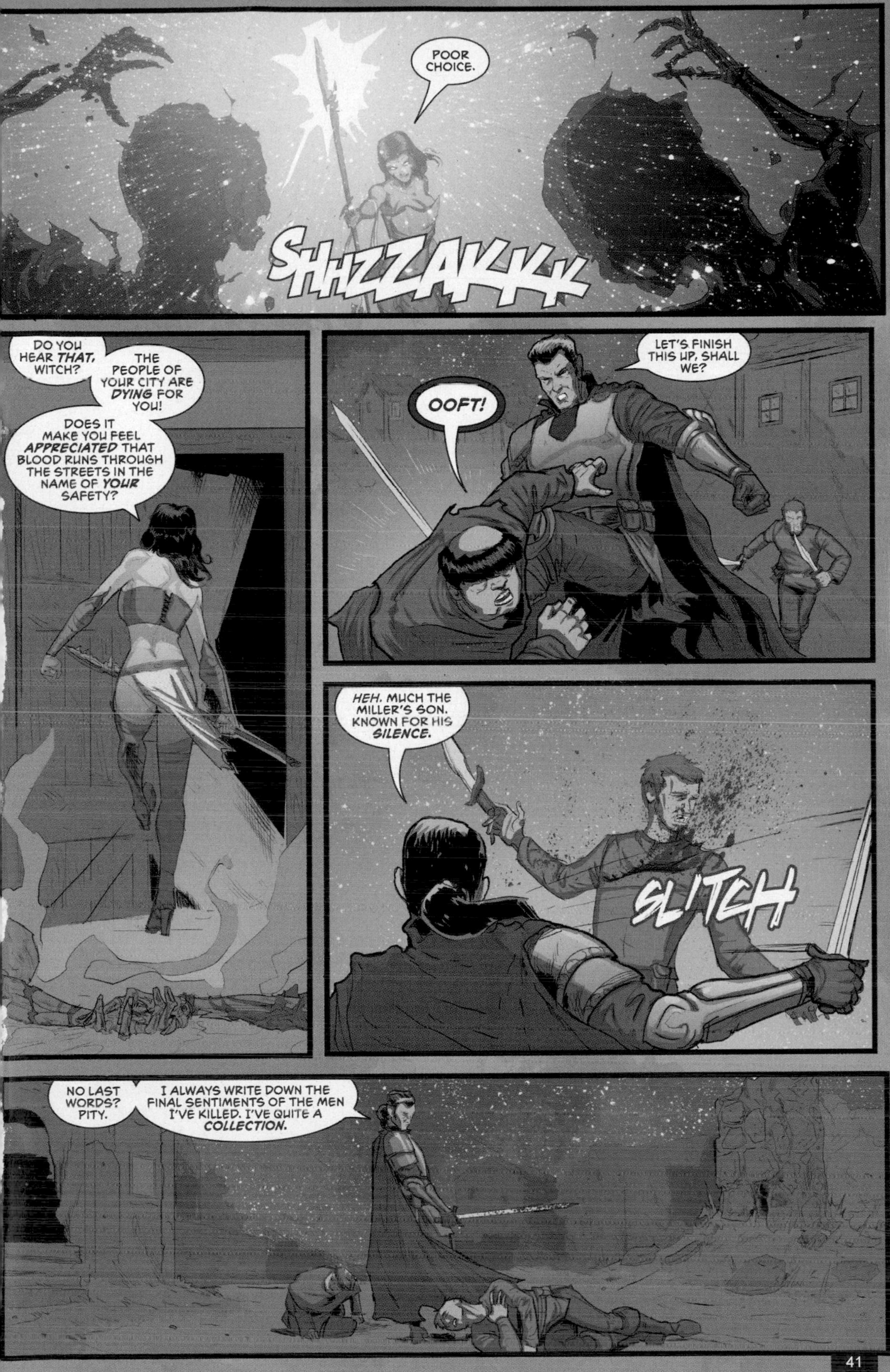
POOR CHOICE.
SHHZZAKKK
DO YOU HEAR *THAT,* WITCH?
THE PEOPLE OF YOUR CITY ARE *DYING* FOR YOU!
DOES IT MAKE YOU FEEL *APPRECIATED* THAT BLOOD RUNS THROUGH THE STREETS IN THE NAME OF *YOUR* SAFETY?
LET'S FINISH THIS UP, SHALL WE?
OOFT!
*HEH.* MUCH THE MILLER'S SON. KNOWN FOR HIS *SILENCE.*
SLITCH
NO LAST WORDS? PITY.
I ALWAYS WRITE DOWN THE FINAL SENTIMENTS OF THE MEN I'VE KILLED. I'VE QUITE A *COLLECTION.*

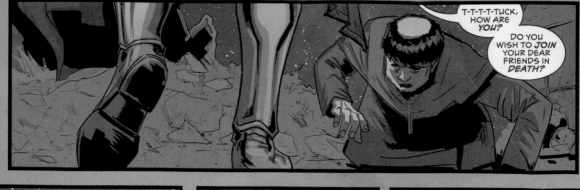

T-T-T-T-TUCK, HOW ARE YOU?

DO YOU WISH TO JOIN YOUR DEAR FRIENDS IN DEATH?

I-I-I... BY THE G-G-GRACES OF GOD--

QUIET, BUFFOON. YOUR GOD IS NOT HERE, AS YOU'LL NOTICE. IT'S YOU AND I.

RUN, FAT MAN.

RUN LIKE THE CRAVEN WRETCH YOU ARE.

P-P-PLEASE...

RUN!

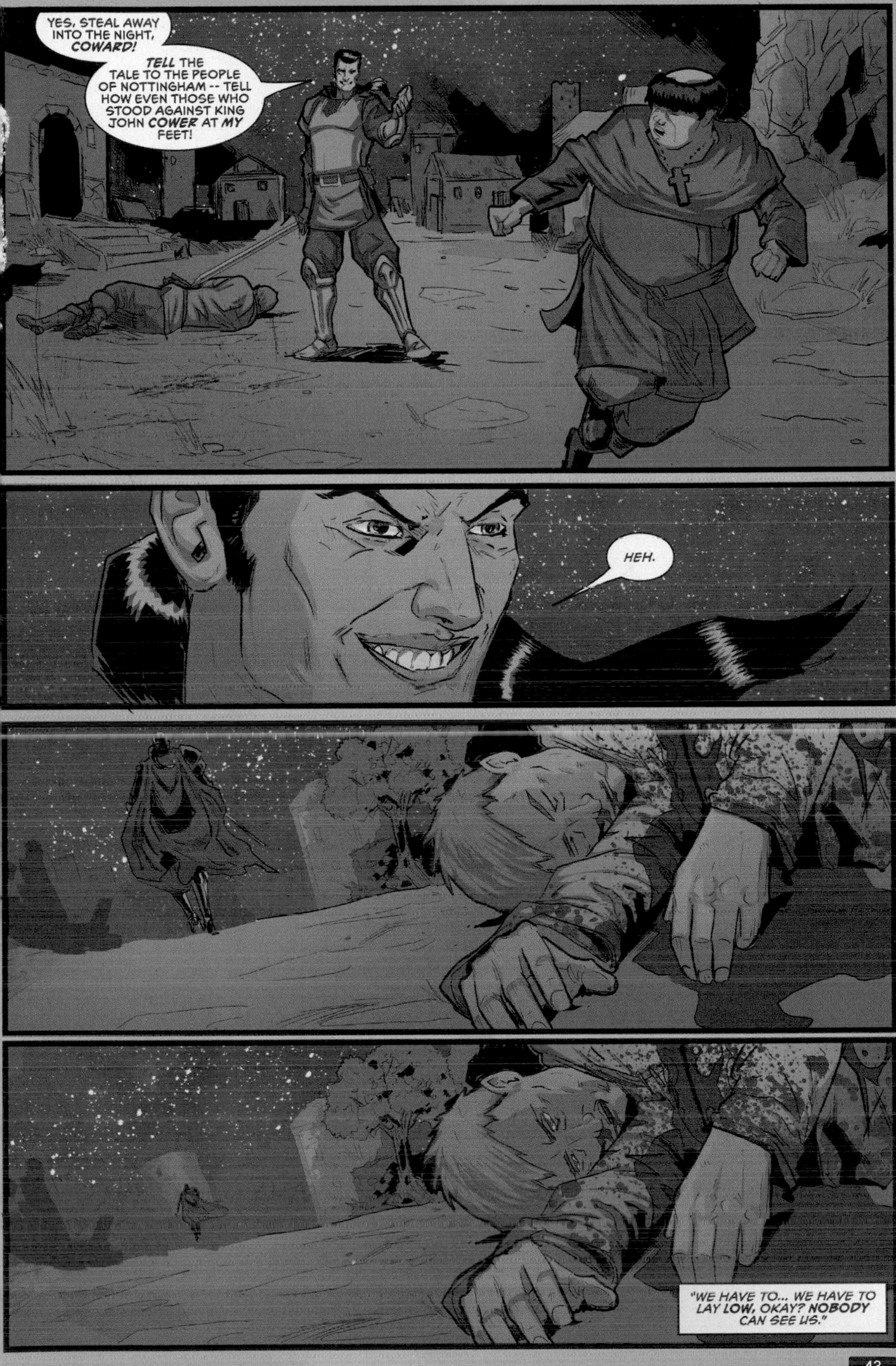
YES, STEAL AWAY INTO THE NIGHT, COWARD!
TELL THE TALE TO THE PEOPLE OF NOTTINGHAM -- TELL HOW EVEN THOSE WHO STOOD AGAINST KING JOHN COWER AT MY FEET!
HEH.
"WE HAVE TO... WE HAVE TO LAY LOW, OKAY? NOBODY CAN SEE US."

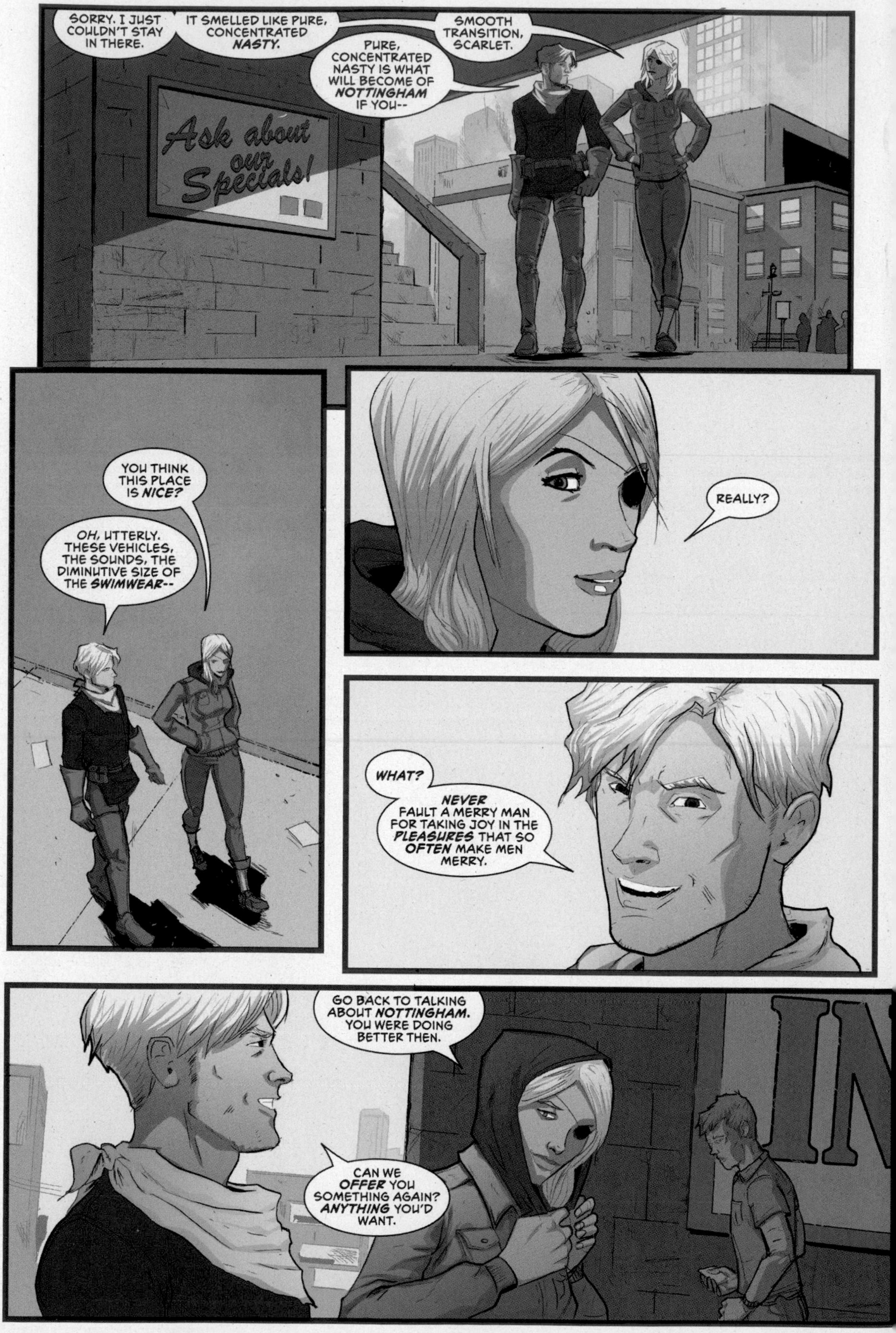
SORRY. I JUST COULDN'T STAY IN THERE.
IT SMELLED LIKE PURE, CONCENTRATED NASTY.
SMOOTH TRANSITION, SCARLET.
PURE, CONCENTRATED NASTY IS WHAT WILL BECOME OF NOTTINGHAM IF YOU--
Ask about our Specials!
YOU THINK THIS PLACE IS NICE?
OH, UTTERLY. THESE VEHICLES, THE SOUNDS, THE DIMINUTIVE SIZE OF THE SWIMWEAR--
REALLY?
WHAT?
NEVER FAULT A MERRY MAN FOR TAKING JOY IN THE PLEASURES THAT SO OFTEN MAKE MEN MERRY.
GO BACK TO TALKING ABOUT NOTTINGHAM. YOU WERE DOING BETTER THEN.
CAN WE OFFER YOU SOMETHING AGAIN? ANYTHING YOU'D WANT.

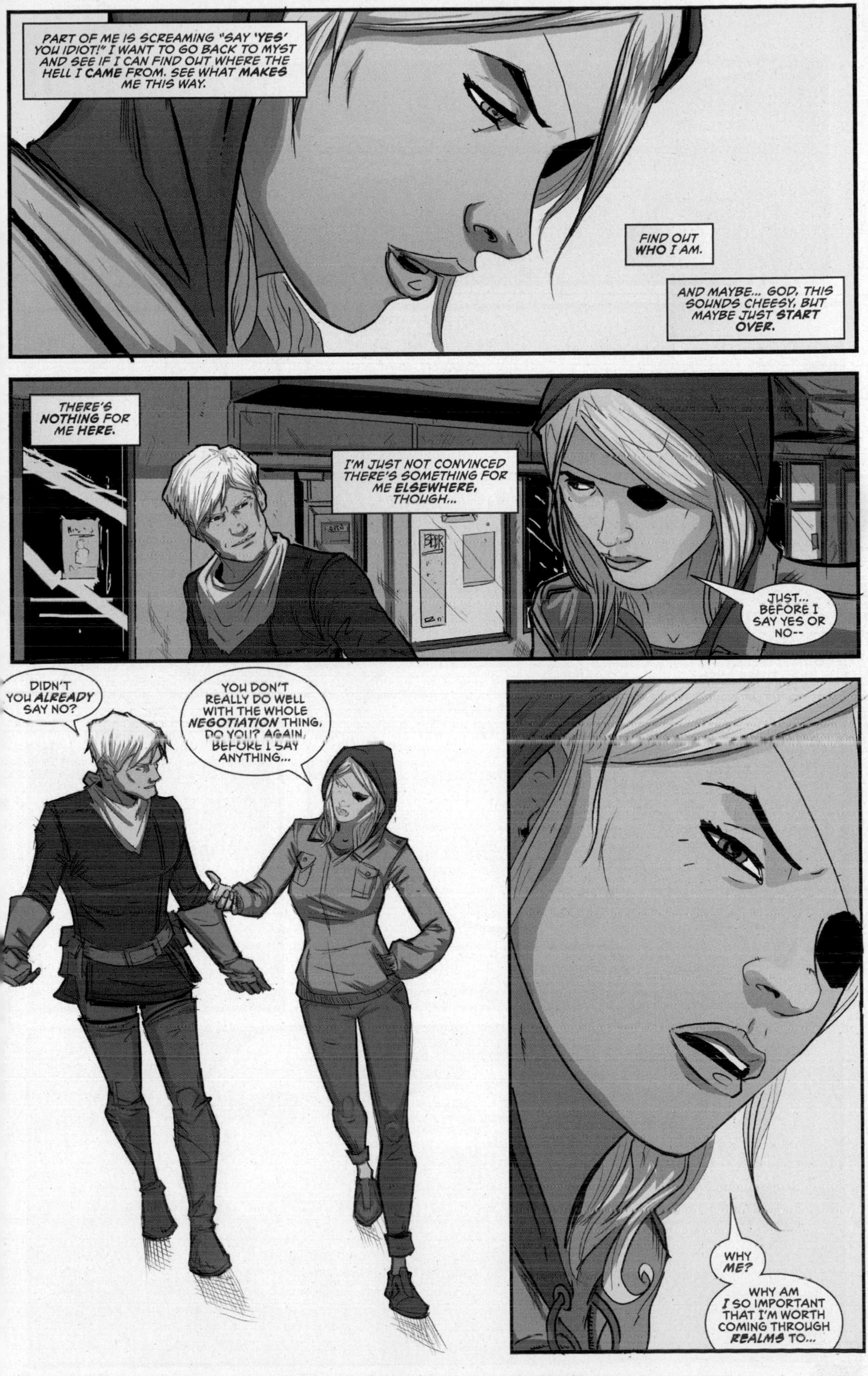
PART OF ME IS SCREAMING "SAY 'YES' YOU IDIOT!" I WANT TO GO BACK TO MYST AND SEE IF I CAN FIND OUT WHERE THE HELL I CAME FROM. SEE WHAT MAKES ME THIS WAY.
FIND OUT WHO I AM.
AND MAYBE... GOD, THIS SOUNDS CHEESY, BUT MAYBE JUST START OVER.
THERE'S NOTHING FOR ME HERE.
I'M JUST NOT CONVINCED THERE'S SOMETHING FOR ME ELSEWHERE, THOUGH...
JUST... BEFORE I SAY YES OR NO--
DIDN'T YOU ALREADY SAY NO?
YOU DON'T REALLY DO WELL WITH THE WHOLE NEGOTIATION THING, DO YOU? AGAIN, BEFORE I SAY ANYTHING...
WHY ME?
WHY AM I SO IMPORTANT THAT I'M WORTH COMING THROUGH REALMS TO...

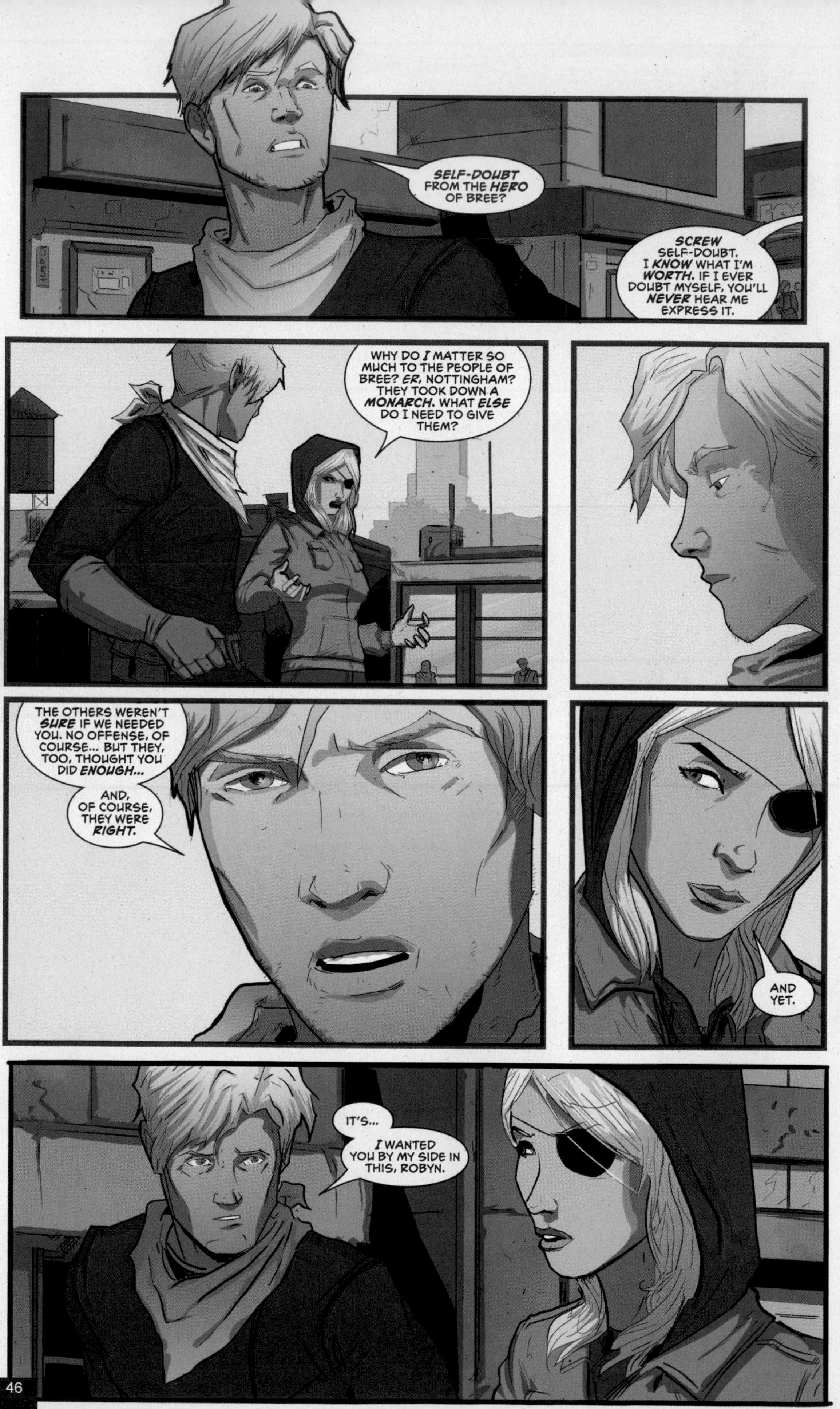

SELF-DOUBT FROM THE HERO OF BREE?
SCREW SELF-DOUBT. I KNOW WHAT I'M WORTH. IF I EVER DOUBT MYSELF, YOU'LL NEVER HEAR ME EXPRESS IT.
WHY DO I MATTER SO MUCH TO THE PEOPLE OF BREE? ER, NOTTINGHAM? THEY TOOK DOWN A MONARCH. WHAT ELSE DO I NEED TO GIVE THEM?
THE OTHERS WEREN'T SURE IF WE NEEDED YOU. NO OFFENSE, OF COURSE... BUT THEY, TOO, THOUGHT YOU DID ENOUGH...
AND, OF COURSE, THEY WERE RIGHT.
AND YET.
IT'S...
I WANTED YOU BY MY SIDE IN THIS, ROBYN.

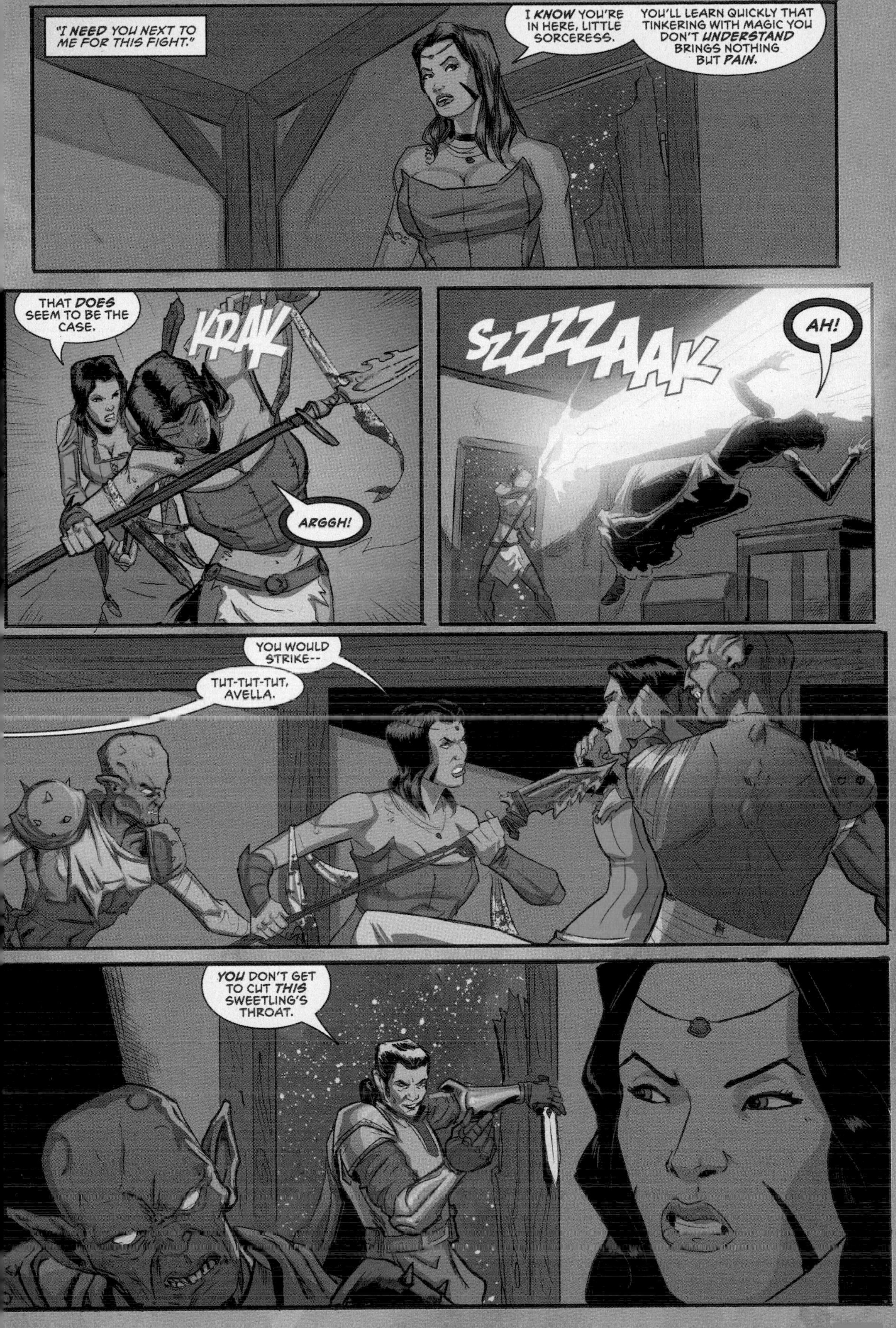
"I NEED YOU NEXT TO ME FOR THIS FIGHT."
I KNOW YOU'RE IN HERE, LITTLE SORCERESS.
YOU'LL LEARN QUICKLY THAT TINKERING WITH MAGIC YOU DON'T UNDERSTAND BRINGS NOTHING BUT PAIN.
THAT DOES SEEM TO BE THE CASE.
KRAK
ARGGH!
SZZZZAAK
AH!
YOU WOULD STRIKE--
TUT-TUT-TUT, AVELLA.
YOU DON'T GET TO CUT THIS SWEETLING'S THROAT.

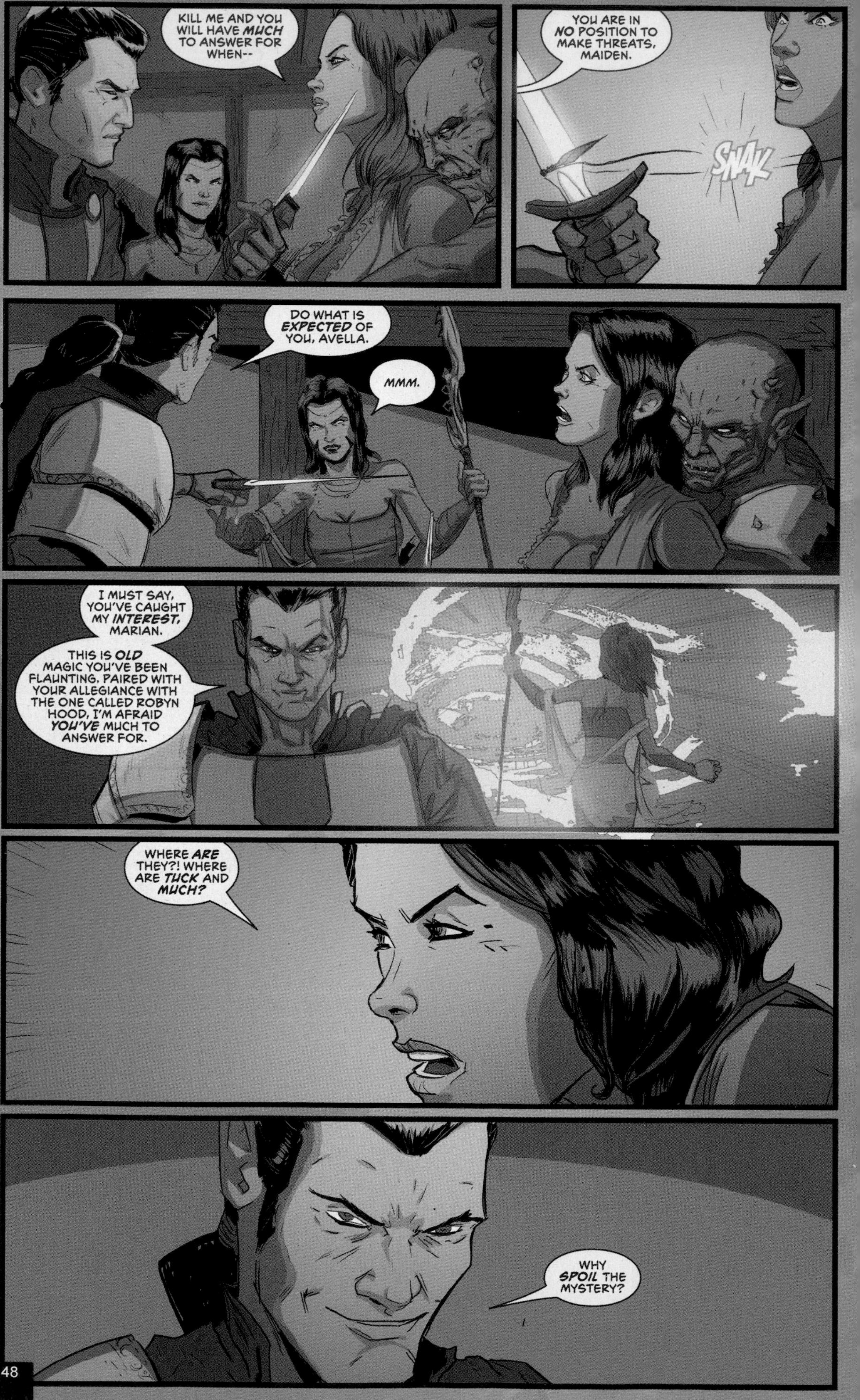
KILL ME AND YOU WILL HAVE MUCH TO ANSWER FOR WHEN--
YOU ARE IN NO POSITION TO MAKE THREATS, MAIDEN.
SNAK
DO WHAT IS EXPECTED OF YOU, AVELLA.
MMM.
I MUST SAY, YOU'VE CAUGHT MY INTEREST, MARIAN.
THIS IS OLD MAGIC YOU'VE BEEN FLAUNTING. PAIRED WITH YOUR ALLEGIANCE WITH THE ONE CALLED ROBYN HOOD, I'M AFRAID YOU'VE MUCH TO ANSWER FOR.
WHERE ARE THEY?! WHERE ARE TUCK AND MUCH?
WHY SPOIL THE MYSTERY?

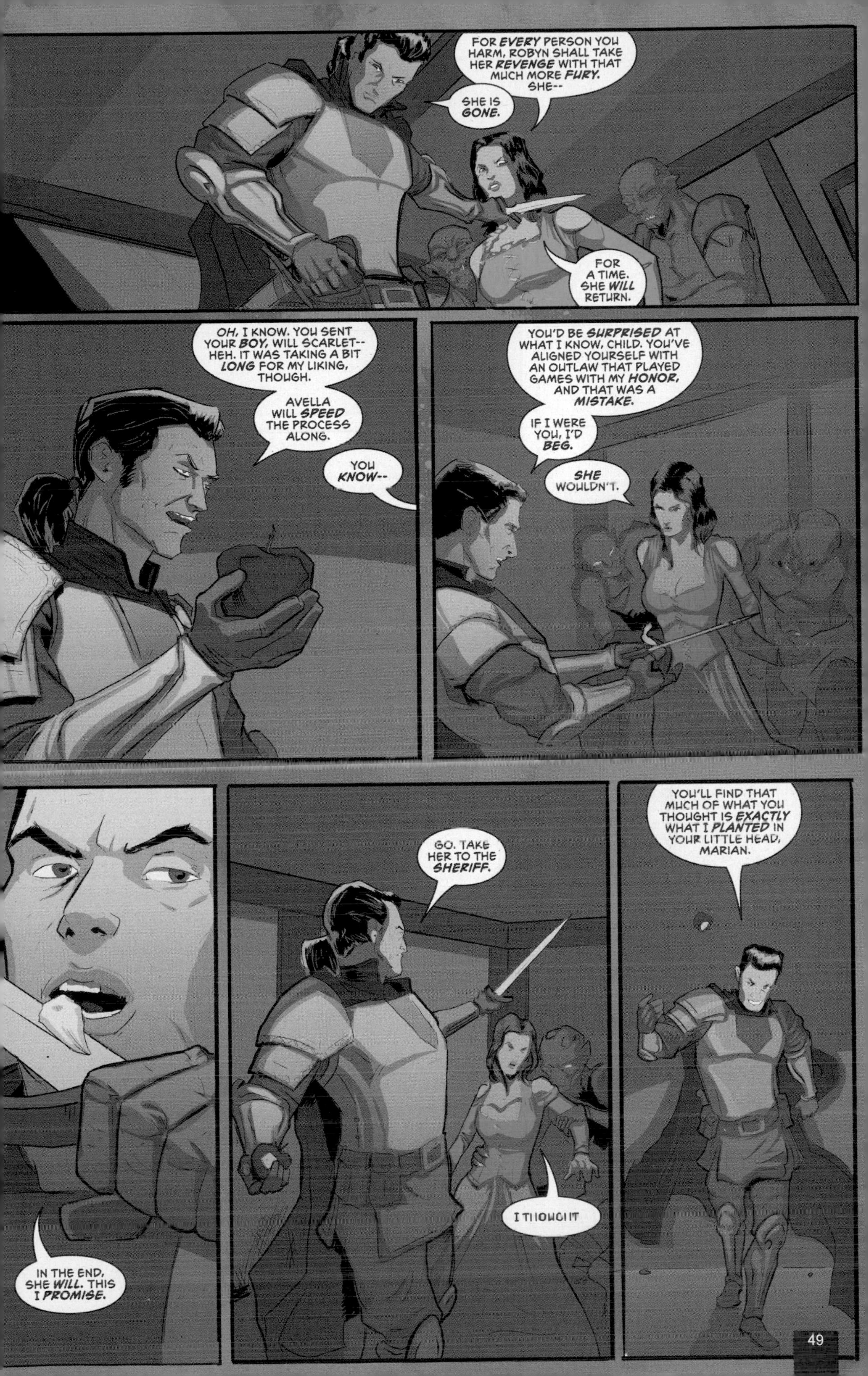
FOR EVERY PERSON YOU HARM, ROBYN SHALL TAKE HER REVENGE WITH THAT MUCH MORE FURY. SHE--
SHE IS GONE.
FOR A TIME. SHE WILL RETURN.
OH, I KNOW. YOU SENT YOUR BOY, WILL SCARLET-- HEH. IT WAS TAKING A BIT LONG FOR MY LIKING, THOUGH.
AVELLA WILL SPEED THE PROCESS ALONG.
YOU KNOW--
YOU'D BE SURPRISED AT WHAT I KNOW, CHILD. YOU'VE ALIGNED YOURSELF WITH AN OUTLAW THAT PLAYED GAMES WITH MY HONOR, AND THAT WAS A MISTAKE.
IF I WERE YOU, I'D BEG.
SHE WOULDN'T.
IN THE END, SHE WILL. THIS I PROMISE.
GO. TAKE HER TO THE SHERIFF.
I THOUGHT
YOU'LL FIND THAT MUCH OF WHAT YOU THOUGHT IS EXACTLY WHAT I PLANTED IN YOUR LITTLE HEAD, MARIAN.

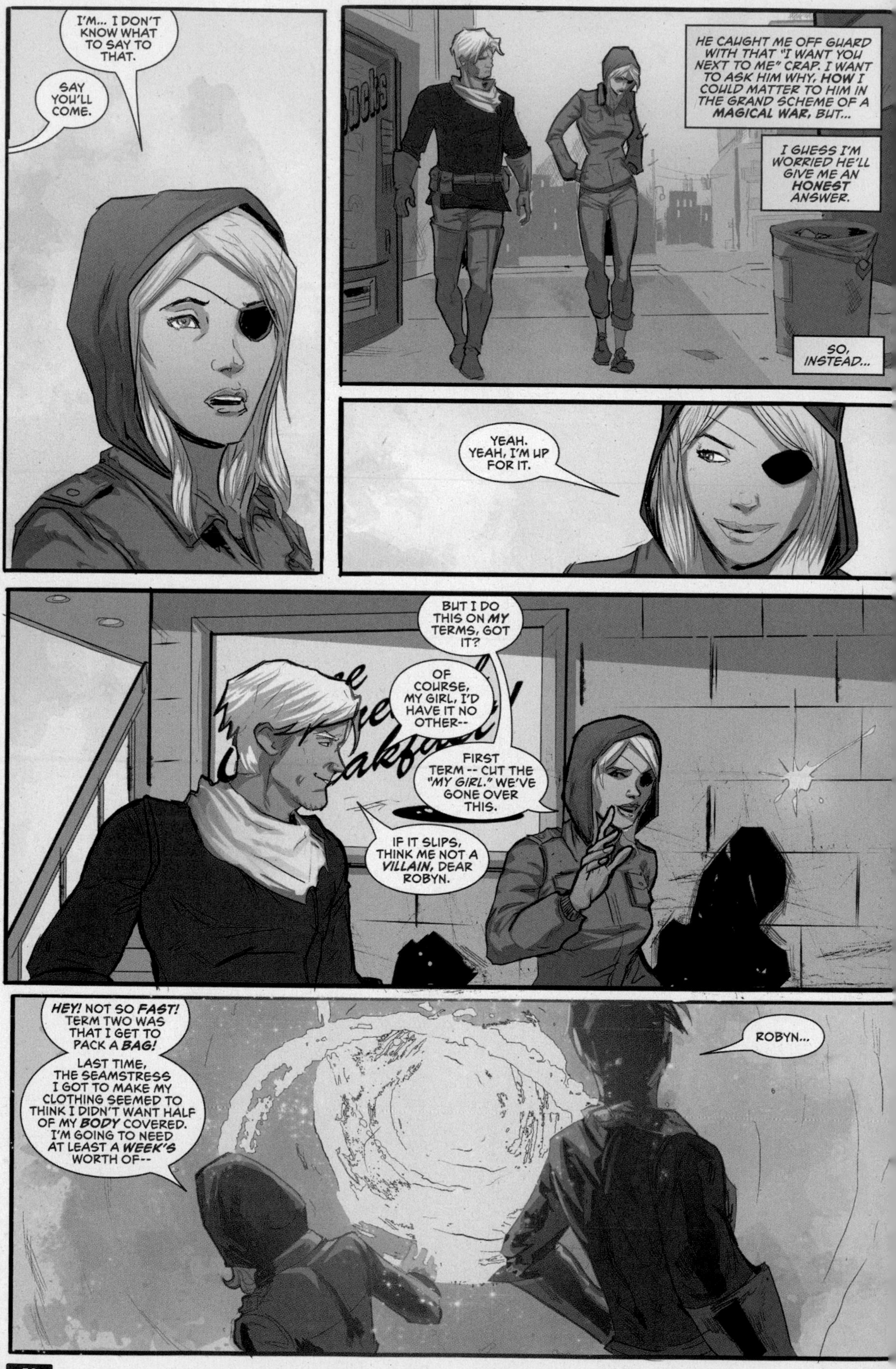

I'M... I DON'T KNOW WHAT TO SAY TO THAT.
SAY YOU'LL COME.
HE CAUGHT ME OFF GUARD WITH THAT "I WANT YOU NEXT TO ME" CRAP. I WANT TO ASK HIM WHY, HOW I COULD MATTER TO HIM IN THE GRAND SCHEME OF A MAGICAL WAR, BUT...
I GUESS I'M WORRIED HE'LL GIVE ME AN HONEST ANSWER.
SO, INSTEAD...
YEAH. YEAH, I'M UP FOR IT.
BUT I DO THIS ON MY TERMS, GOT IT?
OF COURSE, MY GIRL, I'D HAVE IT NO OTHER--
FIRST TERM -- CUT THE "MY GIRL." WE'VE GONE OVER THIS.
IF IT SLIPS, THINK ME NOT A VILLAIN, DEAR ROBYN.
HEY! NOT SO FAST! TERM TWO WAS THAT I GET TO PACK A BAG!
LAST TIME, THE SEAMSTRESS I GOT TO MAKE MY CLOTHING SEEMED TO THINK I DIDN'T WANT HALF OF MY BODY COVERED. I'M GOING TO NEED AT LEAST A WEEK'S WORTH OF--
ROBYN...

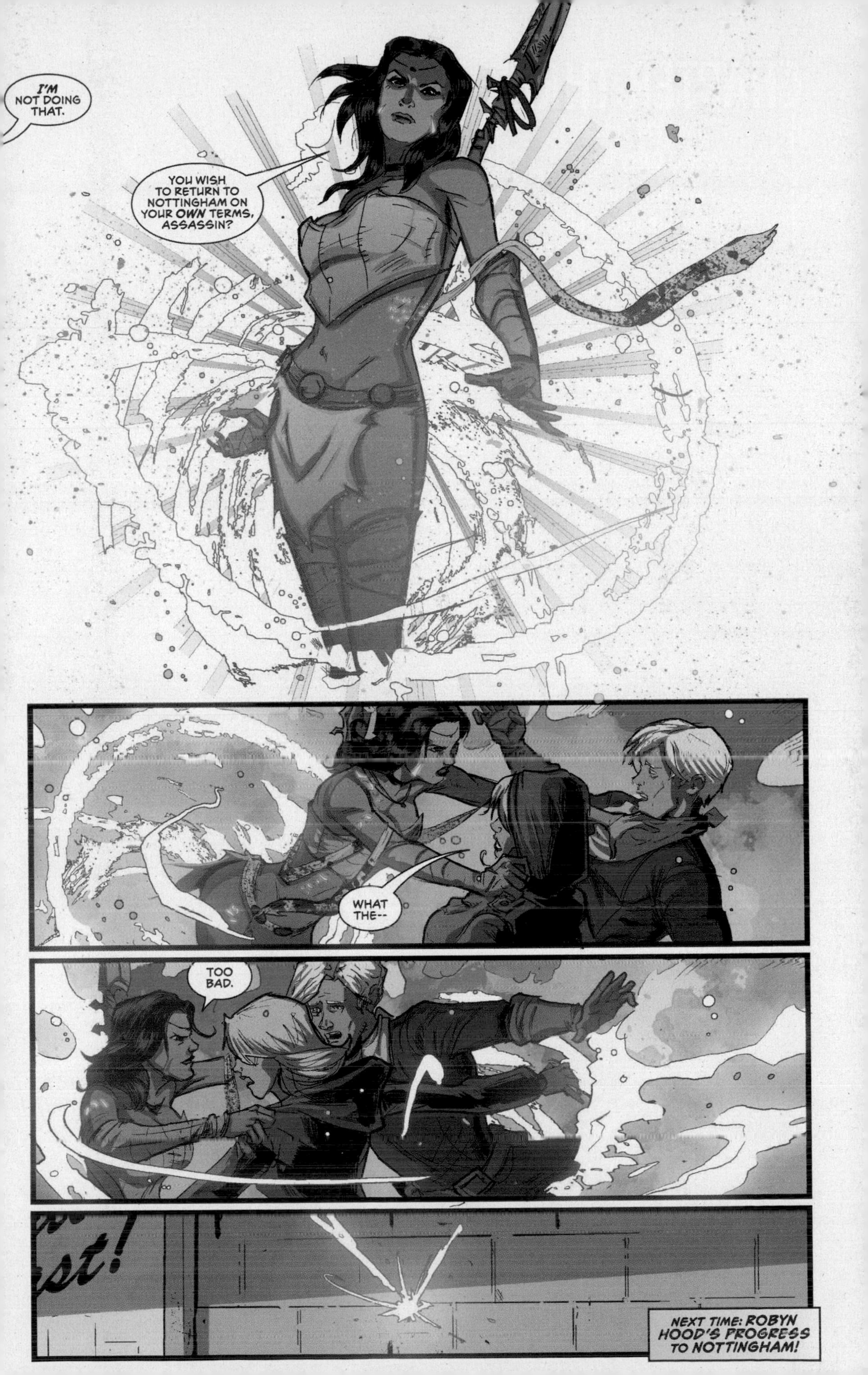
I'M NOT DOING THAT.
YOU WISH TO RETURN TO NOTTINGHAM ON YOUR OWN TERMS, ASSASSIN?
WHAT THE--
TOO BAD.
NEXT TIME: ROBYN HOOD'S PROGRESS TO NOTTINGHAM!

# CHAPTER THREE

*Writer* Pat Shand
*Artwork* Larry Watts
*Colors* Nick Filardi
*Letters* Jim Campbell

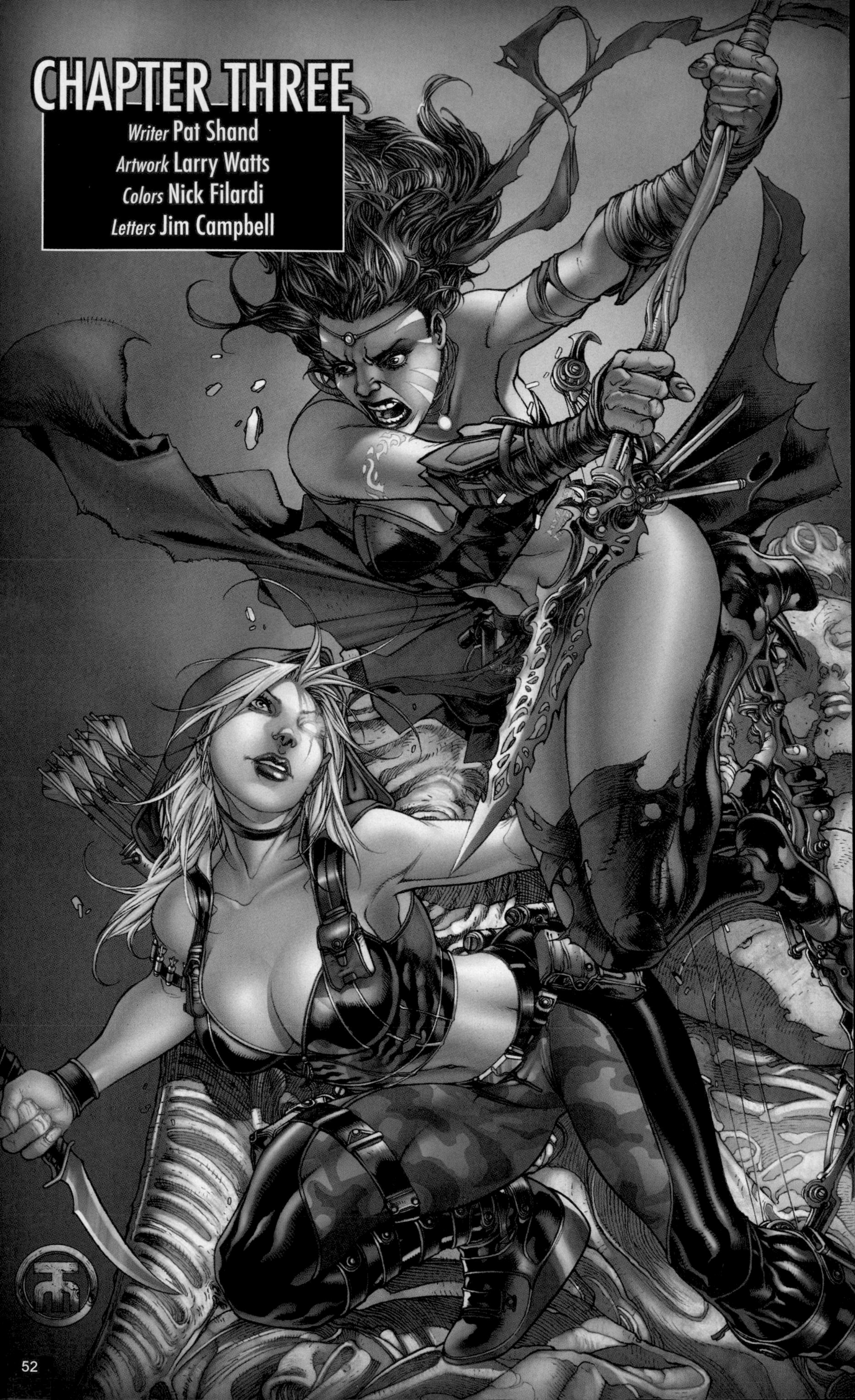

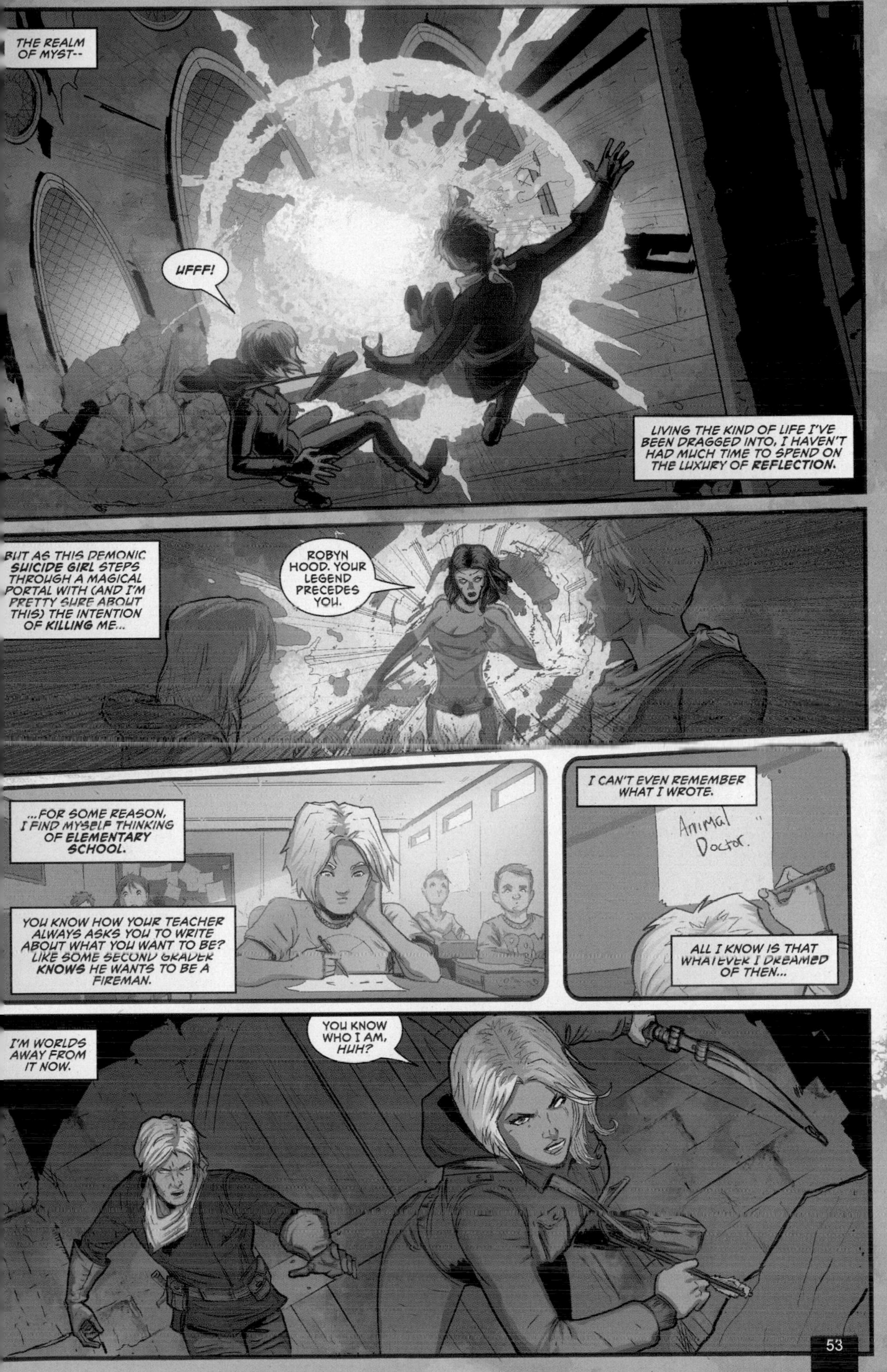
THE REALM OF MYST--
UFFF!
LIVING THE KIND OF LIFE I'VE BEEN DRAGGED INTO, I HAVEN'T HAD MUCH TIME TO SPEND ON THE LUXURY OF REFLECTION.
BUT AS THIS DEMONIC SUICIDE GIRL STEPS THROUGH A MAGICAL PORTAL WITH (AND I'M PRETTY SURE ABOUT THIS) THE INTENTION OF KILLING ME...
ROBYN HOOD. YOUR LEGEND PRECEDES YOU.
...FOR SOME REASON, I FIND MYSELF THINKING OF ELEMENTARY SCHOOL.
YOU KNOW HOW YOUR TEACHER ALWAYS ASKS YOU TO WRITE ABOUT WHAT YOU WANT TO BE? LIKE SOME SECOND GRADER KNOWS HE WANTS TO BE A FIREMAN.
I CAN'T EVEN REMEMBER WHAT I WROTE.
Animal Doctor.
ALL I KNOW IS THAT WHATEVER I DREAMED OF THEN...
I'M WORLDS AWAY FROM IT NOW.
YOU KNOW WHO I AM, HUH?

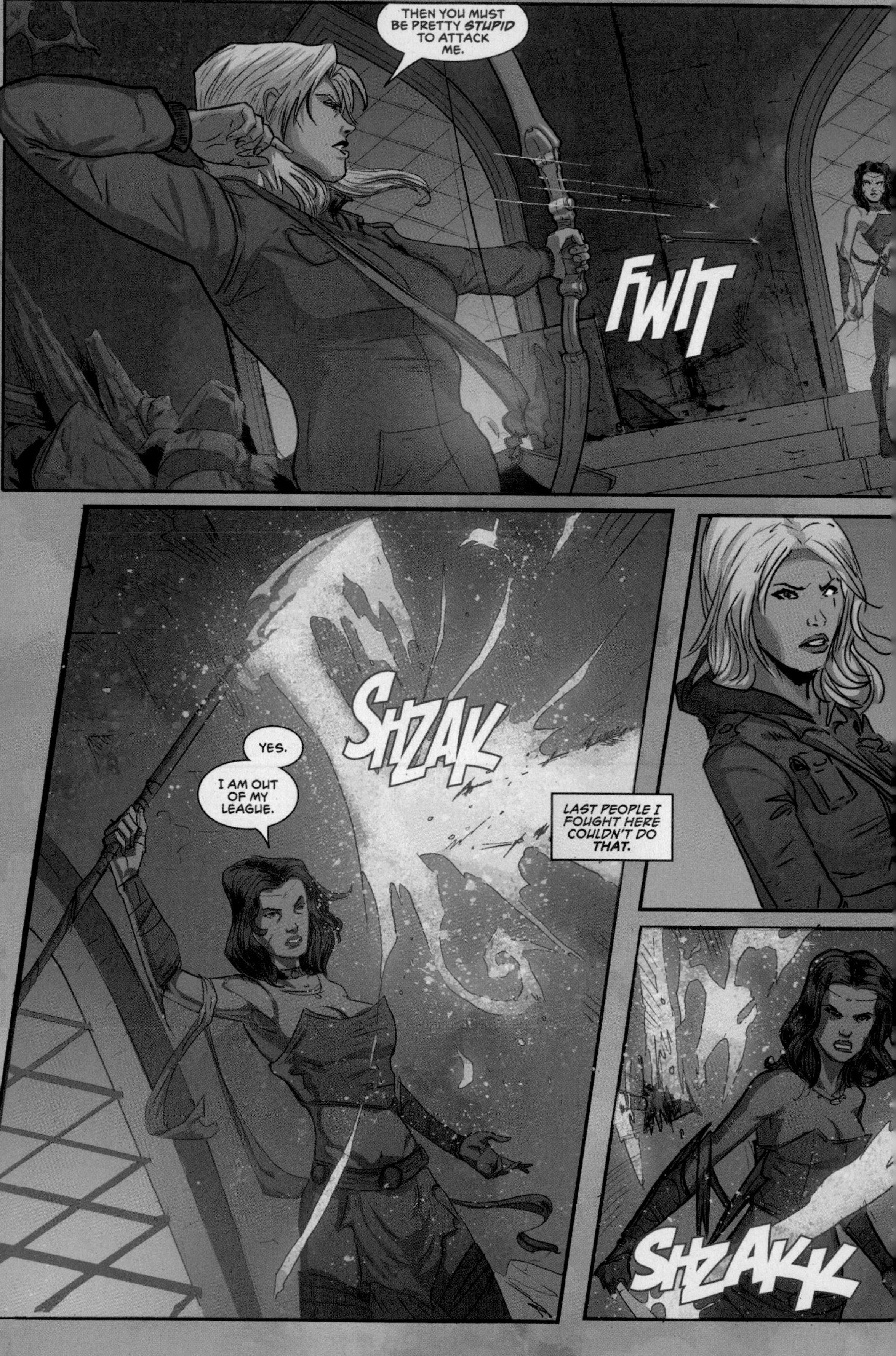
THEN YOU MUST BE PRETTY STUPID TO ATTACK ME.
FWIT
SHZAK
YES.
I AM OUT OF MY LEAGUE.
LAST PEOPLE I FOUGHT HERE COULDN'T DO THAT.
SHZAKK

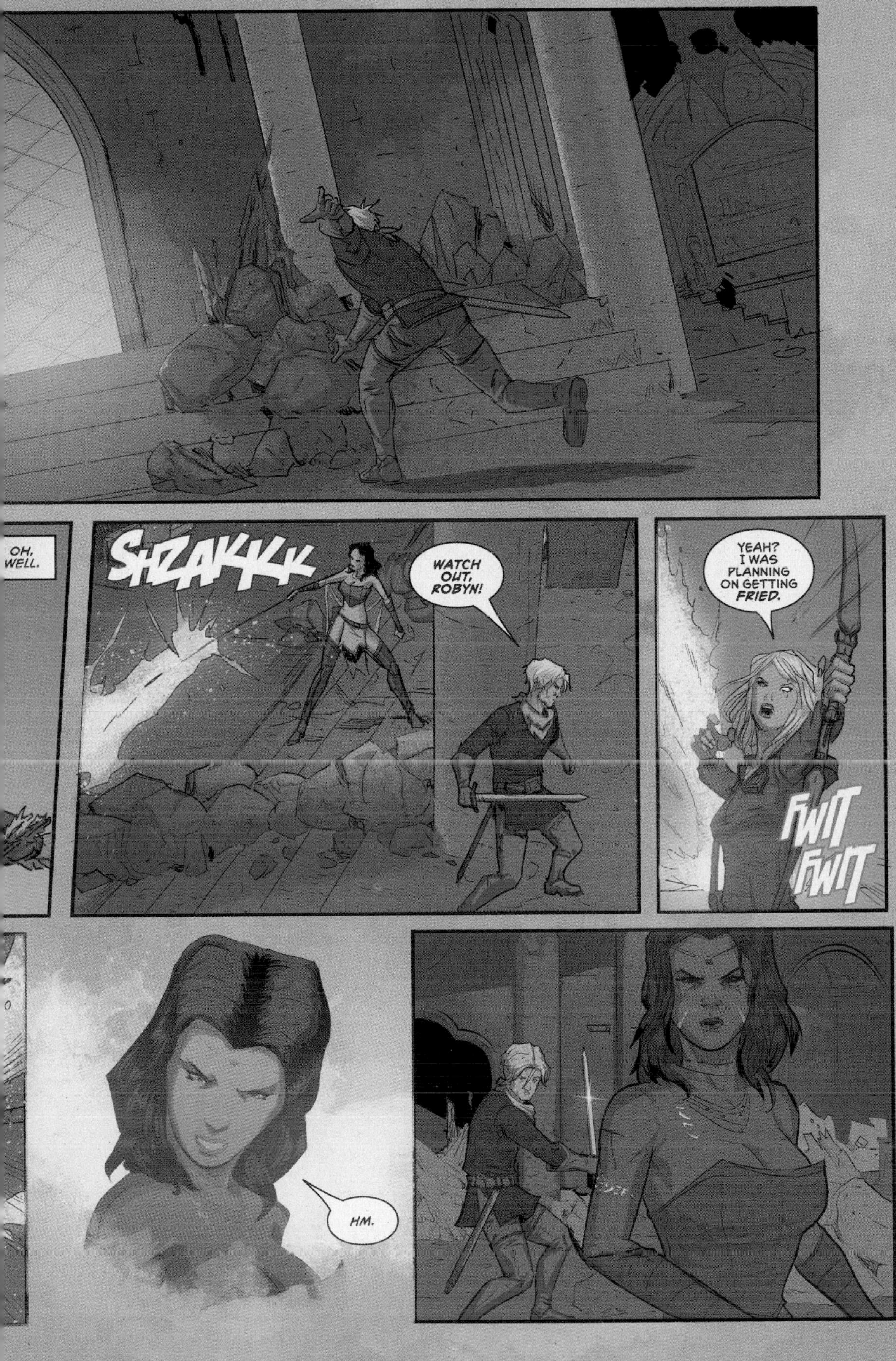
OH, WELL.
SHZAKKK
WATCH OUT, ROBYN!
YEAH? I WAS PLANNING ON GETTING FRIED.
FWIT FWIT
HM.

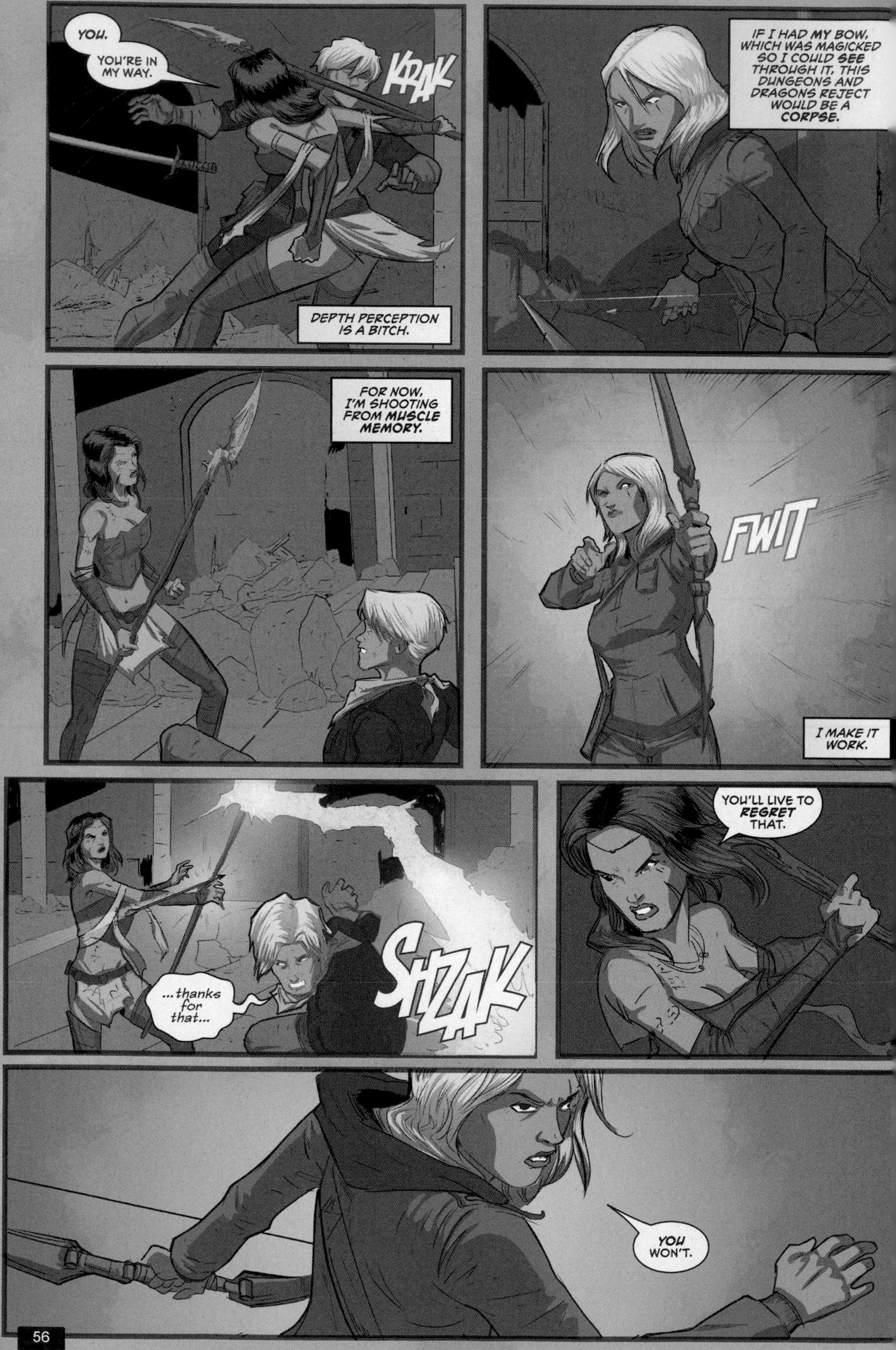

YOU.
YOU'RE IN MY WAY.
KRAK
DEPTH PERCEPTION IS A BITCH.
IF I HAD MY BOW, WHICH WAS MAGICKED SO I COULD SEE THROUGH IT, THIS DUNGEONS AND DRAGONS REJECT WOULD BE A CORPSE.
FOR NOW, I'M SHOOTING FROM MUSCLE MEMORY.
FWIT
I MAKE IT WORK.
SHZAK
...thanks for that...
YOU'LL LIVE TO REGRET THAT.
YOU WON'T.

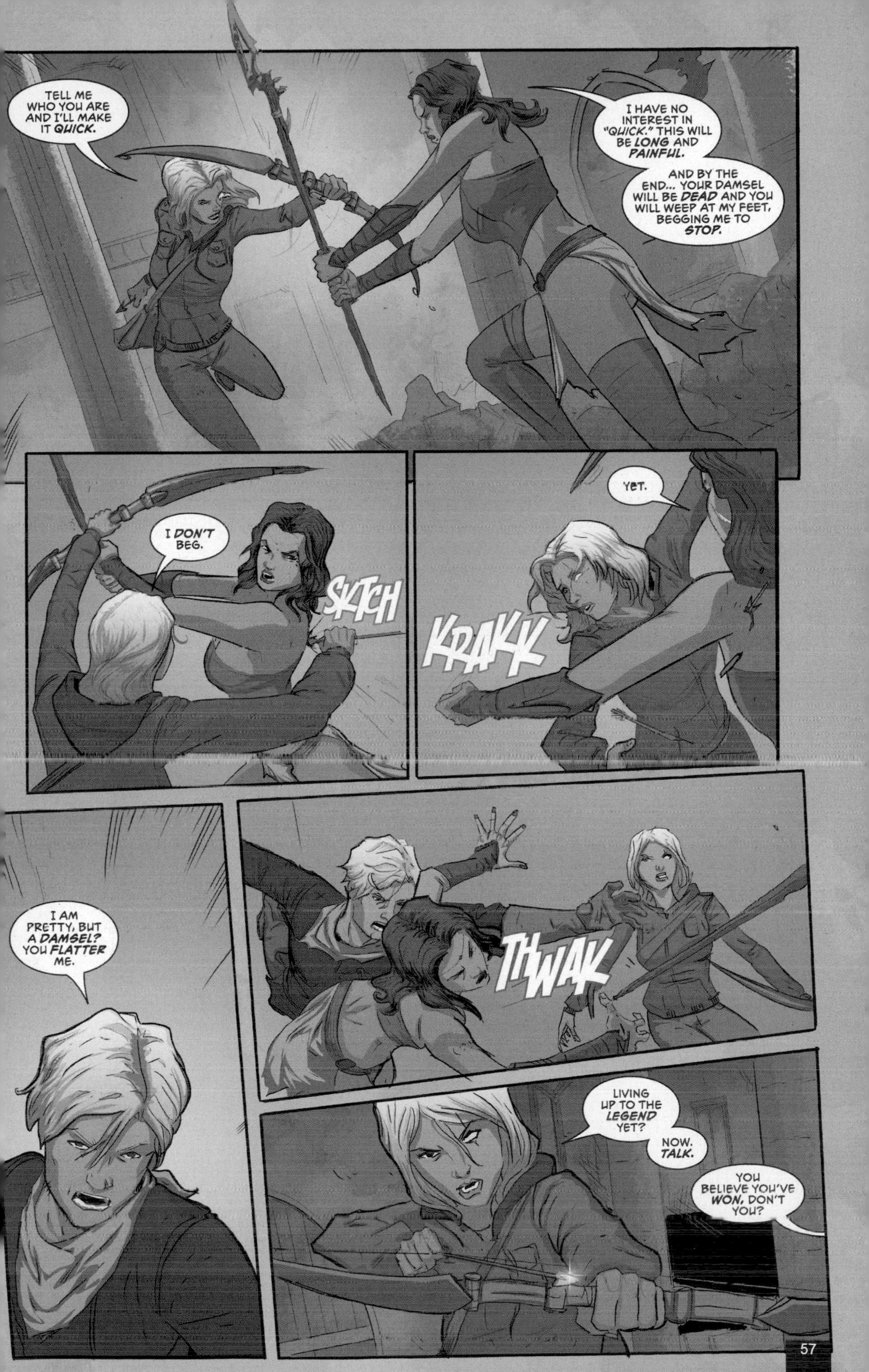
TELL ME WHO YOU ARE AND I'LL MAKE IT QUICK.
I HAVE NO INTEREST IN "QUICK." THIS WILL BE LONG AND PAINFUL.
AND BY THE END... YOUR DAMSEL WILL BE DEAD AND YOU WILL WEEP AT MY FEET, BEGGING ME TO STOP.
I DON'T BEG.
SKTCH
YET.
KRAKK
I AM PRETTY, BUT A DAMSEL? YOU FLATTER ME.
THWAK
LIVING UP TO THE LEGEND YET?
NOW. TALK.
YOU BELIEVE YOU'VE WON, DON'T YOU?

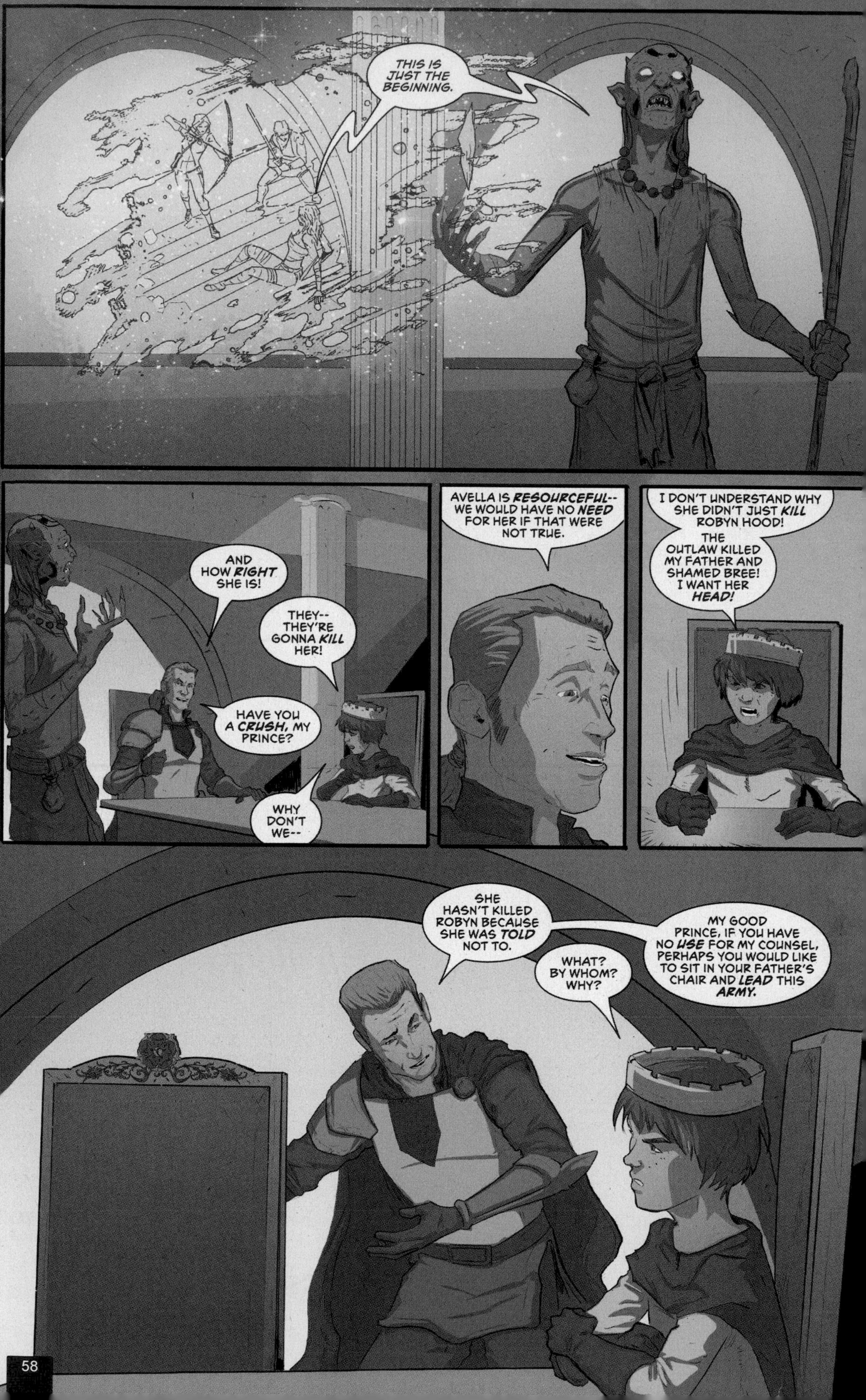
THIS IS JUST THE BEGINNING.
AND HOW RIGHT SHE IS!
THEY-- THEY'RE GONNA KILL HER!
HAVE YOU A CRUSH, MY PRINCE?
WHY DON'T WE--
AVELLA IS RESOURCEFUL-- WE WOULD HAVE NO NEED FOR HER IF THAT WERE NOT TRUE.
I DON'T UNDERSTAND WHY SHE DIDN'T JUST KILL ROBYN HOOD!
THE OUTLAW KILLED MY FATHER AND SHAMED BREE! I WANT HER HEAD!
SHE HASN'T KILLED ROBYN BECAUSE SHE WAS TOLD NOT TO.
WHAT? BY WHOM? WHY?
MY GOOD PRINCE, IF YOU HAVE NO USE FOR MY COUNSEL, PERHAPS YOU WOULD LIKE TO SIT IN YOUR FATHER'S CHAIR AND LEAD THIS ARMY.

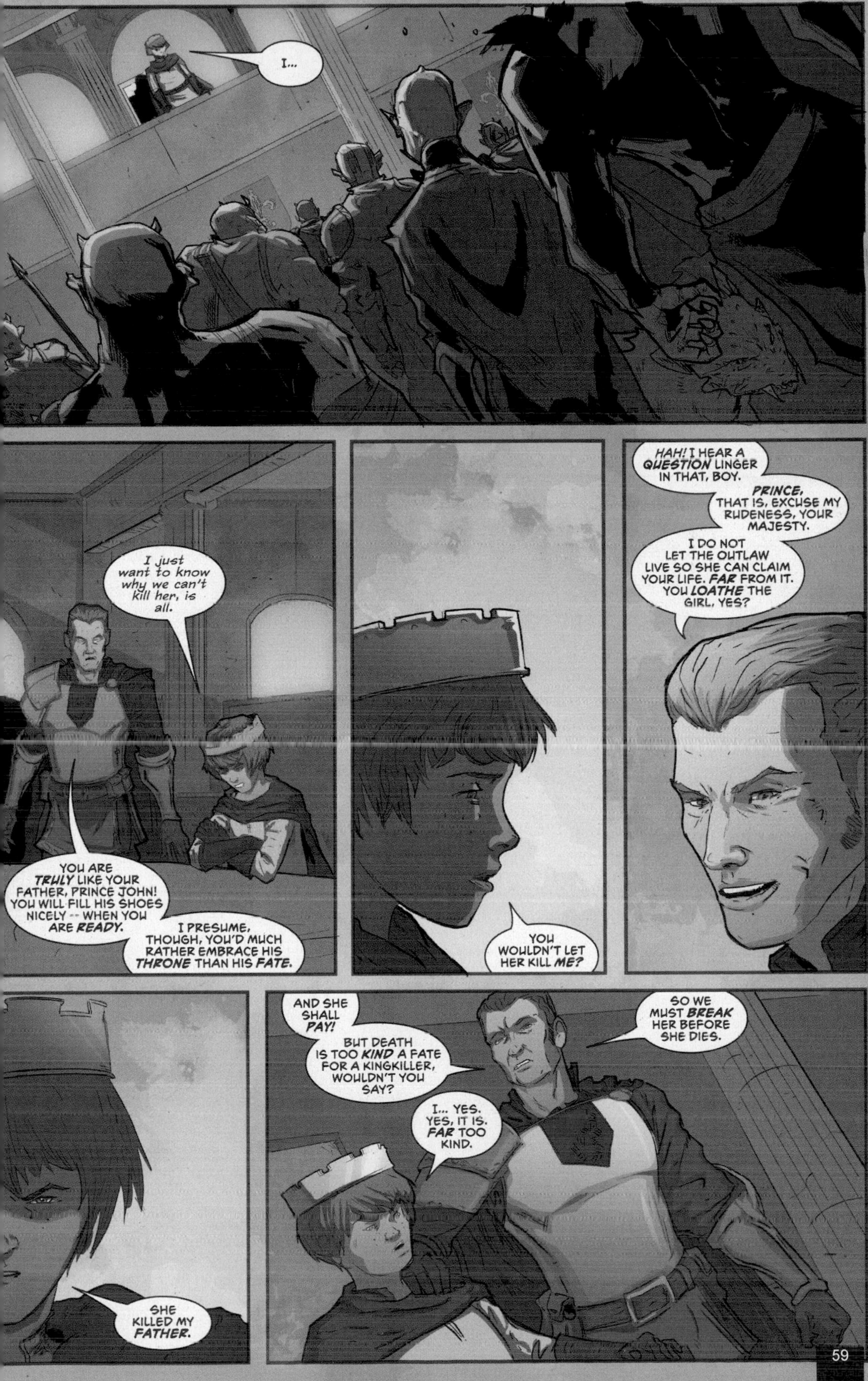
I...
I just want to know why we can't kill her, is all.
YOU ARE TRULY LIKE YOUR FATHER, PRINCE JOHN! YOU WILL FILL HIS SHOES NICELY -- WHEN YOU ARE READY.
I PRESUME, THOUGH, YOU'D MUCH RATHER EMBRACE HIS THRONE THAN HIS FATE.
YOU WOULDN'T LET HER KILL ME?
HAH! I HEAR A QUESTION LINGER IN THAT, BOY.
PRINCE, THAT IS, EXCUSE MY RUDENESS, YOUR MAJESTY.
I DO NOT LET THE OUTLAW LIVE SO SHE CAN CLAIM YOUR LIFE. FAR FROM IT. YOU LOATHE THE GIRL, YES?
SHE KILLED MY FATHER.
AND SHE SHALL PAY!
BUT DEATH IS TOO KIND A FATE FOR A KINGKILLER, WOULDN'T YOU SAY?
I... YES. YES, IT IS. FAR TOO KIND.
SO WE MUST BREAK HER BEFORE SHE DIES.

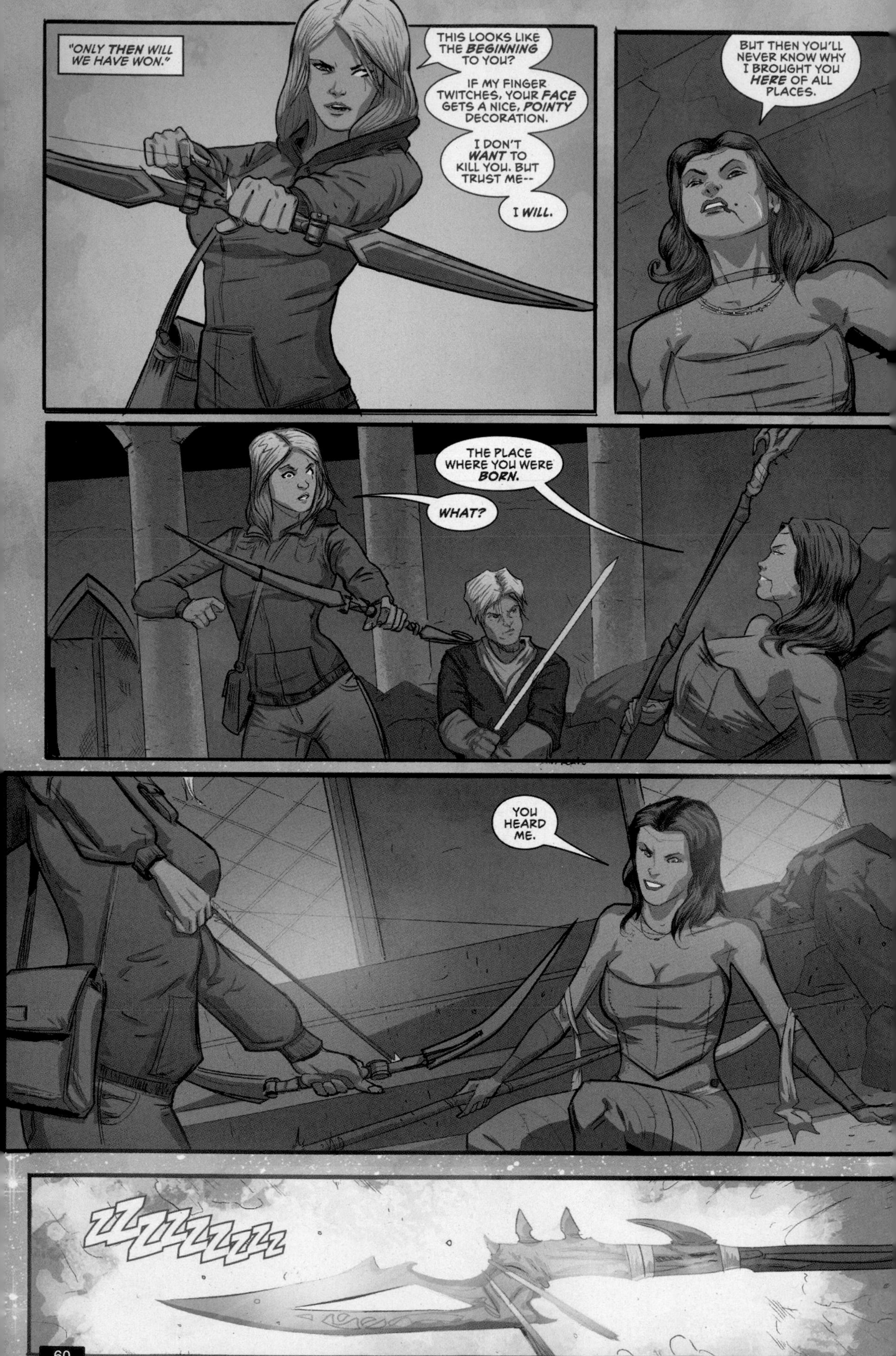
"ONLY THEN WILL WE HAVE WON."
THIS LOOKS LIKE THE BEGINNING TO YOU?
IF MY FINGER TWITCHES, YOUR FACE GETS A NICE, POINTY DECORATION.
I DON'T WANT TO KILL YOU. BUT TRUST ME--
I WILL.
BUT THEN YOU'LL NEVER KNOW WHY I BROUGHT YOU HERE OF ALL PLACES.
THE PLACE WHERE YOU WERE BORN.
WHAT?
YOU HEARD ME.
ZZZZZZZZZZ

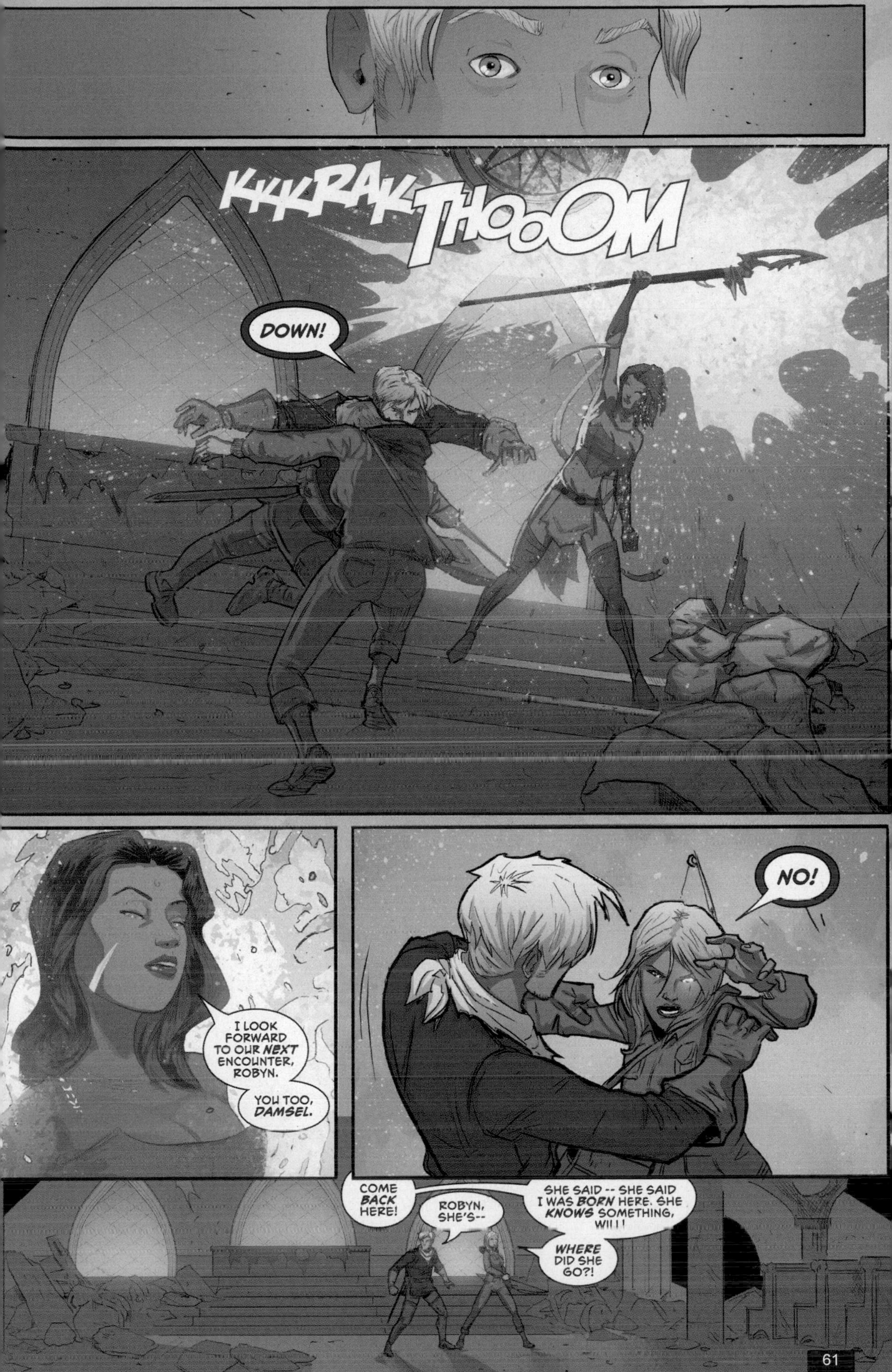
KKKRAK
THOOOM
DOWN!
I LOOK FORWARD TO OUR NEXT ENCOUNTER, ROBYN.
YOU TOO, DAMSEL.
NO!
COME BACK HERE!
ROBYN, SHE'S--
SHE SAID -- SHE SAID I WAS BORN HERE. SHE KNOWS SOMETHING, WILL!
WHERE DID SHE GO?!

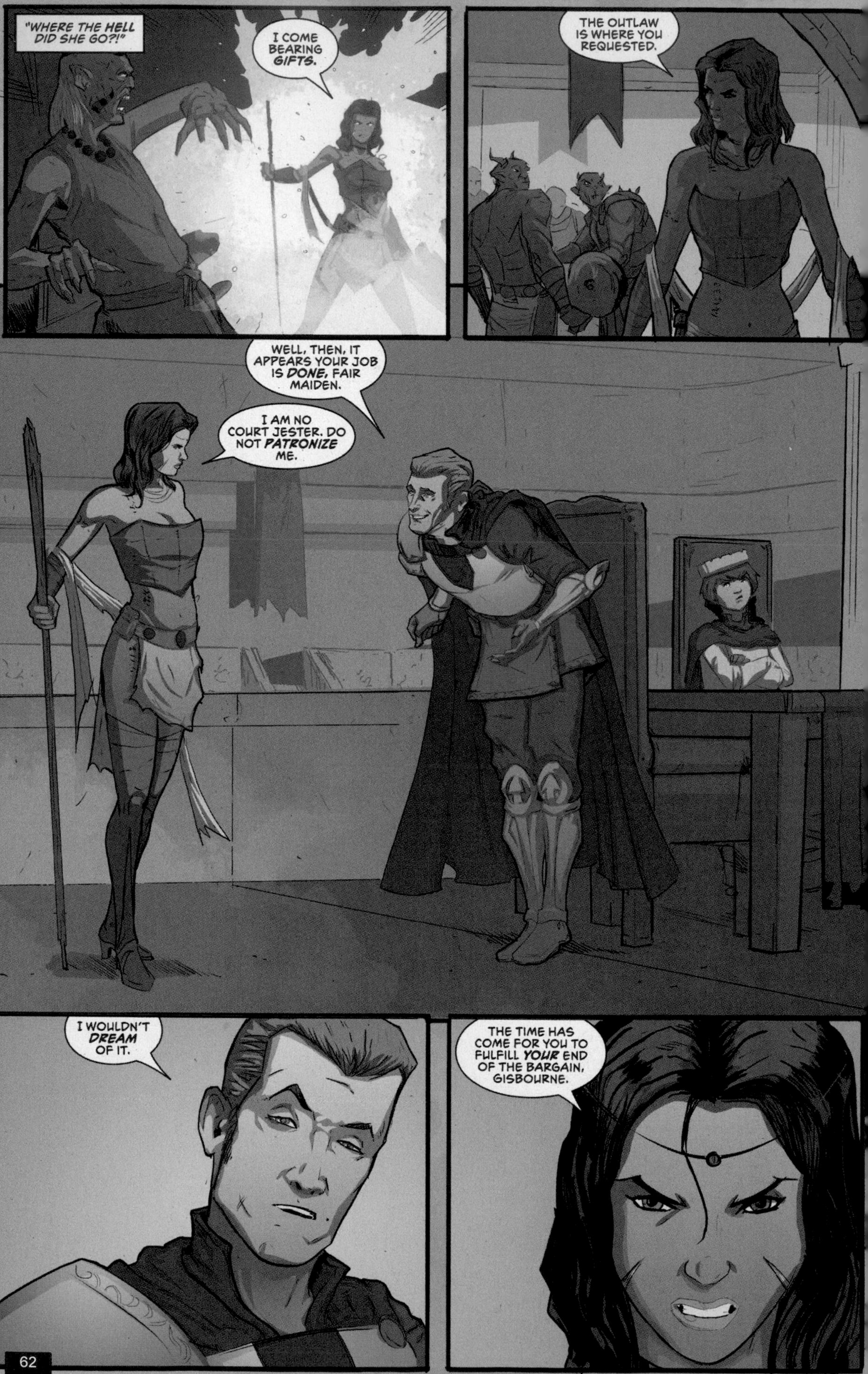
"WHERE THE HELL DID SHE GO?!"
I COME BEARING GIFTS.
THE OUTLAW IS WHERE YOU REQUESTED.
WELL, THEN, IT APPEARS YOUR JOB IS DONE, FAIR MAIDEN.
I AM NO COURT JESTER. DO NOT PATRONIZE ME.
I WOULDN'T DREAM OF IT.
THE TIME HAS COME FOR YOU TO FULFILL YOUR END OF THE BARGAIN, GISBOURNE.

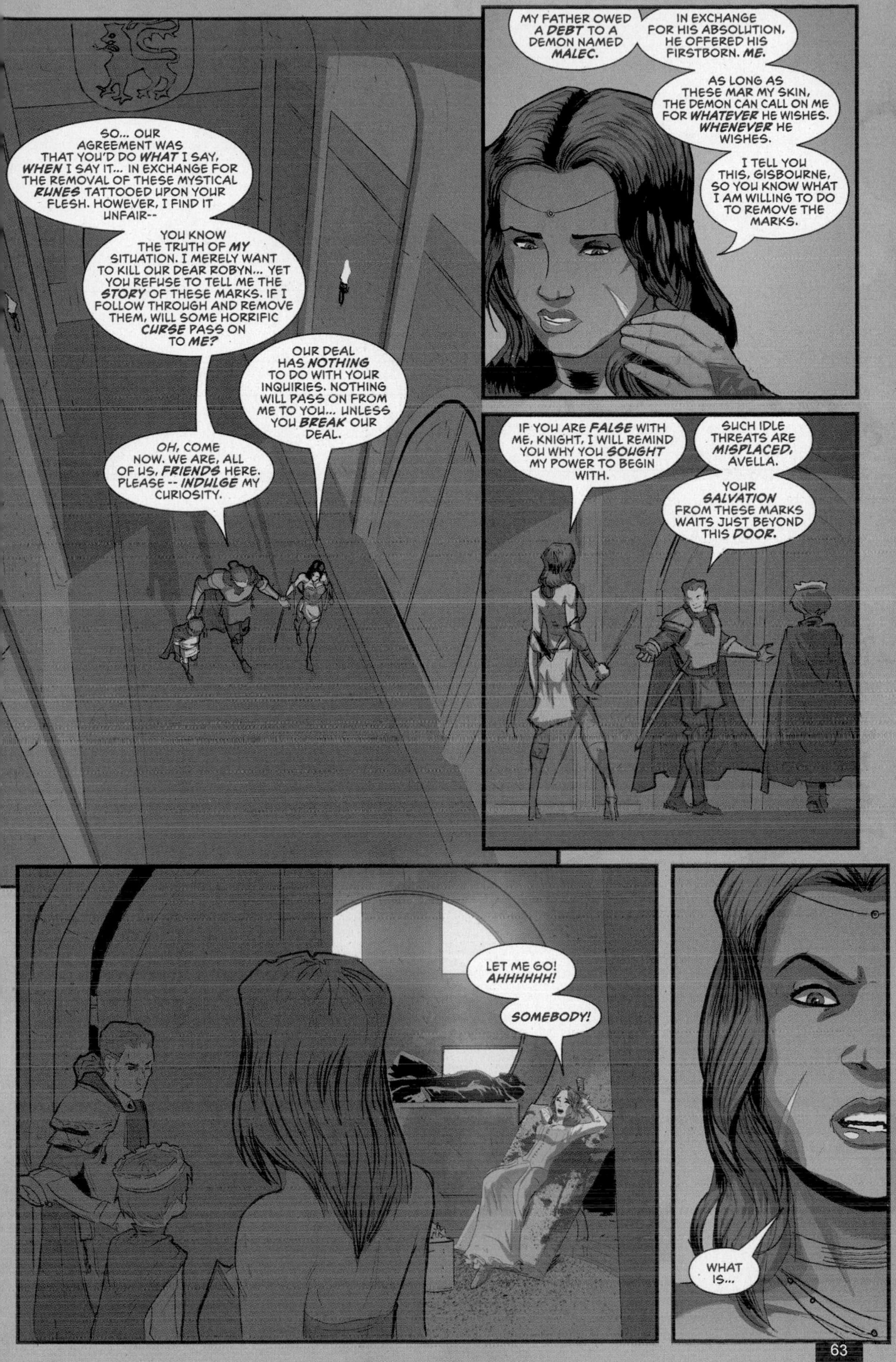

SO... OUR AGREEMENT WAS THAT YOU'D DO WHAT I SAY, WHEN I SAY IT... IN EXCHANGE FOR THE REMOVAL OF THESE MYSTICAL RUNES TATTOOED UPON YOUR FLESH. HOWEVER, I FIND IT UNFAIR--
YOU KNOW THE TRUTH OF MY SITUATION. I MERELY WANT TO KILL OUR DEAR ROBYN... YET YOU REFUSE TO TELL ME THE STORY OF THESE MARKS. IF I FOLLOW THROUGH AND REMOVE THEM, WILL SOME HORRIFIC CURSE PASS ON TO ME?
OUR DEAL HAS NOTHING TO DO WITH YOUR INQUIRIES. NOTHING WILL PASS ON FROM ME TO YOU... UNLESS YOU BREAK OUR DEAL.
OH, COME NOW. WE ARE, ALL OF US, FRIENDS HERE. PLEASE -- INDULGE MY CURIOSITY.
MY FATHER OWED A DEBT TO A DEMON NAMED MALEC.
IN EXCHANGE FOR HIS ABSOLUTION, HE OFFERED HIS FIRSTBORN. ME.
AS LONG AS THESE MAR MY SKIN, THE DEMON CAN CALL ON ME FOR WHATEVER HE WISHES. WHENEVER HE WISHES.
I TELL YOU THIS, GISBOURNE, SO YOU KNOW WHAT I AM WILLING TO DO TO REMOVE THE MARKS.
IF YOU ARE FALSE WITH ME, KNIGHT, I WILL REMIND YOU WHY YOU SOUGHT MY POWER TO BEGIN WITH.
SUCH IDLE THREATS ARE MISPLACED, AVELLA.
YOUR SALVATION FROM THESE MARKS WAITS JUST BEYOND THIS DOOR.
LET ME GO! AHHHHHH!
SOMEBODY!
WHAT IS...

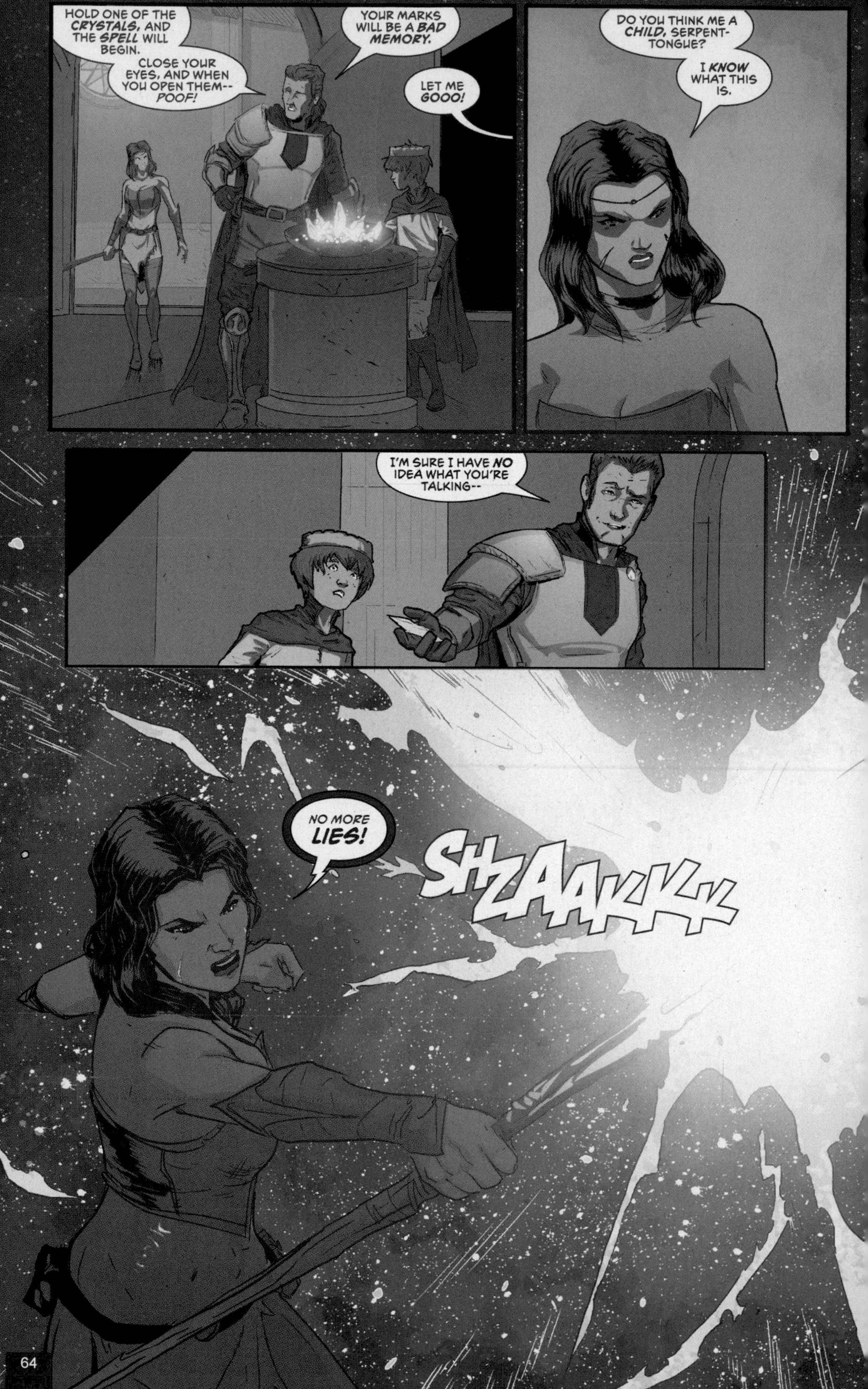
HOLD ONE OF THE CRYSTALS, AND THE SPELL WILL BEGIN.
CLOSE YOUR EYES, AND WHEN YOU OPEN THEM-- POOF!
YOUR MARKS WILL BE A BAD MEMORY.
LET ME GOOO!
DO YOU THINK ME A CHILD, SERPENT-TONGUE?
I KNOW WHAT THIS IS.
I'M SURE I HAVE NO IDEA WHAT YOU'RE TALKING--
NO MORE LIES!
SHZAAKKK

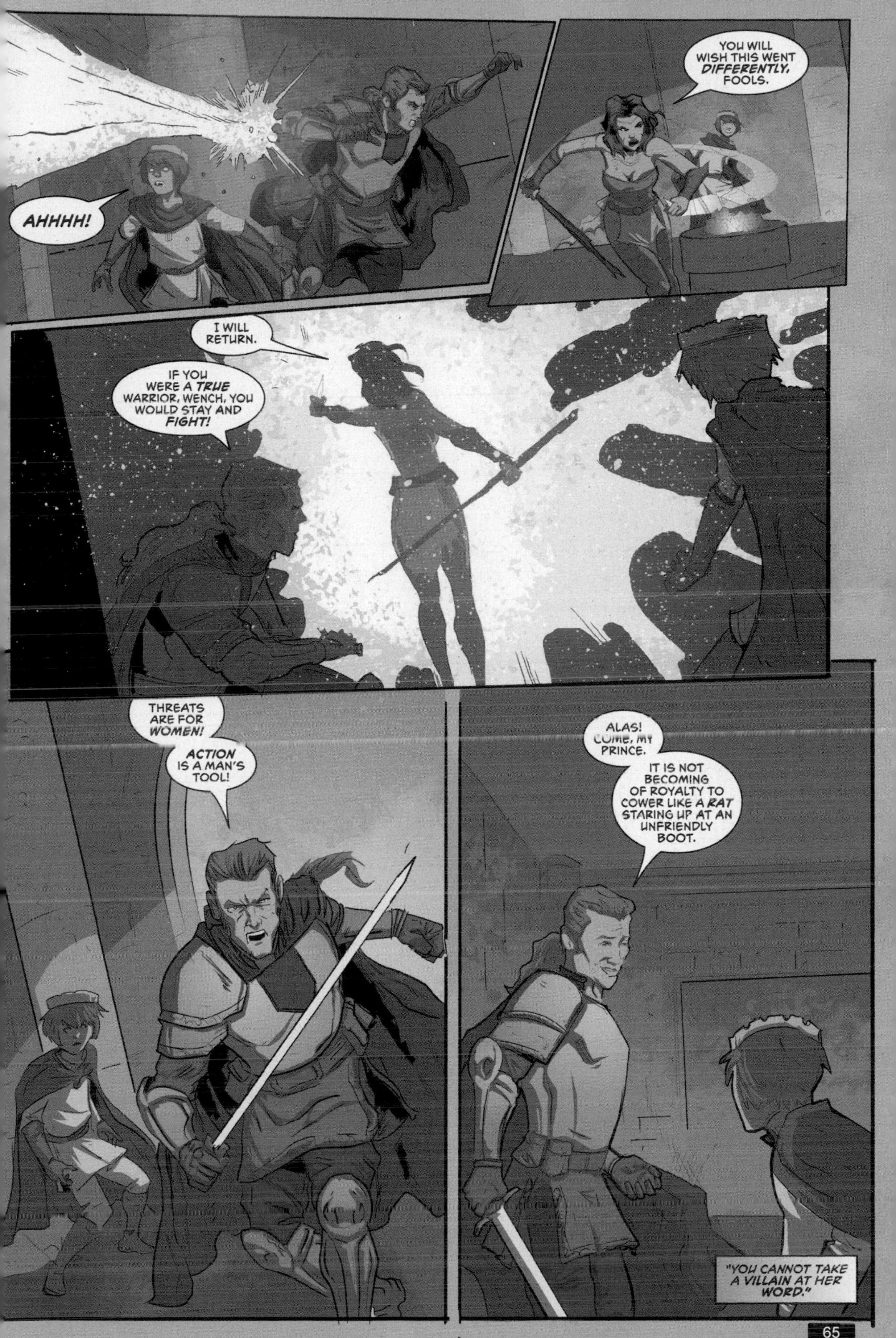
AHHHH!
YOU WILL WISH THIS WENT *DIFFERENTLY,* FOOLS.
I WILL RETURN.
IF YOU WERE A *TRUE* WARRIOR, WENCH, YOU WOULD STAY AND *FIGHT!*
THREATS ARE FOR *WOMEN!*
*ACTION* IS A MAN'S TOOL!
ALAS! COME, MY PRINCE.
IT IS NOT BECOMING OF ROYALTY TO COWER LIKE A *RAT* STARING UP AT AN UNFRIENDLY BOOT.
"YOU CANNOT TAKE A *VILLAIN* AT HER *WORD.*"

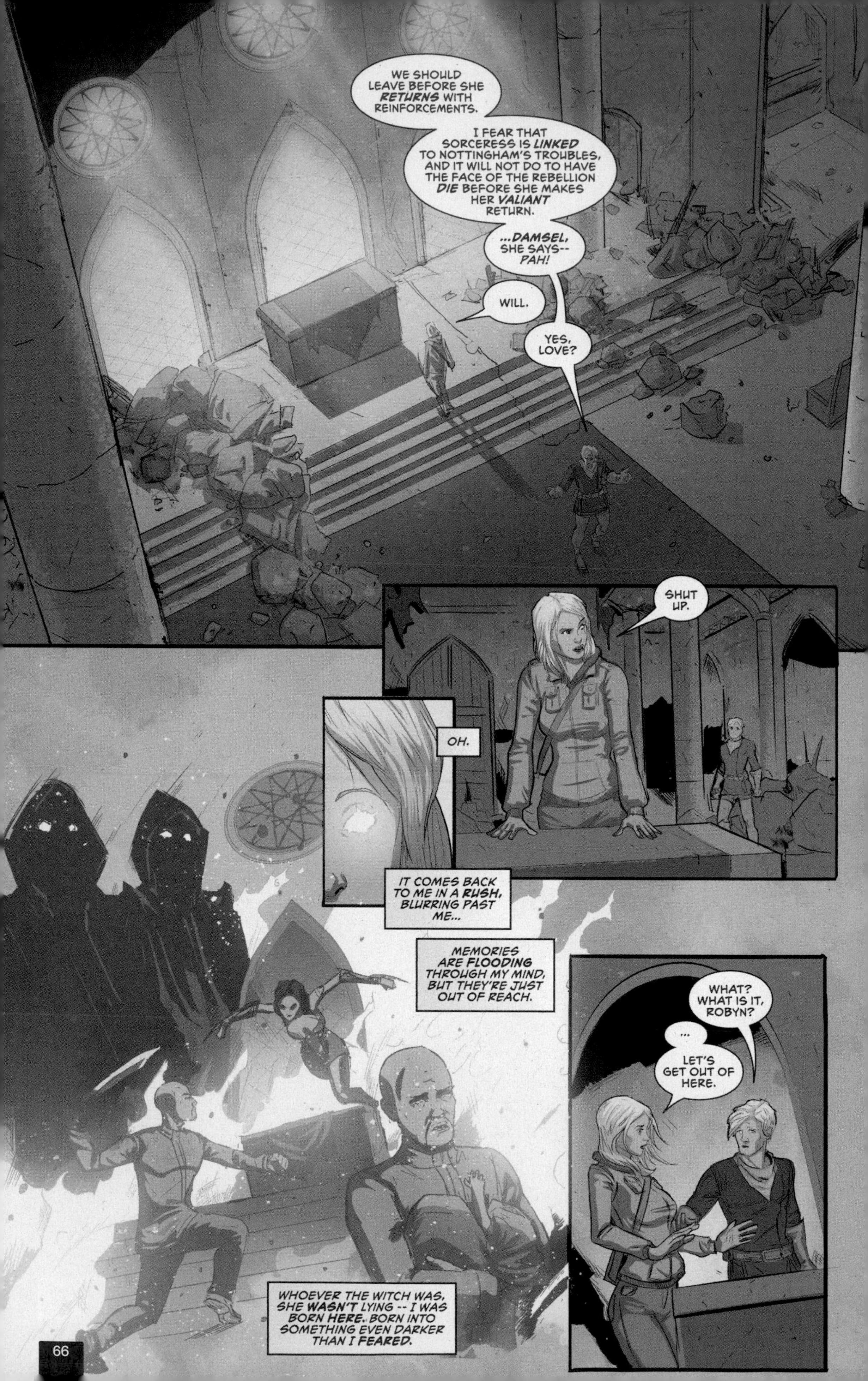

WE SHOULD LEAVE BEFORE SHE RETURNS WITH REINFORCEMENTS.
I FEAR THAT SORCERESS IS LINKED TO NOTTINGHAM'S TROUBLES, AND IT WILL NOT DO TO HAVE THE FACE OF THE REBELLION DIE BEFORE SHE MAKES HER VALIANT RETURN.
...DAMSEL, SHE SAYS-- PAH!
WILL.
YES, LOVE?
SHUT UP.
OH.
IT COMES BACK TO ME IN A RUSH, BLURRING PAST ME...
MEMORIES ARE FLOODING THROUGH MY MIND, BUT THEY'RE JUST OUT OF REACH.
WHAT? WHAT IS IT, ROBYN?
...
LET'S GET OUT OF HERE.
WHOEVER THE WITCH WAS, SHE WASN'T LYING -- I WAS BORN HERE. BORN INTO SOMETHING EVEN DARKER THAN I FEARED.

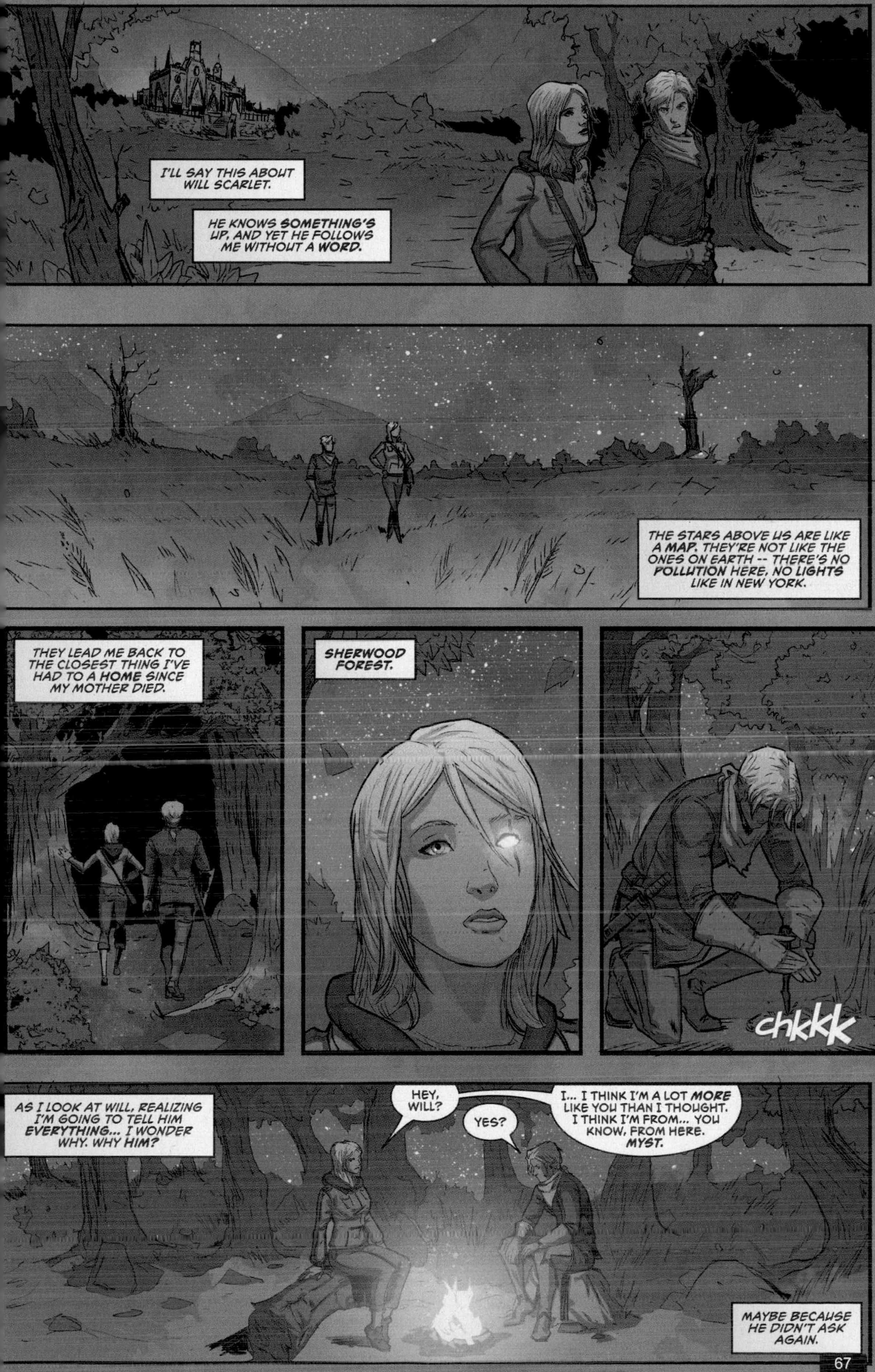
I'LL SAY THIS ABOUT WILL SCARLET.
HE KNOWS SOMETHING'S UP, AND YET HE FOLLOWS ME WITHOUT A WORD.
THE STARS ABOVE US ARE LIKE A MAP. THEY'RE NOT LIKE THE ONES ON EARTH -- THERE'S NO POLLUTION HERE, NO LIGHTS LIKE IN NEW YORK.
THEY LEAD ME BACK TO THE CLOSEST THING I'VE HAD TO A HOME SINCE MY MOTHER DIED.
SHERWOOD FOREST.
chkkk
AS I LOOK AT WILL, REALIZING I'M GOING TO TELL HIM EVERYTHING... I WONDER WHY. WHY HIM?
HEY, WILL?
YES?
I... I THINK I'M A LOT MORE LIKE YOU THAN I THOUGHT. I THINK I'M FROM... YOU KNOW, FROM HERE. MYST.
MAYBE BECAUSE HE DIDN'T ASK AGAIN.

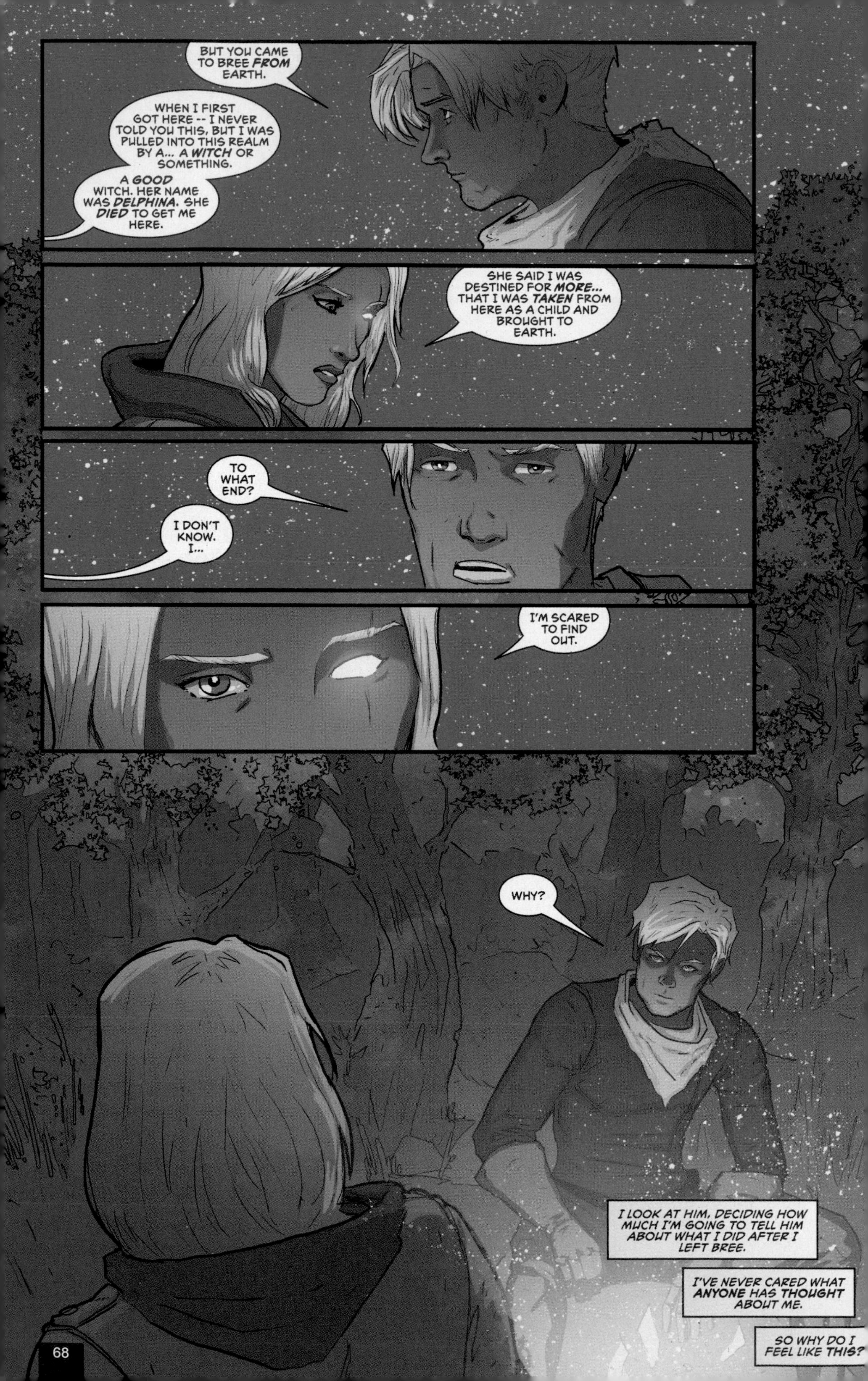
BUT YOU CAME TO BREE *FROM* EARTH.
WHEN I FIRST GOT HERE -- I NEVER TOLD YOU THIS, BUT I WAS PULLED INTO THIS REALM BY A... A *WITCH* OR SOMETHING.
A *GOOD* WITCH. HER NAME WAS *DELPHINA*. SHE *DIED* TO GET ME HERE.
SHE SAID I WAS DESTINED FOR *MORE*... THAT I WAS *TAKEN* FROM HERE AS A CHILD AND BROUGHT TO EARTH.
TO WHAT END?
I DON'T KNOW. I...
I'M SCARED TO FIND OUT.
WHY?
*I LOOK AT HIM, DECIDING HOW MUCH I'M GOING TO TELL HIM ABOUT WHAT I DID AFTER I LEFT BREE.*
*I'VE NEVER CARED WHAT **ANYONE** HAS **THOUGHT** ABOUT ME.*
*SO WHY DO I FEEL LIKE **THIS?***

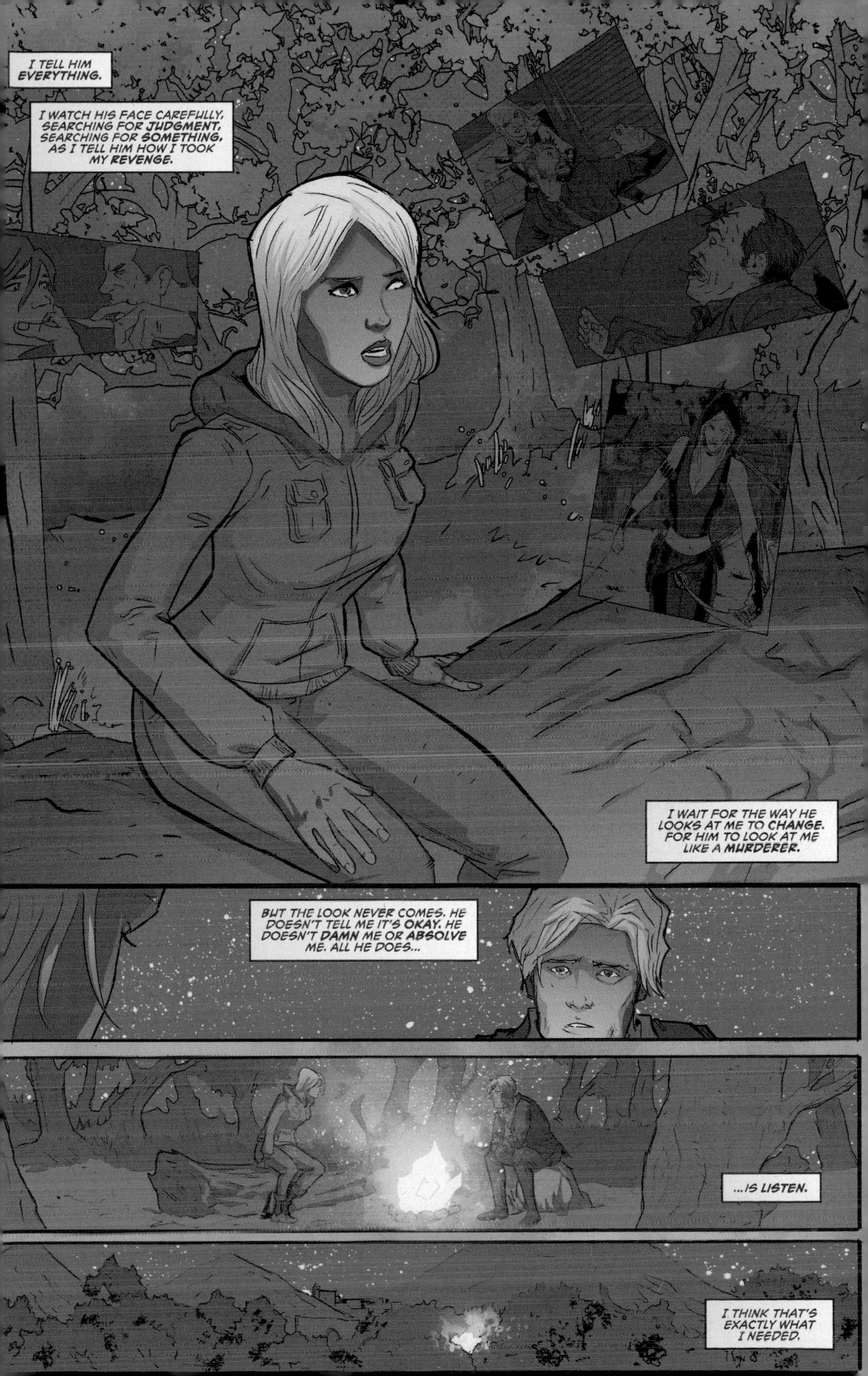
I TELL HIM EVERYTHING.
I WATCH HIS FACE CAREFULLY, SEARCHING FOR JUDGMENT, SEARCHING FOR SOMETHING, AS I TELL HIM HOW I TOOK MY REVENGE.
I WAIT FOR THE WAY HE LOOKS AT ME TO CHANGE. FOR HIM TO LOOK AT ME LIKE A MURDERER.
BUT THE LOOK NEVER COMES. HE DOESN'T TELL ME IT'S OKAY. HE DOESN'T DAMN ME OR ABSOLVE ME. ALL HE DOES...
...IS LISTEN.
I THINK THAT'S EXACTLY WHAT I NEEDED.

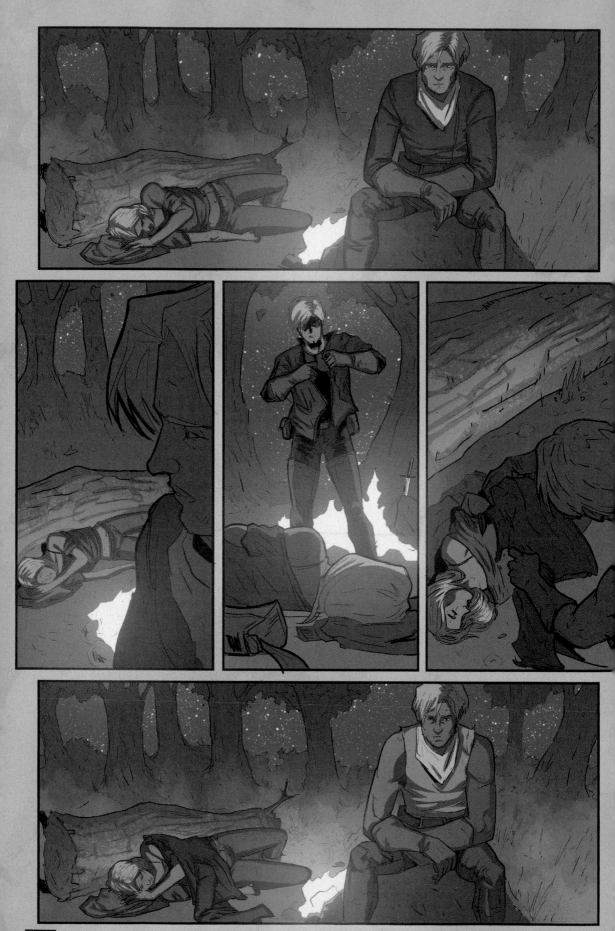

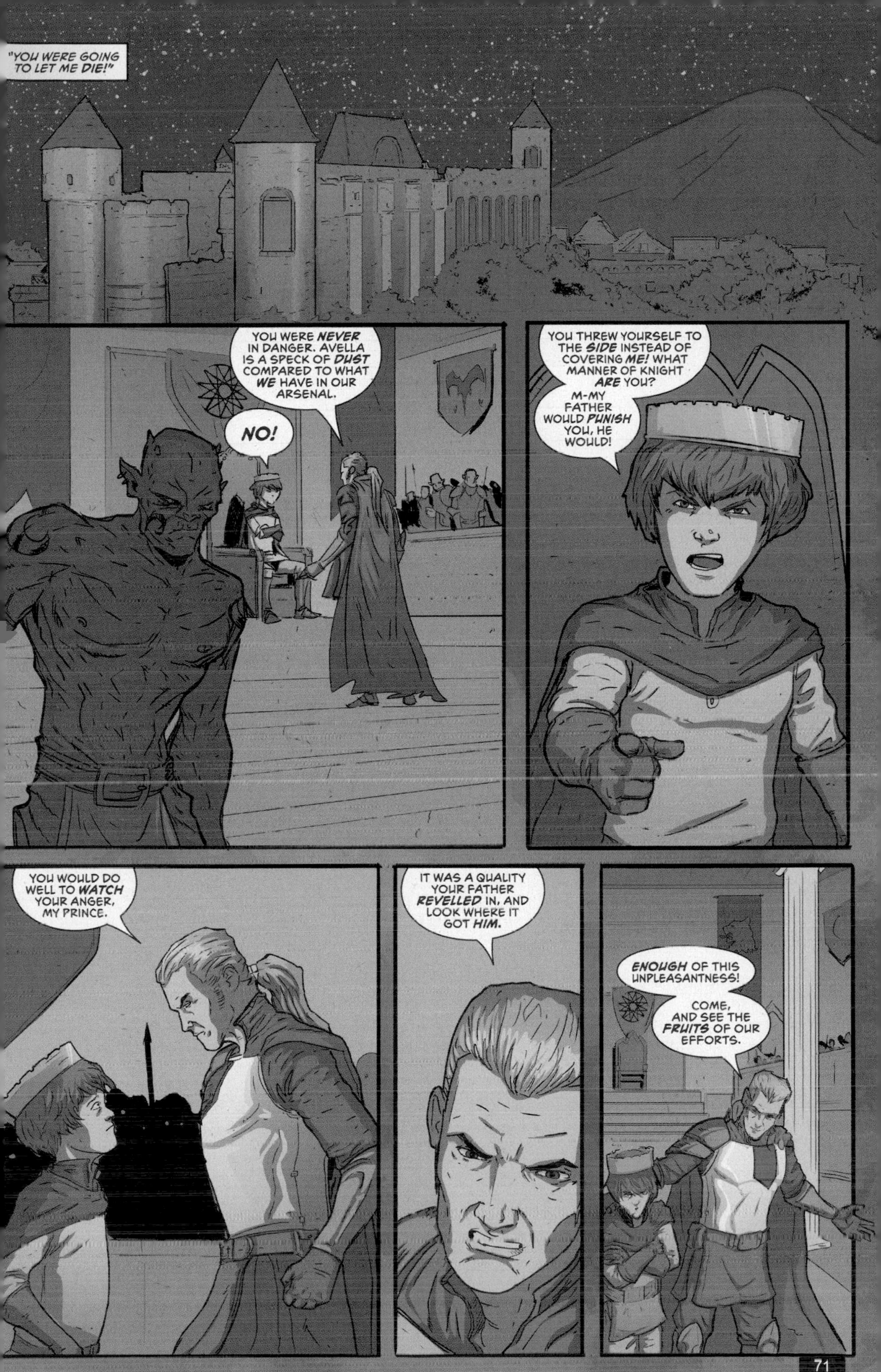
"YOU WERE GOING TO LET ME DIE!"
YOU WERE NEVER IN DANGER. AVELLA IS A SPECK OF DUST COMPARED TO WHAT WE HAVE IN OUR ARSENAL.
NO!
YOU THREW YOURSELF TO THE SIDE INSTEAD OF COVERING ME! WHAT MANNER OF KNIGHT ARE YOU?
M-MY FATHER WOULD PUNISH YOU, HE WOULD!
YOU WOULD DO WELL TO WATCH YOUR ANGER, MY PRINCE.
IT WAS A QUALITY YOUR FATHER REVELLED IN, AND LOOK WHERE IT GOT HIM.
ENOUGH OF THIS UNPLEASANTNESS!
COME, AND SEE THE FRUITS OF OUR EFFORTS.

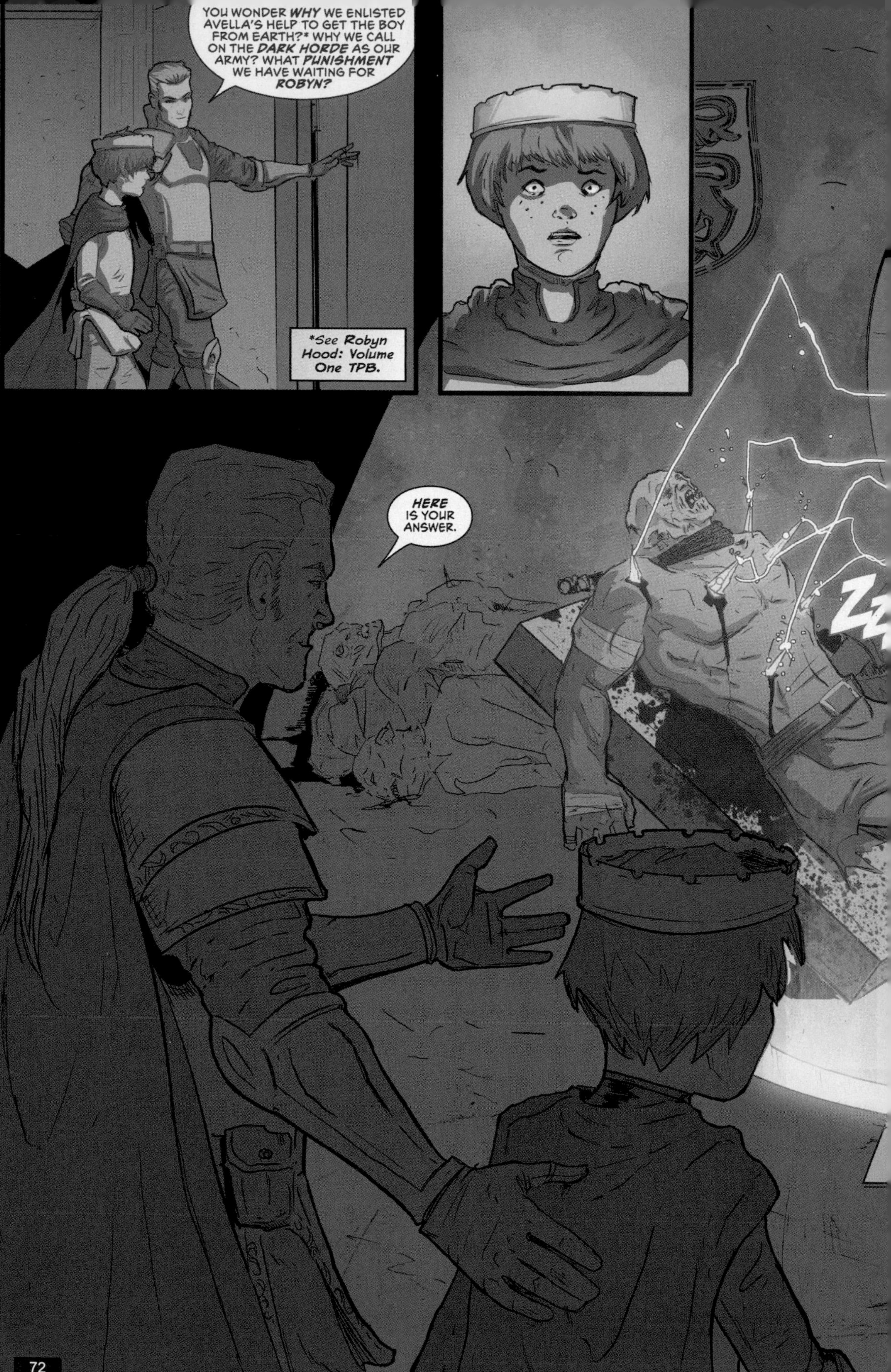

YOU WONDER WHY WE ENLISTED AVELLA'S HELP TO GET THE BOY FROM EARTH?* WHY WE CALL ON THE DARK HORDE AS OUR ARMY? WHAT PUNISHMENT WE HAVE WAITING FOR ROBYN?
*See Robyn Hood: Volume One TPB.
HERE IS YOUR ANSWER.
ZZ

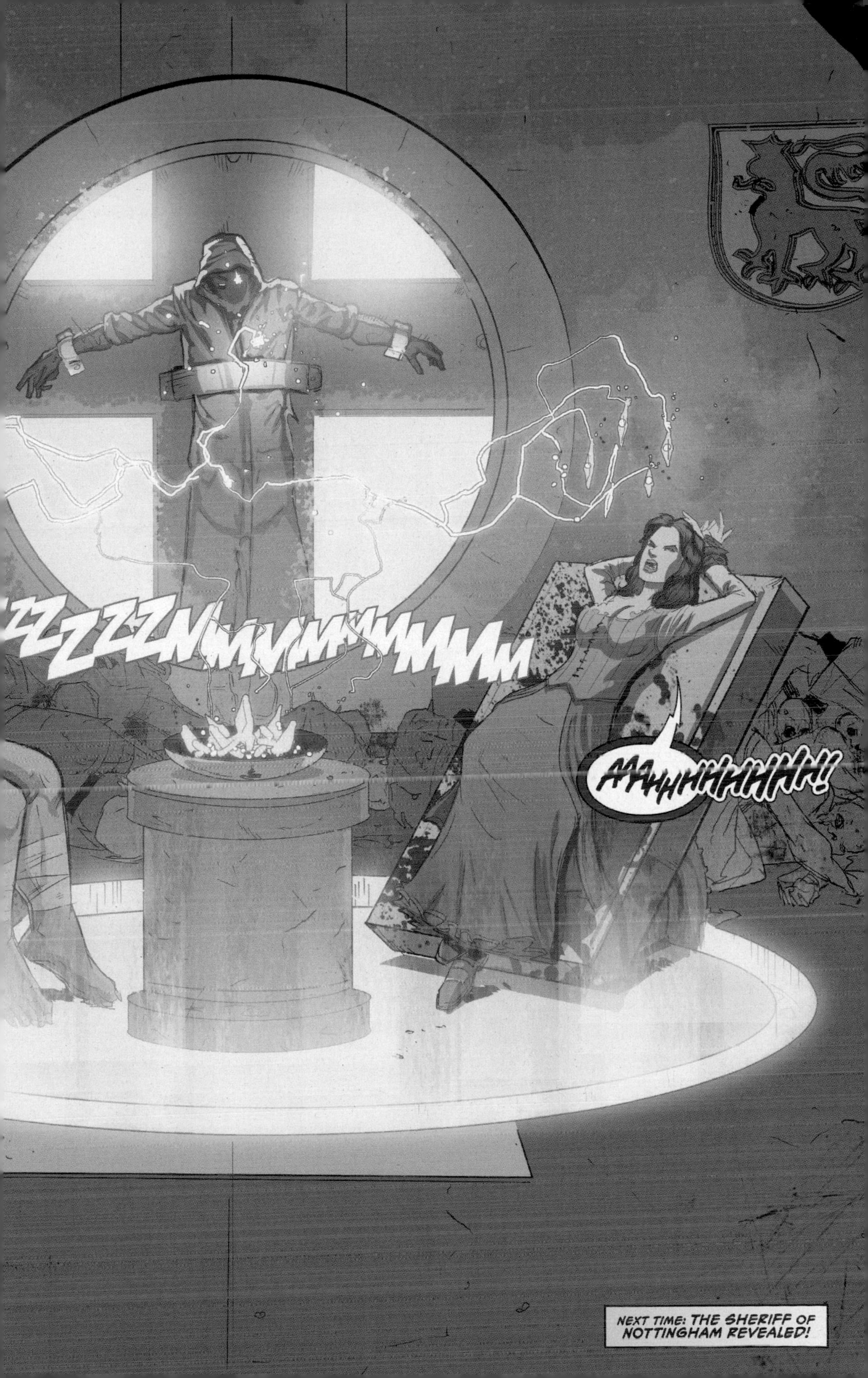
ZZZZZNMMMMMMMMMM
AAAHHHHHHH!
NEXT TIME: THE SHERIFF OF NOTTINGHAM REVEALED!

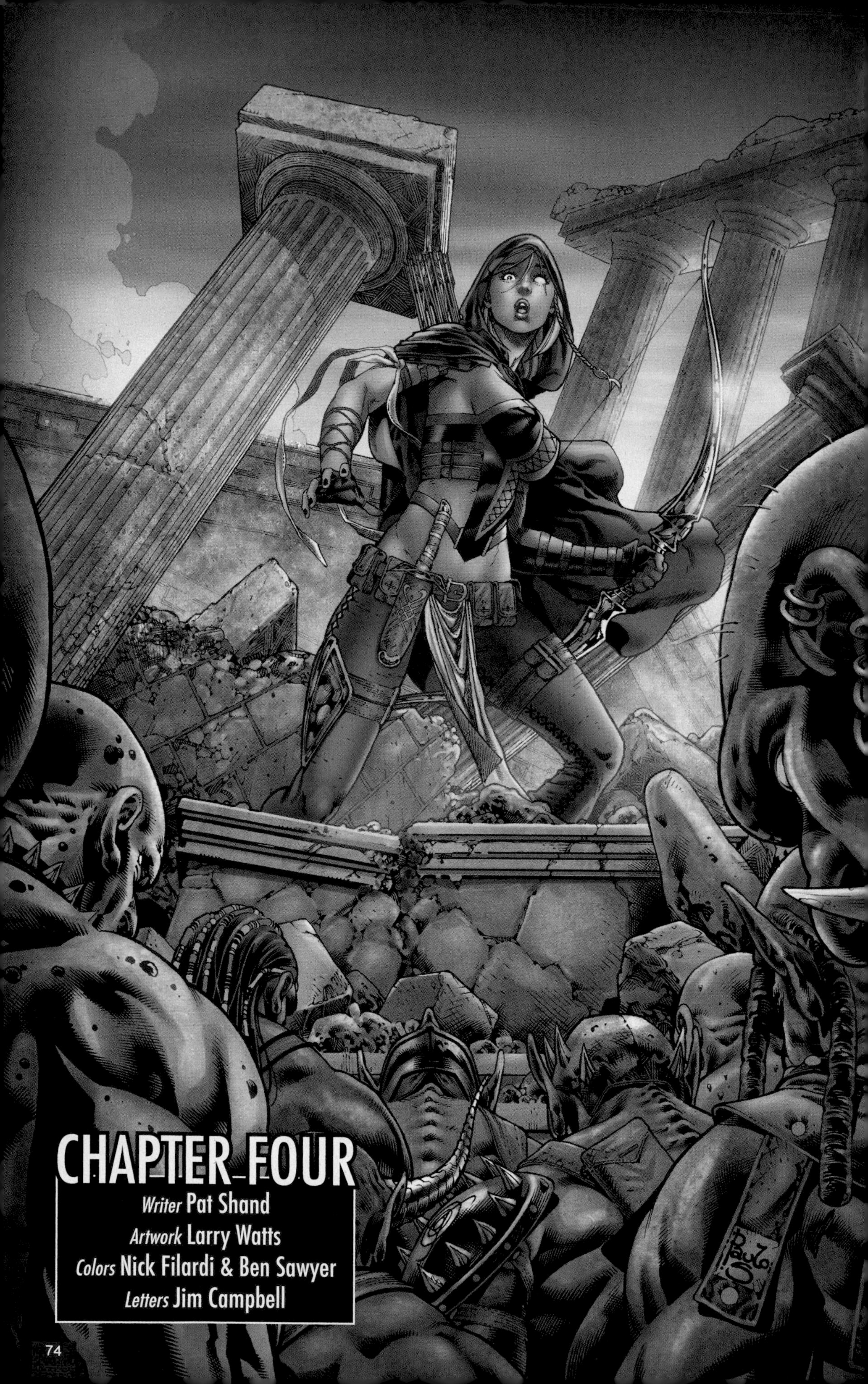

# CHAPTER FOUR

*Writer* Pat Shand
*Artwork* Larry Watts
*Colors* Nick Filardi & Ben Sawyer
*Letters* Jim Campbell

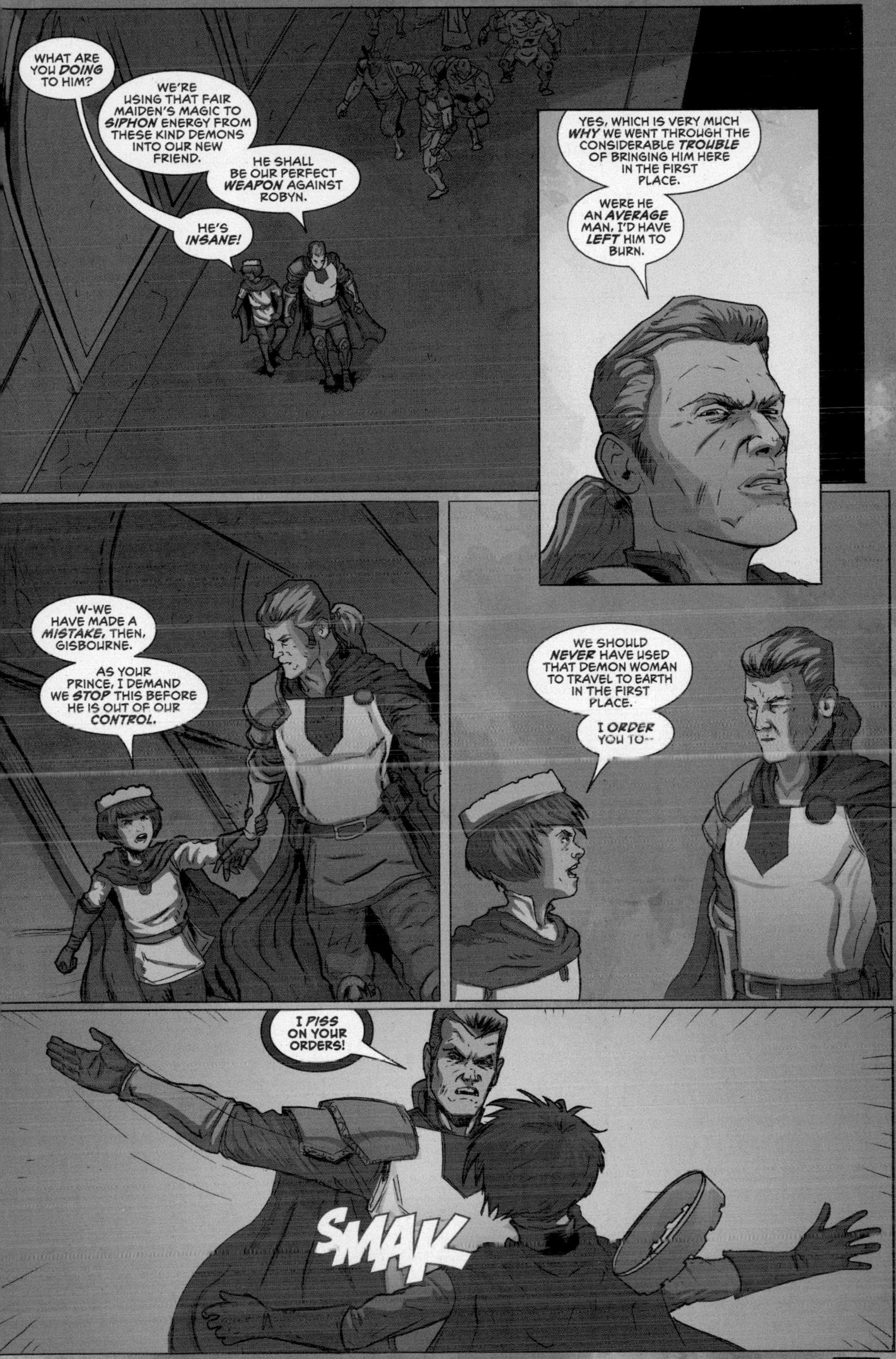

WHAT ARE YOU DOING TO HIM?
WE'RE USING THAT FAIR MAIDEN'S MAGIC TO SIPHON ENERGY FROM THESE KIND DEMONS INTO OUR NEW FRIEND.
HE SHALL BE OUR PERFECT WEAPON AGAINST ROBYN.
HE'S INSANE!
YES, WHICH IS VERY MUCH WHY WE WENT THROUGH THE CONSIDERABLE TROUBLE OF BRINGING HIM HERE IN THE FIRST PLACE.
WERE HE AN AVERAGE MAN, I'D HAVE LEFT HIM TO BURN.
W-WE HAVE MADE A MISTAKE, THEN, GISBOURNE.
AS YOUR PRINCE, I DEMAND WE STOP THIS BEFORE HE IS OUT OF OUR CONTROL.
WE SHOULD NEVER HAVE USED THAT DEMON WOMAN TO TRAVEL TO EARTH IN THE FIRST PLACE.
I ORDER YOU TO--
I PISS ON YOUR ORDERS!
SMAK

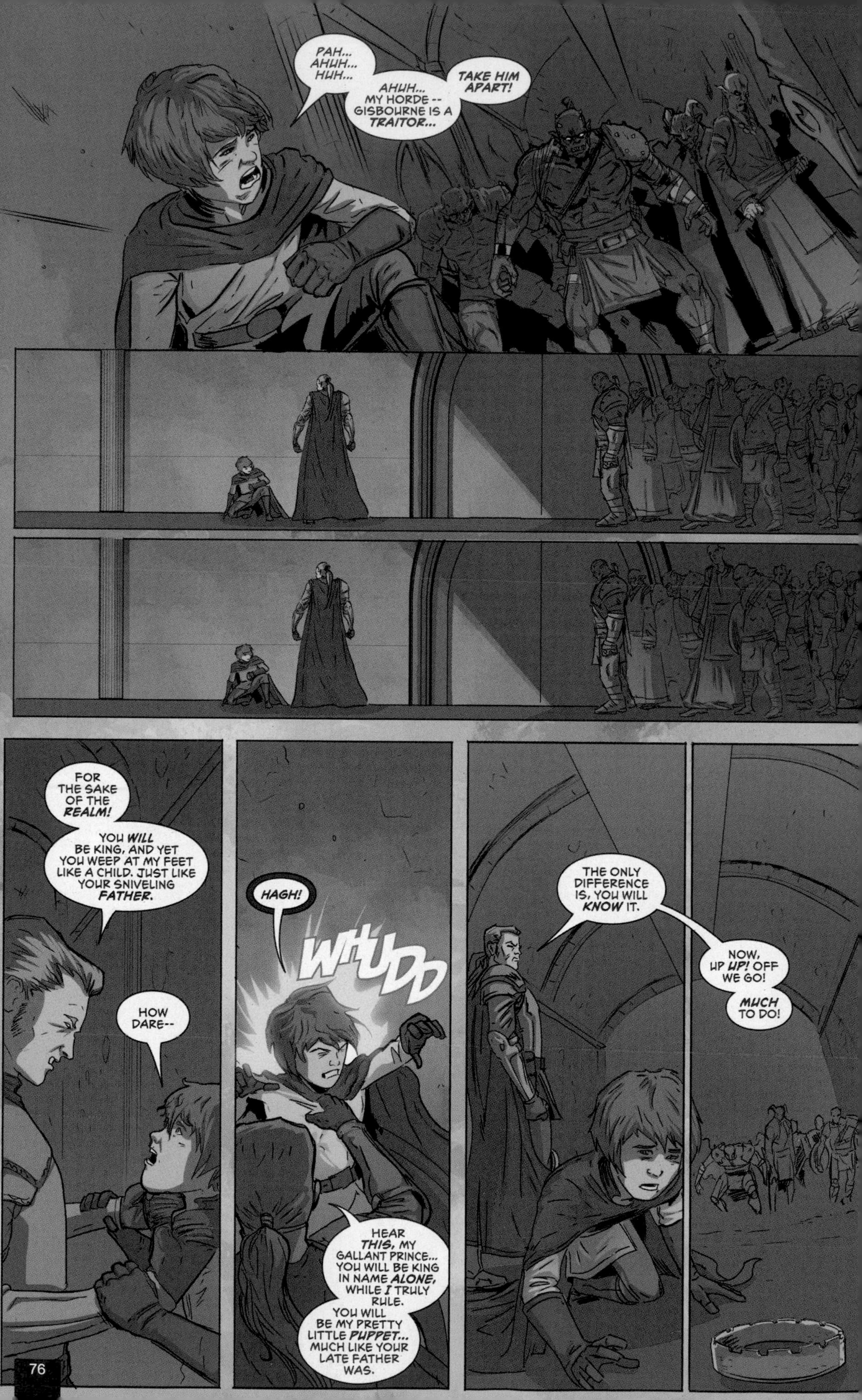
PAH... AHUH... HUH...
AHUH... MY HORDE -- GISBOURNE IS A TRAITOR...
TAKE HIM APART!
FOR THE SAKE OF THE REALM!
YOU WILL BE KING, AND YET YOU WEEP AT MY FEET LIKE A CHILD. JUST LIKE YOUR SNIVELING FATHER.
HOW DARE--
HAGH!
WHUDD
HEAR THIS, MY GALLANT PRINCE... YOU WILL BE KING IN NAME ALONE, WHILE I TRULY RULE. YOU WILL BE MY PRETTY LITTLE PUPPET... MUCH LIKE YOUR LATE FATHER WAS.
THE ONLY DIFFERENCE IS, YOU WILL KNOW IT.
NOW, UP UP! OFF WE GO!
MUCH TO DO!

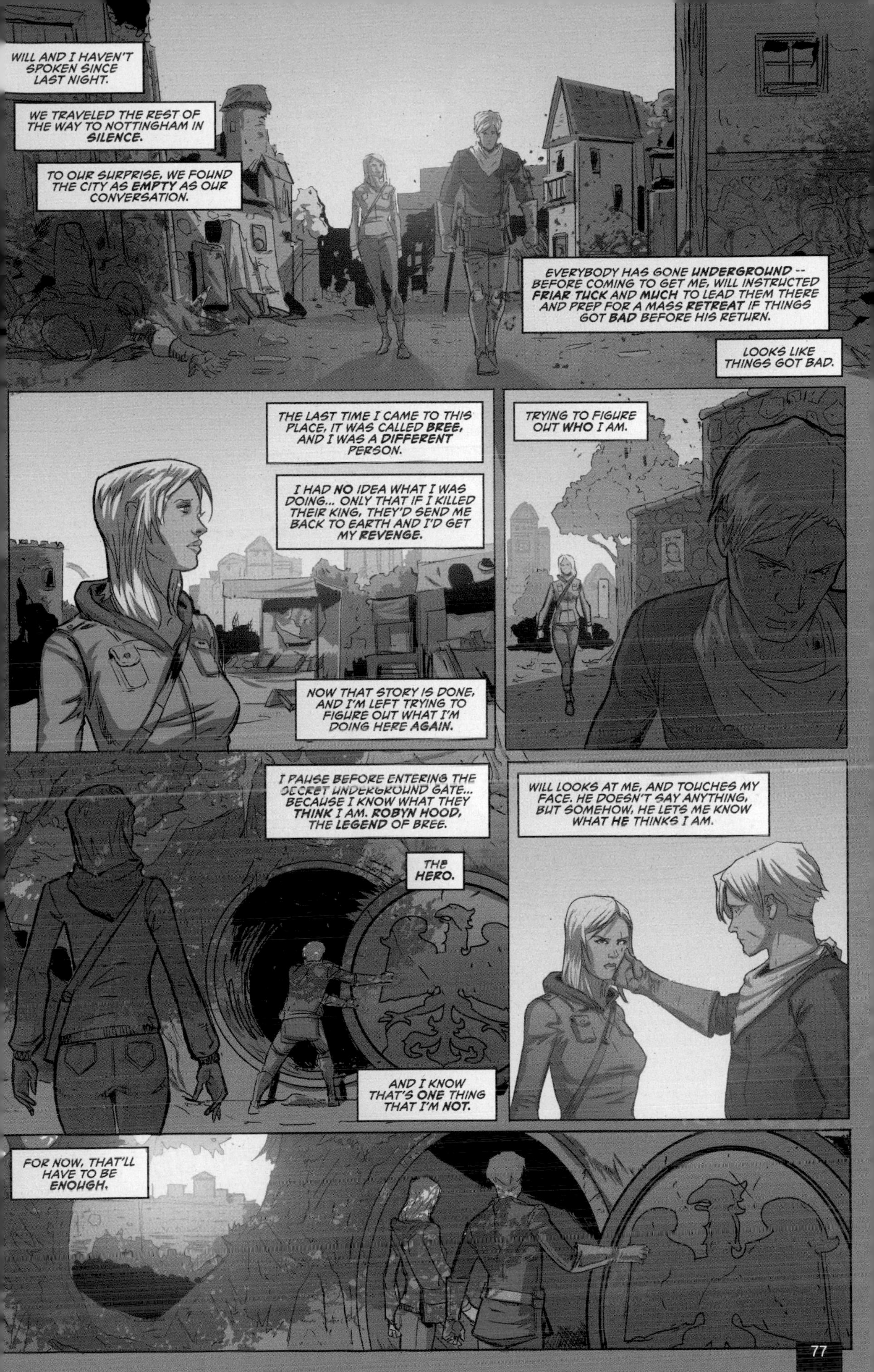
WILL AND I HAVEN'T SPOKEN SINCE LAST NIGHT.
WE TRAVELED THE REST OF THE WAY TO NOTTINGHAM IN SILENCE.
TO OUR SURPRISE, WE FOUND THE CITY AS EMPTY AS OUR CONVERSATION.
EVERYBODY HAS GONE UNDERGROUND -- BEFORE COMING TO GET ME, WILL INSTRUCTED FRIAR TUCK AND MUCH TO LEAD THEM THERE AND PREP FOR A MASS RETREAT IF THINGS GOT BAD BEFORE HIS RETURN.
LOOKS LIKE THINGS GOT BAD.
THE LAST TIME I CAME TO THIS PLACE, IT WAS CALLED BREE, AND I WAS A DIFFERENT PERSON.
I HAD NO IDEA WHAT I WAS DOING... ONLY THAT IF I KILLED THEIR KING, THEY'D SEND ME BACK TO EARTH AND I'D GET MY REVENGE.
NOW THAT STORY IS DONE, AND I'M LEFT TRYING TO FIGURE OUT WHAT I'M DOING HERE AGAIN.
TRYING TO FIGURE OUT WHO I AM.
I PAUSE BEFORE ENTERING THE SECRET UNDERGROUND GATE... BECAUSE I KNOW WHAT THEY THINK I AM. ROBYN HOOD, THE LEGEND OF BREE.
THE HERO.
AND I KNOW THAT'S ONE THING THAT I'M NOT.
WILL LOOKS AT ME, AND TOUCHES MY FACE. HE DOESN'T SAY ANYTHING, BUT SOMEHOW, HE LETS ME KNOW WHAT HE THINKS I AM.
FOR NOW, THAT'LL HAVE TO BE ENOUGH.

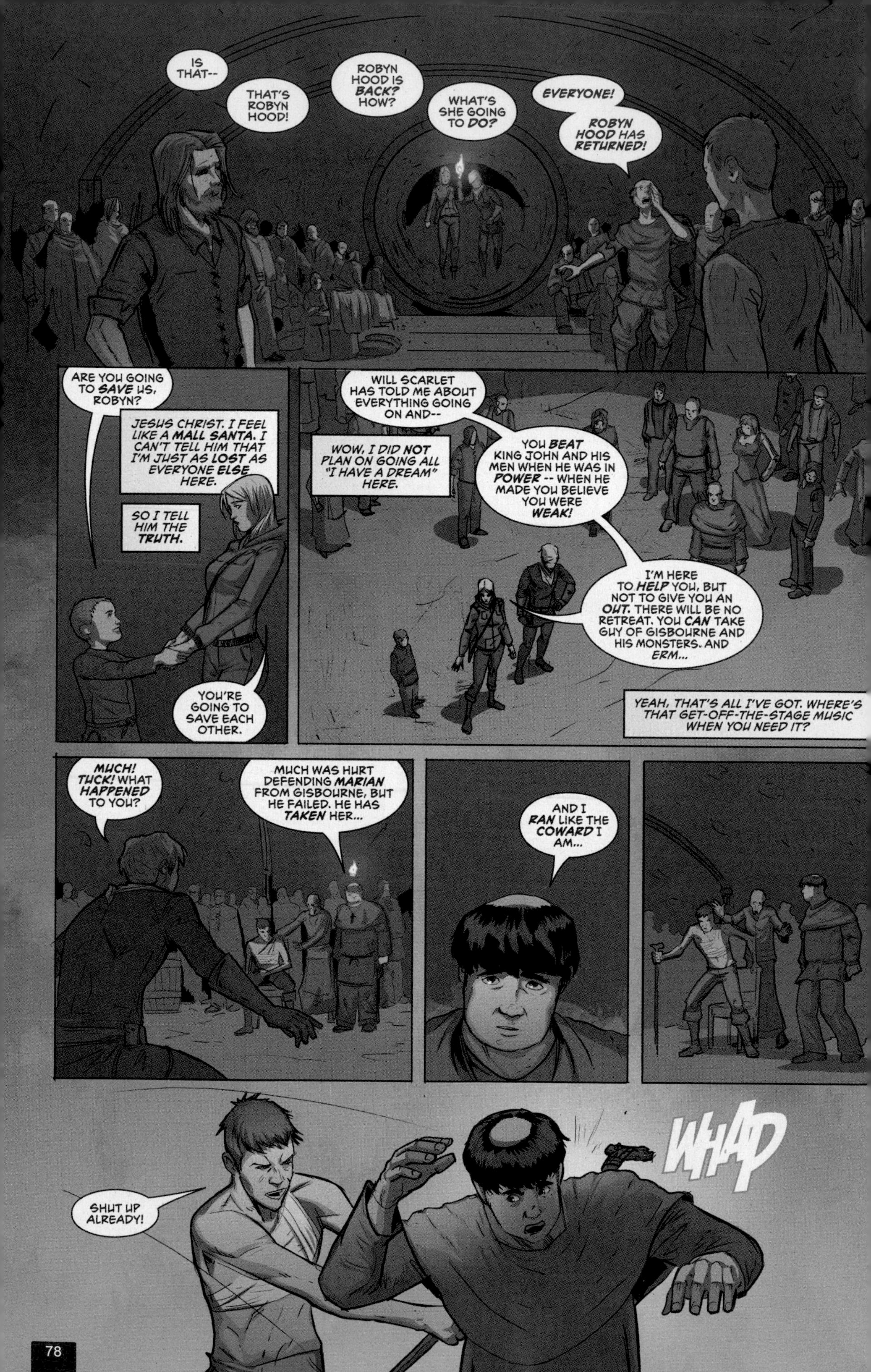

IS THAT--
THAT'S ROBYN HOOD!
ROBYN HOOD IS BACK? HOW?
WHAT'S SHE GOING TO DO?
EVERYONE!
ROBYN HOOD HAS RETURNED!
ARE YOU GOING TO SAVE US, ROBYN?
JESUS CHRIST. I FEEL LIKE A MALL SANTA. I CAN'T TELL HIM THAT I'M JUST AS LOST AS EVERYONE ELSE HERE.
SO I TELL HIM THE TRUTH.
YOU'RE GOING TO SAVE EACH OTHER.
WILL SCARLET HAS TOLD ME ABOUT EVERYTHING GOING ON AND--
WOW, I DID NOT PLAN ON GOING ALL "I HAVE A DREAM" HERE.
YOU BEAT KING JOHN AND HIS MEN WHEN HE WAS IN POWER -- WHEN HE MADE YOU BELIEVE YOU WERE WEAK!
I'M HERE TO HELP YOU, BUT NOT TO GIVE YOU AN OUT. THERE WILL BE NO RETREAT. YOU CAN TAKE GUY OF GISBOURNE AND HIS MONSTERS. AND ERM...
YEAH, THAT'S ALL I'VE GOT. WHERE'S THAT GET-OFF-THE-STAGE MUSIC WHEN YOU NEED IT?
MUCH! TUCK! WHAT HAPPENED TO YOU?
MUCH WAS HURT DEFENDING MARIAN FROM GISBOURNE, BUT HE FAILED. HE HAS TAKEN HER...
AND I RAN LIKE THE COWARD I AM...
WHAP
SHUT UP ALREADY!

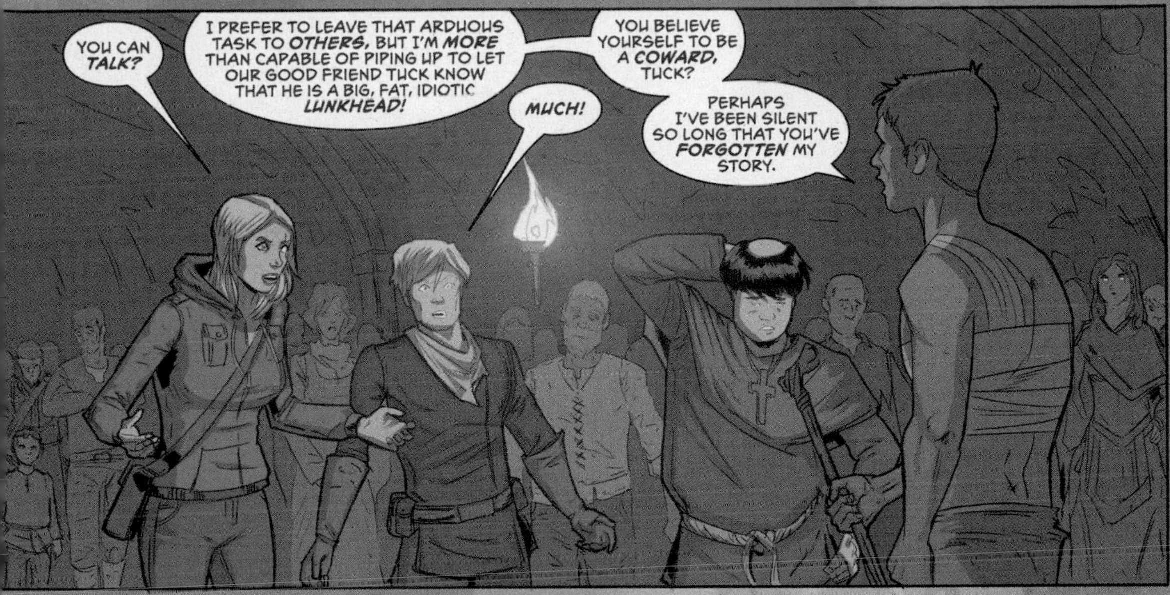
YOU CAN TALK?
I PREFER TO LEAVE THAT ARDUOUS TASK TO OTHERS, BUT I'M MORE THAN CAPABLE OF PIPING UP TO LET OUR GOOD FRIEND TUCK KNOW THAT HE IS A BIG, FAT, IDIOTIC LUNKHEAD!
MUCH!
YOU BELIEVE YOURSELF TO BE A COWARD, TUCK?
PERHAPS I'VE BEEN SILENT SO LONG THAT YOU'VE FORGOTTEN MY STORY.

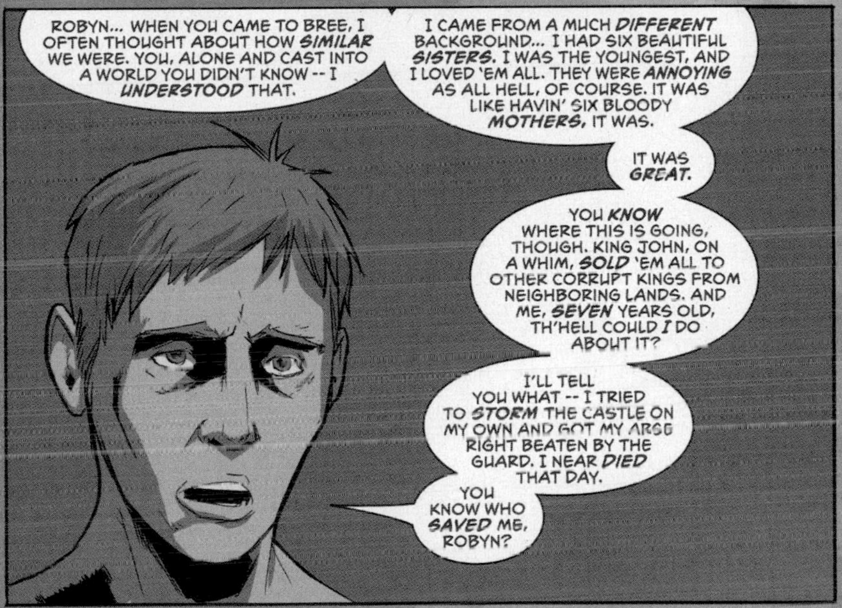
ROBYN... WHEN YOU CAME TO BREE, I OFTEN THOUGHT ABOUT HOW SIMILAR WE WERE. YOU, ALONE AND CAST INTO A WORLD YOU DIDN'T KNOW -- I UNDERSTOOD THAT.
I CAME FROM A MUCH DIFFERENT BACKGROUND... I HAD SIX BEAUTIFUL SISTERS. I WAS THE YOUNGEST, AND I LOVED 'EM ALL. THEY WERE ANNOYING AS ALL HELL, OF COURSE. IT WAS LIKE HAVIN' SIX BLOODY MOTHERS, IT WAS.
IT WAS GREAT.
YOU KNOW WHERE THIS IS GOING, THOUGH. KING JOHN, ON A WHIM, SOLD 'EM ALL TO OTHER CORRUPT KINGS FROM NEIGHBORING LANDS. AND ME, SEVEN YEARS OLD, TH'HELL COULD I DO ABOUT IT?
I'LL TELL YOU WHAT -- I TRIED TO STORM THE CASTLE ON MY OWN AND GOT MY ARSE RIGHT BEATEN BY THE GUARD. I NEAR DIED THAT DAY.
YOU KNOW WHO SAVED ME, ROBYN?

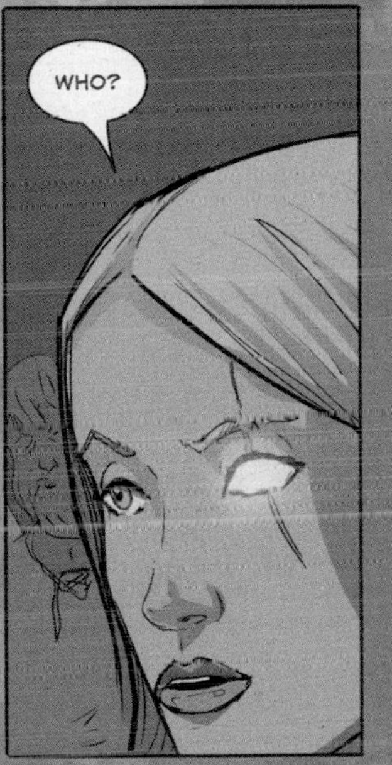
WHO?

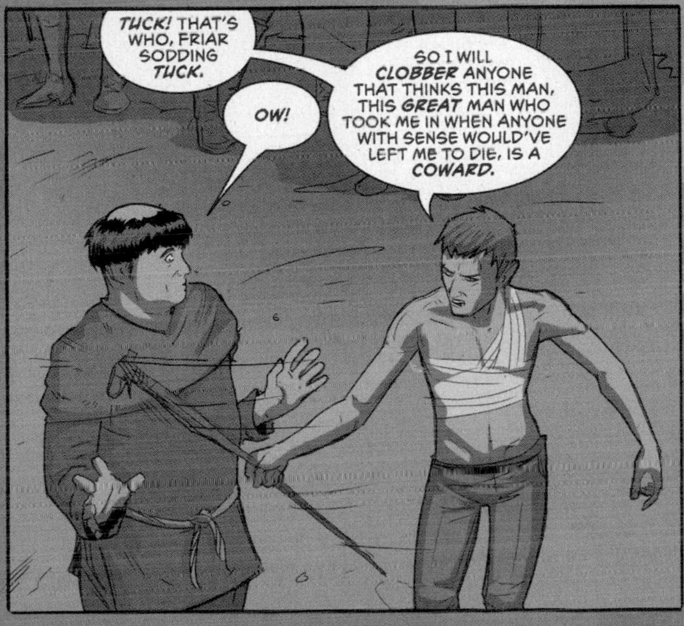
TUCK! THAT'S WHO. FRIAR SODDING TUCK.
OW!
SO I WILL CLOBBER ANYONE THAT THINKS THIS MAN, THIS GREAT MAN WHO TOOK ME IN WHEN ANYONE WITH SENSE WOULD'VE LEFT ME TO DIE, IS A COWARD.

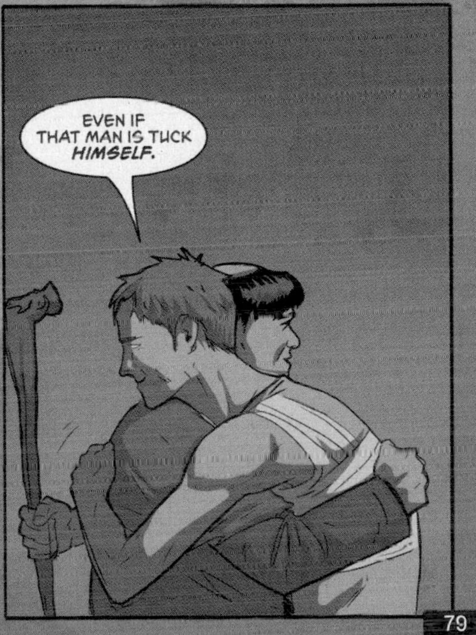
EVEN IF THAT MAN IS TUCK HIMSELF.

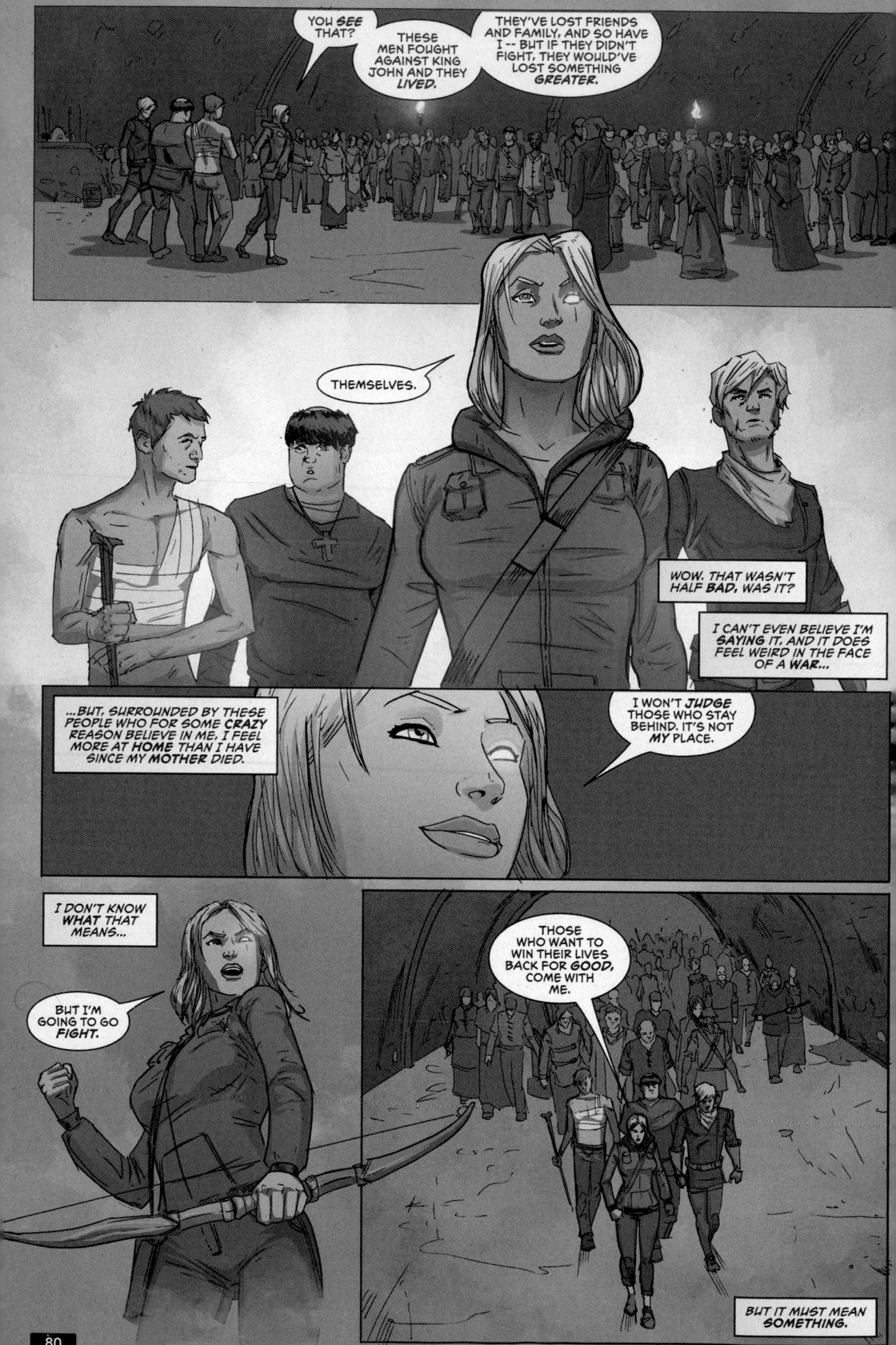

YOU SEE THAT?
THESE MEN FOUGHT AGAINST KING JOHN AND THEY LIVED.
THEY'VE LOST FRIENDS AND FAMILY, AND SO HAVE I -- BUT IF THEY DIDN'T FIGHT, THEY WOULD'VE LOST SOMETHING GREATER.
THEMSELVES.
WOW. THAT WASN'T HALF BAD, WAS IT?
I CAN'T EVEN BELIEVE I'M SAYING IT, AND IT DOES FEEL WEIRD IN THE FACE OF A WAR...
...BUT, SURROUNDED BY THESE PEOPLE WHO FOR SOME CRAZY REASON BELIEVE IN ME, I FEEL MORE AT HOME THAN I HAVE SINCE MY MOTHER DIED.
I WON'T JUDGE THOSE WHO STAY BEHIND. IT'S NOT MY PLACE.
I DON'T KNOW WHAT THAT MEANS...
BUT I'M GOING TO GO FIGHT.
THOSE WHO WANT TO WIN THEIR LIVES BACK FOR GOOD, COME WITH ME.
BUT IT MUST MEAN SOMETHING.

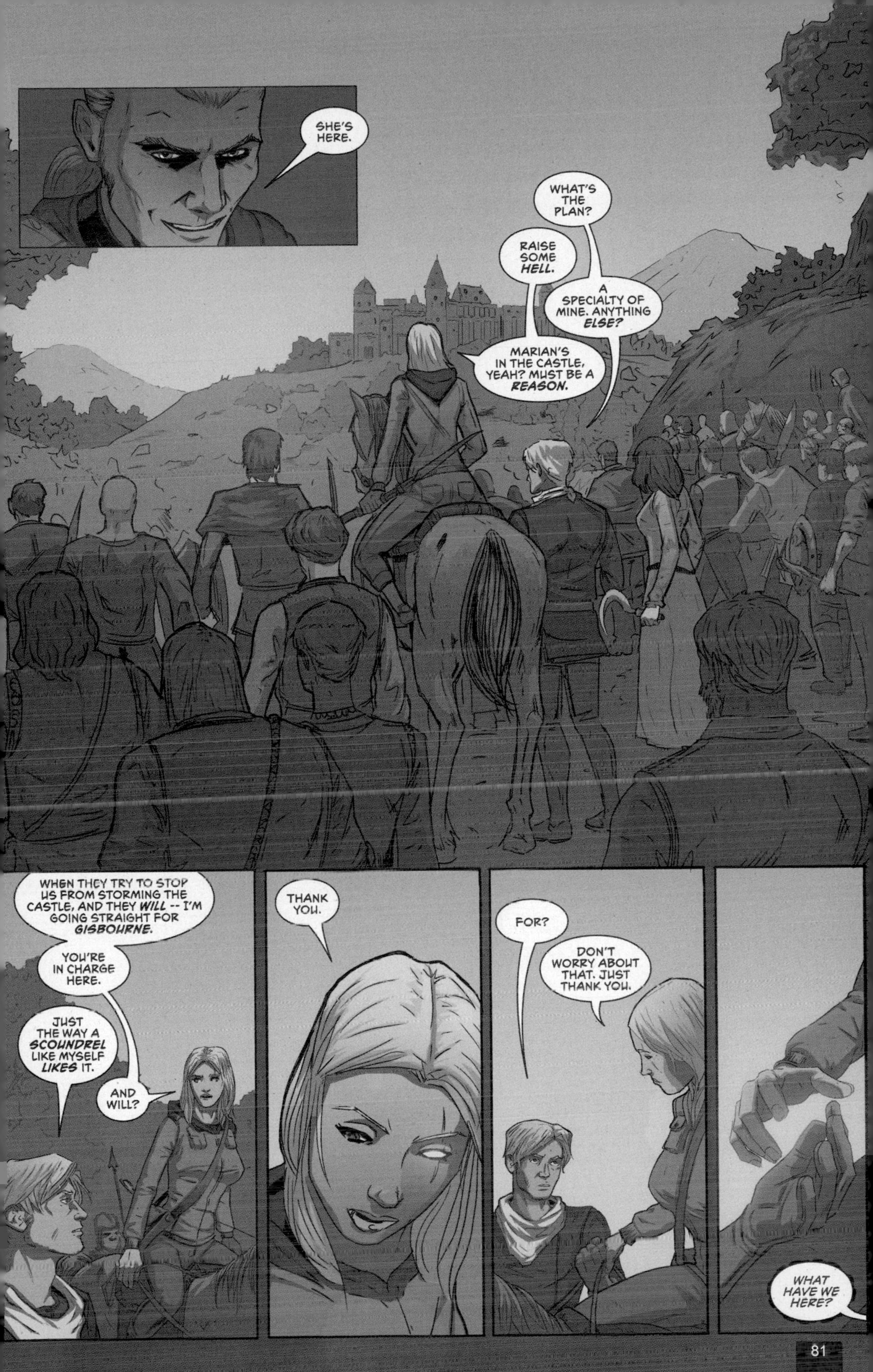
SHE'S HERE.
WHAT'S THE PLAN?
RAISE SOME HELL.
A SPECIALTY OF MINE. ANYTHING ELSE?
MARIAN'S IN THE CASTLE, YEAH? MUST BE A REASON.
WHEN THEY TRY TO STOP US FROM STORMING THE CASTLE, AND THEY WILL -- I'M GOING STRAIGHT FOR GISBOURNE.
YOU'RE IN CHARGE HERE.
JUST THE WAY A SCOUNDREL LIKE MYSELF LIKES IT.
AND WILL?
THANK YOU.
FOR?
DON'T WORRY ABOUT THAT. JUST THANK YOU.
WHAT HAVE WE HERE?

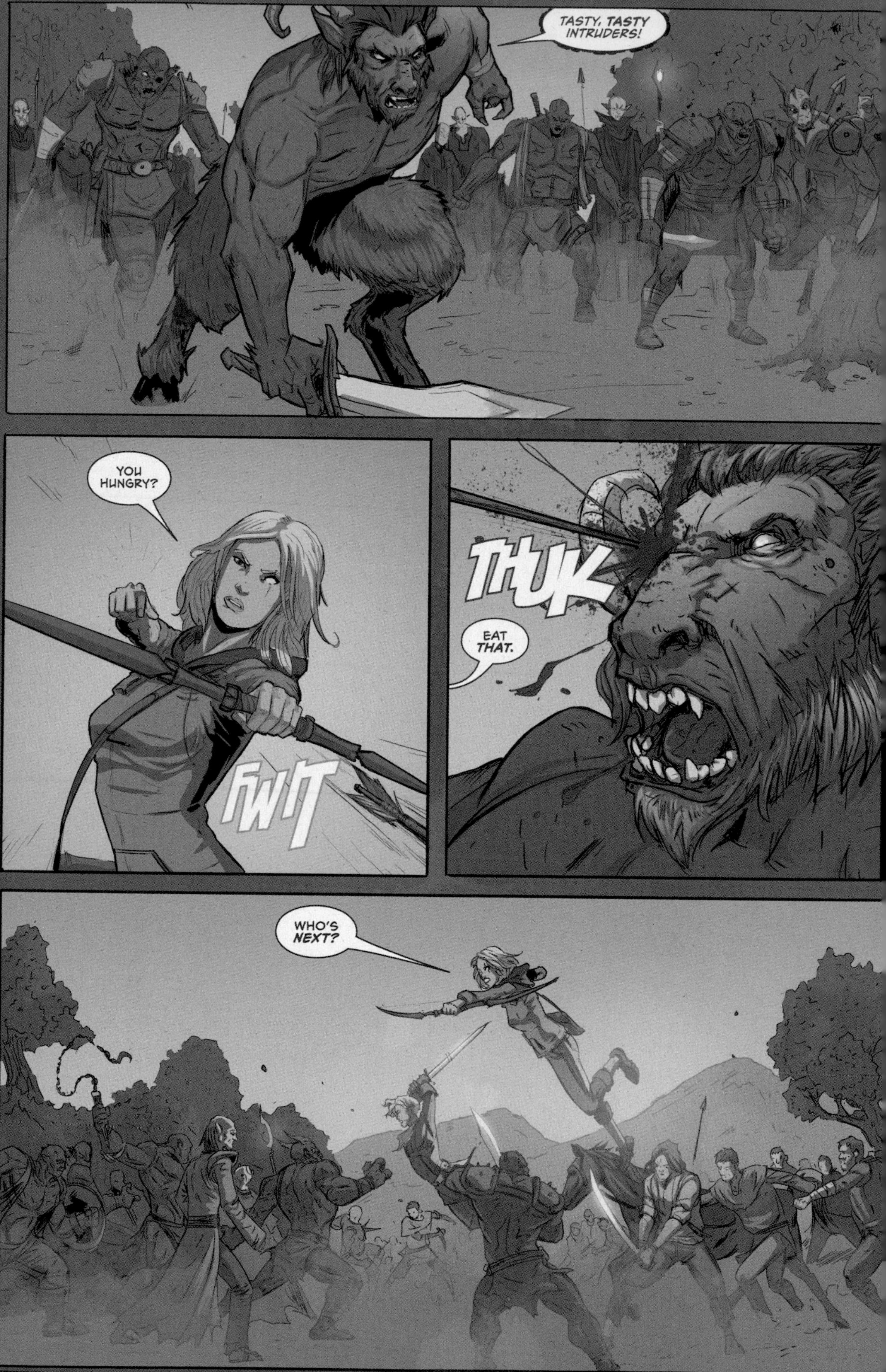
TASTY, TASTY INTRUDERS!
YOU HUNGRY?
FWIT
THUK
EAT THAT.
WHO'S NEXT?

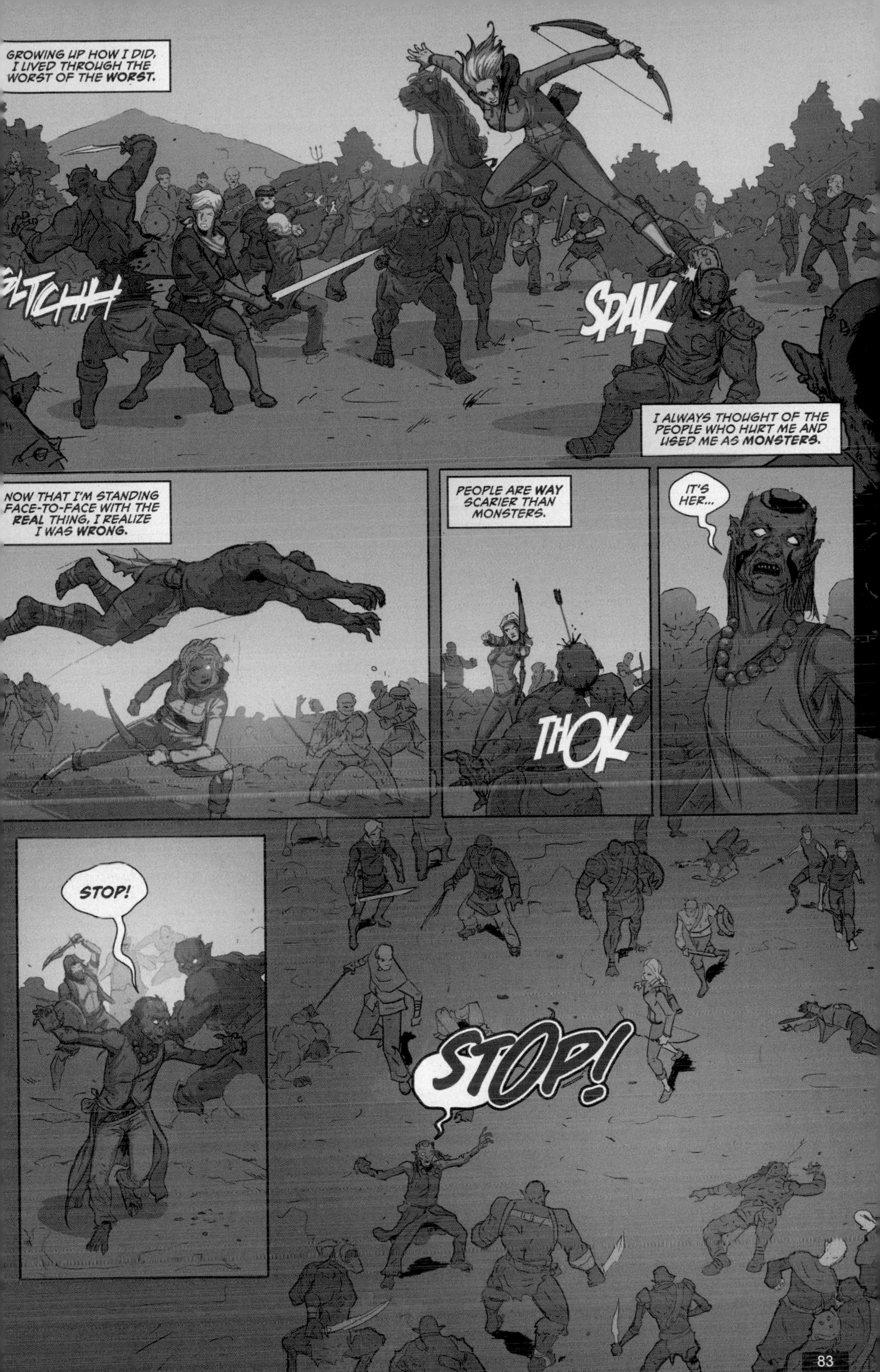
GROWING UP HOW I DID, I LIVED THROUGH THE WORST OF THE WORST.
SLTCHH
SPAK
I ALWAYS THOUGHT OF THE PEOPLE WHO HURT ME AND USED ME AS MONSTERS.
NOW THAT I'M STANDING FACE-TO-FACE WITH THE REAL THING, I REALIZE I WAS WRONG.
PEOPLE ARE WAY SCARIER THAN MONSTERS.
THOK
IT'S HER...
STOP!
STOP!

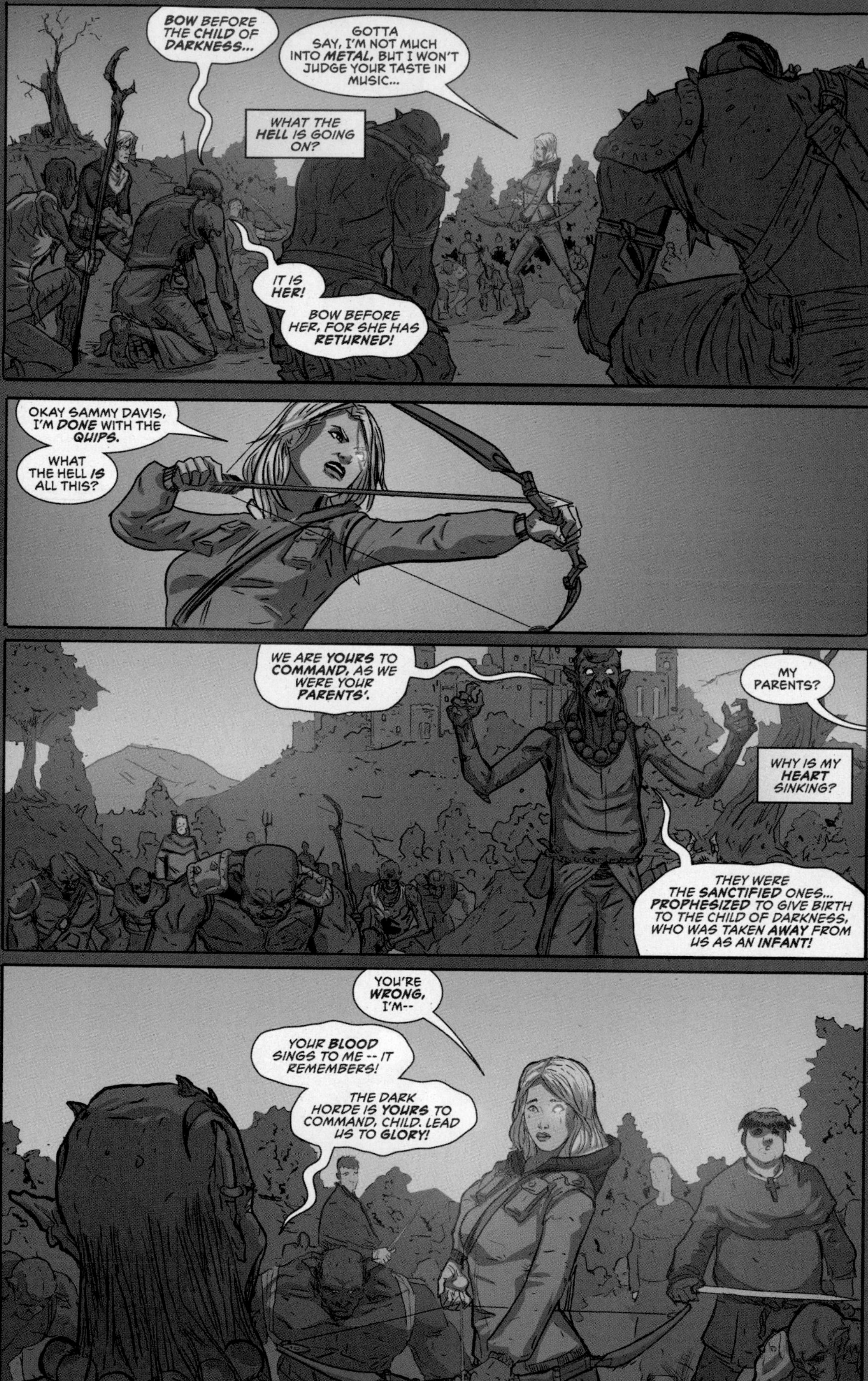
BOW BEFORE THE CHILD OF DARKNESS...
GOTTA SAY, I'M NOT MUCH INTO METAL, BUT I WON'T JUDGE YOUR TASTE IN MUSIC...
WHAT THE HELL IS GOING ON?
IT IS HER!
BOW BEFORE HER, FOR SHE HAS RETURNED!
OKAY SAMMY DAVIS, I'M DONE WITH THE QUIPS.
WHAT THE HELL IS ALL THIS?
WE ARE YOURS TO COMMAND, AS WE WERE YOUR PARENTS'.
MY PARENTS?
WHY IS MY HEART SINKING?
THEY WERE THE SANCTIFIED ONES... PROPHESIZED TO GIVE BIRTH TO THE CHILD OF DARKNESS, WHO WAS TAKEN AWAY FROM US AS AN INFANT!
YOU'RE WRONG, I'M--
YOUR BLOOD SINGS TO ME -- IT REMEMBERS!
THE DARK HORDE IS YOURS TO COMMAND, CHILD. LEAD US TO GLORY!

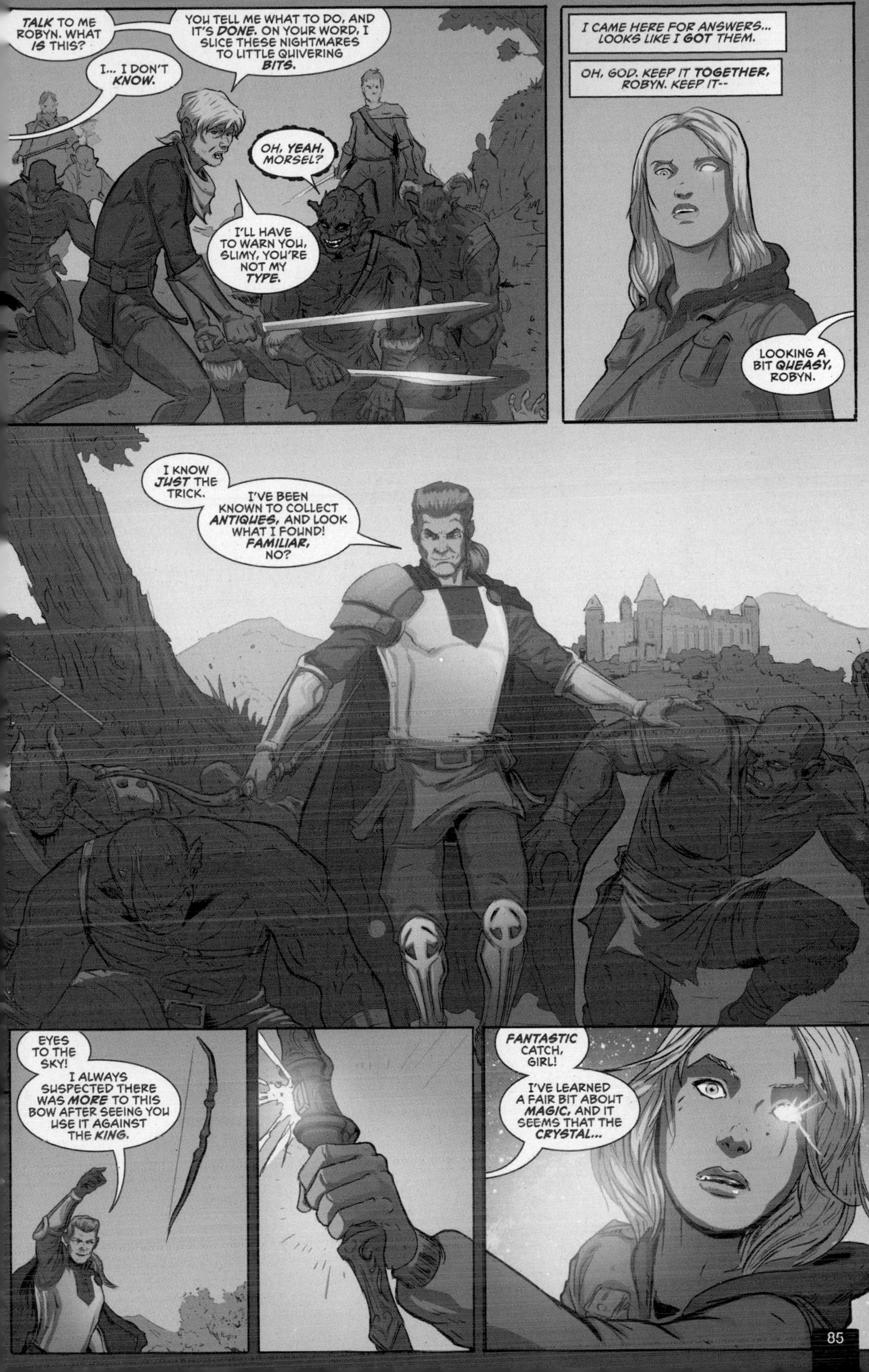
TALK TO ME ROBYN. WHAT IS THIS?
YOU TELL ME WHAT TO DO, AND IT'S DONE. ON YOUR WORD, I SLICE THESE NIGHTMARES TO LITTLE QUIVERING BITS.
I... I DON'T KNOW.
OH, YEAH, MORSEL?
I'LL HAVE TO WARN YOU, SLIMY, YOU'RE NOT MY TYPE.
I CAME HERE FOR ANSWERS... LOOKS LIKE I GOT THEM.
OH, GOD. KEEP IT TOGETHER, ROBYN. KEEP IT--
LOOKING A BIT QUEASY, ROBYN.
I KNOW JUST THE TRICK.
I'VE BEEN KNOWN TO COLLECT ANTIQUES, AND LOOK WHAT I FOUND! FAMILIAR, NO?
EYES TO THE SKY!
I ALWAYS SUSPECTED THERE WAS MORE TO THIS BOW AFTER SEEING YOU USE IT AGAINST THE KING.
FANTASTIC CATCH, GIRL!
I'VE LEARNED A FAIR BIT ABOUT MAGIC, AND IT SEEMS THAT THE CRYSTAL...

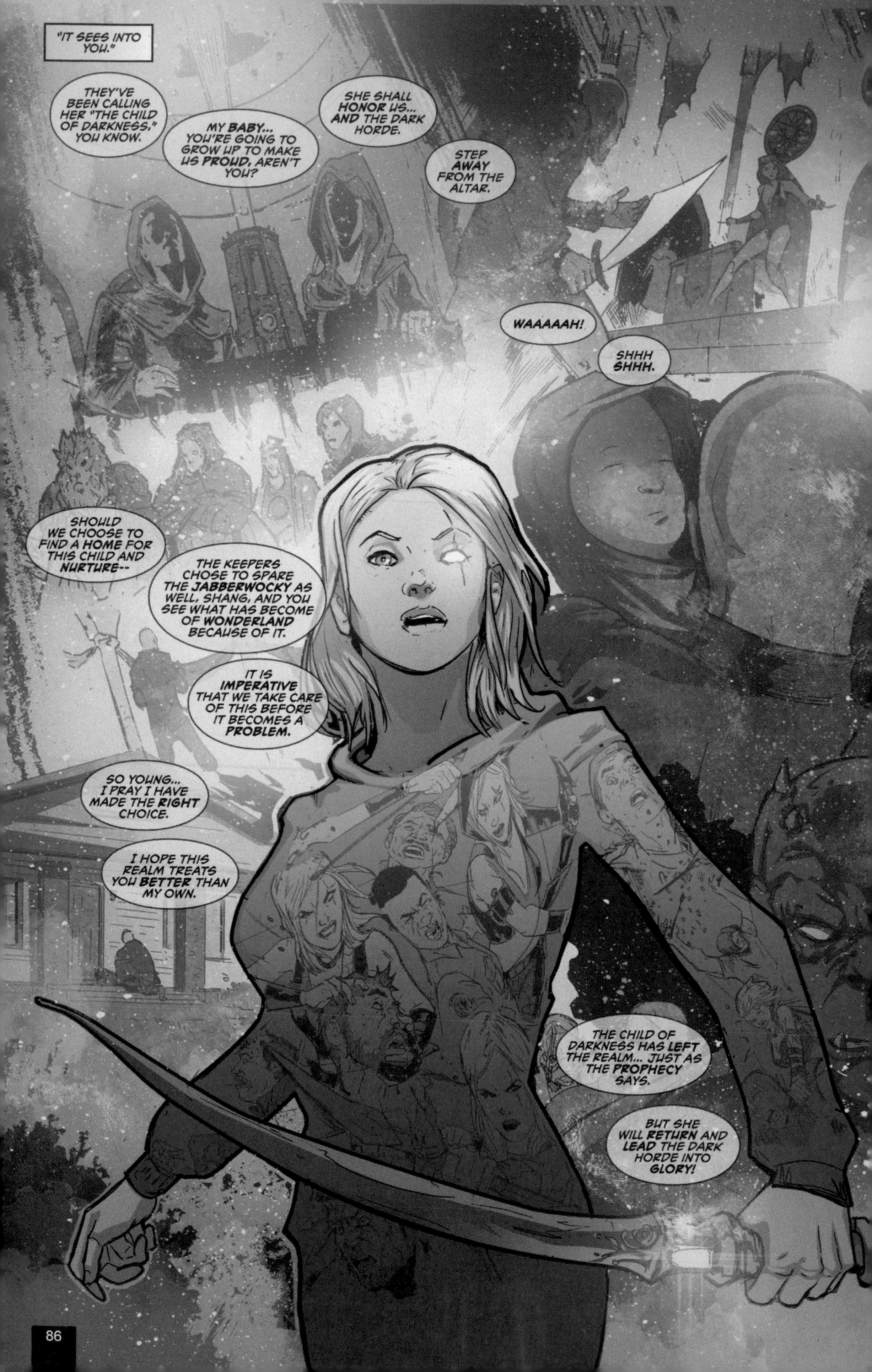

"IT SEES INTO YOU."
THEY'VE BEEN CALLING HER "THE CHILD OF DARKNESS," YOU KNOW.
MY BABY... YOU'RE GOING TO GROW UP TO MAKE US PROUD, AREN'T YOU?
SHE SHALL HONOR US... AND THE DARK HORDE.
STEP AWAY FROM THE ALTAR.
WAAAAAH!
SHHH SHHH.
SHOULD WE CHOOSE TO FIND A HOME FOR THIS CHILD AND NURTURE--
THE KEEPERS CHOSE TO SPARE THE JABBERWOCKY AS WELL, SHANG, AND YOU SEE WHAT HAS BECOME OF WONDERLAND BECAUSE OF IT.
IT IS IMPERATIVE THAT WE TAKE CARE OF THIS BEFORE IT BECOMES A PROBLEM.
SO YOUNG... I PRAY I HAVE MADE THE RIGHT CHOICE.
I HOPE THIS REALM TREATS YOU BETTER THAN MY OWN.
THE CHILD OF DARKNESS HAS LEFT THE REALM... JUST AS THE PROPHECY SAYS.
BUT SHE WILL RETURN AND LEAD THE DARK HORDE INTO GLORY!

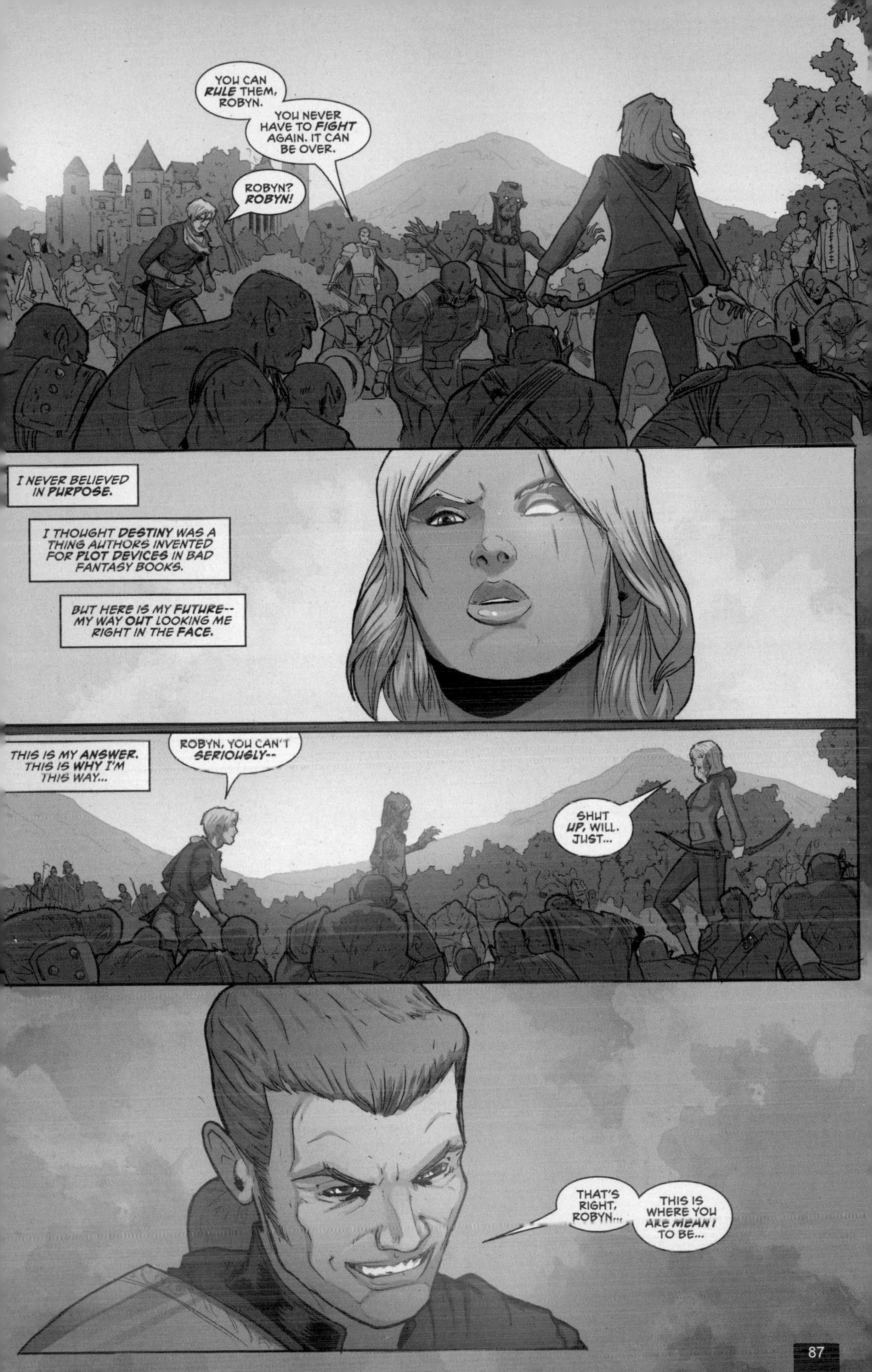
YOU CAN RULE THEM, ROBYN.
YOU NEVER HAVE TO FIGHT AGAIN. IT CAN BE OVER.
ROBYN? ROBYN!
I NEVER BELIEVED IN PURPOSE.
I THOUGHT DESTINY WAS A THING AUTHORS INVENTED FOR PLOT DEVICES IN BAD FANTASY BOOKS.
BUT HERE IS MY FUTURE-- MY WAY OUT LOOKING ME RIGHT IN THE FACE.
THIS IS MY ANSWER. THIS IS WHY I'M THIS WAY...
ROBYN, YOU CAN'T SERIOUSLY--
SHUT UP, WILL. JUST...
THAT'S RIGHT, ROBYN...
THIS IS WHERE YOU ARE MEANT TO BE...

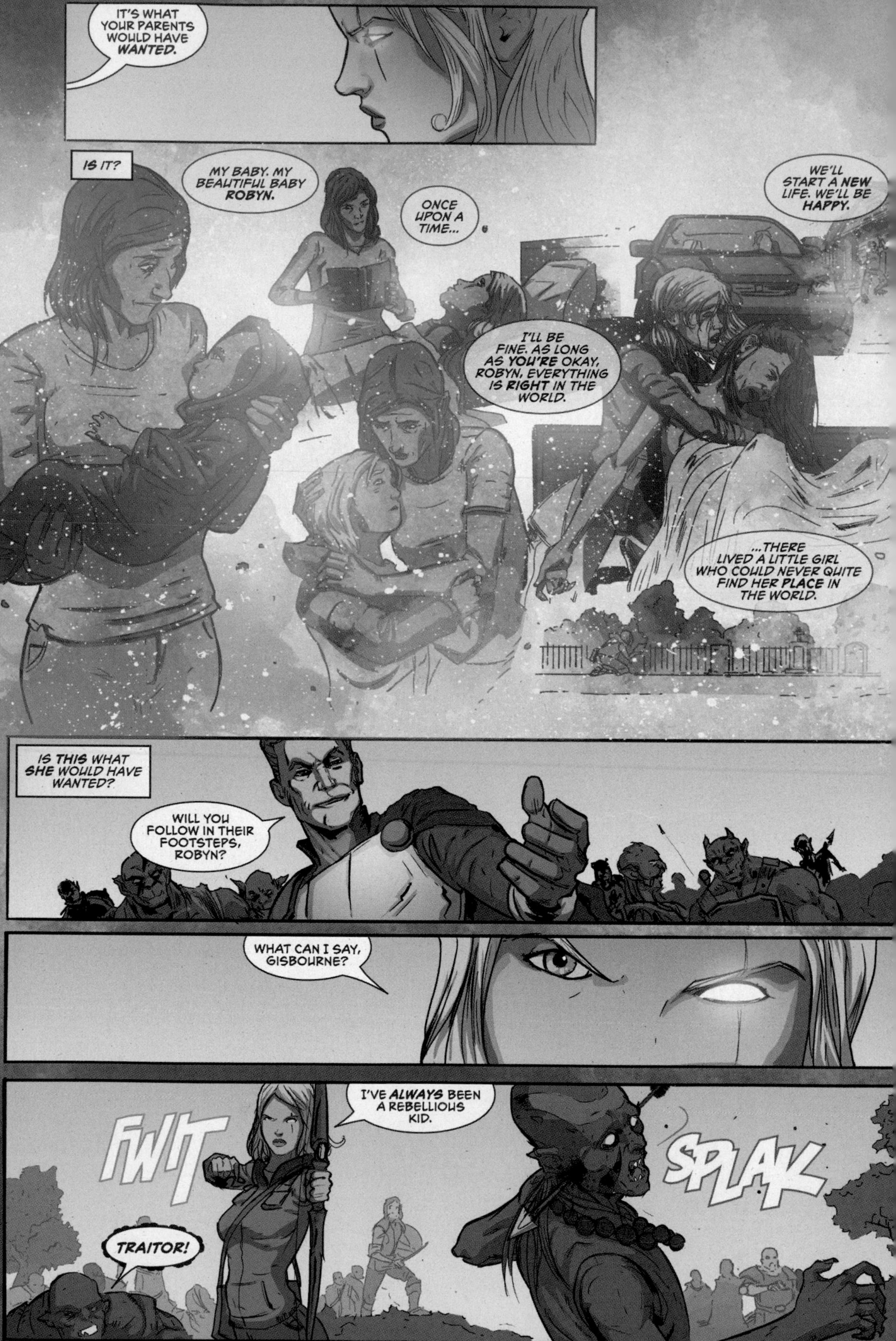
IT'S WHAT YOUR PARENTS WOULD HAVE WANTED.
IS IT?
MY BABY. MY BEAUTIFUL BABY ROBYN.
ONCE UPON A TIME...
WE'LL START A NEW LIFE. WE'LL BE HAPPY.
I'LL BE FINE. AS LONG AS YOU'RE OKAY, ROBYN, EVERYTHING IS RIGHT IN THE WORLD.
...THERE LIVED A LITTLE GIRL WHO COULD NEVER QUITE FIND HER PLACE IN THE WORLD.
IS THIS WHAT SHE WOULD HAVE WANTED?
WILL YOU FOLLOW IN THEIR FOOTSTEPS, ROBYN?
WHAT CAN I SAY, GISBOURNE?
FWIT
I'VE ALWAYS BEEN A REBELLIOUS KID.
SPLAK
TRAITOR!

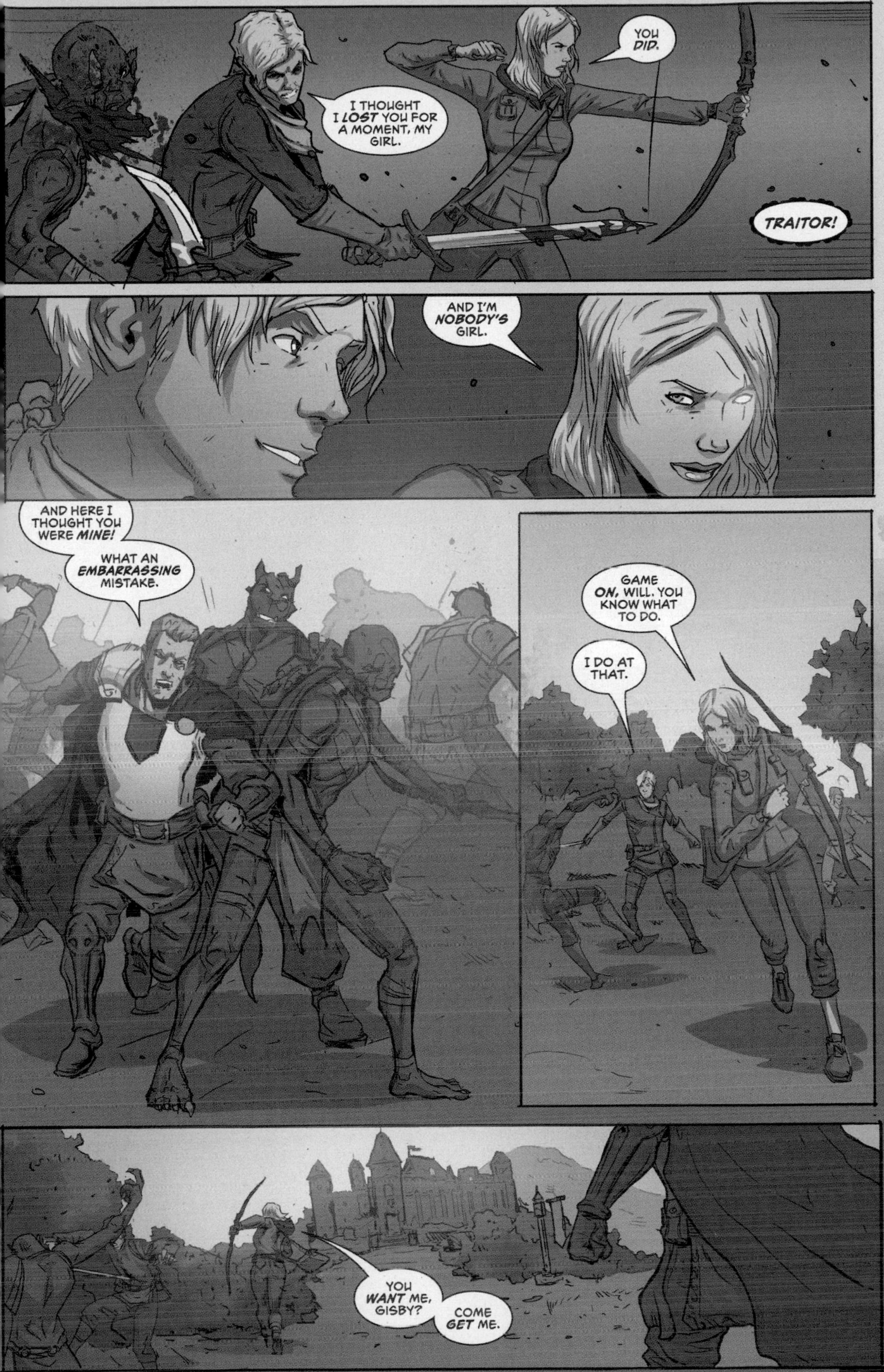
I THOUGHT I LOST YOU FOR A MOMENT, MY GIRL.
YOU DID.
TRAITOR!
AND I'M NOBODY'S GIRL.
AND HERE I THOUGHT YOU WERE MINE!
WHAT AN EMBARRASSING MISTAKE.
GAME ON, WILL. YOU KNOW WHAT TO DO.
I DO AT THAT.
YOU WANT ME, GISBY?
COME GET ME.

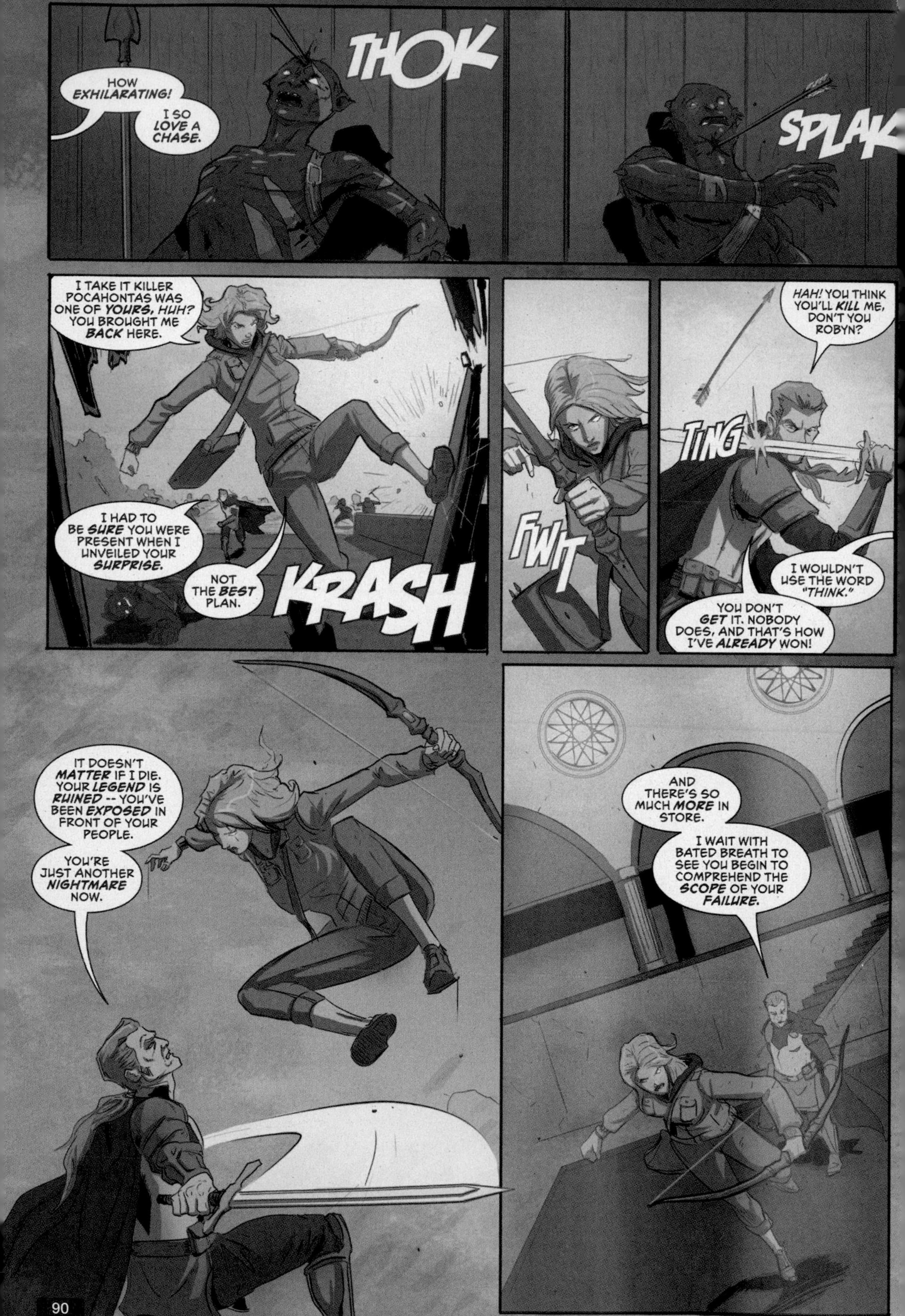
THOK
HOW EXHILARATING!
I SO LOVE A CHASE.
SPLAK
I TAKE IT KILLER POCAHONTAS WAS ONE OF YOURS, HUH? YOU BROUGHT ME BACK HERE.
I HAD TO BE SURE YOU WERE PRESENT WHEN I UNVEILED YOUR SURPRISE.
NOT THE BEST PLAN.
KRASH
FWIT
HAH! YOU THINK YOU'LL KILL ME, DON'T YOU ROBYN?
TING
I WOULDN'T USE THE WORD "THINK."
YOU DON'T GET IT. NOBODY DOES, AND THAT'S HOW I'VE ALREADY WON!
IT DOESN'T MATTER IF I DIE. YOUR LEGEND IS RUINED -- YOU'VE BEEN EXPOSED IN FRONT OF YOUR PEOPLE.
YOU'RE JUST ANOTHER NIGHTMARE NOW.
AND THERE'S SO MUCH MORE IN STORE.
I WAIT WITH BATED BREATH TO SEE YOU BEGIN TO COMPREHEND THE SCOPE OF YOUR FAILURE.

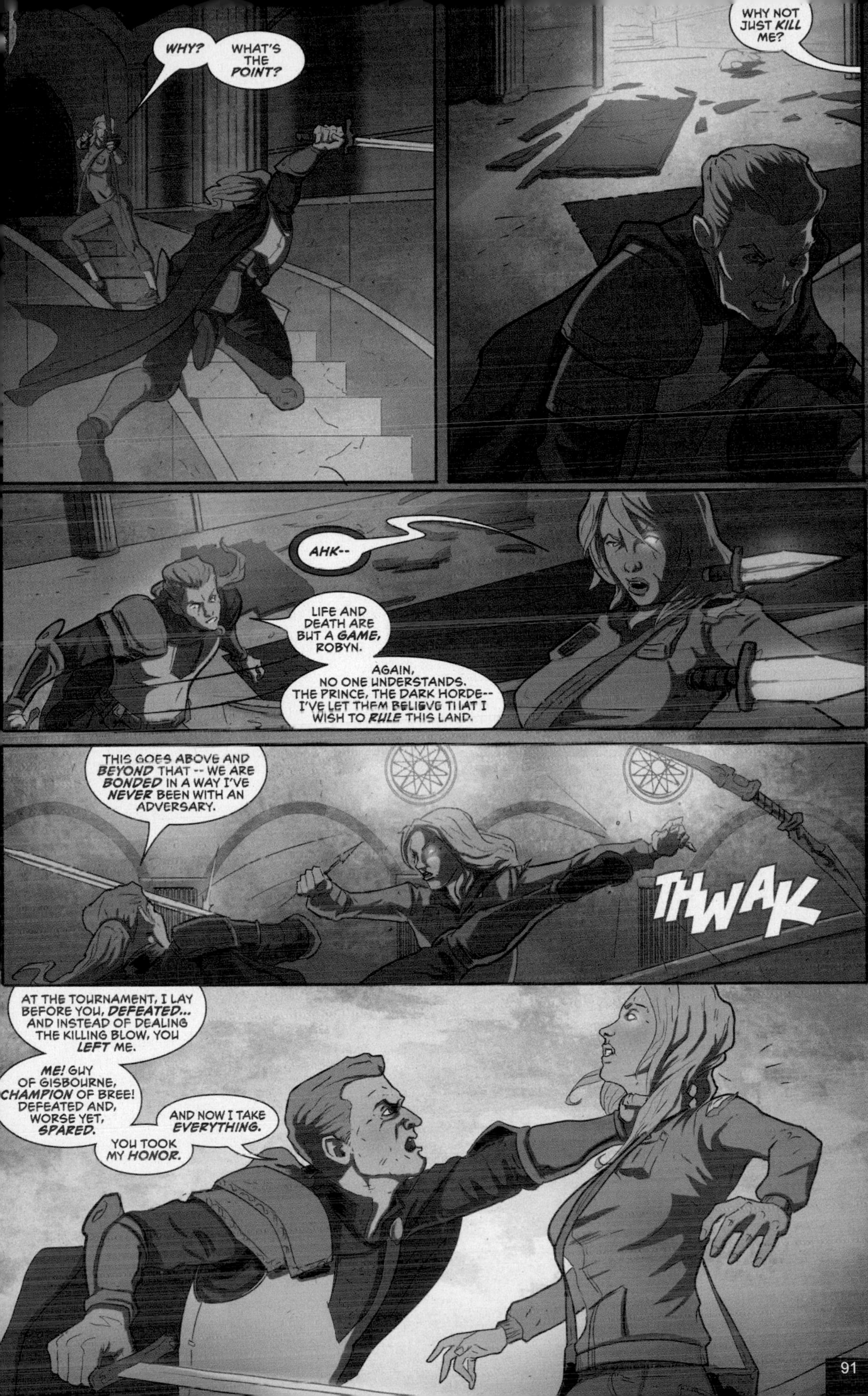
WHY? WHAT'S THE POINT?
WHY NOT JUST KILL ME?
AHK--
LIFE AND DEATH ARE BUT A GAME, ROBYN.
AGAIN, NO ONE UNDERSTANDS. THE PRINCE, THE DARK HORDE-- I'VE LET THEM BELIEVE THAT I WISH TO RULE THIS LAND.
THIS GOES ABOVE AND BEYOND THAT -- WE ARE BONDED IN A WAY I'VE NEVER BEEN WITH AN ADVERSARY.
THWAK
AT THE TOURNAMENT, I LAY BEFORE YOU, DEFEATED... AND INSTEAD OF DEALING THE KILLING BLOW, YOU LEFT ME.
ME! GUY OF GISBOURNE, CHAMPION OF BREE! DEFEATED AND, WORSE YET, SPARED.
YOU TOOK MY HONOR.
AND NOW I TAKE EVERYTHING.

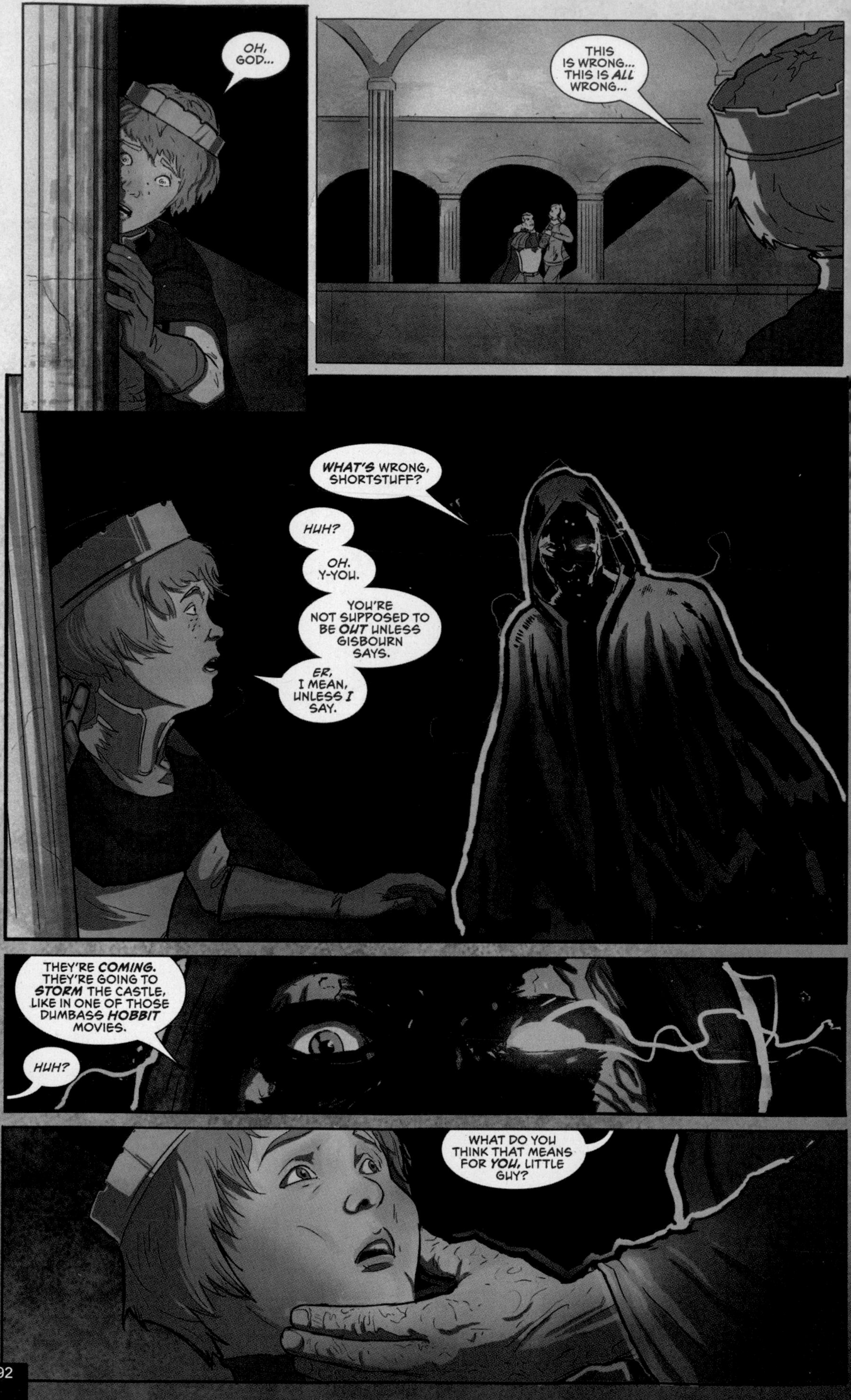
OH, GOD...
THIS IS WRONG... THIS IS ALL WRONG...
WHAT'S WRONG, SHORTSTUFF?
HUH?
OH. Y-YOU.
YOU'RE NOT SUPPOSED TO BE OUT UNLESS GISBOURN SAYS.
ER, I MEAN, UNLESS I SAY.
THEY'RE COMING. THEY'RE GOING TO STORM THE CASTLE, LIKE IN ONE OF THOSE DUMBASS HOBBIT MOVIES.
HUH?
WHAT DO YOU THINK THAT MEANS FOR YOU, LITTLE GUY?

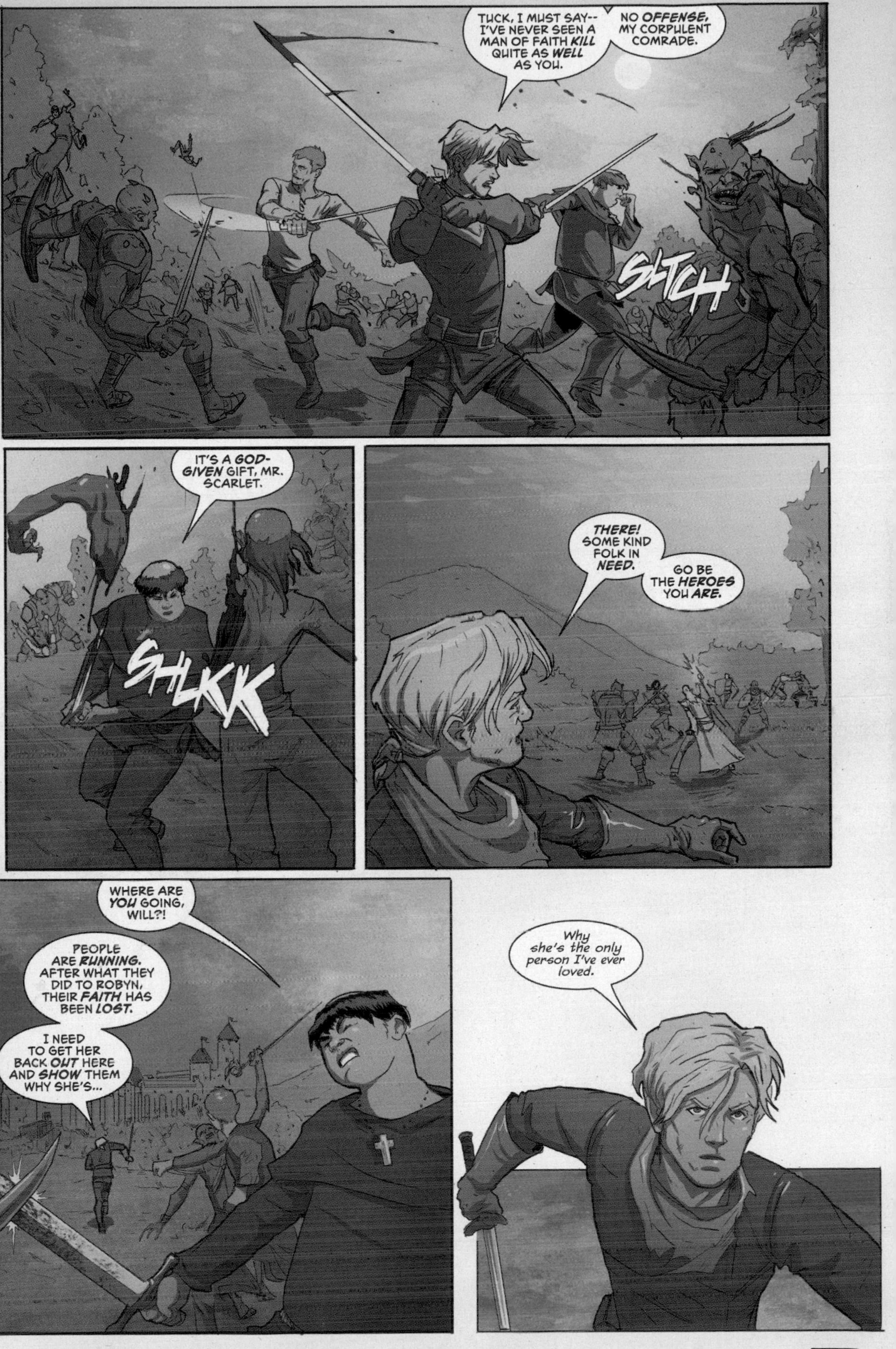
TUCK, I MUST SAY-- I'VE NEVER SEEN A MAN OF FAITH KILL QUITE AS WELL AS YOU.
NO OFFENSE, MY CORPULENT COMRADE.
SLTCH
IT'S A GOD-GIVEN GIFT, MR. SCARLET.
SHLKK
THERE! SOME KIND FOLK IN NEED.
GO BE THE HEROES YOU ARE.
WHERE ARE YOU GOING, WILL?!
PEOPLE ARE RUNNING. AFTER WHAT THEY DID TO ROBYN, THEIR FAITH HAS BEEN LOST.
I NEED TO GET HER BACK OUT HERE AND SHOW THEM WHY SHE'S...
Why she's the only person I've ever loved.

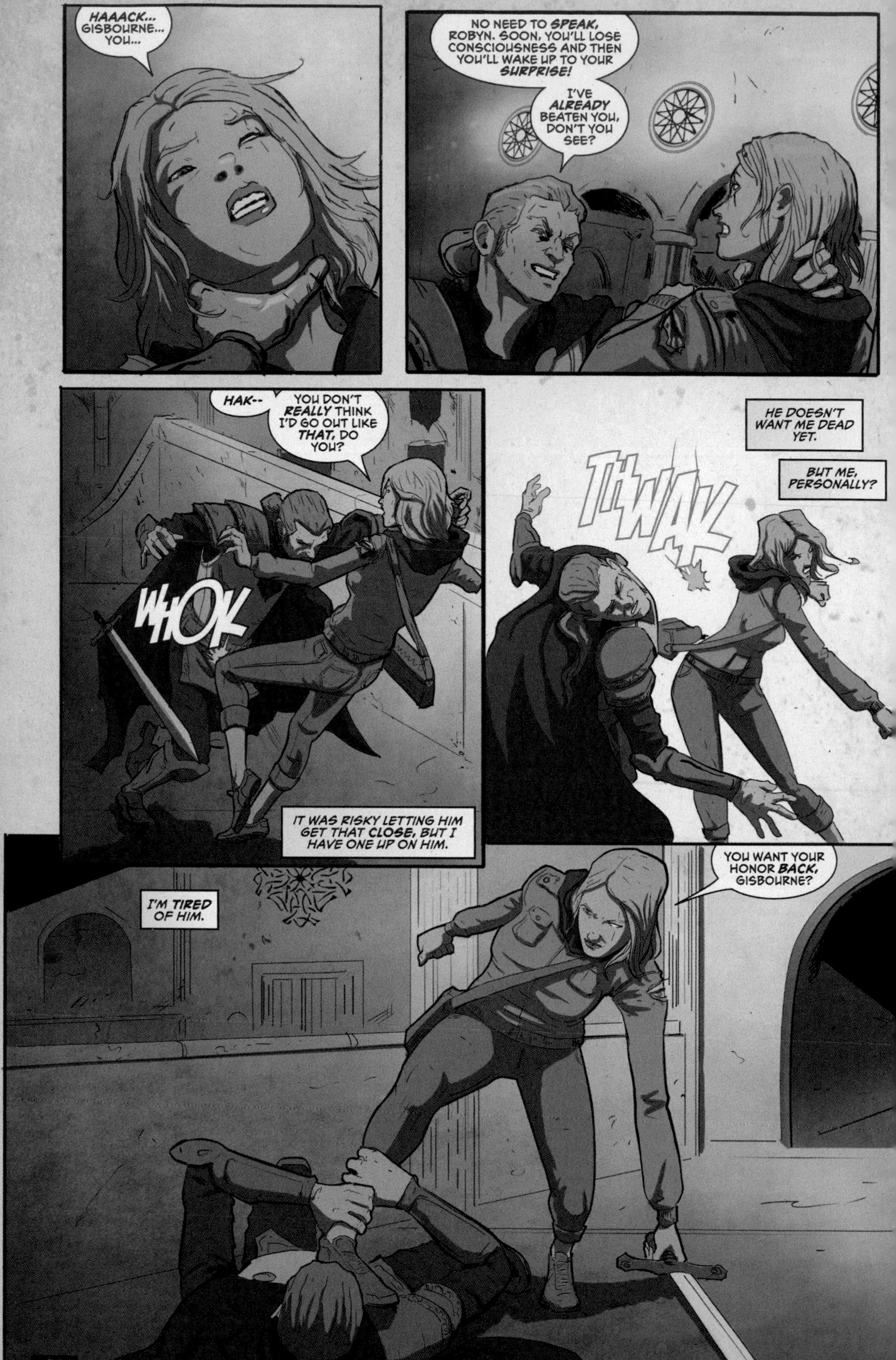
HAAACK... GISBOURNE... YOU...
NO NEED TO SPEAK, ROBYN. SOON, YOU'LL LOSE CONSCIOUSNESS AND THEN YOU'LL WAKE UP TO YOUR SURPRISE!
I'VE ALREADY BEATEN YOU, DON'T YOU SEE?
HAK--
YOU DON'T REALLY THINK I'D GO OUT LIKE THAT, DO YOU?
WHOK
IT WAS RISKY LETTING HIM GET THAT CLOSE, BUT I HAVE ONE UP ON HIM.
HE DOESN'T WANT ME DEAD YET.
BUT ME, PERSONALLY?
THWAK
I'M TIRED OF HIM.
YOU WANT YOUR HONOR BACK, GISBOURNE?

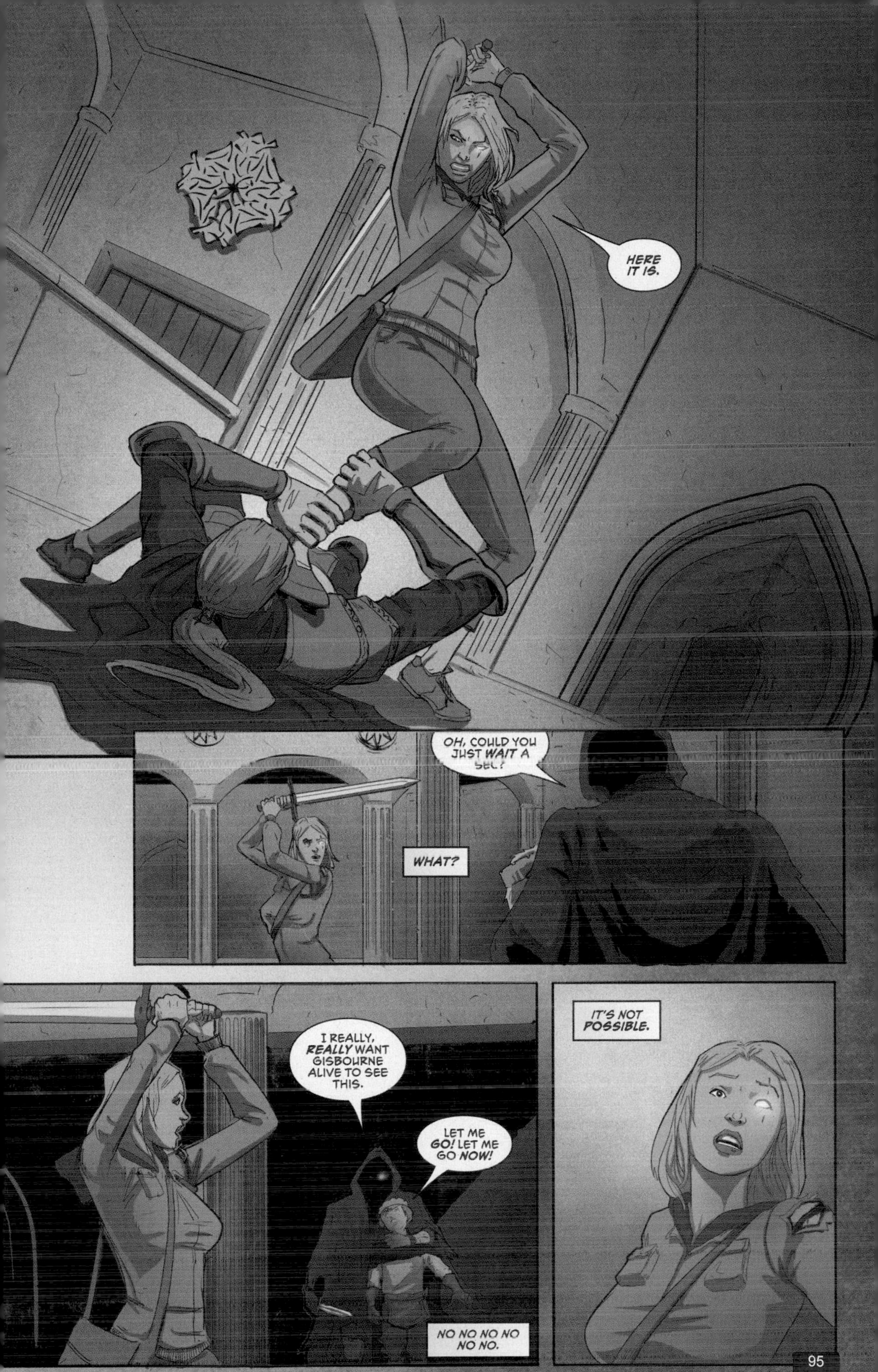
HERE IT IS.
OH, COULD YOU JUST WAIT A SEC?
WHAT?
I REALLY, REALLY WANT GISBOURNE ALIVE TO SEE THIS.
LET ME GO! LET ME GO NOW!
NO NO NO NO NO NO.
IT'S NOT POSSIBLE.

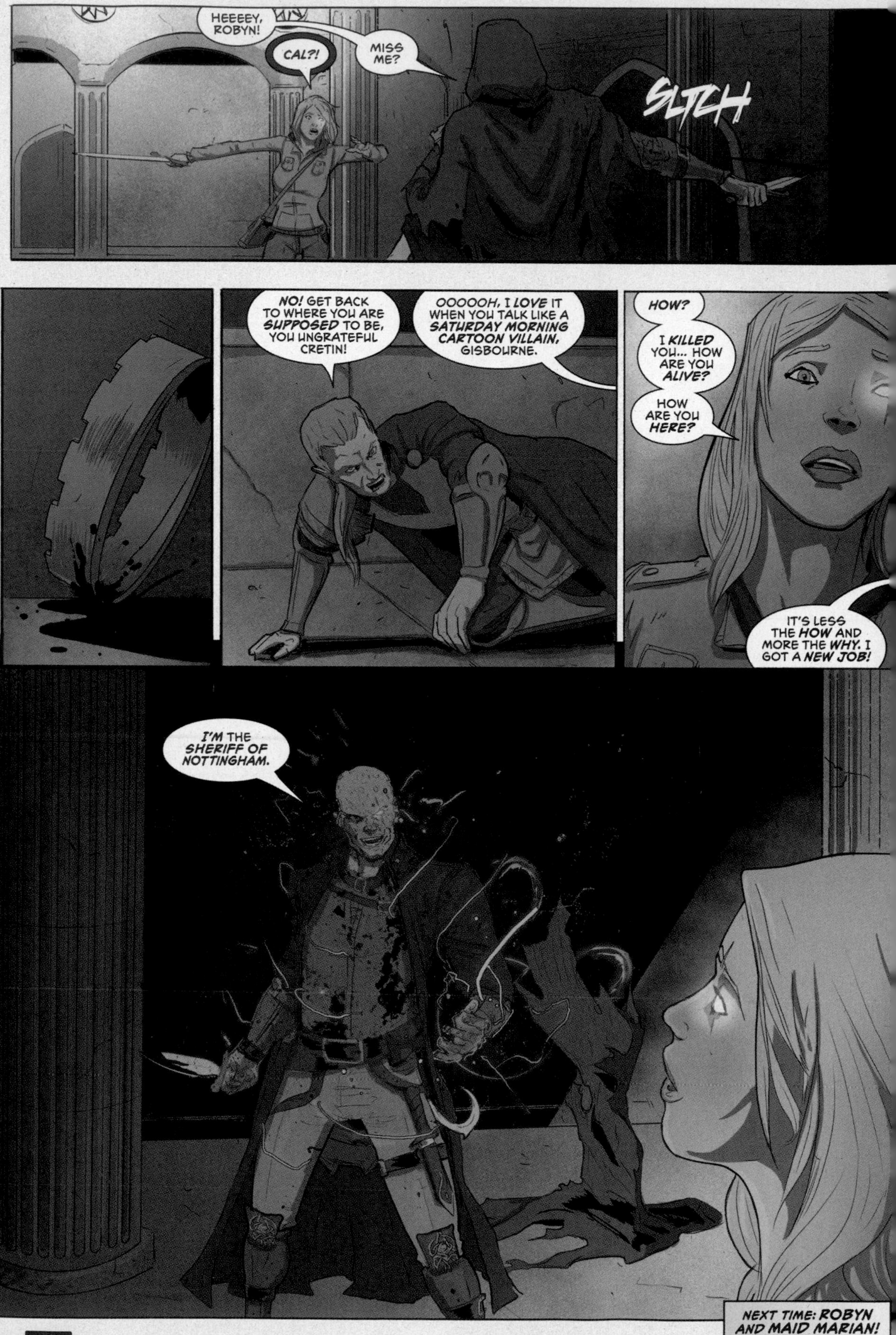
HEEEEY, ROBYN!
CAL?!
MISS ME?
SLTCH
NO! GET BACK TO WHERE YOU ARE SUPPOSED TO BE, YOU UNGRATEFUL CRETIN!
OOOOOH, I LOVE IT WHEN YOU TALK LIKE A SATURDAY MORNING CARTOON VILLAIN, GISBOURNE.
HOW?
I KILLED YOU... HOW ARE YOU ALIVE?
HOW ARE YOU HERE?
IT'S LESS THE HOW AND MORE THE WHY. I GOT A NEW JOB!
I'M THE SHERIFF OF NOTTINGHAM.
NEXT TIME: ROBYN AND MAID MARIAN!

Grimm Fairy Tales presents:

# ROBYN HOOD

## WANTED

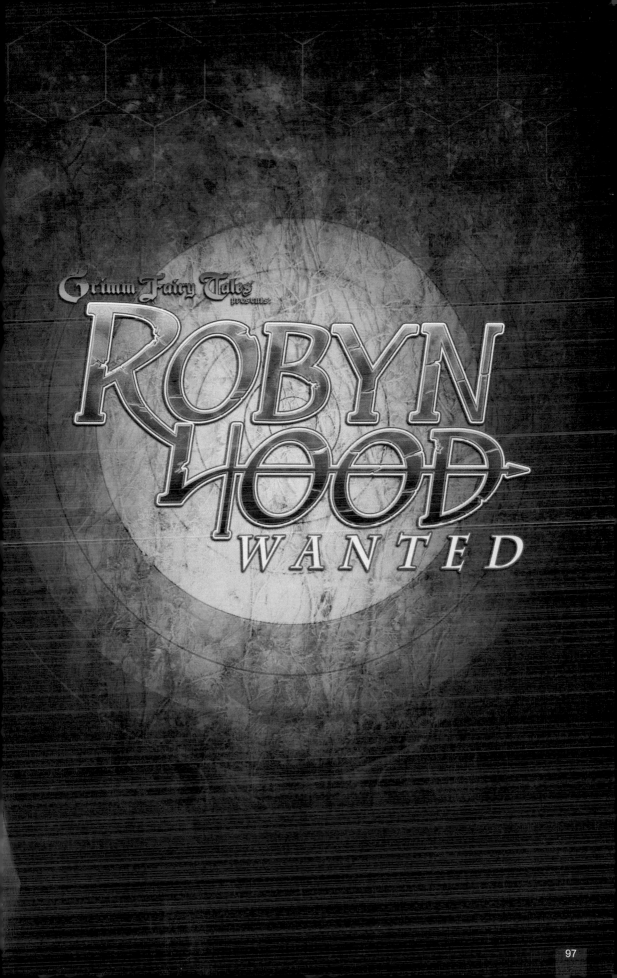

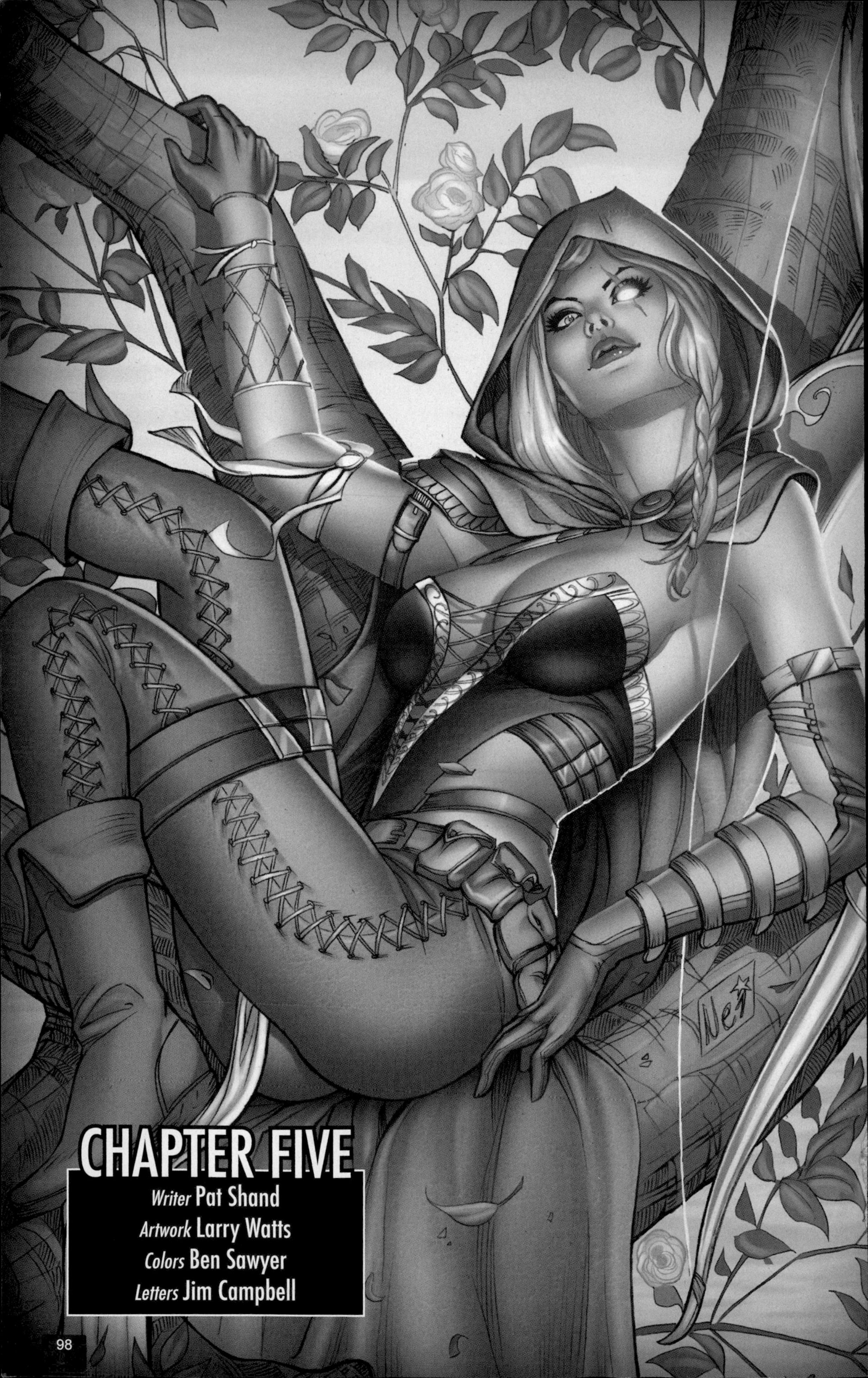

# CHAPTER FIVE

*Writer* Pat Shand
*Artwork* Larry Watts
*Colors* Ben Sawyer
*Letters* Jim Campbell

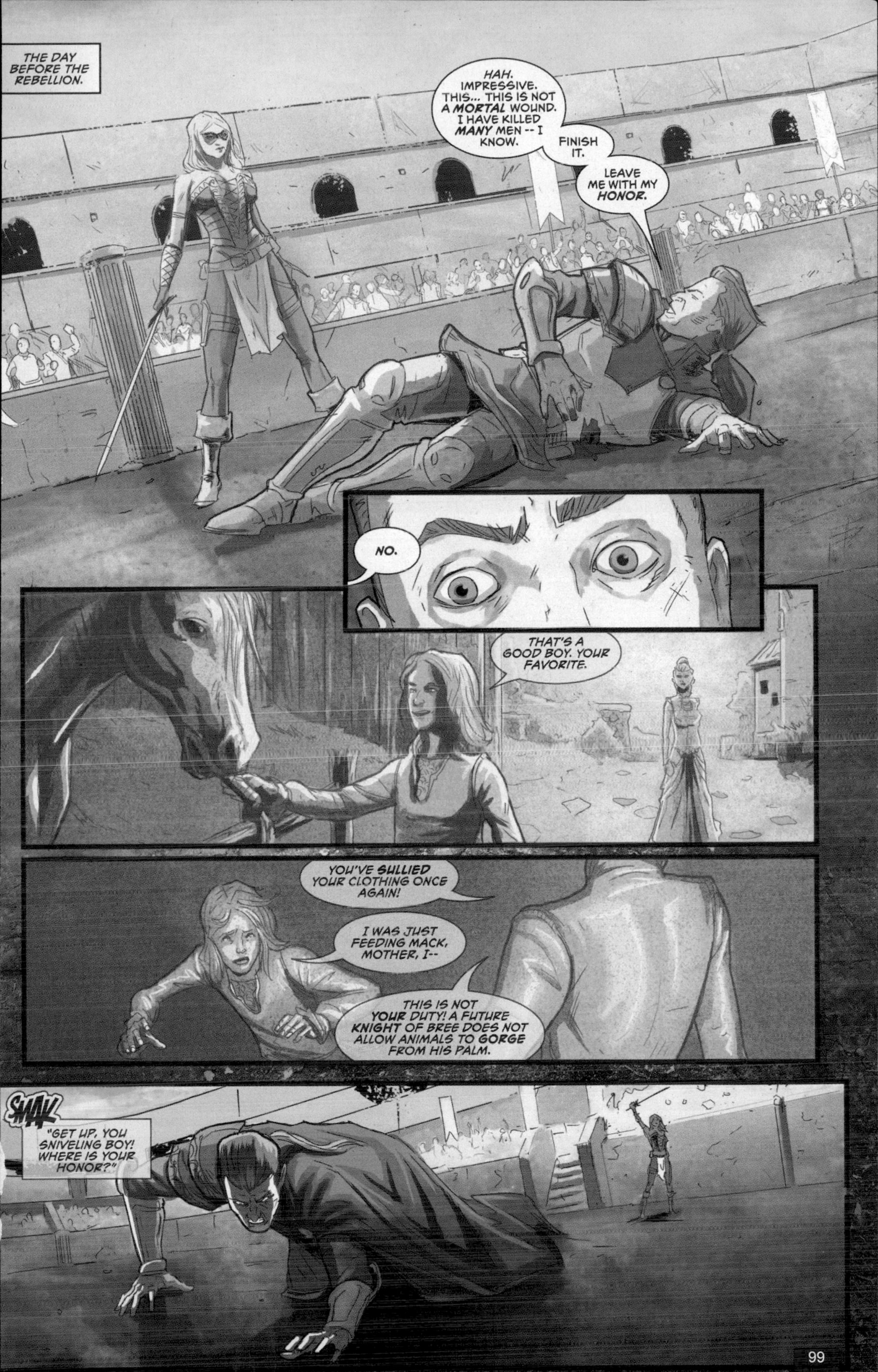
THE DAY BEFORE THE REBELLION.
HAH. IMPRESSIVE. THIS... THIS IS NOT A MORTAL WOUND. I HAVE KILLED MANY MEN -- I KNOW.
FINISH IT.
LEAVE ME WITH MY HONOR.
NO.
THAT'S A GOOD BOY. YOUR FAVORITE.
YOU'VE SULLIED YOUR CLOTHING ONCE AGAIN!
I WAS JUST FEEDING MACK, MOTHER, I--
THIS IS NOT YOUR DUTY! A FUTURE KNIGHT OF BREE DOES NOT ALLOW ANIMALS TO GORGE FROM HIS PALM.
SMAK
"GET UP, YOU SNIVELING BOY! WHERE IS YOUR HONOR?"

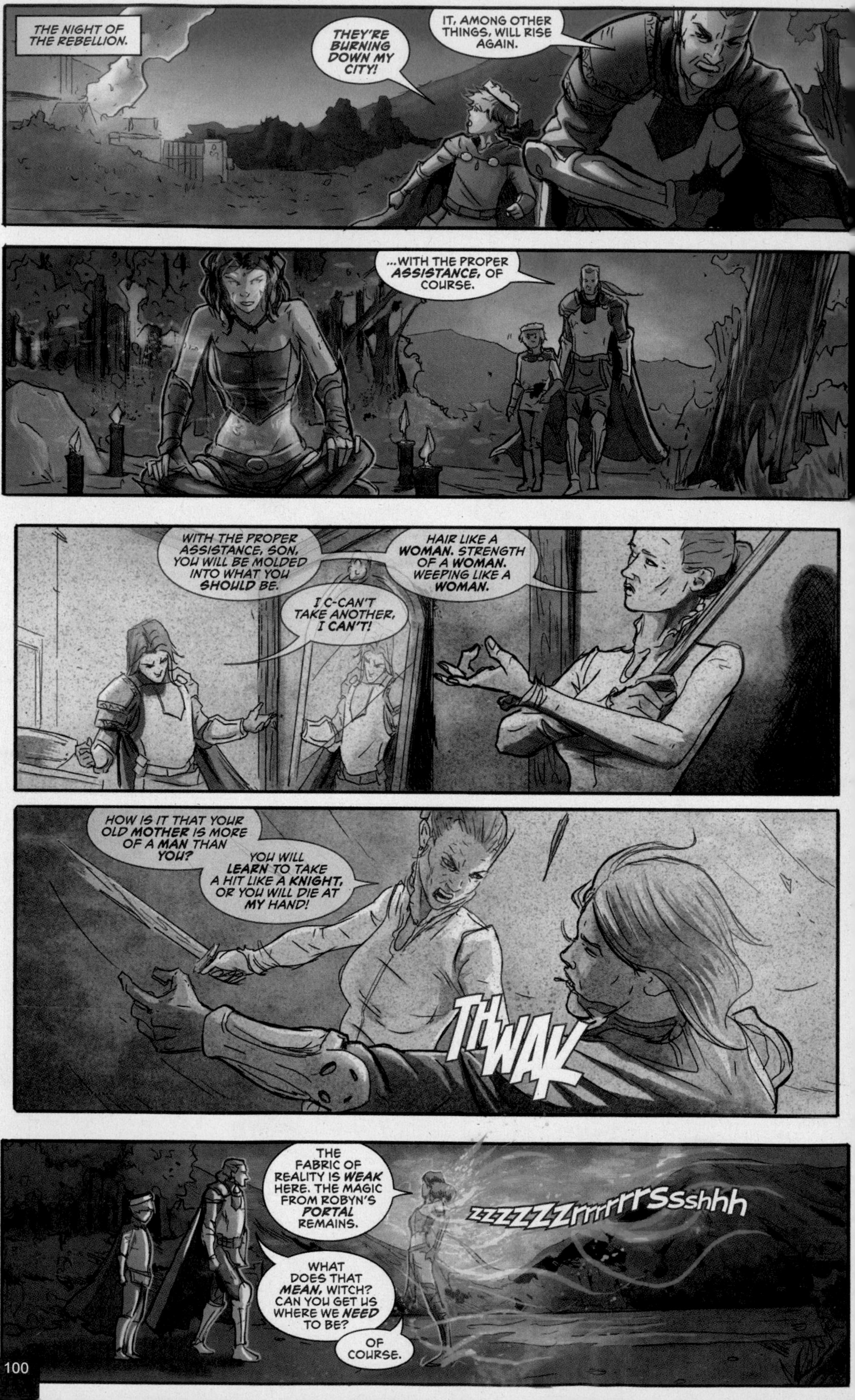
THE NIGHT OF THE REBELLION.
THEY'RE BURNING DOWN MY CITY!
IT, AMONG OTHER THINGS, WILL RISE AGAIN.
...WITH THE PROPER ASSISTANCE, OF COURSE.
WITH THE PROPER ASSISTANCE, SON, YOU WILL BE MOLDED INTO WHAT YOU SHOULD BE.
I C-CAN'T TAKE ANOTHER, I CAN'T!
HAIR LIKE A WOMAN. STRENGTH OF A WOMAN. WEEPING LIKE A WOMAN.
HOW IS IT THAT YOUR OLD MOTHER IS MORE OF A MAN THAN YOU?
YOU WILL LEARN TO TAKE A HIT LIKE A KNIGHT, OR YOU WILL DIE AT MY HAND!
THWAK
THE FABRIC OF REALITY IS WEAK HERE. THE MAGIC FROM ROBYN'S PORTAL REMAINS.
ZZZZZZrrrrrrSsshhh
WHAT DOES THAT MEAN, WITCH? CAN YOU GET US WHERE WE NEED TO BE?
OF COURSE.

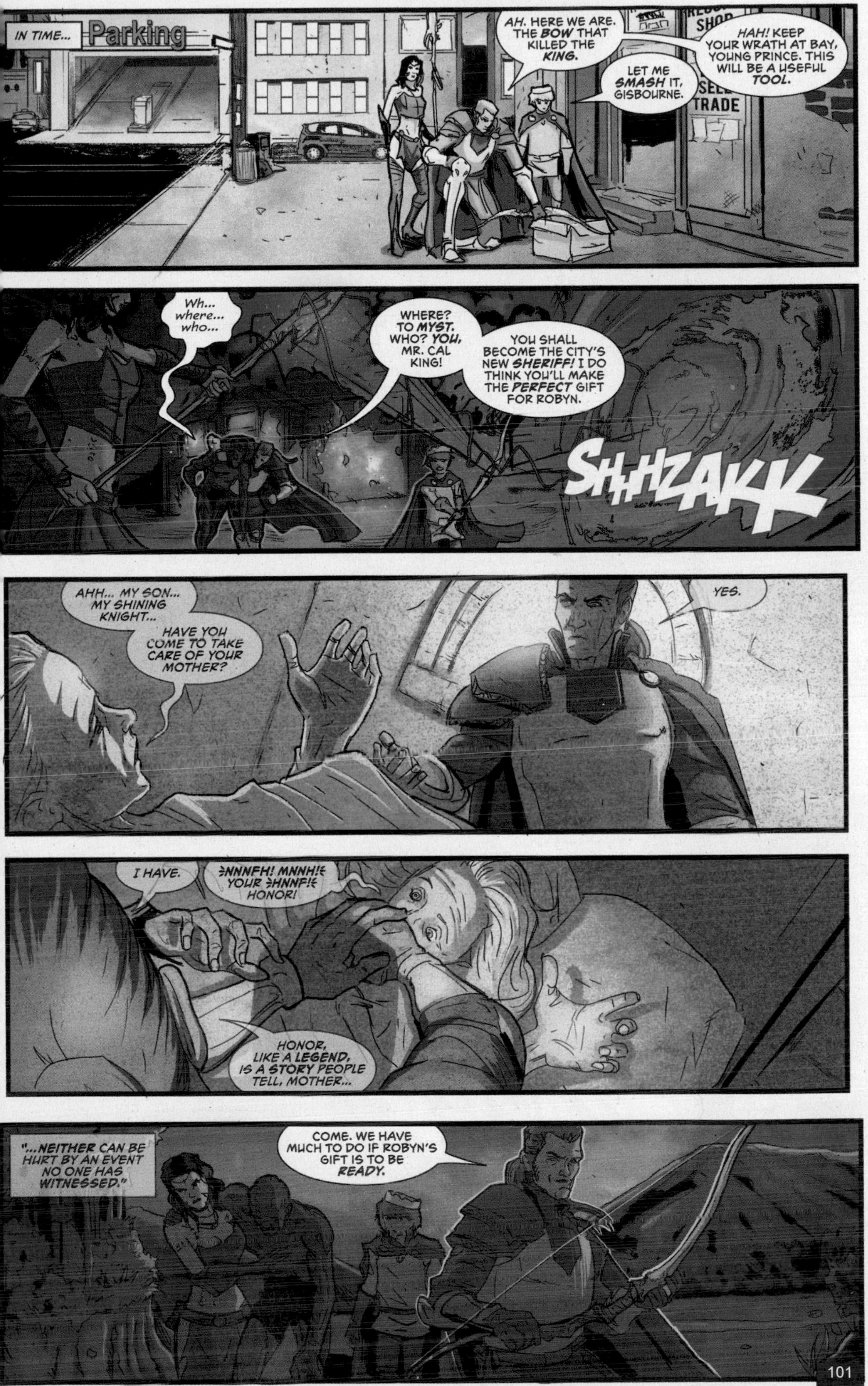
IN TIME...
Parking
AH. HERE WE ARE. THE BOW THAT KILLED THE KING.
LET ME SMASH IT, GISBOURNE.
HAH! KEEP YOUR WRATH AT BAY, YOUNG PRINCE. THIS WILL BE A USEFUL TOOL.
SHOP
TRADE
Wh... where... who...
WHERE? TO MYST. WHO? YOU, MR. CAL KING!
YOU SHALL BECOME THE CITY'S NEW SHERIFF! I DO THINK YOU'LL MAKE THE PERFECT GIFT FOR ROBYN.
SHHZAKK
AHH... MY SON... MY SHINING KNIGHT...
HAVE YOU COME TO TAKE CARE OF YOUR MOTHER?
YES.
I HAVE.
NNNFH! MNNH! YOUR HNNF! HONOR!
HONOR, LIKE A LEGEND, IS A STORY PEOPLE TELL, MOTHER...
"...NEITHER CAN BE HURT BY AN EVENT NO ONE HAS WITNESSED."
COME. WE HAVE MUCH TO DO IF ROBYN'S GIFT IS TO BE READY.

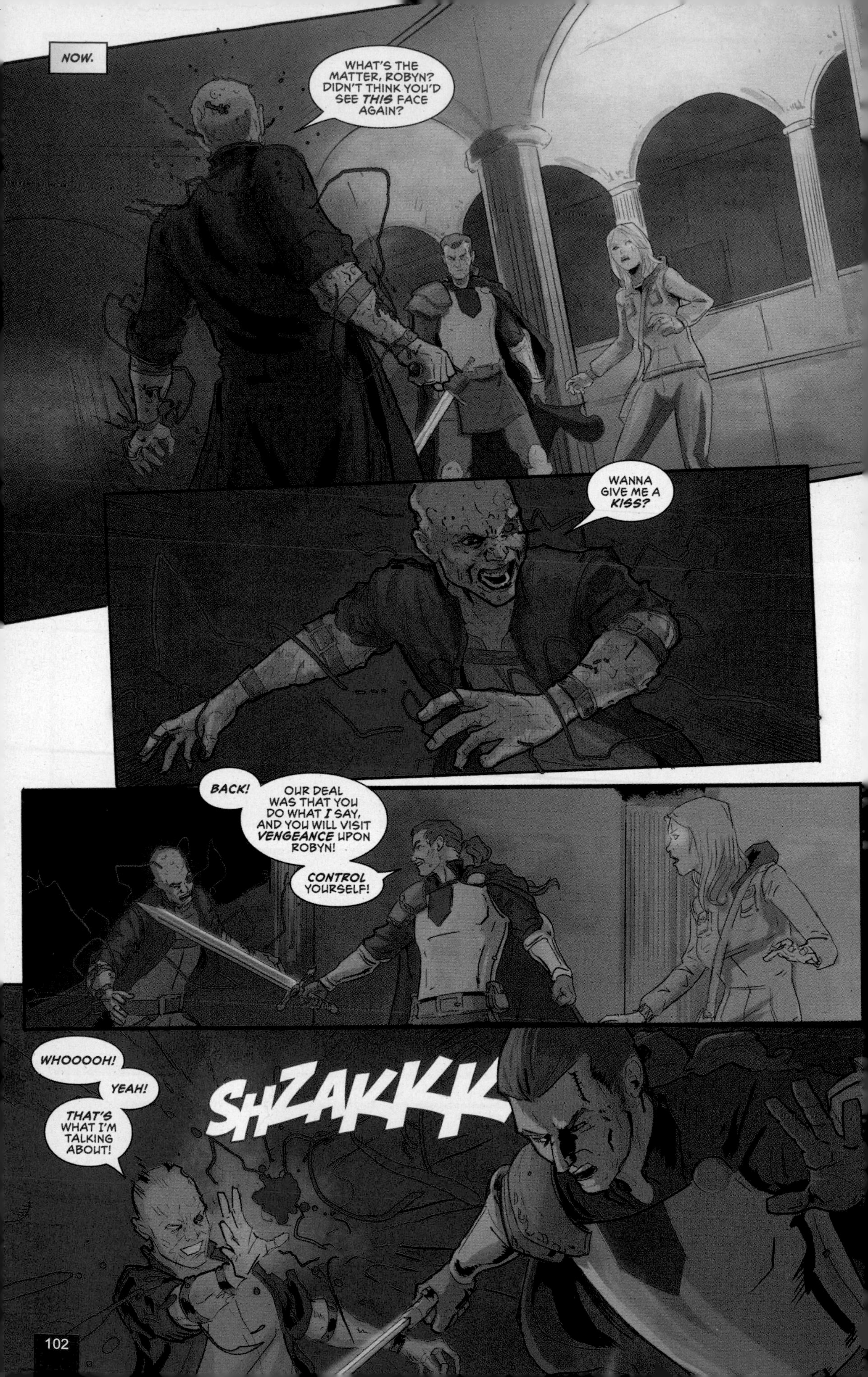
NOW.
WHAT'S THE MATTER, ROBYN? DIDN'T THINK YOU'D SEE THIS FACE AGAIN?
WANNA GIVE ME A KISS?
BACK!
OUR DEAL WAS THAT YOU DO WHAT I SAY, AND YOU WILL VISIT VENGEANCE UPON ROBYN!
CONTROL YOURSELF!
WHOOOOH!
YEAH!
THAT'S WHAT I'M TALKING ABOUT!
SHZAKKK

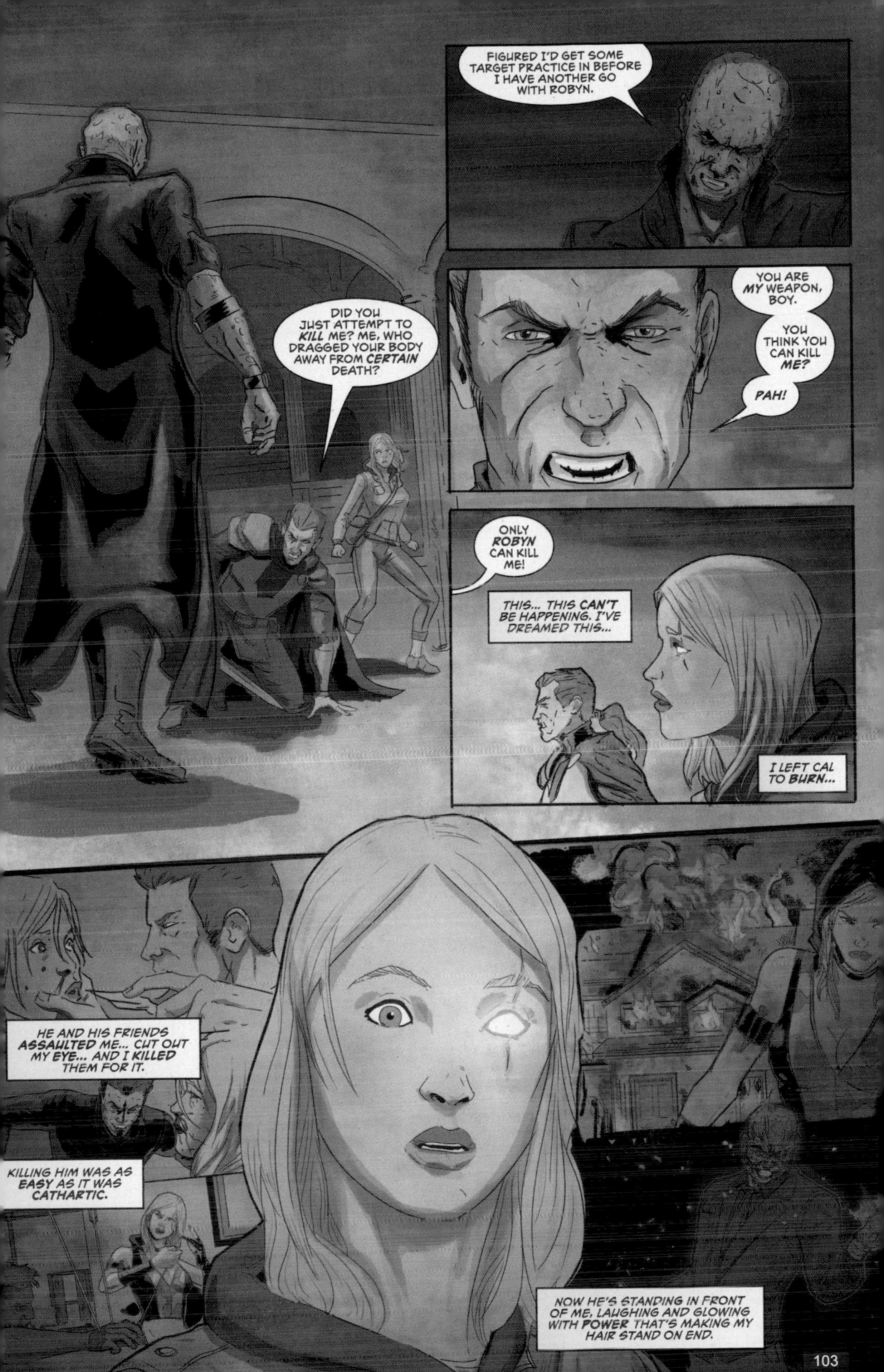
FIGURED I'D GET SOME TARGET PRACTICE IN BEFORE I HAVE ANOTHER GO WITH ROBYN.
DID YOU JUST ATTEMPT TO KILL ME? ME, WHO DRAGGED YOUR BODY AWAY FROM CERTAIN DEATH?
YOU ARE MY WEAPON, BOY.
YOU THINK YOU CAN KILL ME?
PAH!
ONLY ROBYN CAN KILL ME!
THIS... THIS CAN'T BE HAPPENING. I'VE DREAMED THIS...
I LEFT CAL TO BURN...
HE AND HIS FRIENDS ASSAULTED ME... CUT OUT MY EYE... AND I KILLED THEM FOR IT.
KILLING HIM WAS AS EASY AS IT WAS CATHARTIC.
NOW HE'S STANDING IN FRONT OF ME, LAUGHING AND GLOWING WITH POWER THAT'S MAKING MY HAIR STAND ON END.

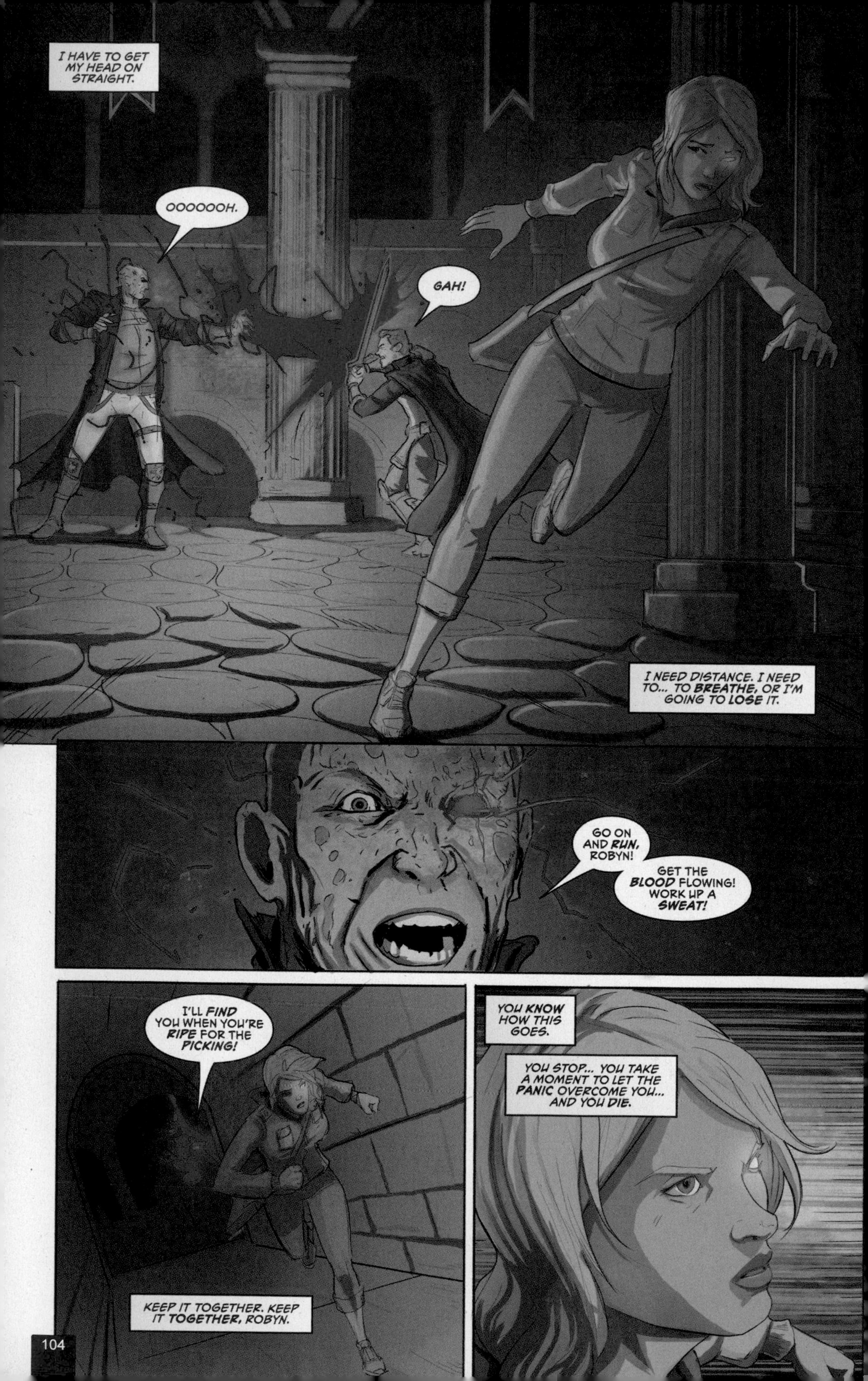
I HAVE TO GET MY HEAD ON STRAIGHT.
OOOOOOH.
GAH!
I NEED DISTANCE. I NEED TO... TO BREATHE, OR I'M GOING TO LOSE IT.
GO ON AND RUN, ROBYN!
GET THE BLOOD FLOWING! WORK UP A SWEAT!
I'LL FIND YOU WHEN YOU'RE RIPE FOR THE PICKING!
KEEP IT TOGETHER. KEEP IT TOGETHER, ROBYN.
YOU KNOW HOW THIS GOES.
YOU STOP... YOU TAKE A MOMENT TO LET THE PANIC OVERCOME YOU... AND YOU DIE.

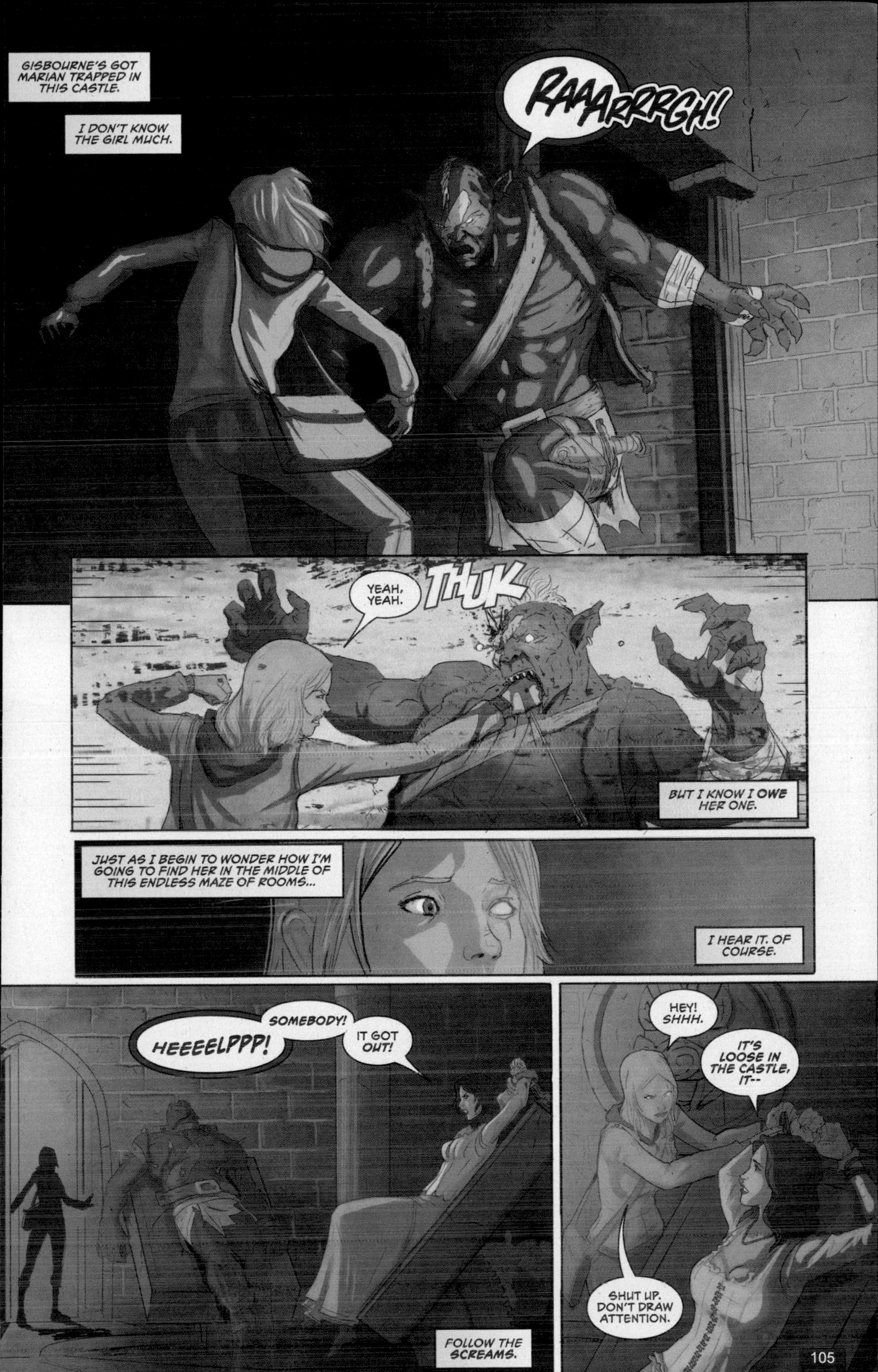
GISBOURNE'S GOT MARIAN TRAPPED IN THIS CASTLE.
I DON'T KNOW THE GIRL MUCH.
RAAAARRRRGH!
YEAH, YEAH.
THUK
BUT I KNOW I OWE HER ONE.
JUST AS I BEGIN TO WONDER HOW I'M GOING TO FIND HER IN THE MIDDLE OF THIS ENDLESS MAZE OF ROOMS...
I HEAR IT, OF COURSE.
HEEEELPPP!
SOMEBODY!
IT GOT OUT!
FOLLOW THE SCREAMS.
HEY! SHHH.
IT'S LOOSE IN THE CASTLE, IT--
SHUT UP. DON'T DRAW ATTENTION.

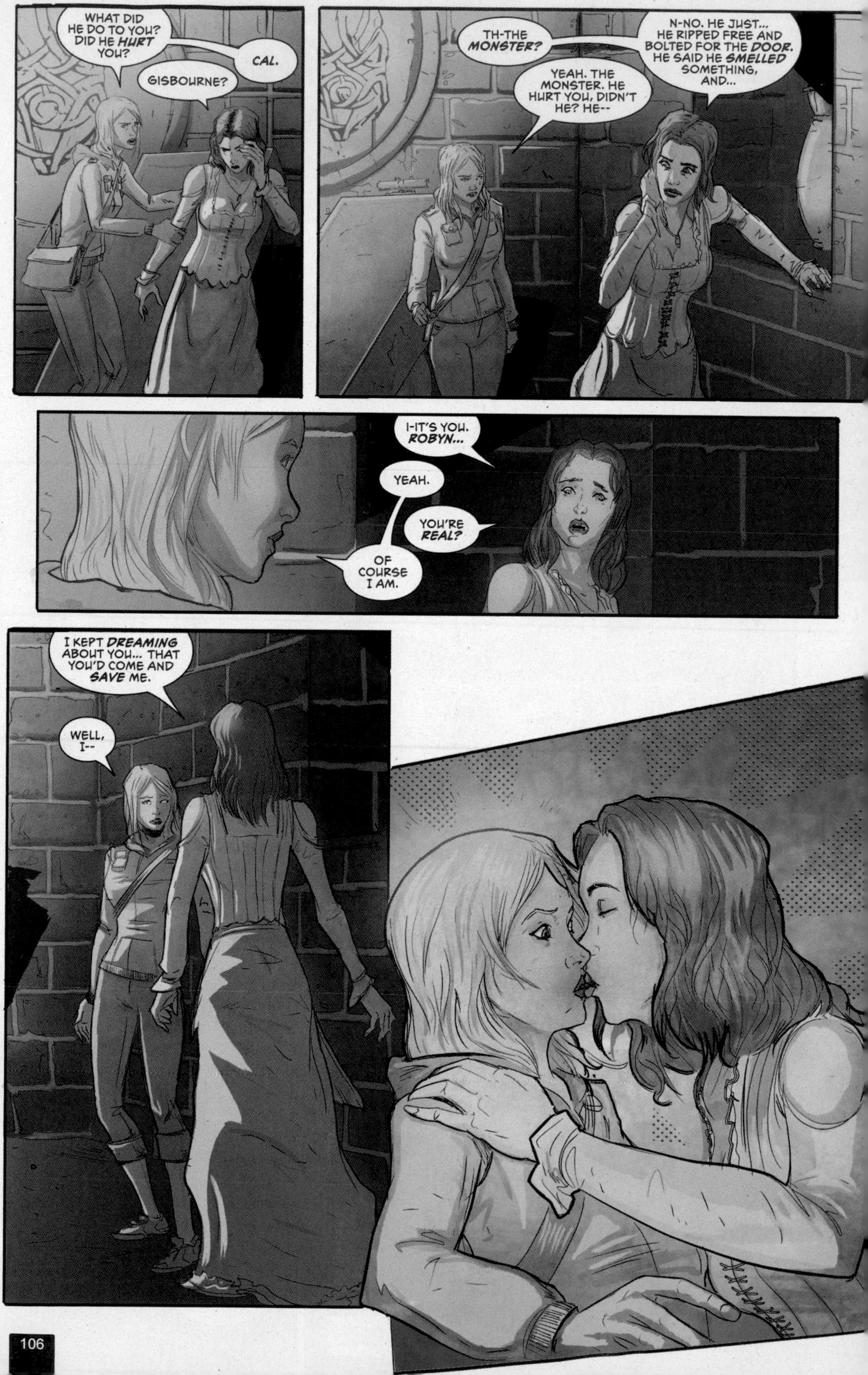
WHAT DID HE DO TO YOU? DID HE HURT YOU?
CAL.
GISBOURNE?
TH-THE MONSTER?
N-NO. HE JUST... HE RIPPED FREE AND BOLTED FOR THE DOOR. HE SAID HE SMELLED SOMETHING, AND...
YEAH. THE MONSTER. HE HURT YOU, DIDN'T HE? HE--
I-IT'S YOU. ROBYN...
YEAH.
YOU'RE REAL?
OF COURSE I AM.
I KEPT DREAMING ABOUT YOU... THAT YOU'D COME AND SAVE ME.
WELL, I--

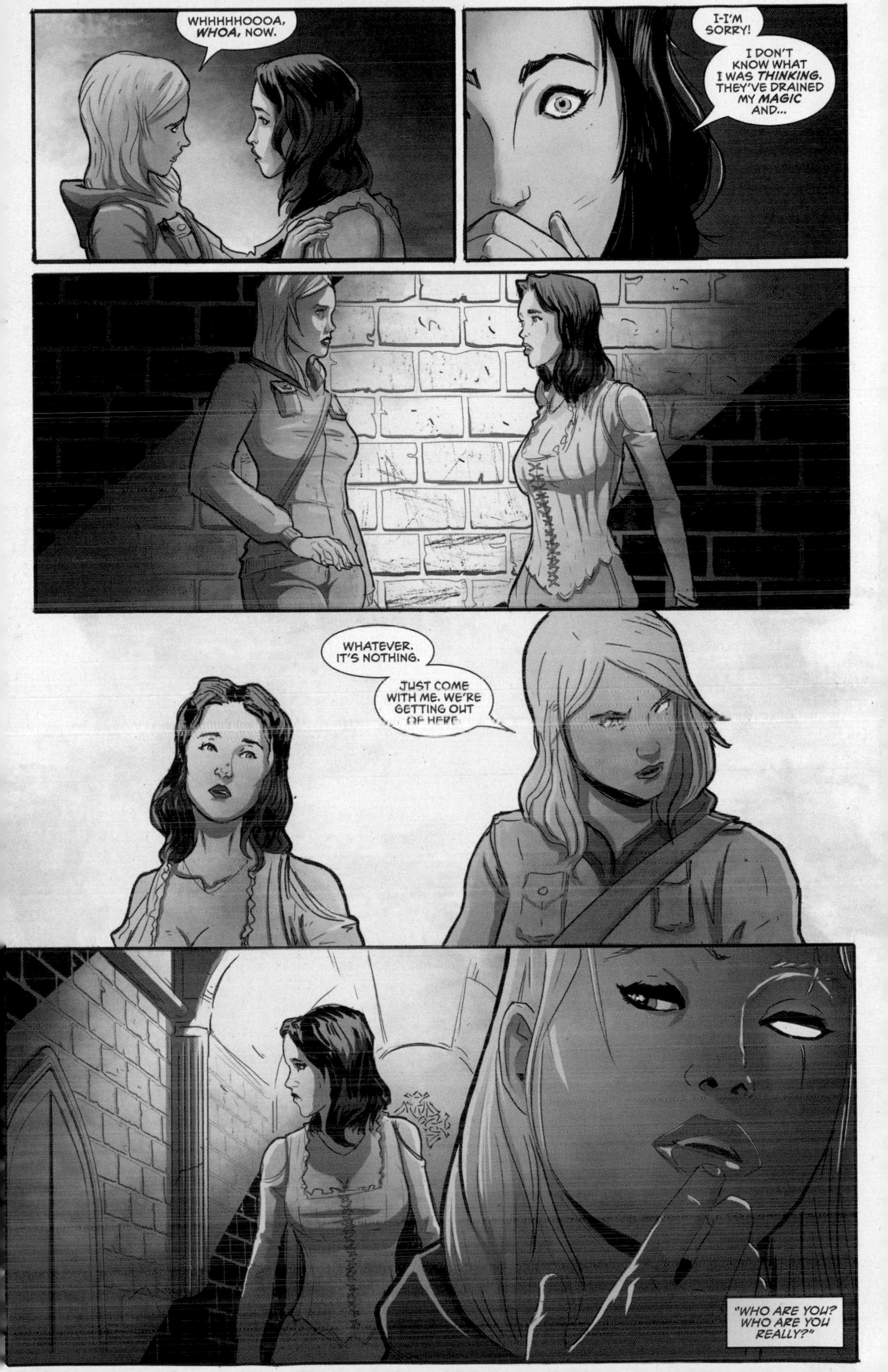
WHHHHHOOOA, *WHOA*, NOW.
I-I'M SORRY!
I DON'T KNOW WHAT I WAS *THINKING*. THEY'VE DRAINED MY *MAGIC* AND...
WHATEVER. IT'S NOTHING.
JUST COME WITH ME. WE'RE GETTING OUT OF HERE.
"WHO ARE YOU? WHO ARE YOU *REALLY*?"

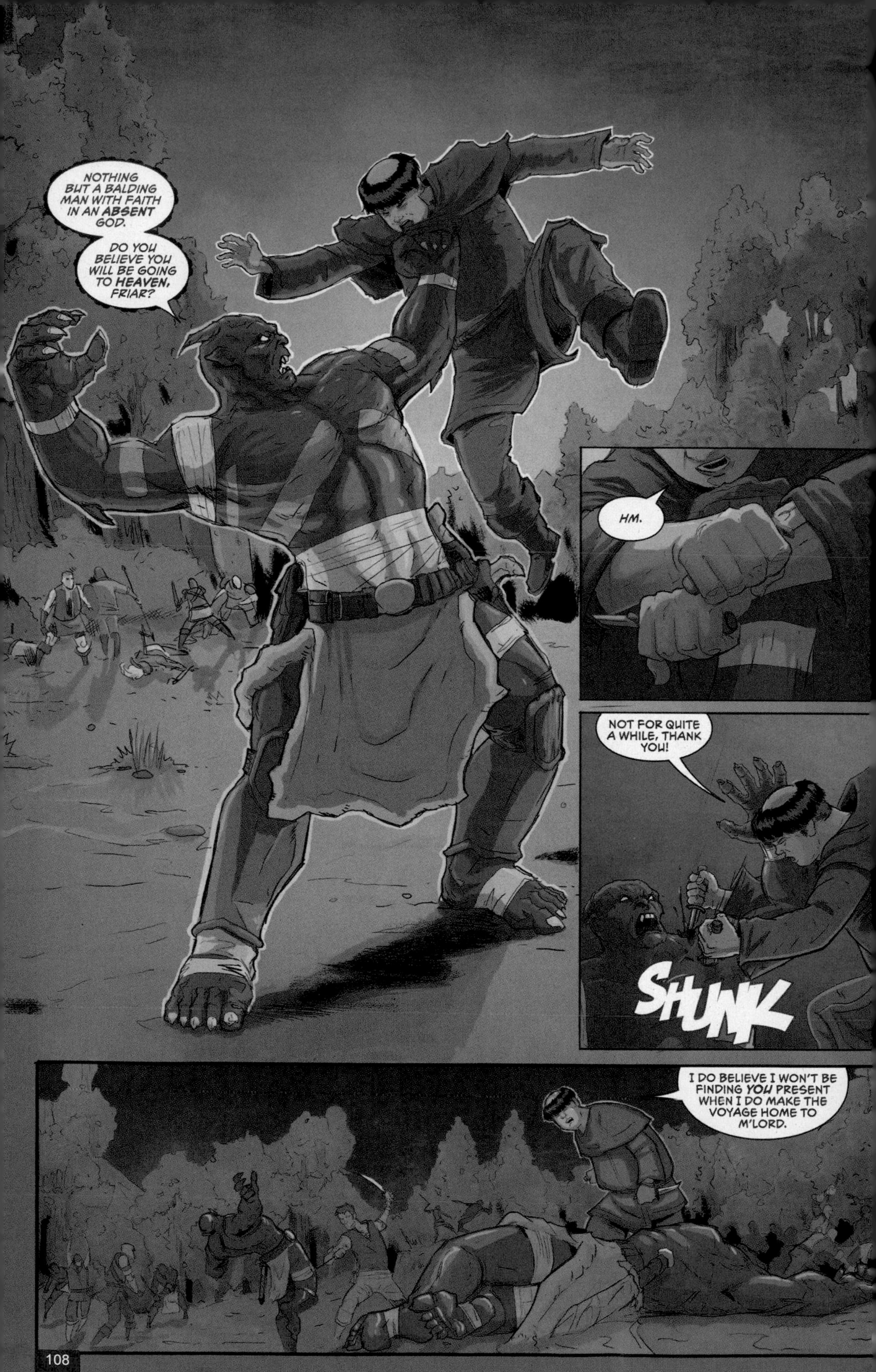
NOTHING BUT A BALDING MAN WITH FAITH IN AN ABSENT GOD.
DO YOU BELIEVE YOU WILL BE GOING TO HEAVEN, FRIAR?
HM.
NOT FOR QUITE A WHILE, THANK YOU!
SHUNK
I DO BELIEVE I WON'T BE FINDING YOU PRESENT WHEN I DO MAKE THE VOYAGE HOME TO M'LORD.

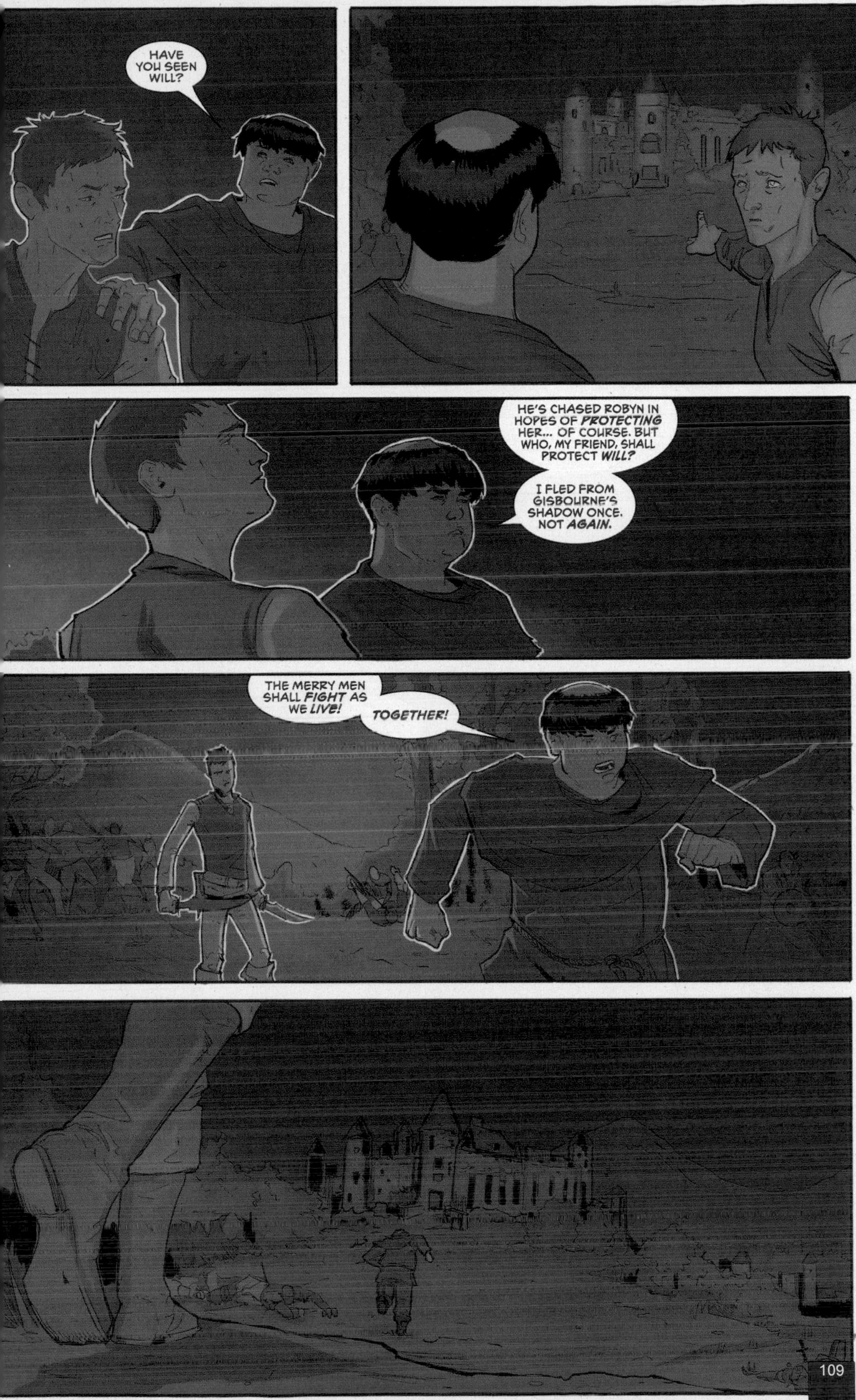
HAVE YOU SEEN WILL?
HE'S CHASED ROBYN IN HOPES OF *PROTECTING* HER... OF COURSE. BUT WHO, MY FRIEND, SHALL PROTECT *WILL?*
I FLED FROM GISBOURNE'S SHADOW ONCE. NOT *AGAIN.*
THE MERRY MEN SHALL *FIGHT* AS WE *LIVE!*
*TOGETHER!*

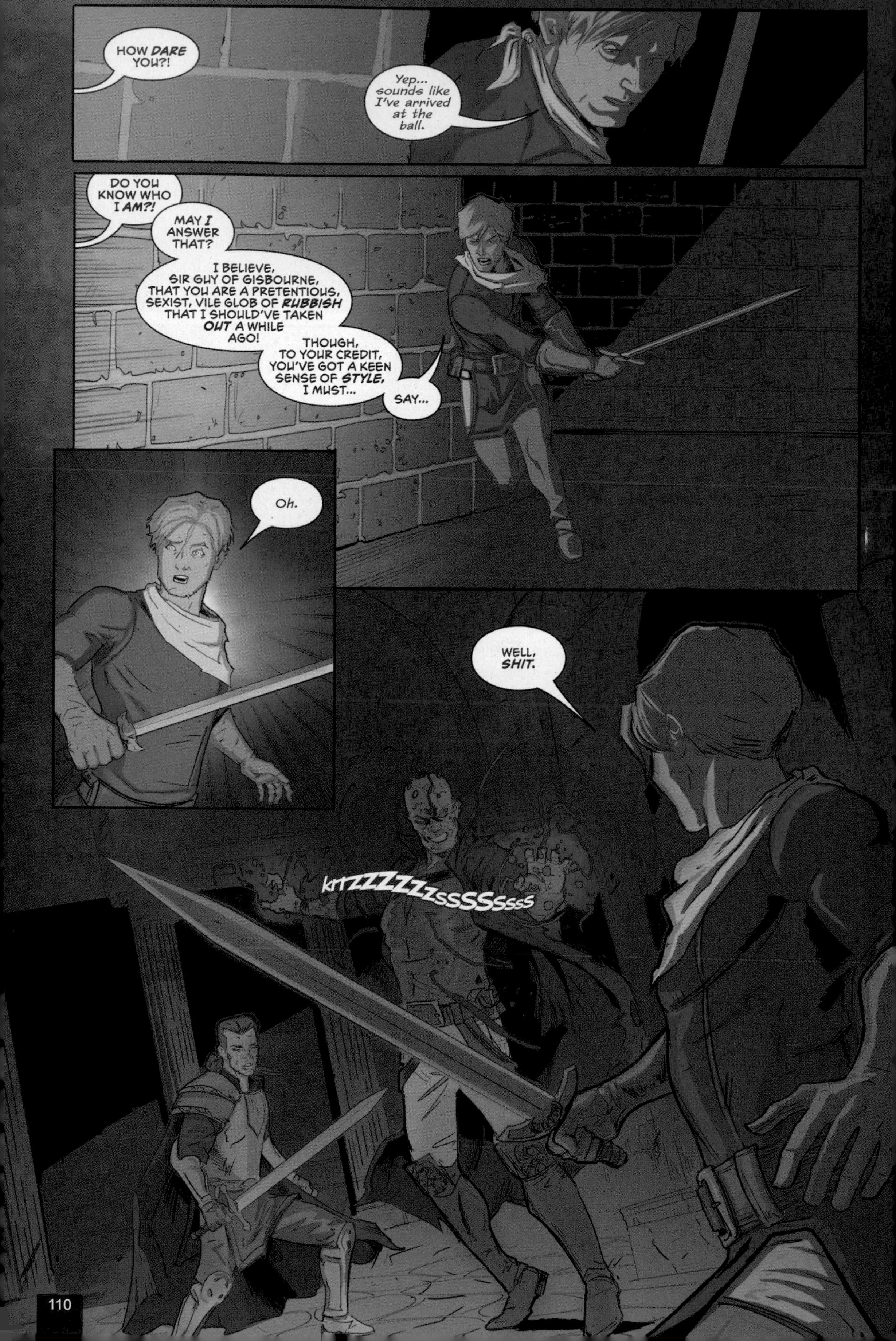
HOW DARE YOU?!
Yep... sounds like I've arrived at the ball.
DO YOU KNOW WHO I AM?!
MAY I ANSWER THAT?
I BELIEVE, SIR GUY OF GISBOURNE, THAT YOU ARE A PRETENTIOUS, SEXIST, VILE GLOB OF RUBBISH THAT I SHOULD'VE TAKEN OUT A WHILE AGO!
THOUGH, TO YOUR CREDIT, YOU'VE GOT A KEEN SENSE OF STYLE, I MUST...
SAY...
Oh.
WELL, SHIT.
krrZZZZZzzsSSSsss

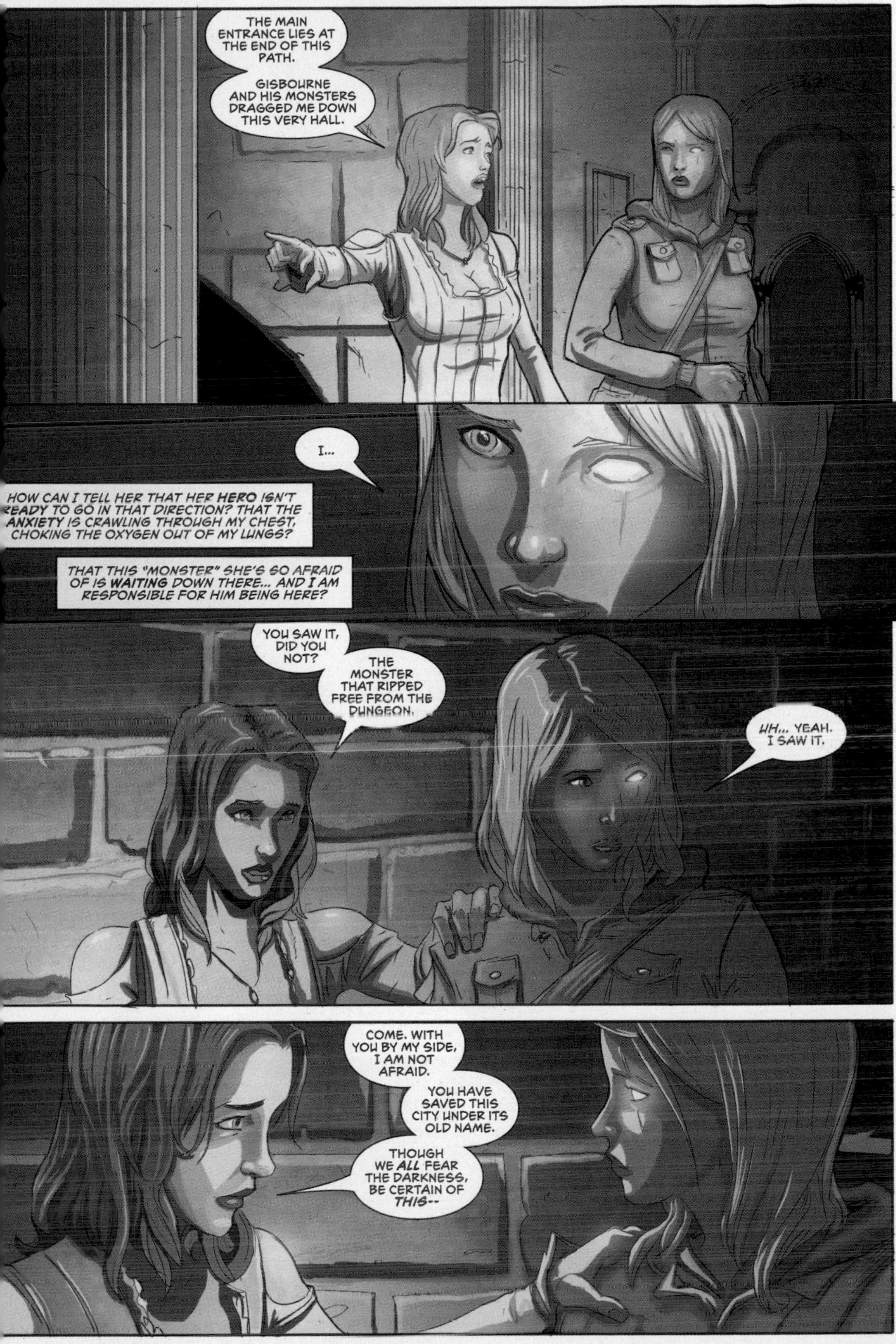
THE MAIN ENTRANCE LIES AT THE END OF THIS PATH.
GISBOURNE AND HIS MONSTERS DRAGGED ME DOWN THIS VERY HALL.
I...
HOW CAN I TELL HER THAT HER HERO ISN'T READY TO GO IN THAT DIRECTION? THAT THE ANXIETY IS CRAWLING THROUGH MY CHEST, CHOKING THE OXYGEN OUT OF MY LUNGS?
THAT THIS "MONSTER" SHE'S SO AFRAID OF IS WAITING DOWN THERE... AND I AM RESPONSIBLE FOR HIM BEING HERE?
YOU SAW IT, DID YOU NOT?
THE MONSTER THAT RIPPED FREE FROM THE DUNGEON.
UH... YEAH. I SAW IT.
COME. WITH YOU BY MY SIDE, I AM NOT AFRAID.
YOU HAVE SAVED THIS CITY UNDER ITS OLD NAME.
THOUGH WE ALL FEAR THE DARKNESS, BE CERTAIN OF THIS--

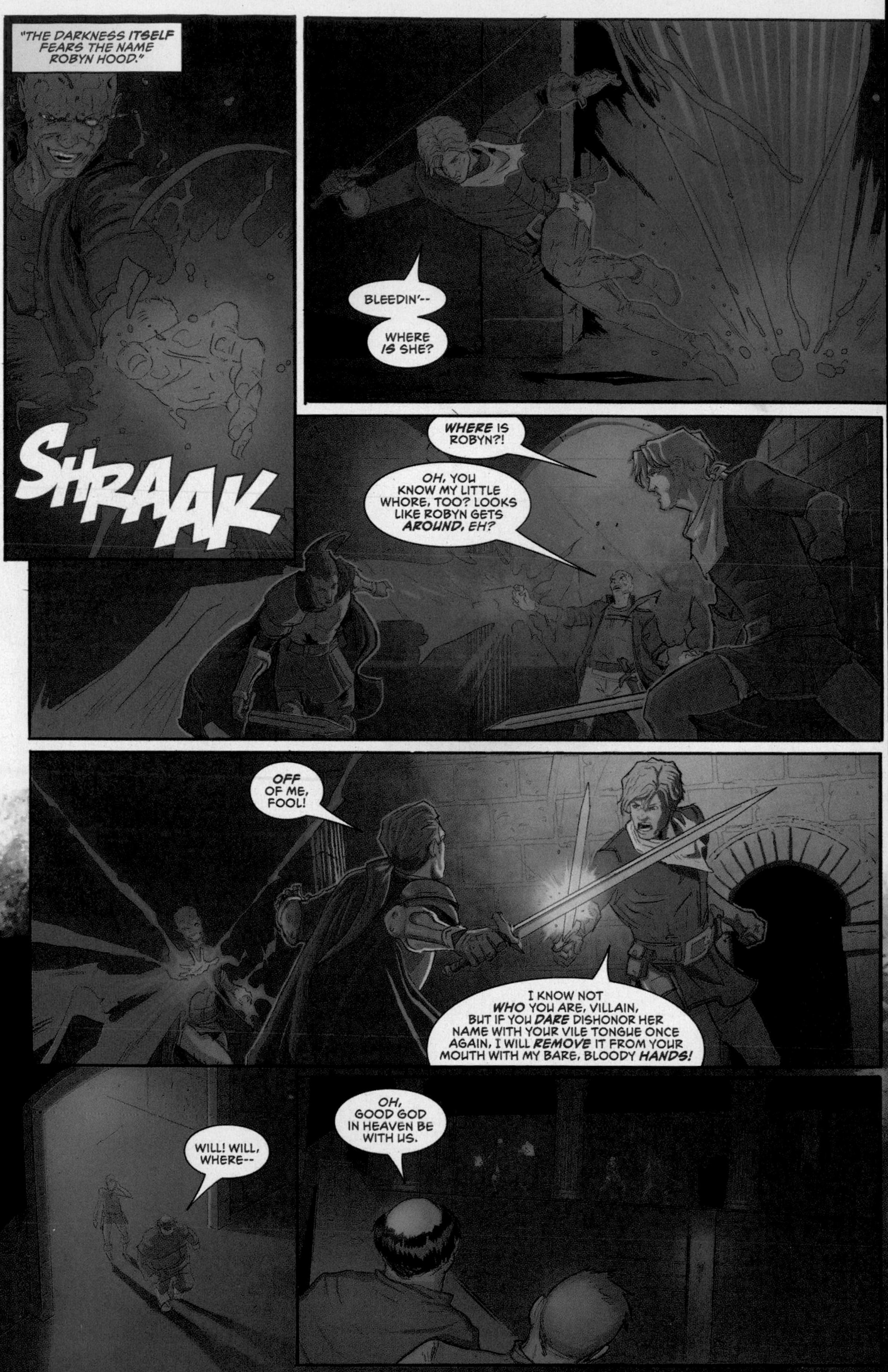
"THE DARKNESS ITSELF FEARS THE NAME ROBYN HOOD."
BLEEDIN'--
WHERE IS SHE?
SHRAAK
WHERE IS ROBYN?!
OH, YOU KNOW MY LITTLE WHORE, TOO? LOOKS LIKE ROBYN GETS AROUND, EH?
OFF OF ME, FOOL!
I KNOW NOT WHO YOU ARE, VILLAIN, BUT IF YOU DARE DISHONOR HER NAME WITH YOUR VILE TONGUE ONCE AGAIN, I WILL REMOVE IT FROM YOUR MOUTH WITH MY BARE, BLOODY HANDS!
WILL! WILL, WHERE--
OH, GOOD GOD IN HEAVEN BE WITH US.

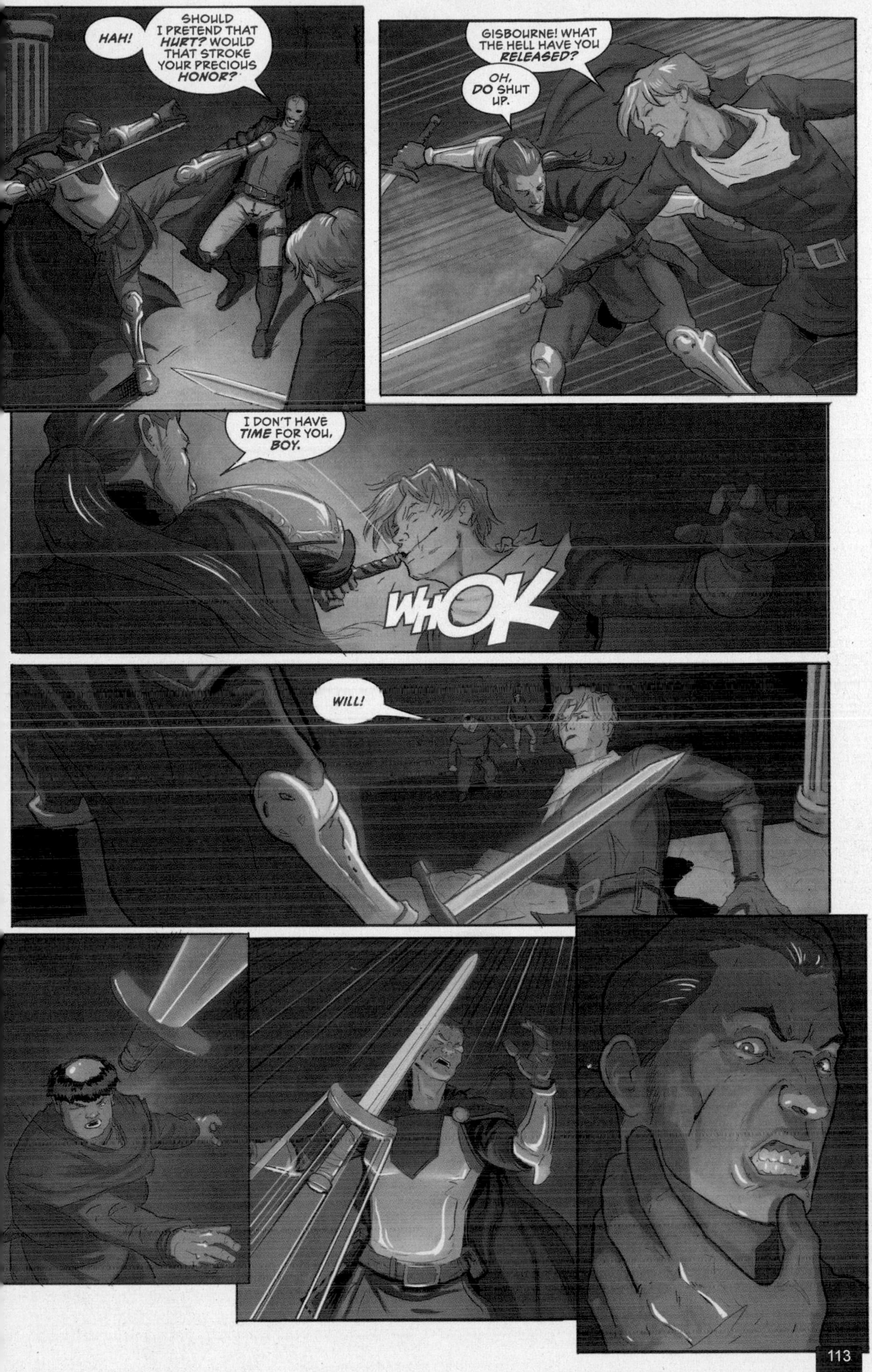
HAH!
SHOULD I PRETEND THAT HURT? WOULD THAT STROKE YOUR PRECIOUS HONOR?
GISBOURNE! WHAT THE HELL HAVE YOU RELEASED?
OH, DO SHUT UP.
I DON'T HAVE TIME FOR YOU, BOY.
WHOK
WILL!

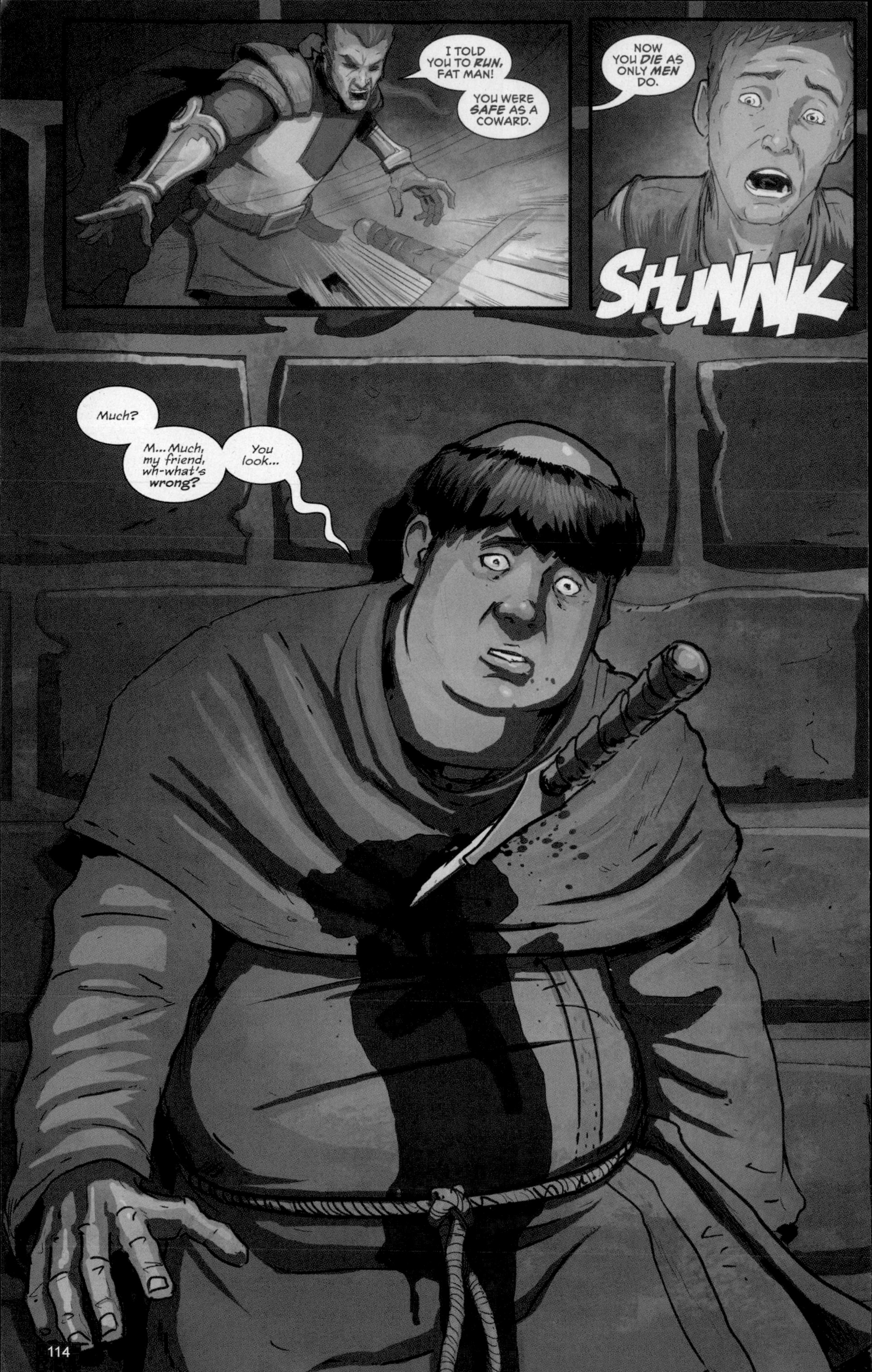
I TOLD YOU TO RUN, FAT MAN!
YOU WERE SAFE AS A COWARD.
NOW YOU DIE AS ONLY MEN DO.
SHUNNK
Much?
M... Much, my friend, wh-what's wrong?
You look...

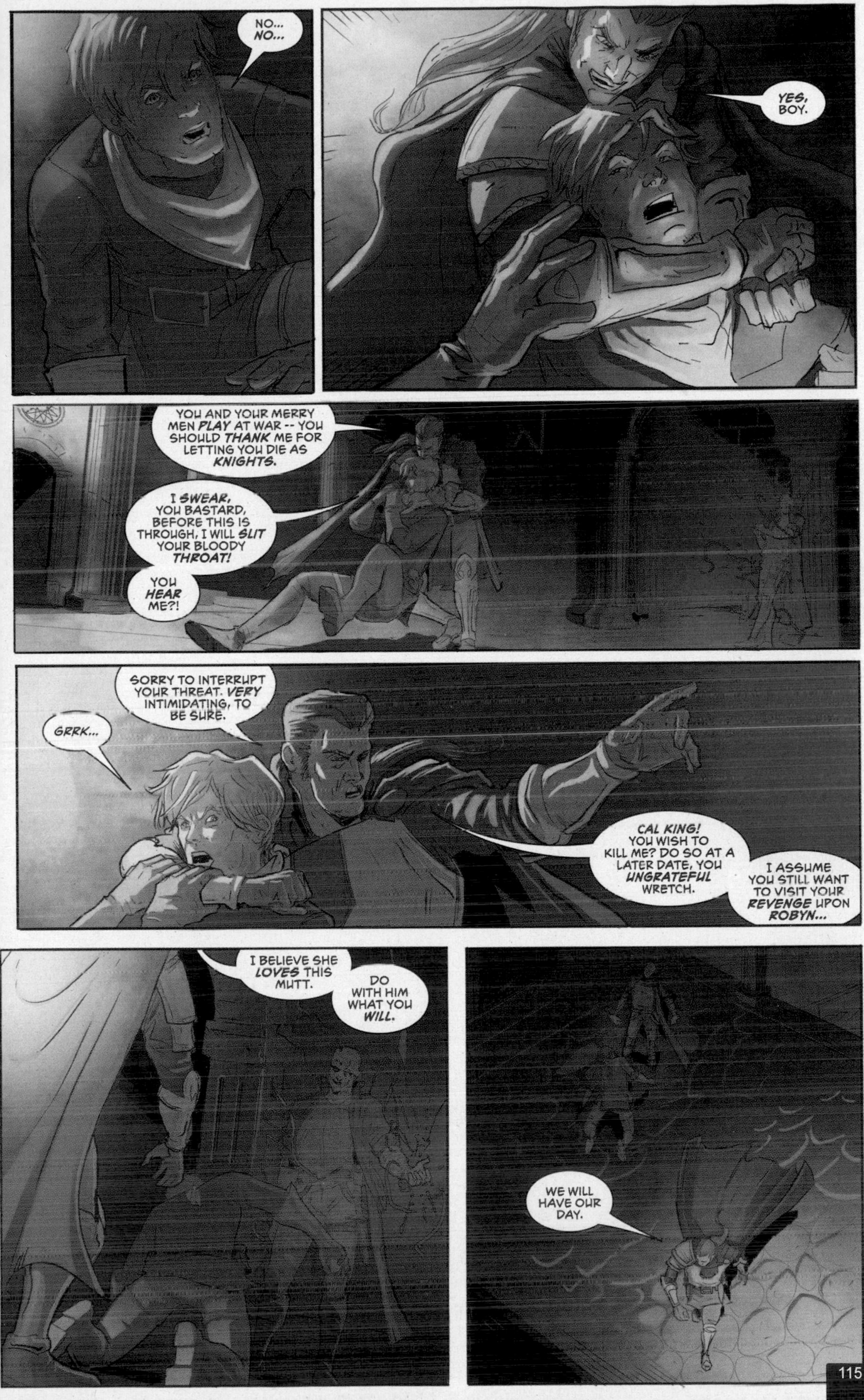

NO... NO...
YES, BOY.
YOU AND YOUR MERRY MEN PLAY AT WAR -- YOU SHOULD THANK ME FOR LETTING YOU DIE AS KNIGHTS.
I SWEAR, YOU BASTARD, BEFORE THIS IS THROUGH, I WILL SLIT YOUR BLOODY THROAT!
YOU HEAR ME?!
SORRY TO INTERRUPT YOUR THREAT. VERY INTIMIDATING, TO BE SURE.
GRRK...
CAL KING! YOU WISH TO KILL ME? DO SO AT A LATER DATE, YOU UNGRATEFUL WRETCH.
I ASSUME YOU STILL WANT TO VISIT YOUR REVENGE UPON ROBYN...
I BELIEVE SHE LOVES THIS MUTT.
DO WITH HIM WHAT YOU WILL.
WE WILL HAVE OUR DAY.

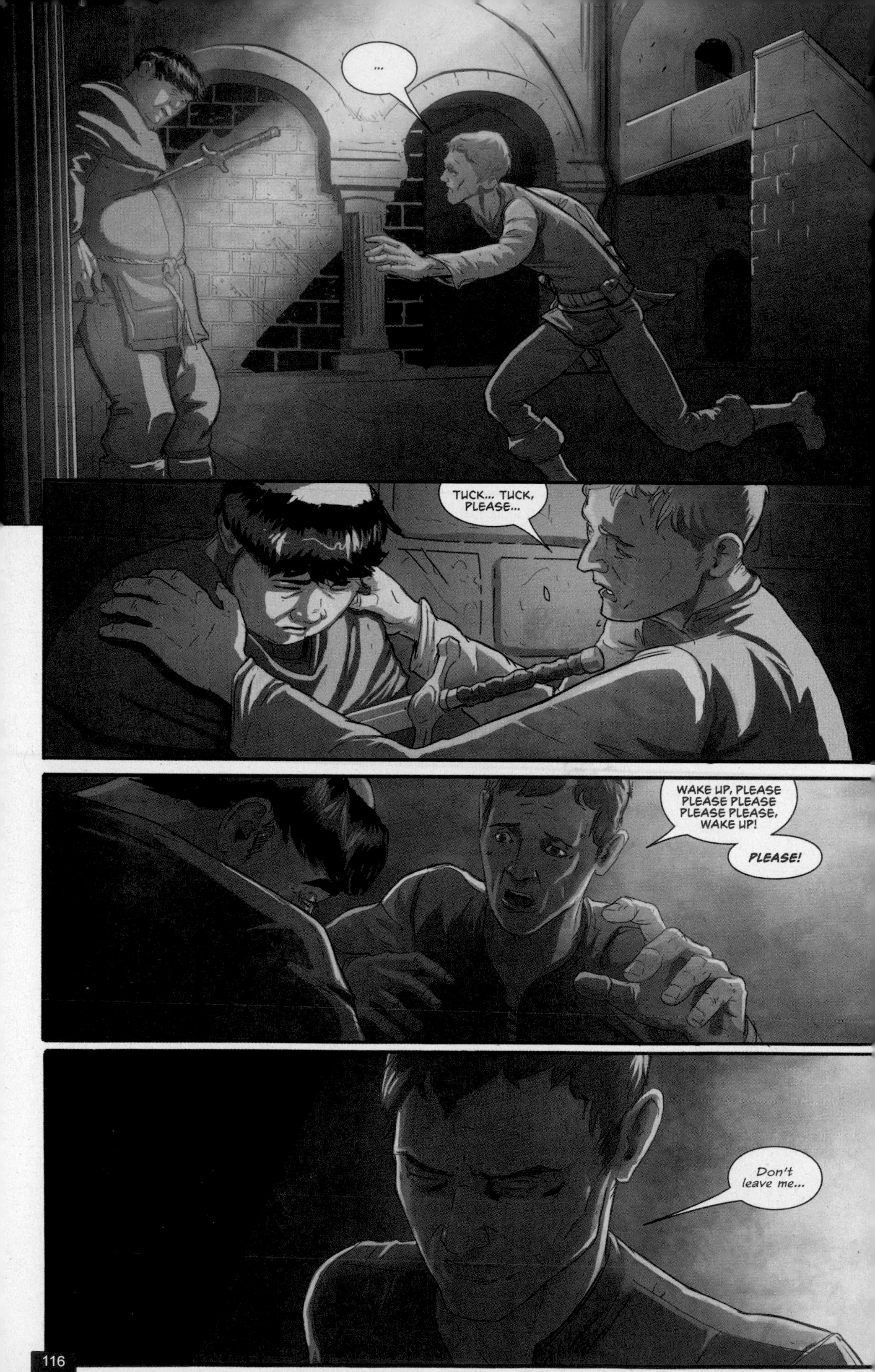
...
TUCK... TUCK, PLEASE...
WAKE UP, PLEASE PLEASE PLEASE PLEASE PLEASE, WAKE UP!
PLEASE!
Don't leave me...

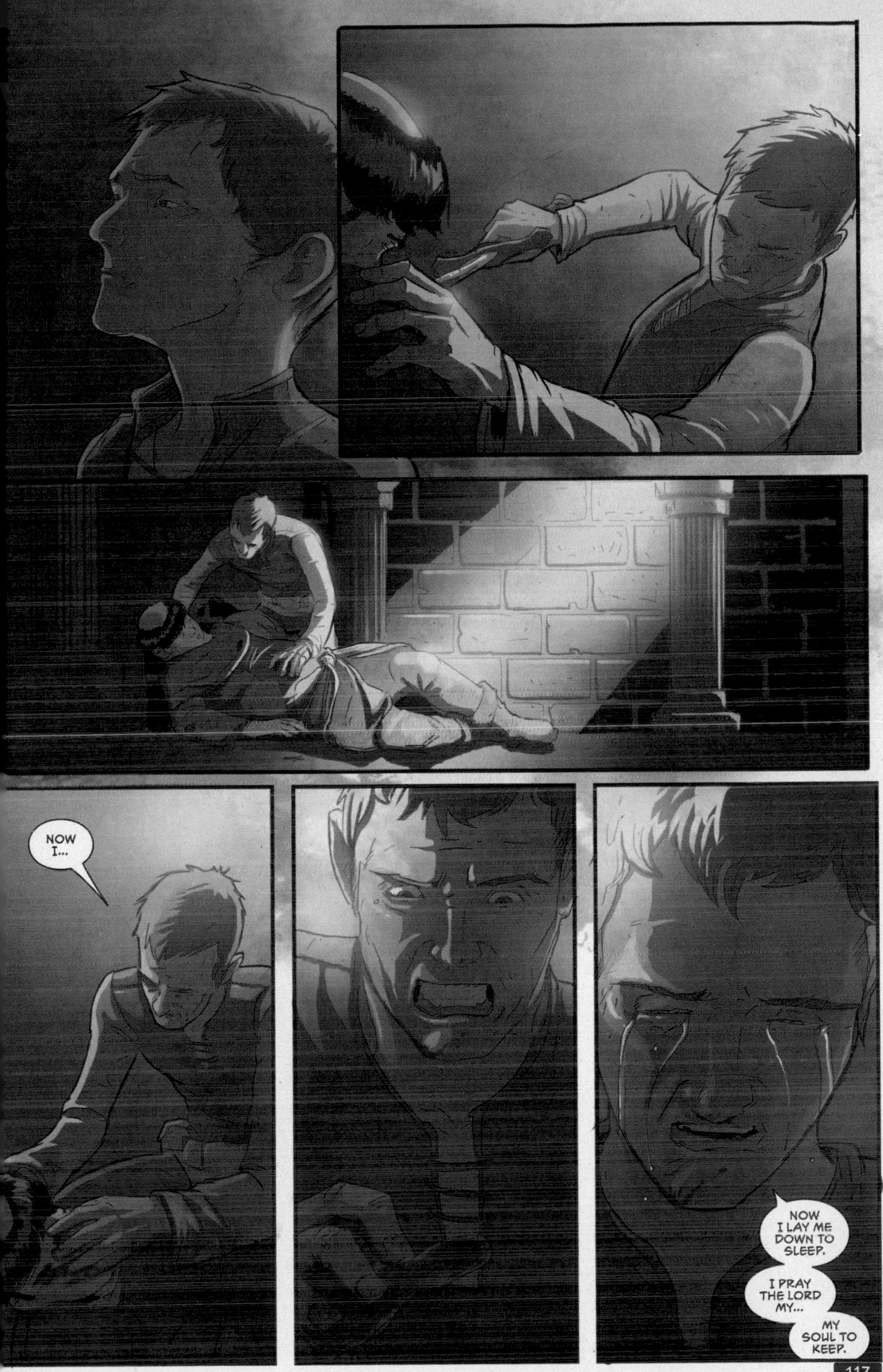
NOW I...
NOW I LAY ME DOWN TO SLEEP.
I PRAY THE LORD MY...
MY SOUL TO KEEP.

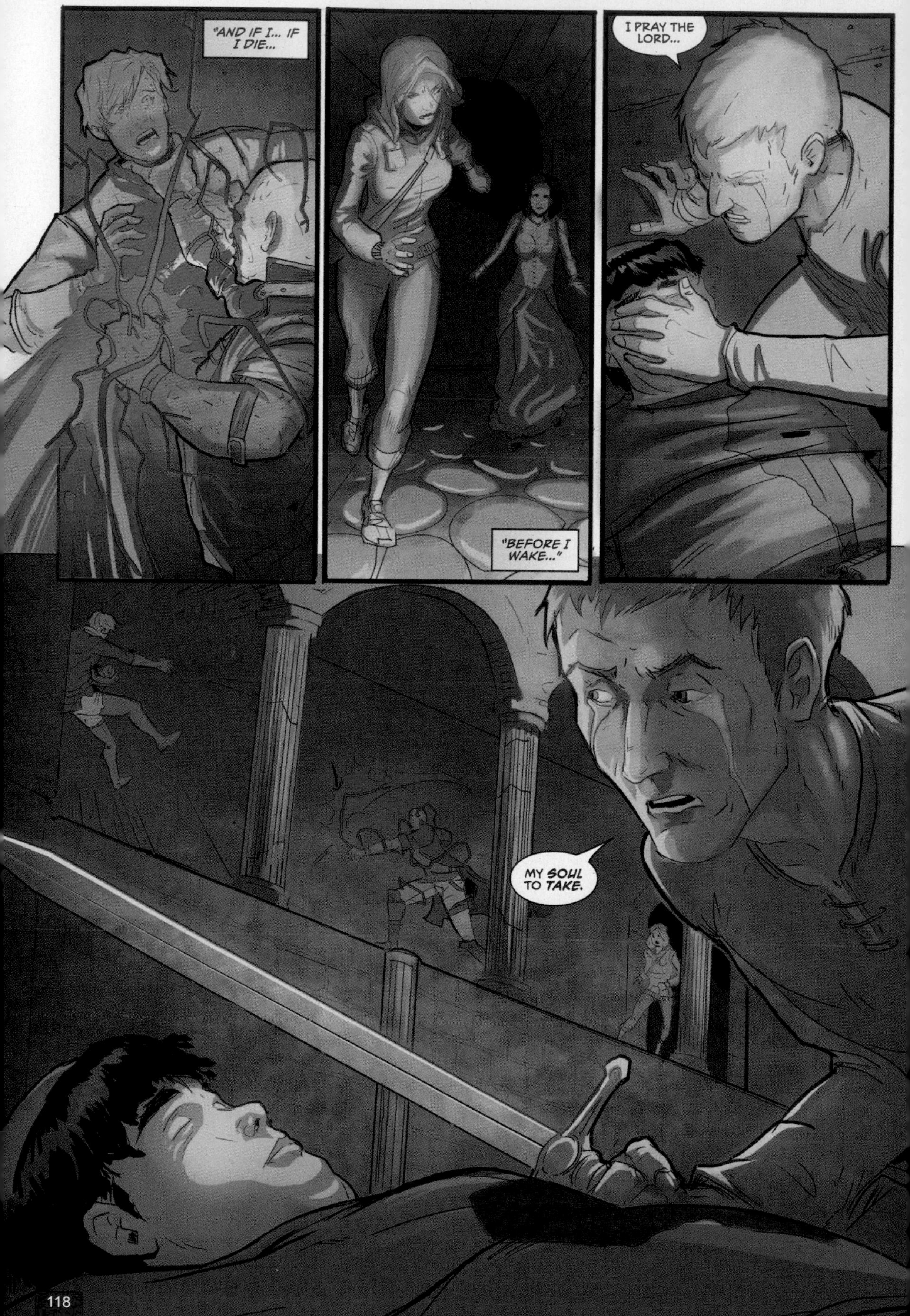
"AND IF I... IF I DIE...
"BEFORE I WAKE..."
I PRAY THE LORD...
MY SOUL TO TAKE.

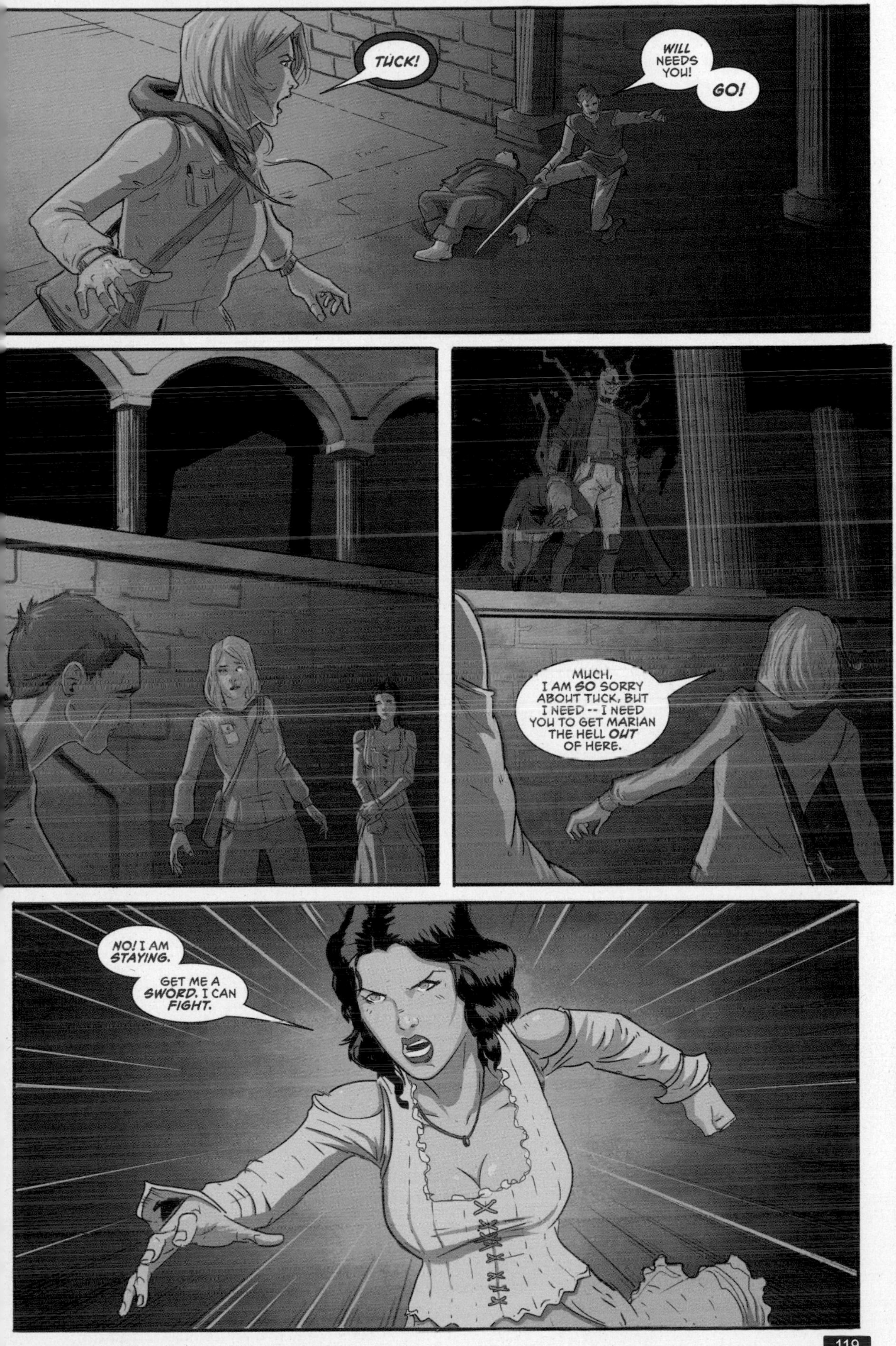
TUCK!
WILL NEEDS YOU!
GO!
MUCH, I AM SO SORRY ABOUT TUCK, BUT I NEED -- I NEED YOU TO GET MARIAN THE HELL OUT OF HERE.
NO! I AM STAYING.
GET ME A SWORD. I CAN FIGHT.

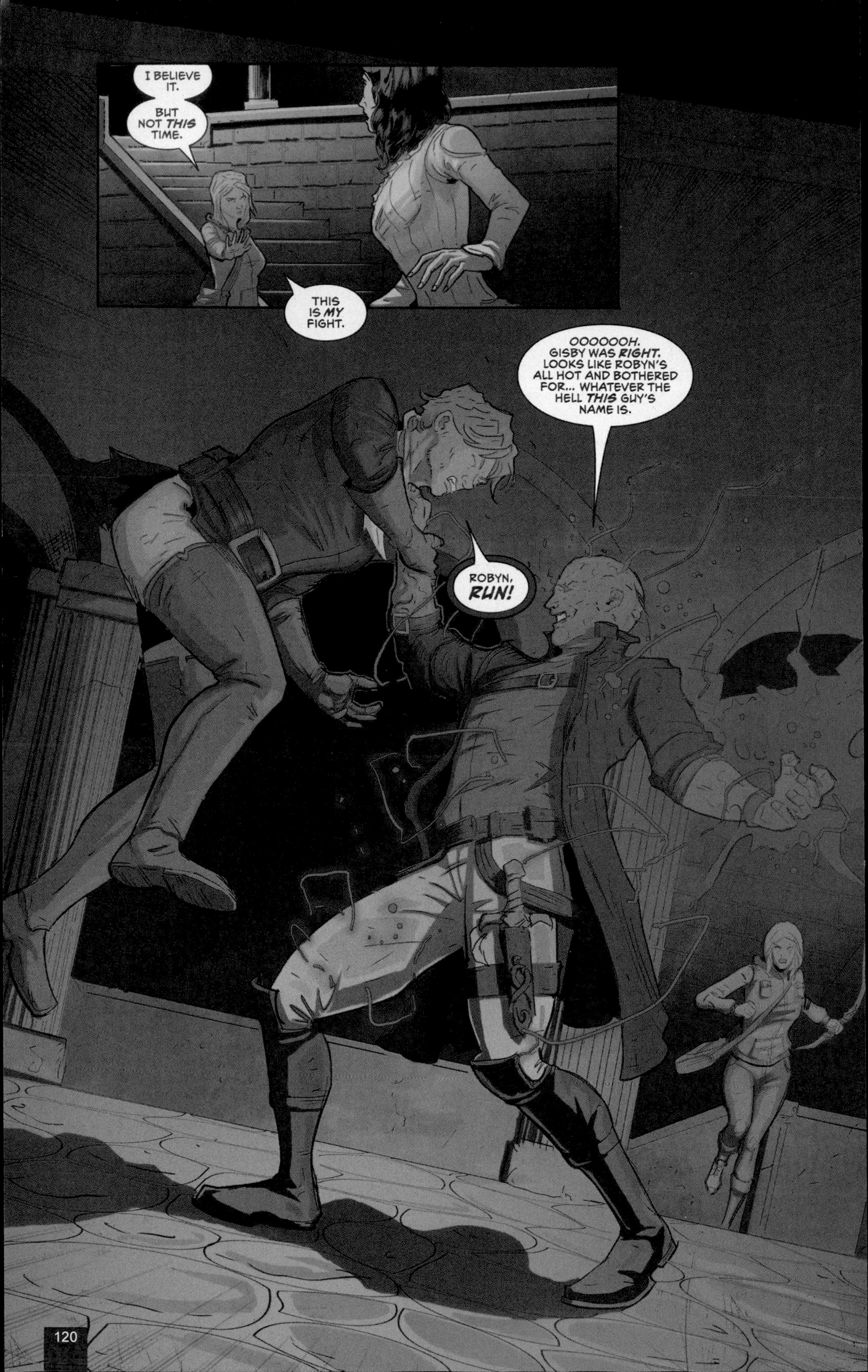

I BELIEVE IT.
BUT NOT *THIS* TIME.
THIS IS *MY* FIGHT.
OOOOOOH. GISBY WAS ***RIGHT***. LOOKS LIKE ROBYN'S ALL HOT AND BOTHERED FOR... WHATEVER THE HELL ***THIS*** GUY'S NAME IS.
ROBYN, ***RUN!***

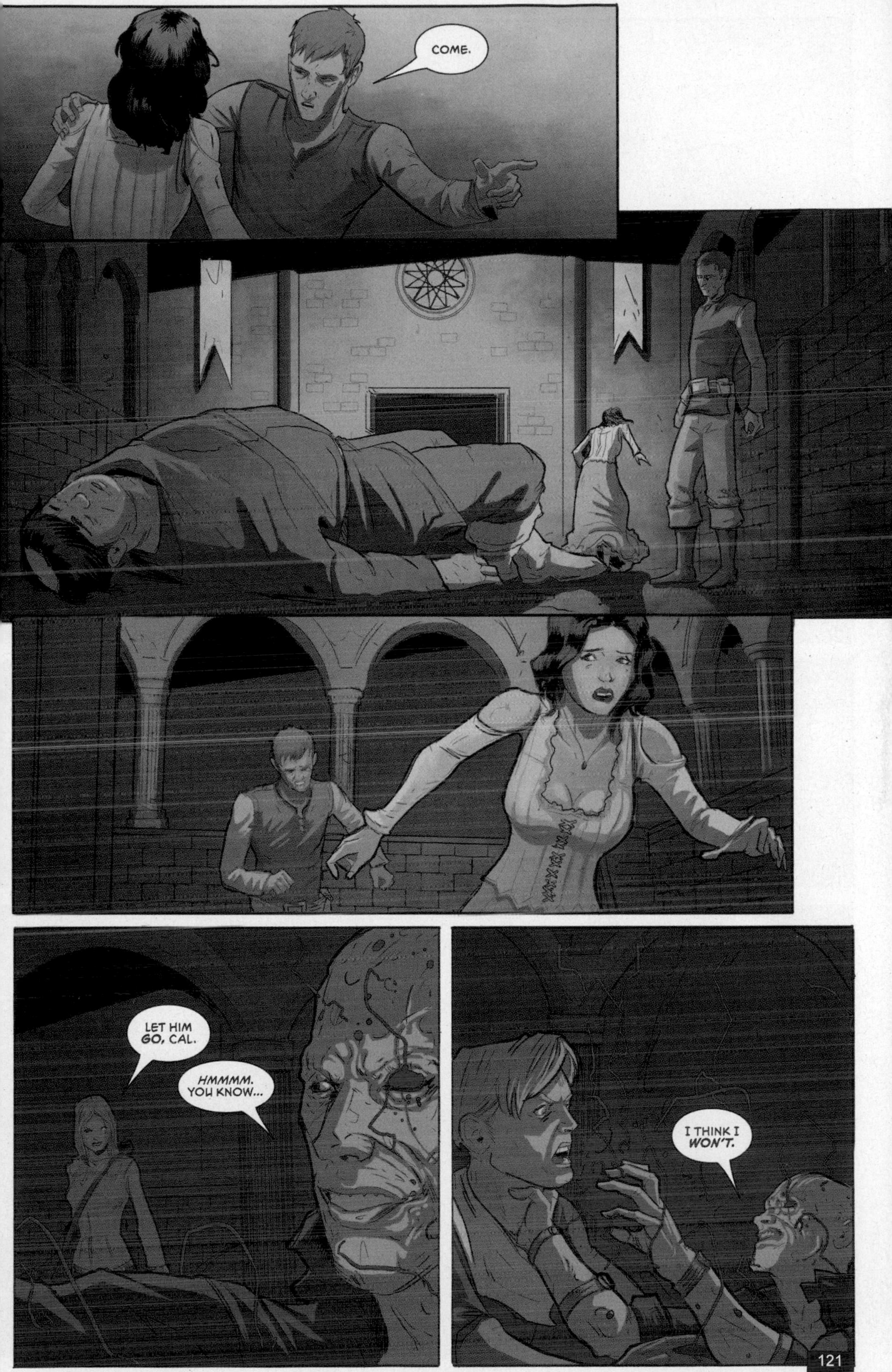
COME.
LET HIM GO, CAL.
HMMMM. YOU KNOW...
I THINK I WON'T.

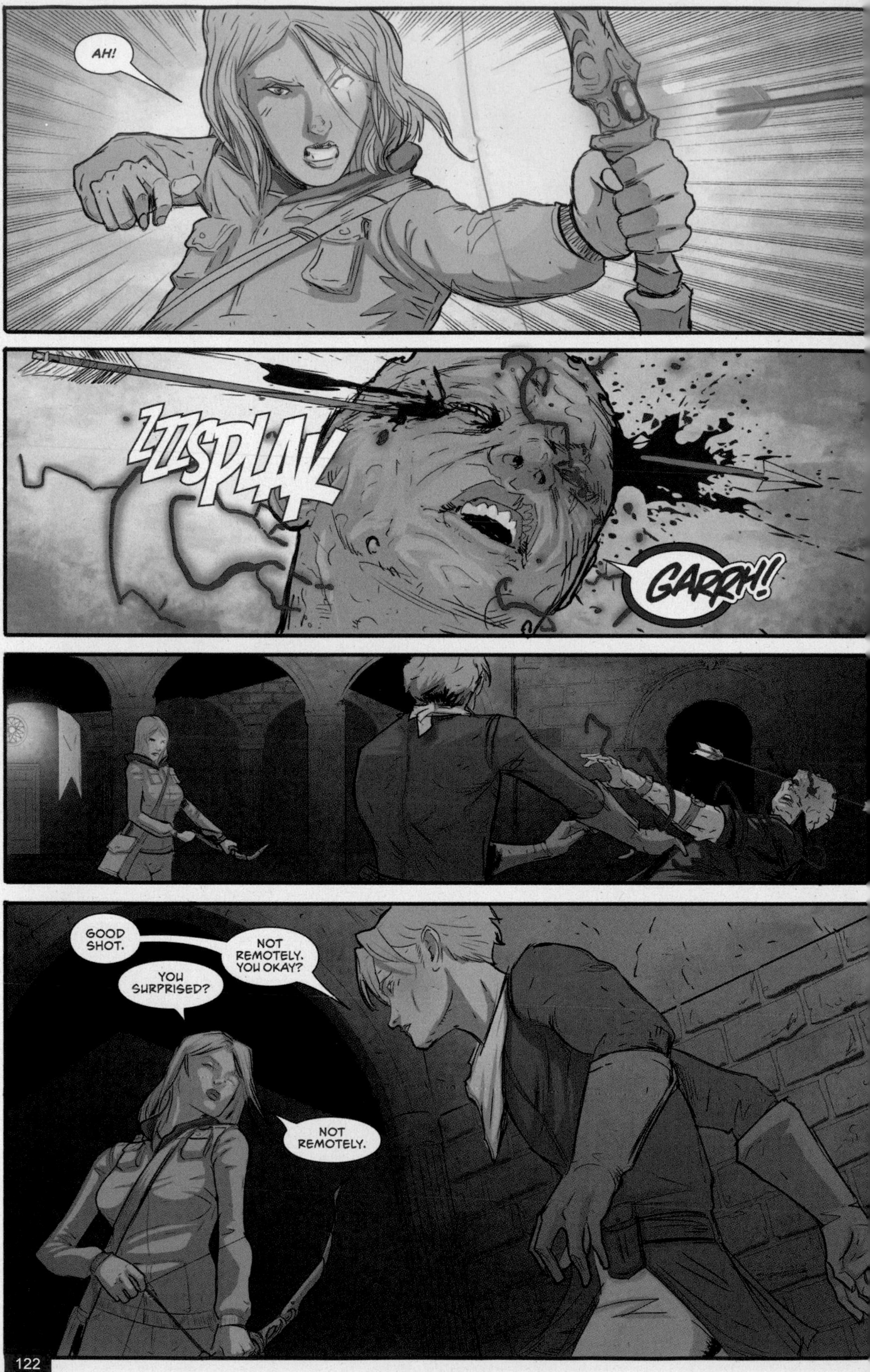
AH!
Z-ZZSPLAK
GARRH!
GOOD SHOT.
NOT REMOTELY. YOU OKAY?
YOU SURPRISED?
NOT REMOTELY.

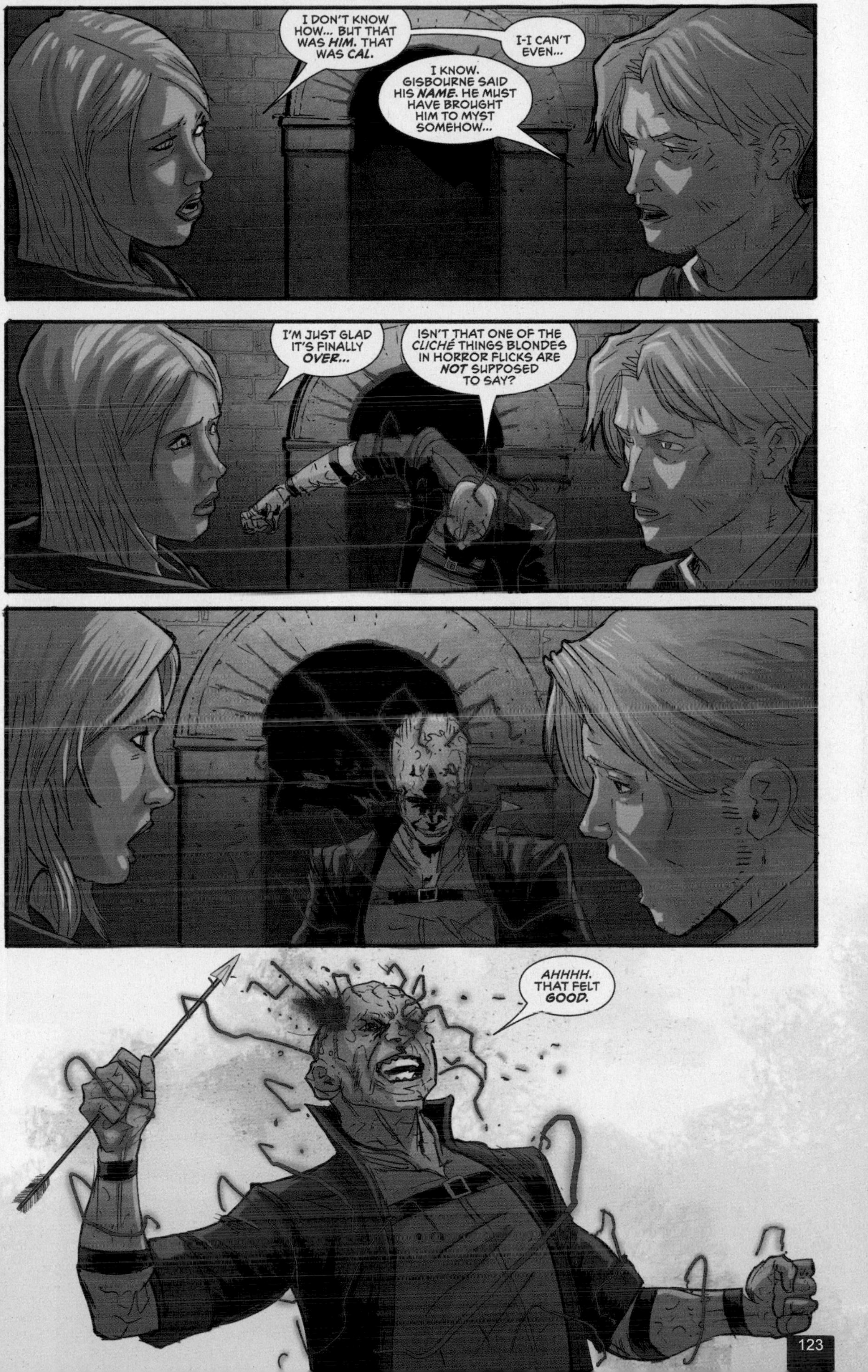
I DON'T KNOW HOW... BUT THAT WAS *HIM*. THAT WAS *CAL*.
I-I CAN'T EVEN...
I KNOW. GISBOURNE SAID HIS *NAME*. HE MUST HAVE BROUGHT HIM TO MYST SOMEHOW...
I'M JUST GLAD IT'S FINALLY *OVER*...
ISN'T THAT ONE OF THE *CLICHÉ* THINGS BLONDES IN HORROR FLICKS ARE *NOT* SUPPOSED TO SAY?
*AHHHH*. THAT FELT *GOOD*.

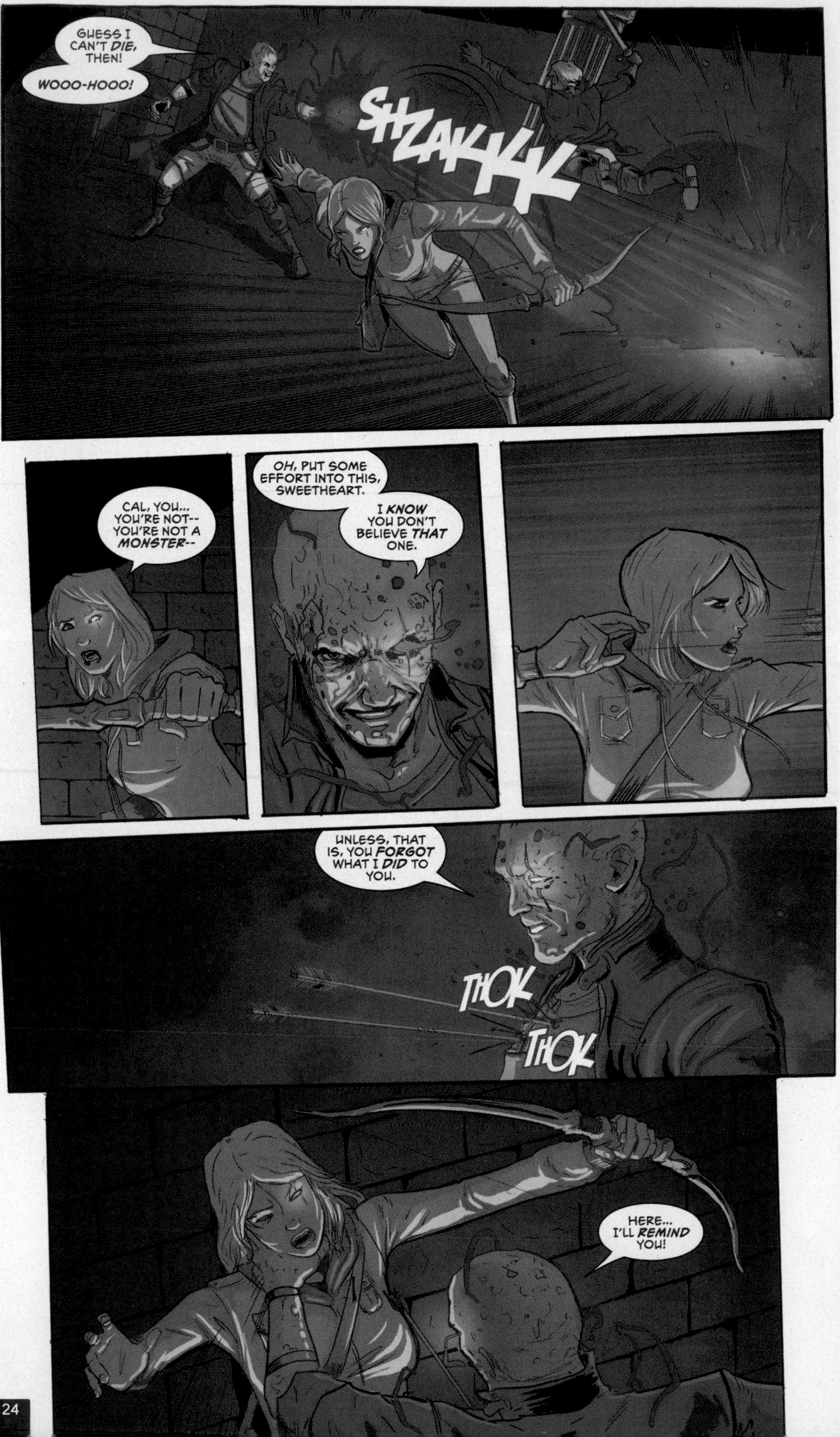
GUESS I CAN'T DIE, THEN!
WOOO-HOOO!
SHZAKKKK
CAL, YOU... YOU'RE NOT-- YOU'RE NOT A MONSTER--
OH, PUT SOME EFFORT INTO THIS, SWEETHEART.
I KNOW YOU DON'T BELIEVE THAT ONE.
UNLESS, THAT IS, YOU FORGOT WHAT I DID TO YOU.
THOK
THOK
HERE... I'LL REMIND YOU!

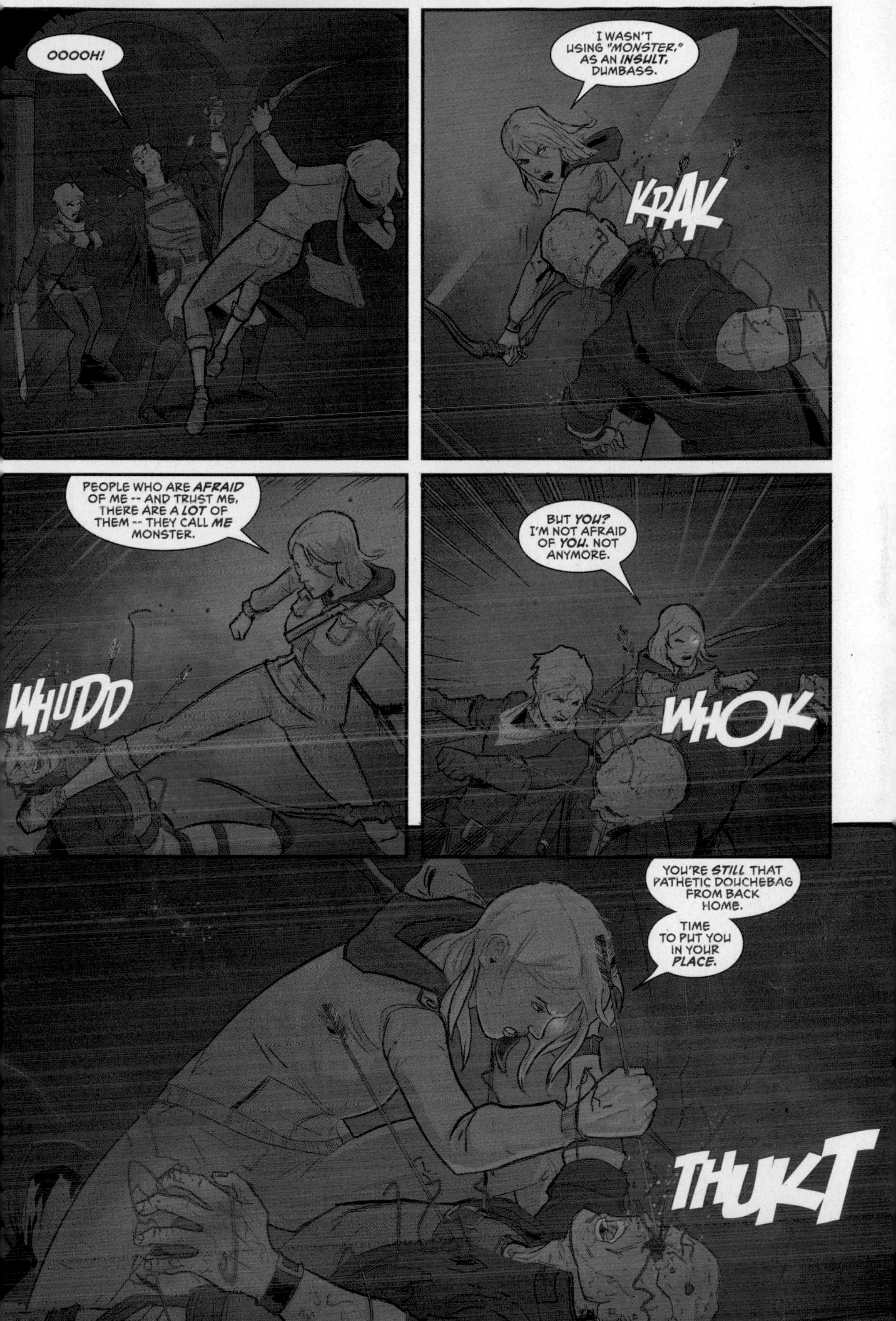
OOOOH!
I WASN'T USING "MONSTER," AS AN INSULT, DUMBASS.
KRAK
PEOPLE WHO ARE AFRAID OF ME -- AND TRUST ME, THERE ARE A LOT OF THEM -- THEY CALL ME MONSTER.
WHUDD
BUT YOU? I'M NOT AFRAID OF YOU. NOT ANYMORE.
WHOK
YOU'RE STILL THAT PATHETIC DOUCHEBAG FROM BACK HOME.
TIME TO PUT YOU IN YOUR PLACE.
THUKT

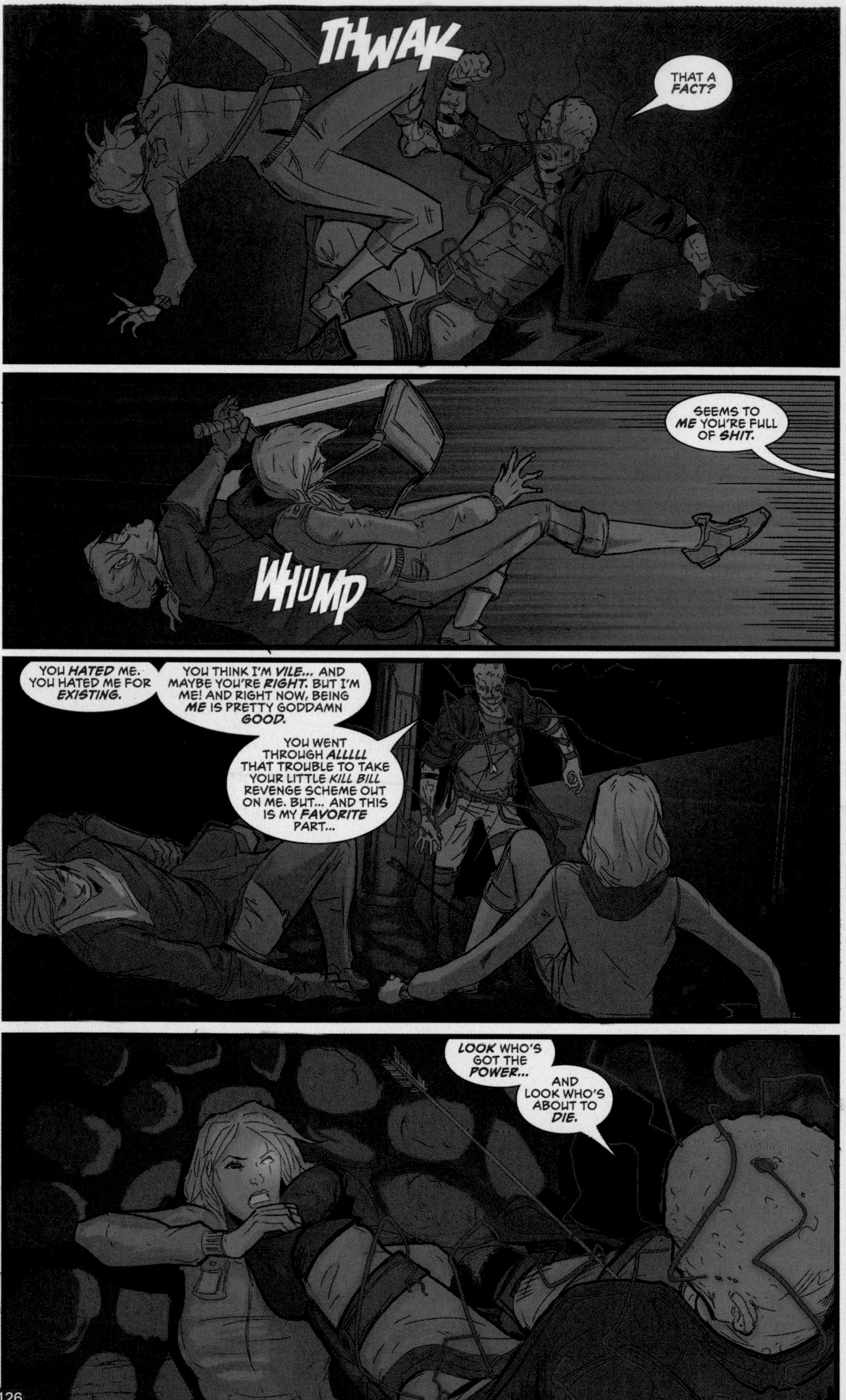
THWAK
THAT A FACT?
SEEMS TO ME YOU'RE FULL OF SHIT.
WHUMP
YOU HATED ME. YOU HATED ME FOR EXISTING.
YOU THINK I'M VILE... AND MAYBE YOU'RE RIGHT. BUT I'M ME! AND RIGHT NOW, BEING ME IS PRETTY GODDAMN GOOD.
YOU WENT THROUGH ALLLLL THAT TROUBLE TO TAKE YOUR LITTLE KILL BILL REVENGE SCHEME OUT ON ME. BUT... AND THIS IS MY FAVORITE PART...
LOOK WHO'S GOT THE POWER...
AND LOOK WHO'S ABOUT TO DIE.

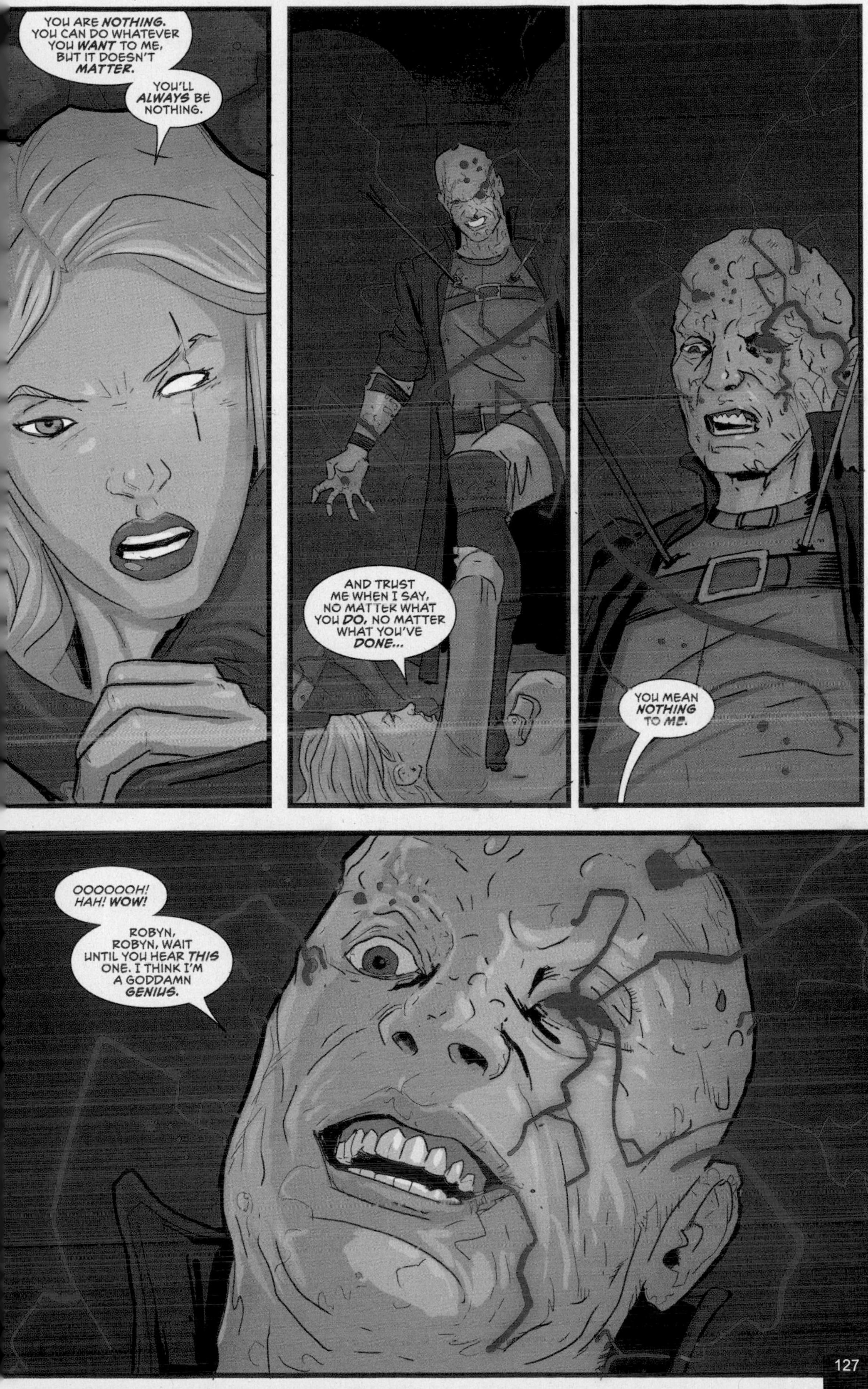
YOU ARE NOTHING. YOU CAN DO WHATEVER YOU WANT TO ME, BUT IT DOESN'T MATTER.
YOU'LL ALWAYS BE NOTHING.
AND TRUST ME WHEN I SAY, NO MATTER WHAT YOU DO, NO MATTER WHAT YOU'VE DONE...
YOU MEAN NOTHING TO ME.
OOOOOOH! HAH! WOW!
ROBYN, ROBYN, WAIT UNTIL YOU HEAR THIS ONE. I THINK I'M A GODDAMN GENIUS.

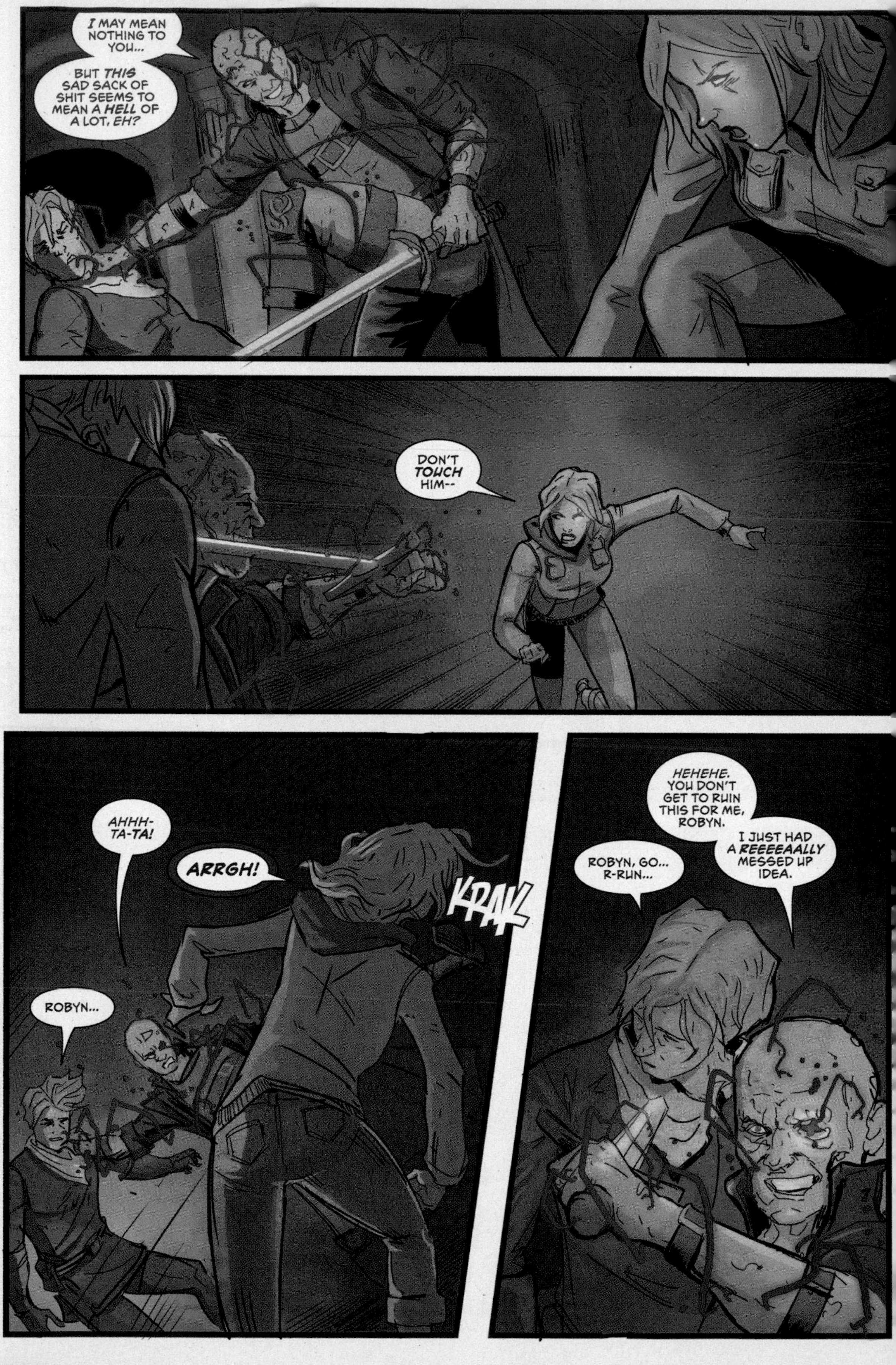
I MAY MEAN NOTHING TO YOU...
BUT THIS SAD SACK OF SHIT SEEMS TO MEAN A HELL OF A LOT, EH?
DON'T TOUCH HIM--
AHHH-TA-TA!
ARRGH!
KRAK
ROBYN...
HEHEHE. YOU DON'T GET TO RUIN THIS FOR ME, ROBYN.
ROBYN, GO... R-RUN...
I JUST HAD A REEEEAALLY MESSED UP IDEA.

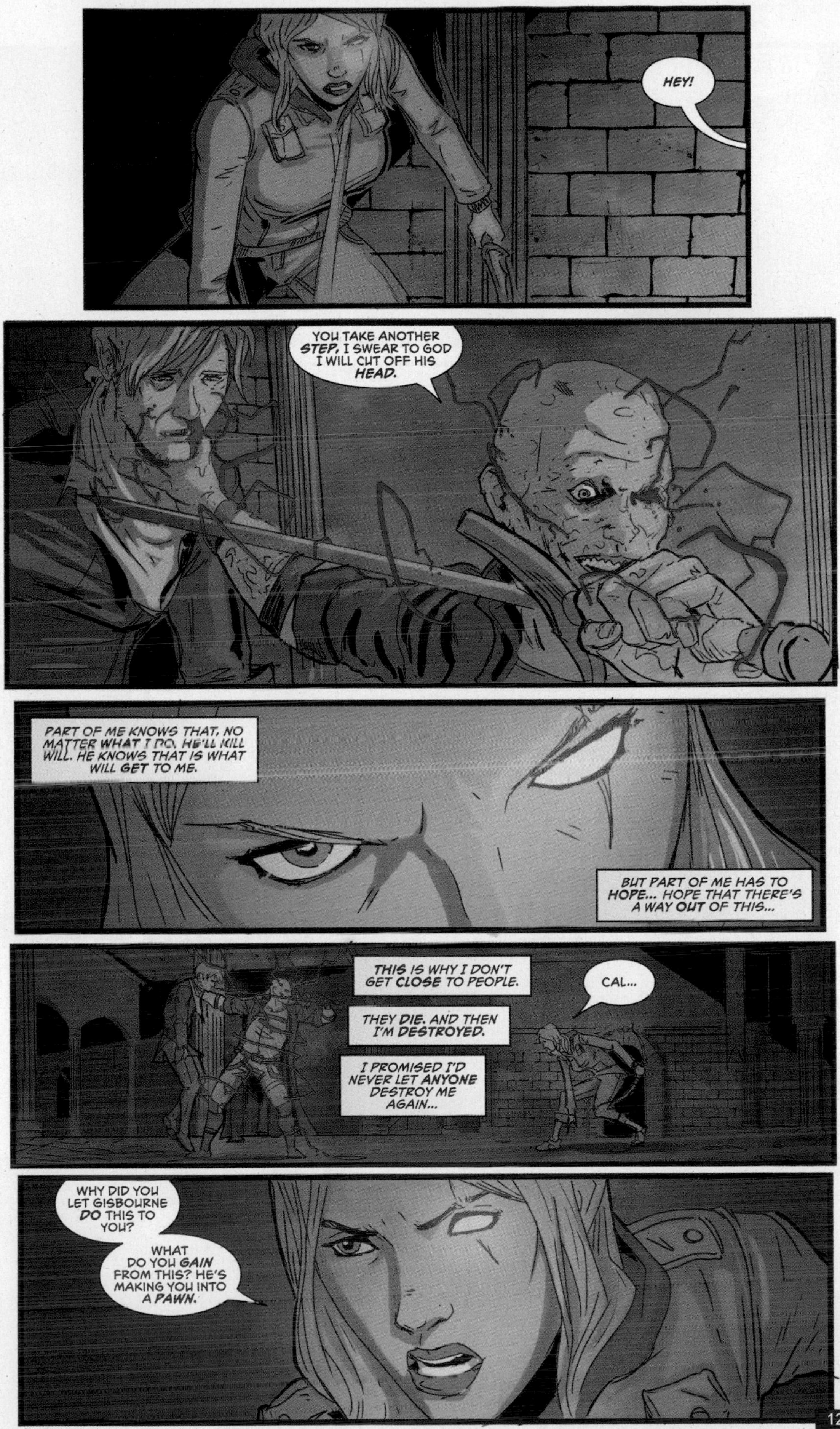
HEY!
YOU TAKE ANOTHER STEP, I SWEAR TO GOD I WILL CUT OFF HIS HEAD.
PART OF ME KNOWS THAT, NO MATTER WHAT I DO, HE'LL KILL WILL. HE KNOWS THAT IS WHAT WILL GET TO ME.
BUT PART OF ME HAS TO HOPE... HOPE THAT THERE'S A WAY OUT OF THIS...
THIS IS WHY I DON'T GET CLOSE TO PEOPLE.
CAL...
THEY DIE. AND THEN I'M DESTROYED.
I PROMISED I'D NEVER LET ANYONE DESTROY ME AGAIN...
WHY DID YOU LET GISBOURNE DO THIS TO YOU?
WHAT DO YOU GAIN FROM THIS? HE'S MAKING YOU INTO A PAWN.

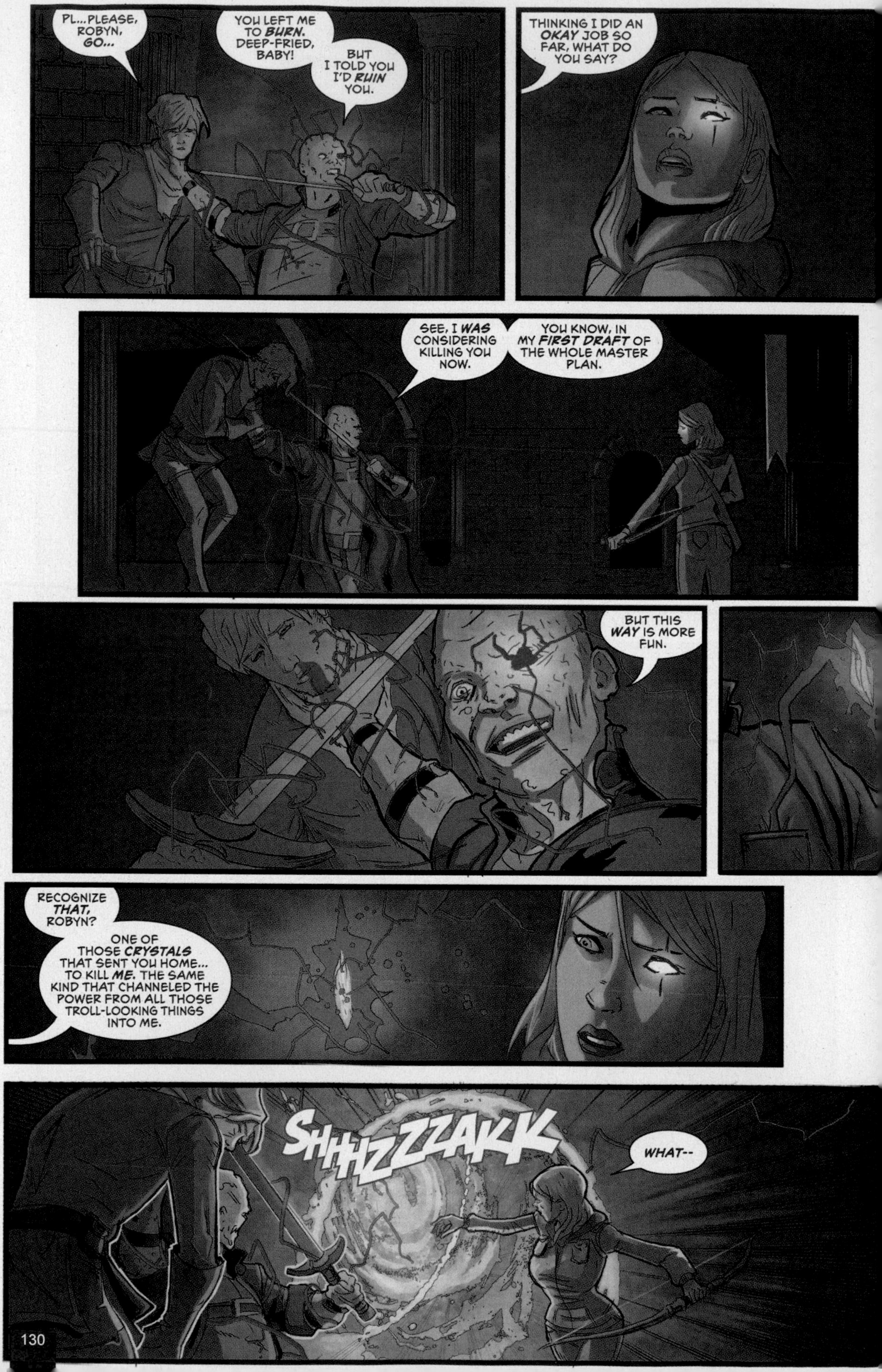
PL...PLEASE, ROBYN, GO...
YOU LEFT ME TO BURN. DEEP-FRIED, BABY!
BUT I TOLD YOU I'D RUIN YOU.
THINKING I DID AN OKAY JOB SO FAR, WHAT DO YOU SAY?
SEE, I WAS CONSIDERING KILLING YOU NOW.
YOU KNOW, IN MY FIRST DRAFT OF THE WHOLE MASTER PLAN.
BUT THIS WAY IS MORE FUN.
RECOGNIZE THAT, ROBYN?
ONE OF THOSE CRYSTALS THAT SENT YOU HOME... TO KILL ME. THE SAME KIND THAT CHANNELED THE POWER FROM ALL THOSE TROLL-LOOKING THINGS INTO ME.
SHHHZZZAKK
WHAT--

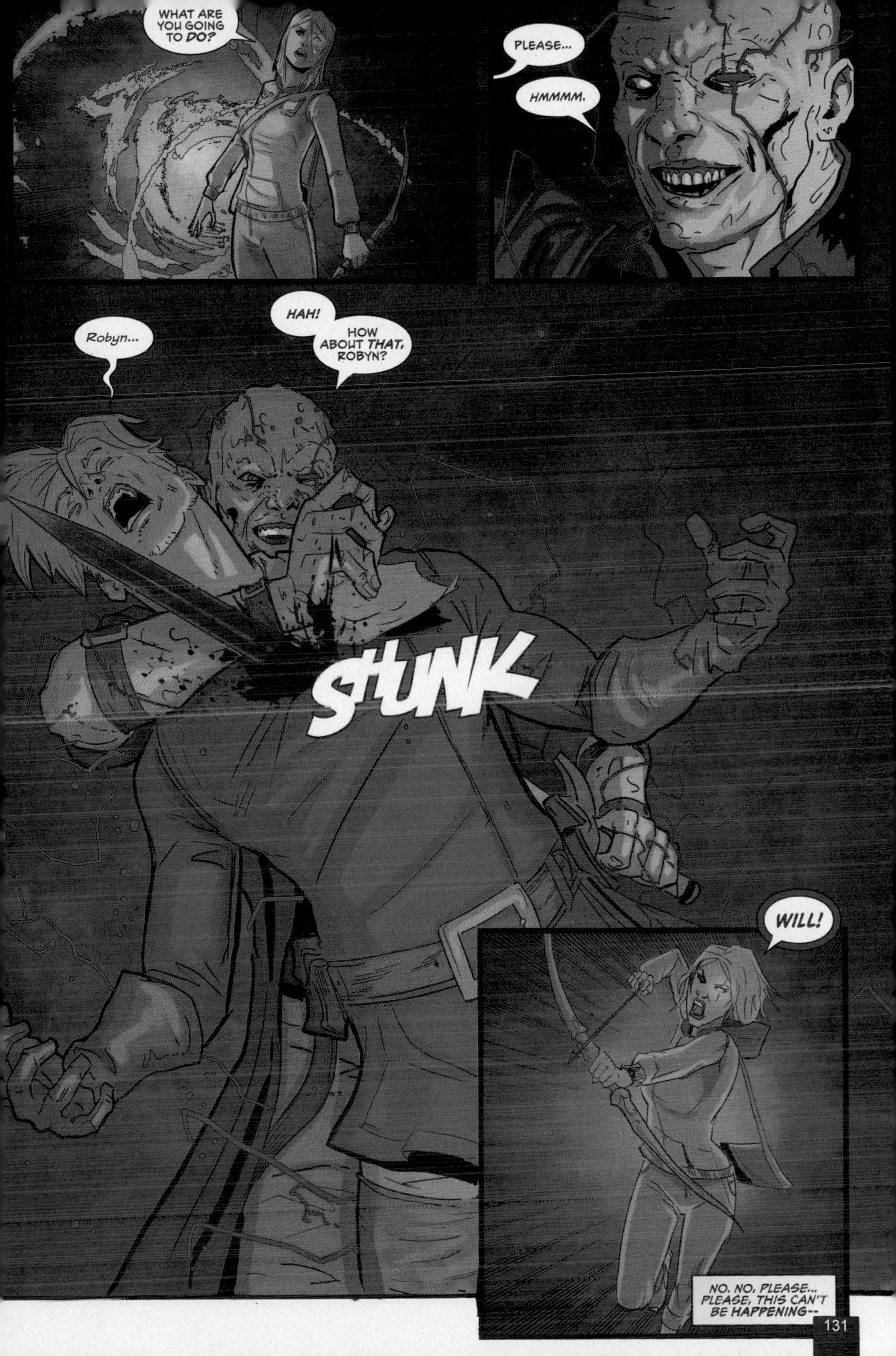
WHAT ARE YOU GOING TO DO?
PLEASE...
HMMMM.
Robyn...
HAH!
HOW ABOUT THAT, ROBYN?
STUNK
WILL!
NO. NO, PLEASE... PLEASE, THIS CAN'T BE HAPPENING--

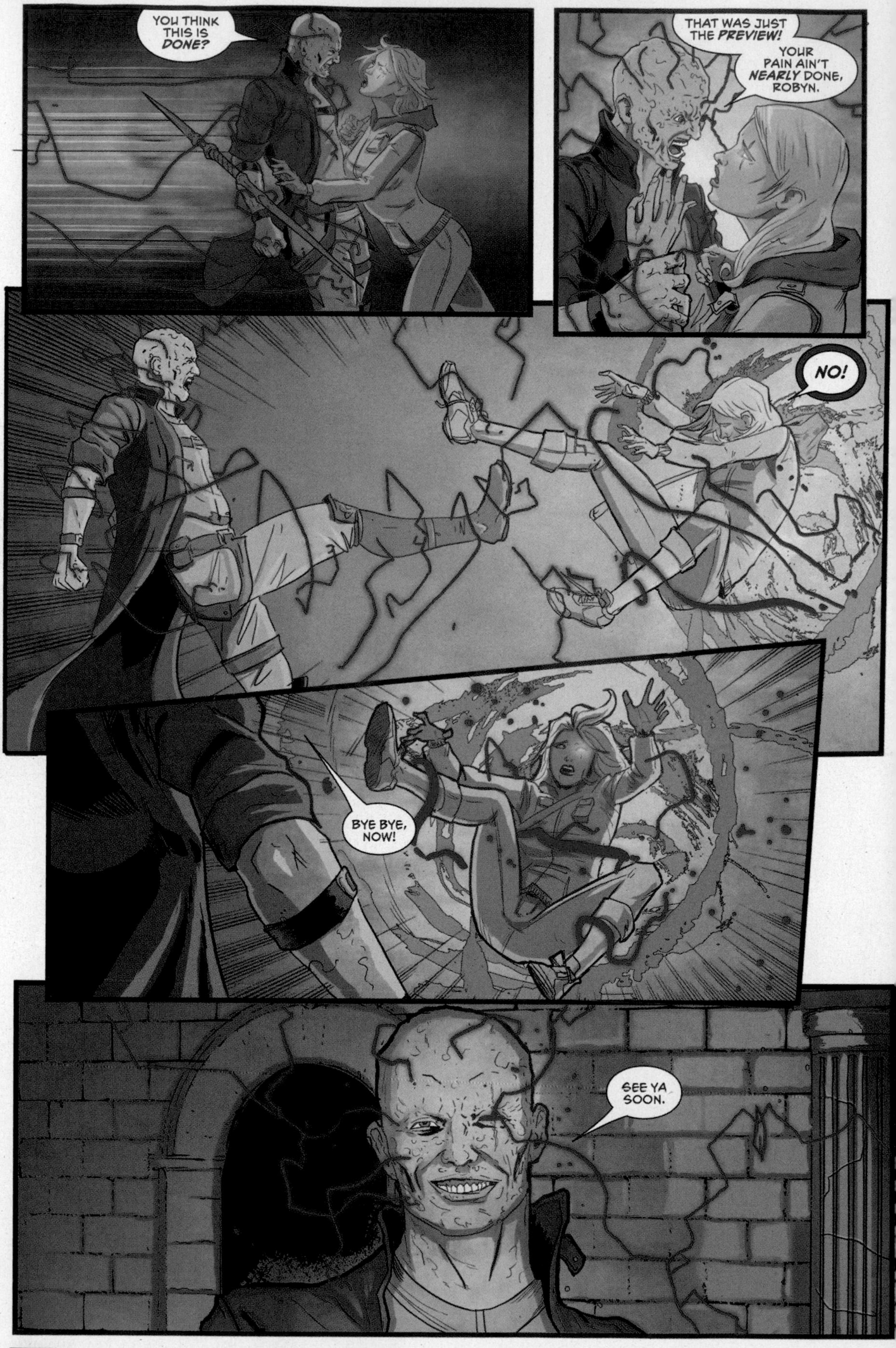
YOU THINK THIS IS DONE?
THAT WAS JUST THE PREVIEW!
YOUR PAIN AIN'T NEARLY DONE, ROBYN.
NO!
BYE BYE, NOW!
SEE YA SOON.

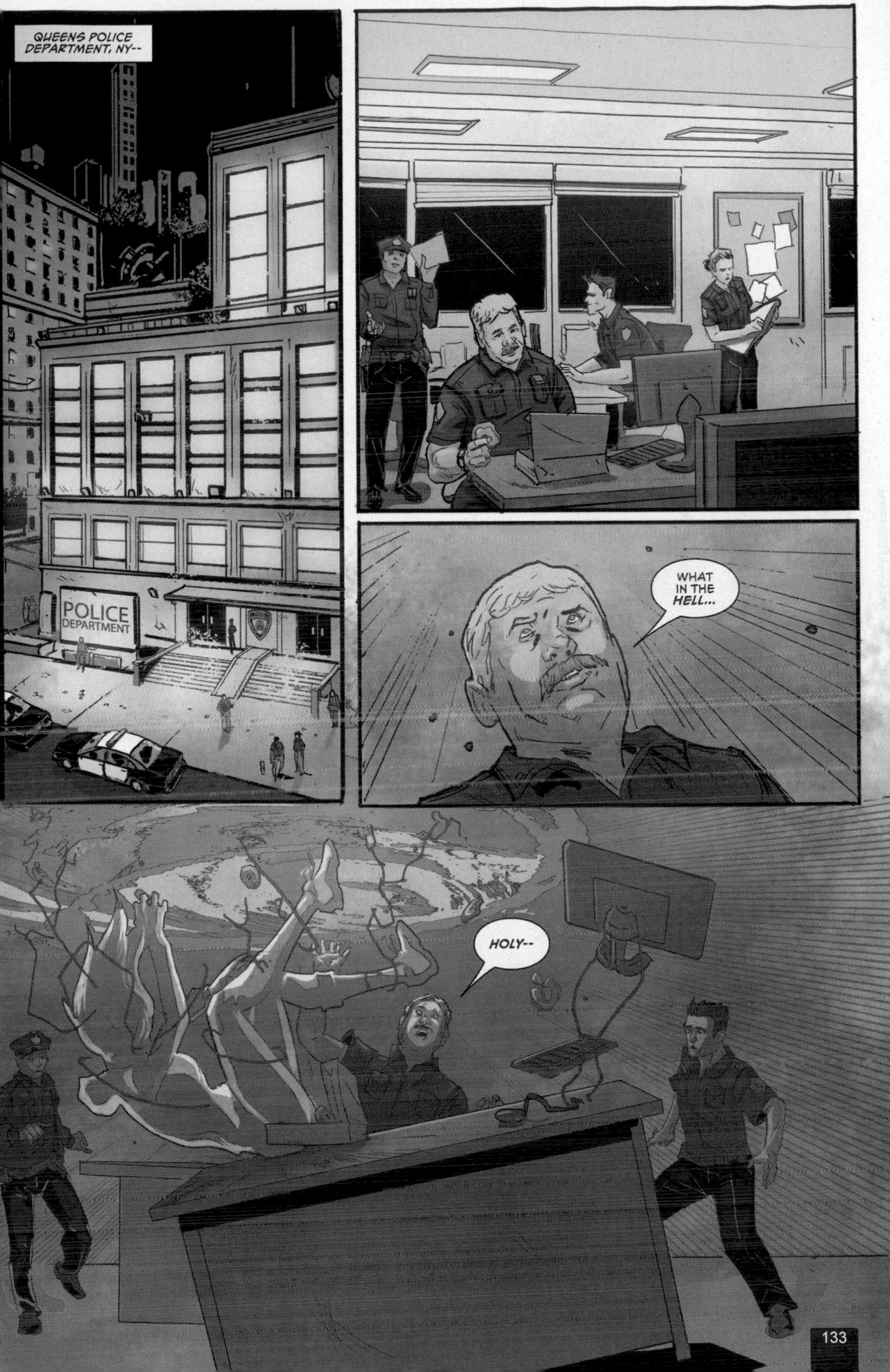
QUEENS POLICE DEPARTMENT, NY--
POLICE DEPARTMENT
WHAT IN THE HELL...
HOLY--

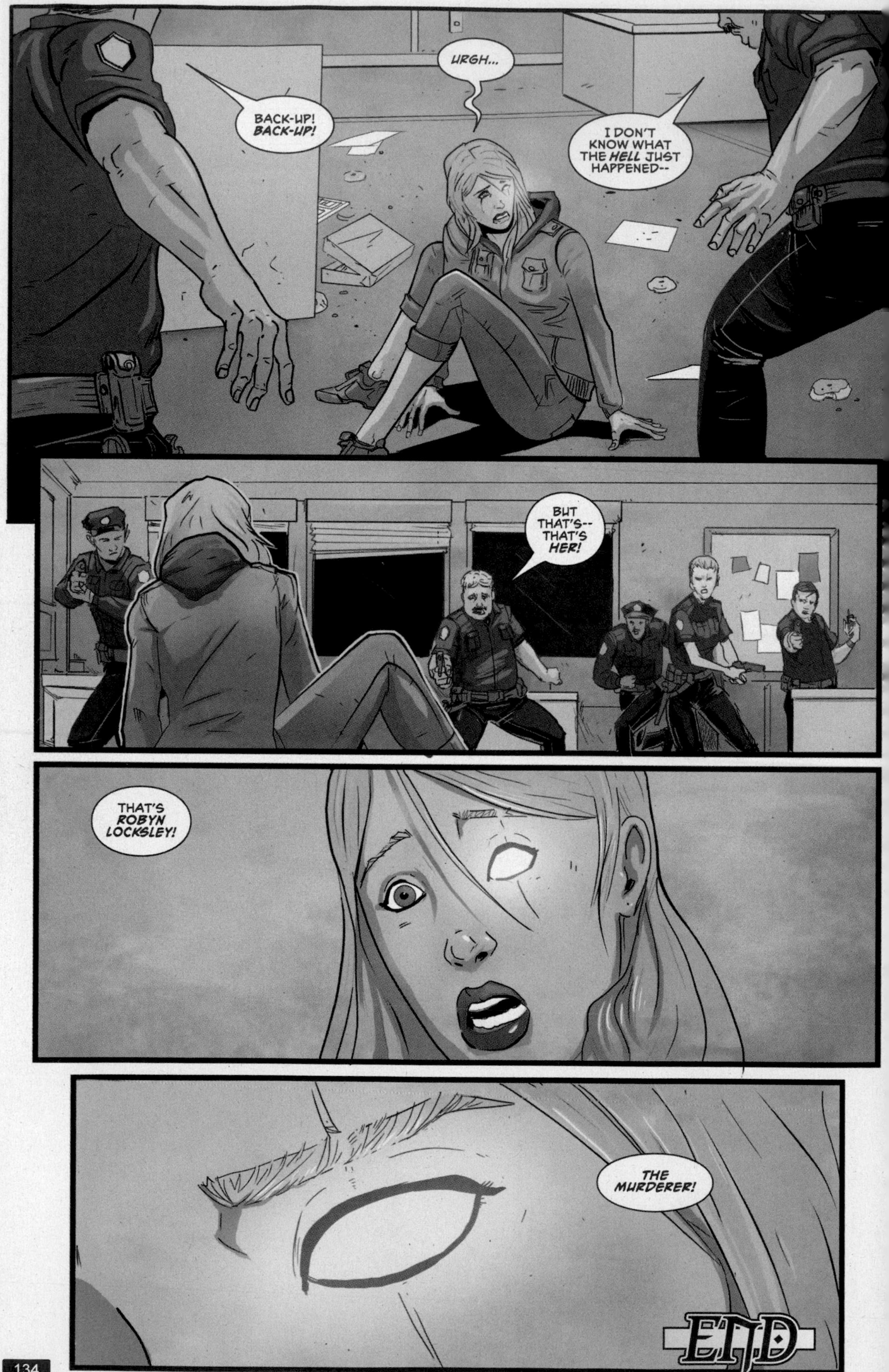
BACK-UP! BACK-UP!
URGH...
I DON'T KNOW WHAT THE HELL JUST HAPPENED--
BUT THAT'S-- THAT'S HER!
THAT'S ROBYN LOCKSLEY!
THE MURDERER!
END

Grimm Fairy Tales presents:

# ROBYN HOOD

## WANTED

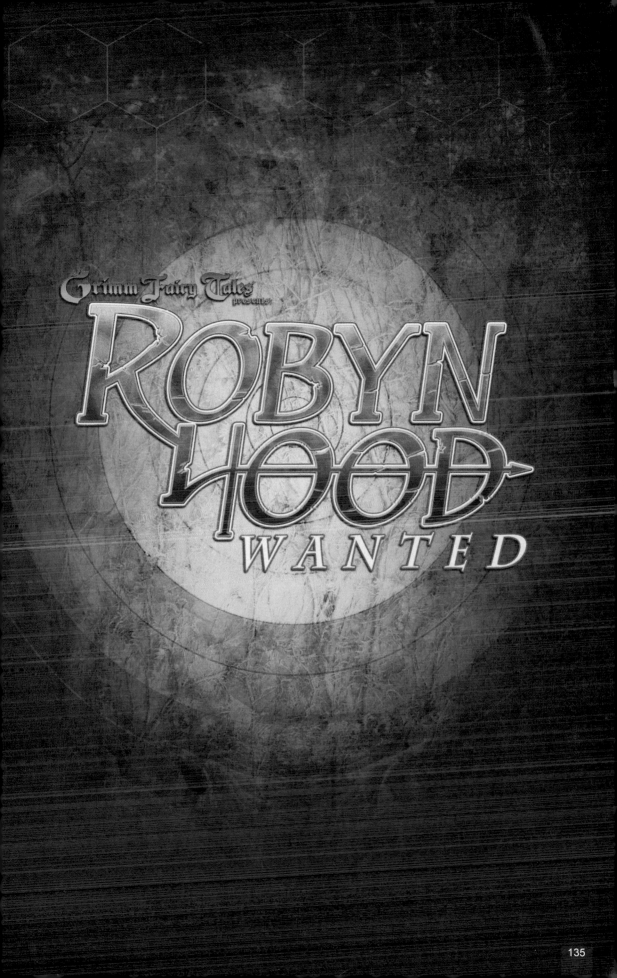

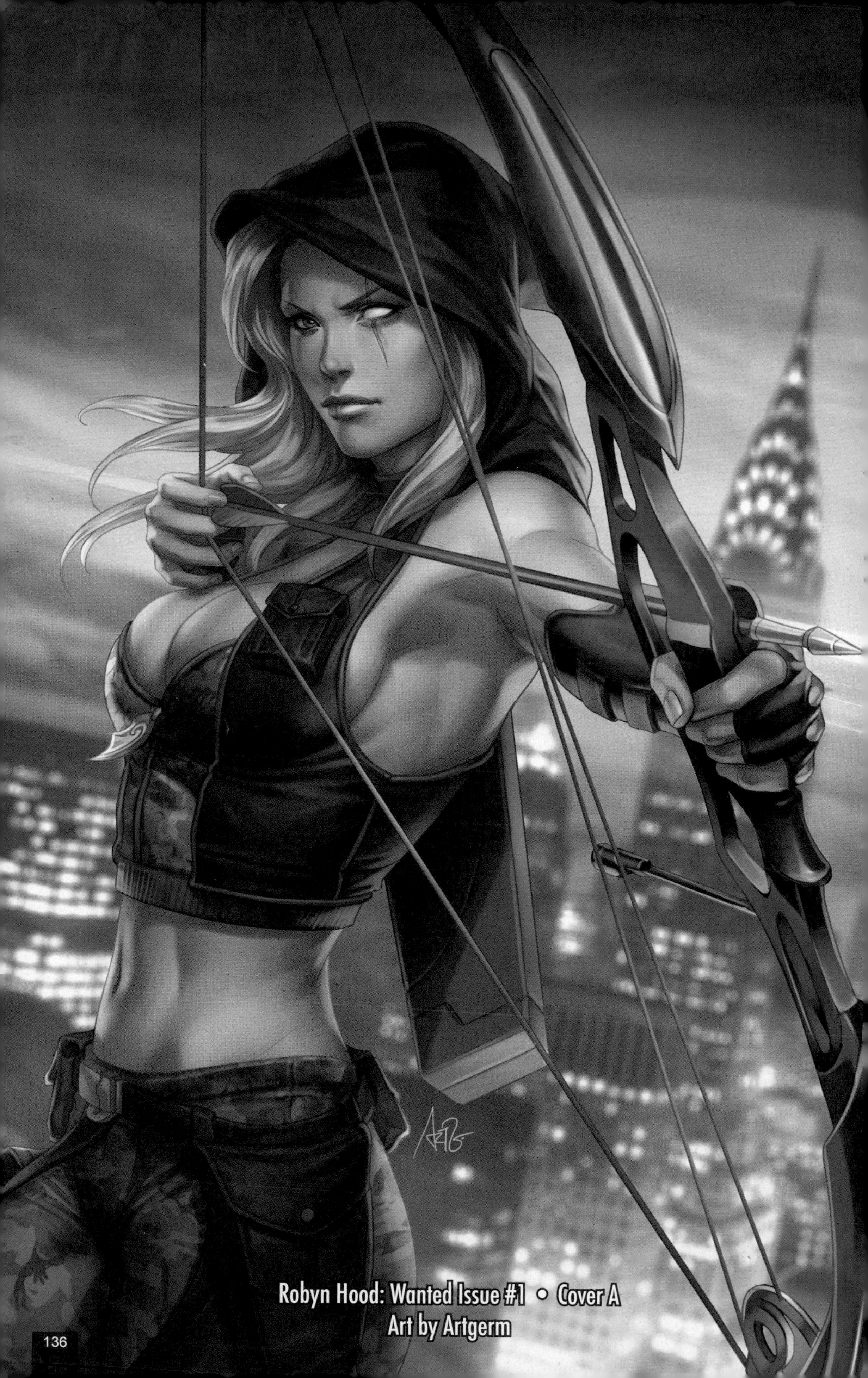

Robyn Hood: Wanted Issue #1 • Cover A
Art by Artgerm

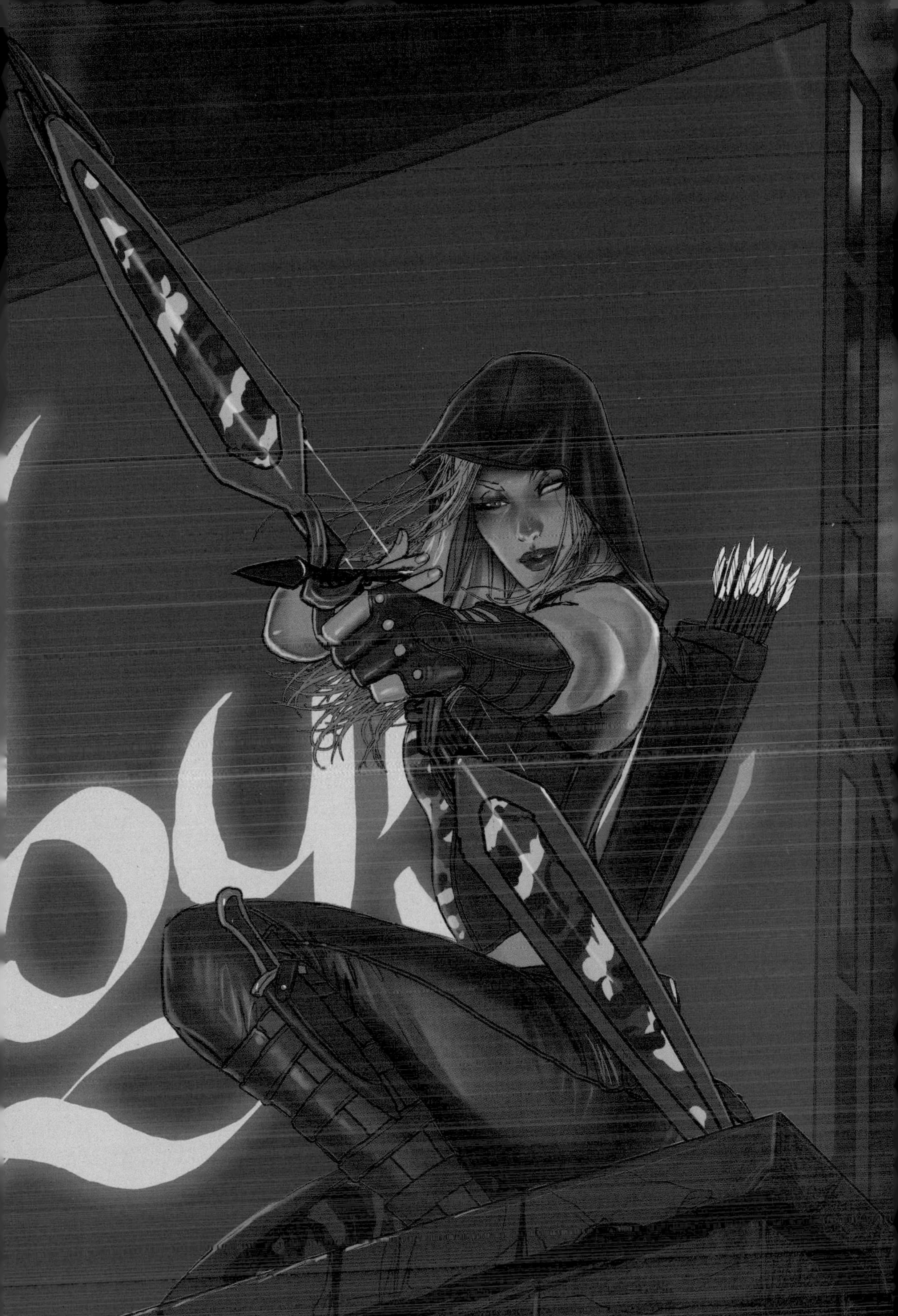

Robyn Hood: Wanted Issue #1 • Cover B
Art by Stjepan Sejic

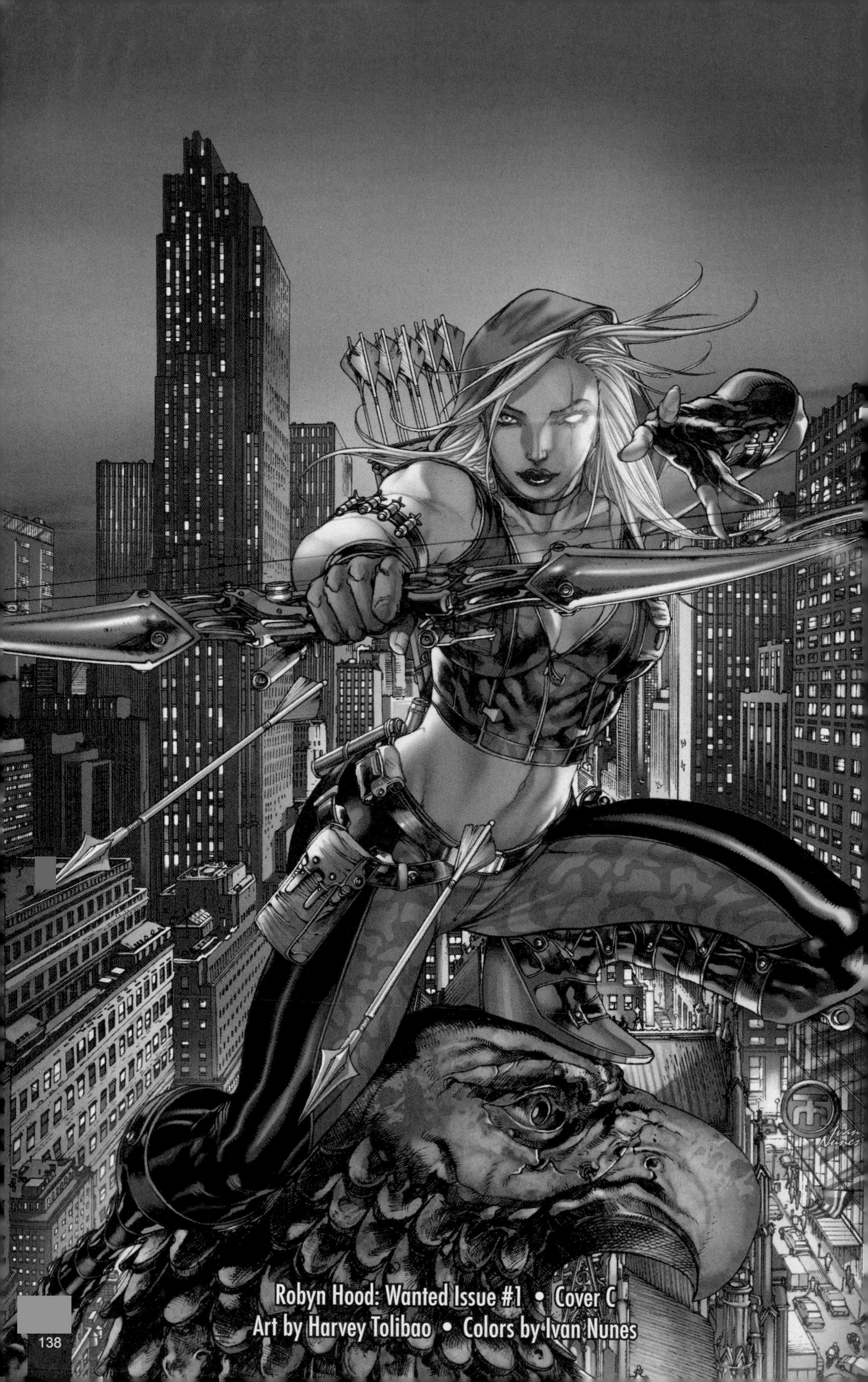

Robyn Hood: Wanted Issue #1 • Cover C
Art by Harvey Tolibao • Colors by Ivan Nunes

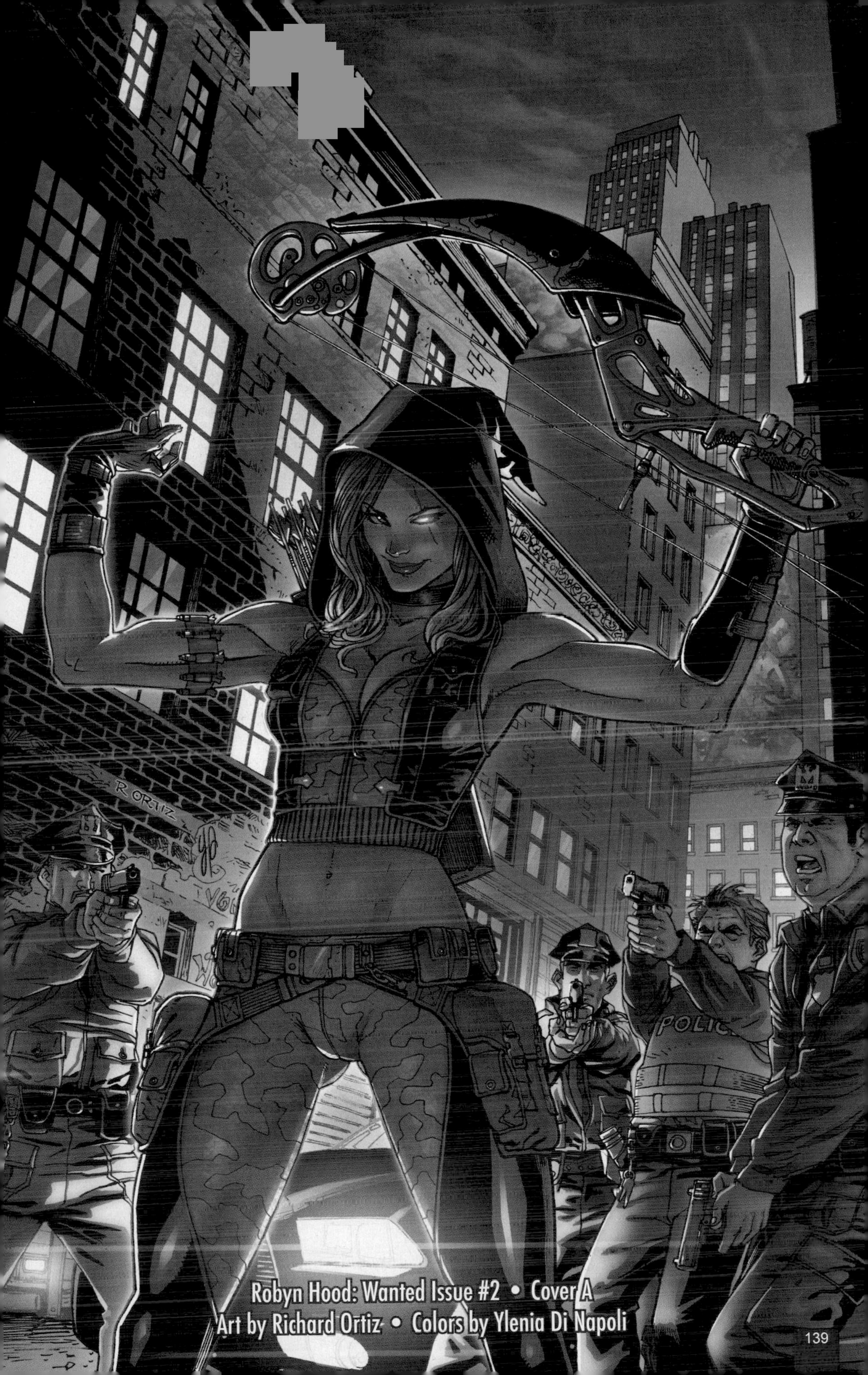
R ORTIZ
POLICE

Robyn Hood: Wanted Issue #2 • Cover A
Art by Richard Ortiz • Colors by Ylenia Di Napoli

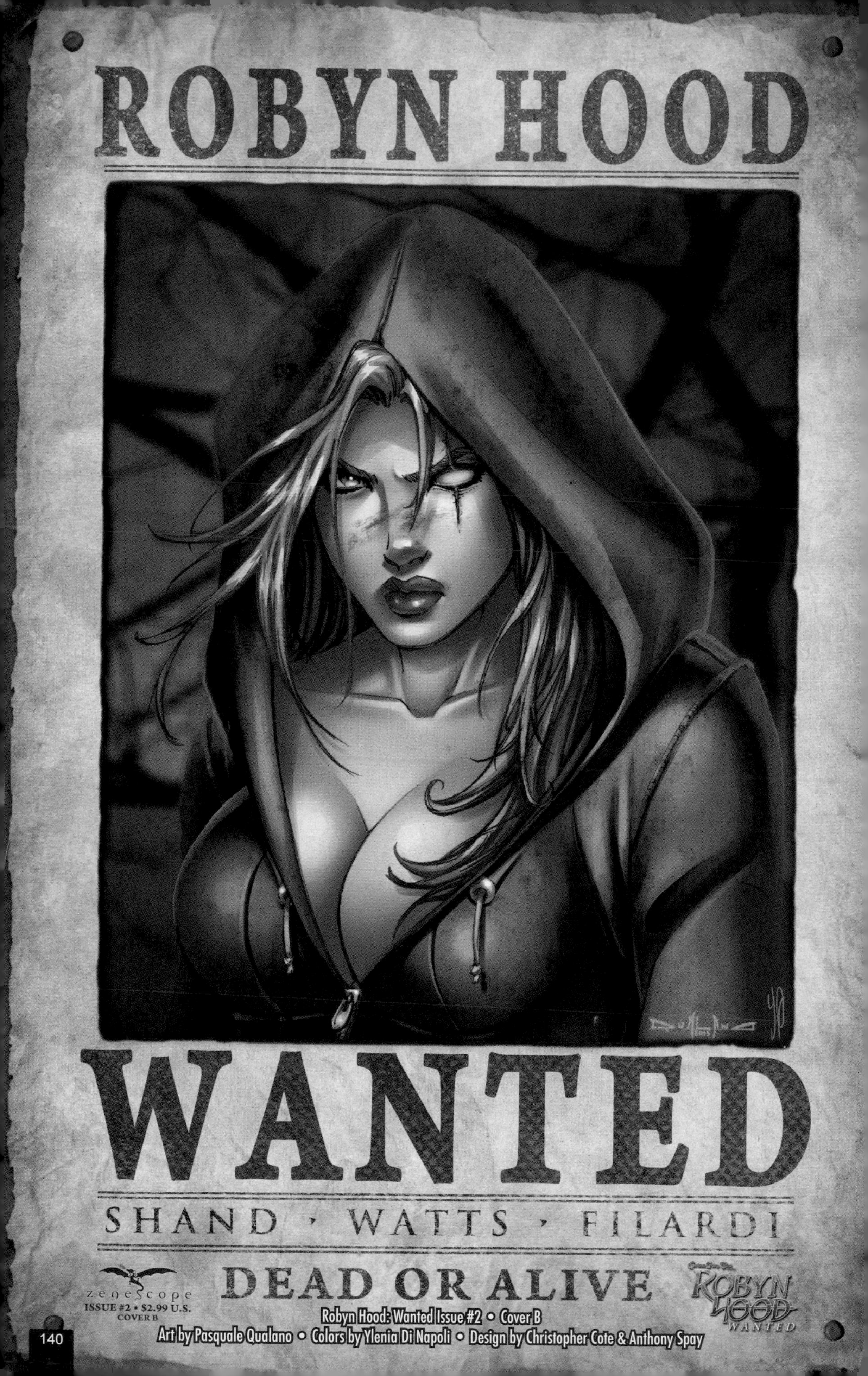
ROBYN HOOD
WANTED
SHAND · WATTS · FILARDI
DEAD OR ALIVE
zenescope
ISSUE #2 • $2.99 U.S.
COVER B
ROBYN HOOD
WANTED
Robyn Hood: Wanted Issue #2 • Cover B
Art by Pasquale Qualano • Colors by Ylenia Di Napoli • Design by Christopher Cote & Anthony Spay

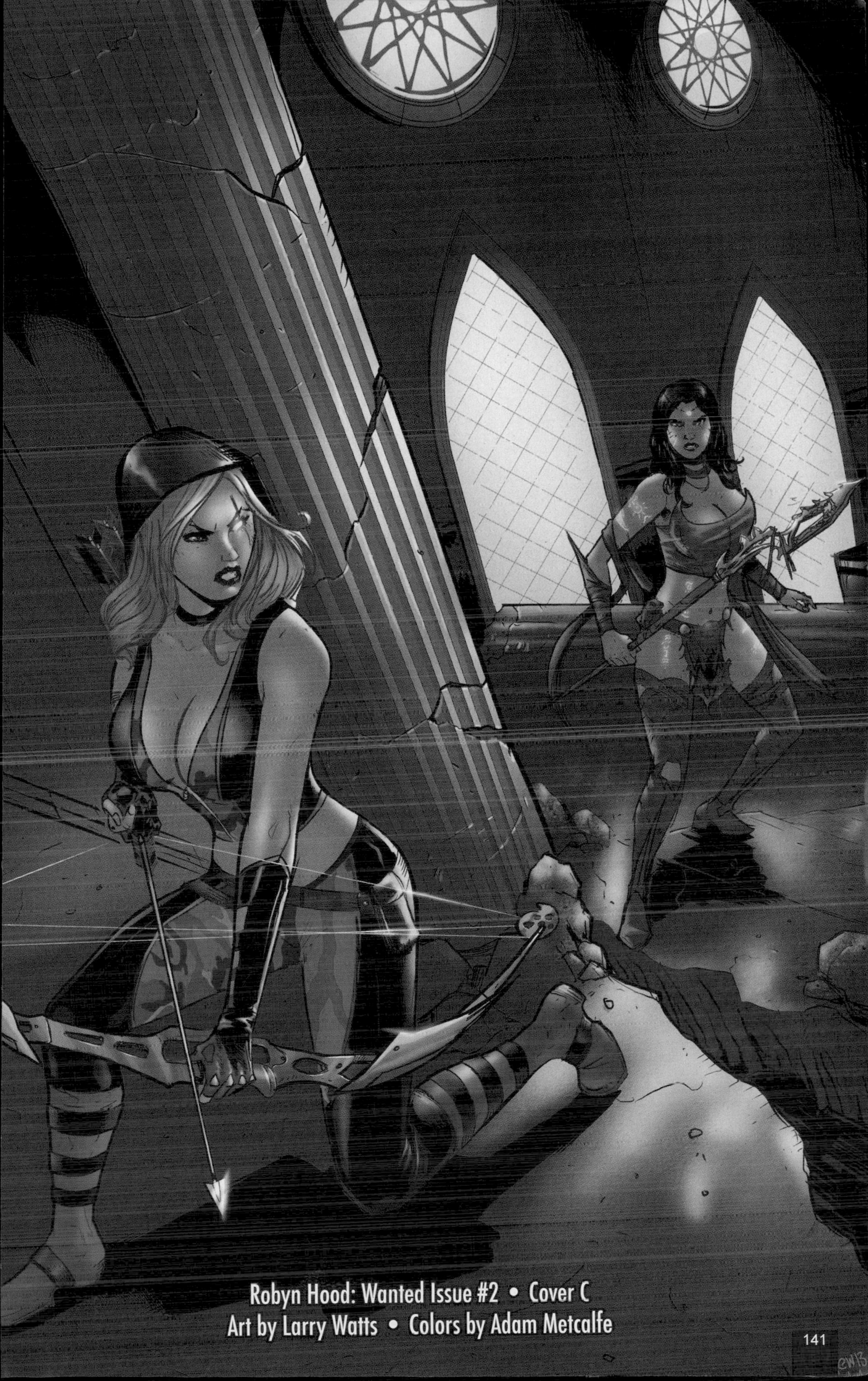

Robyn Hood: Wanted Issue #2 • Cover C
Art by Larry Watts • Colors by Adam Metcalfe

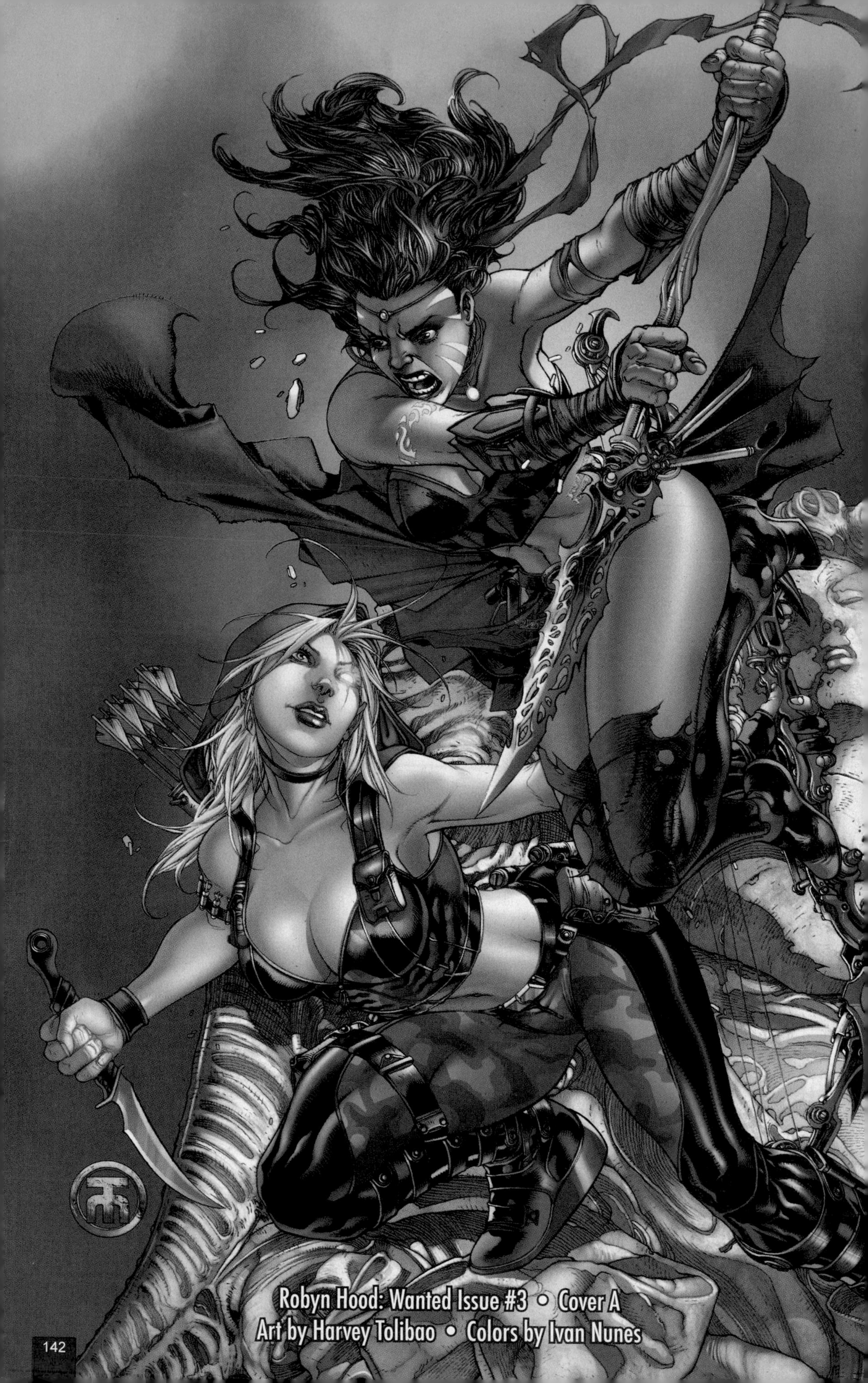

Robyn Hood: Wanted Issue #3 • Cover A
Art by Harvey Tolibao • Colors by Ivan Nunes

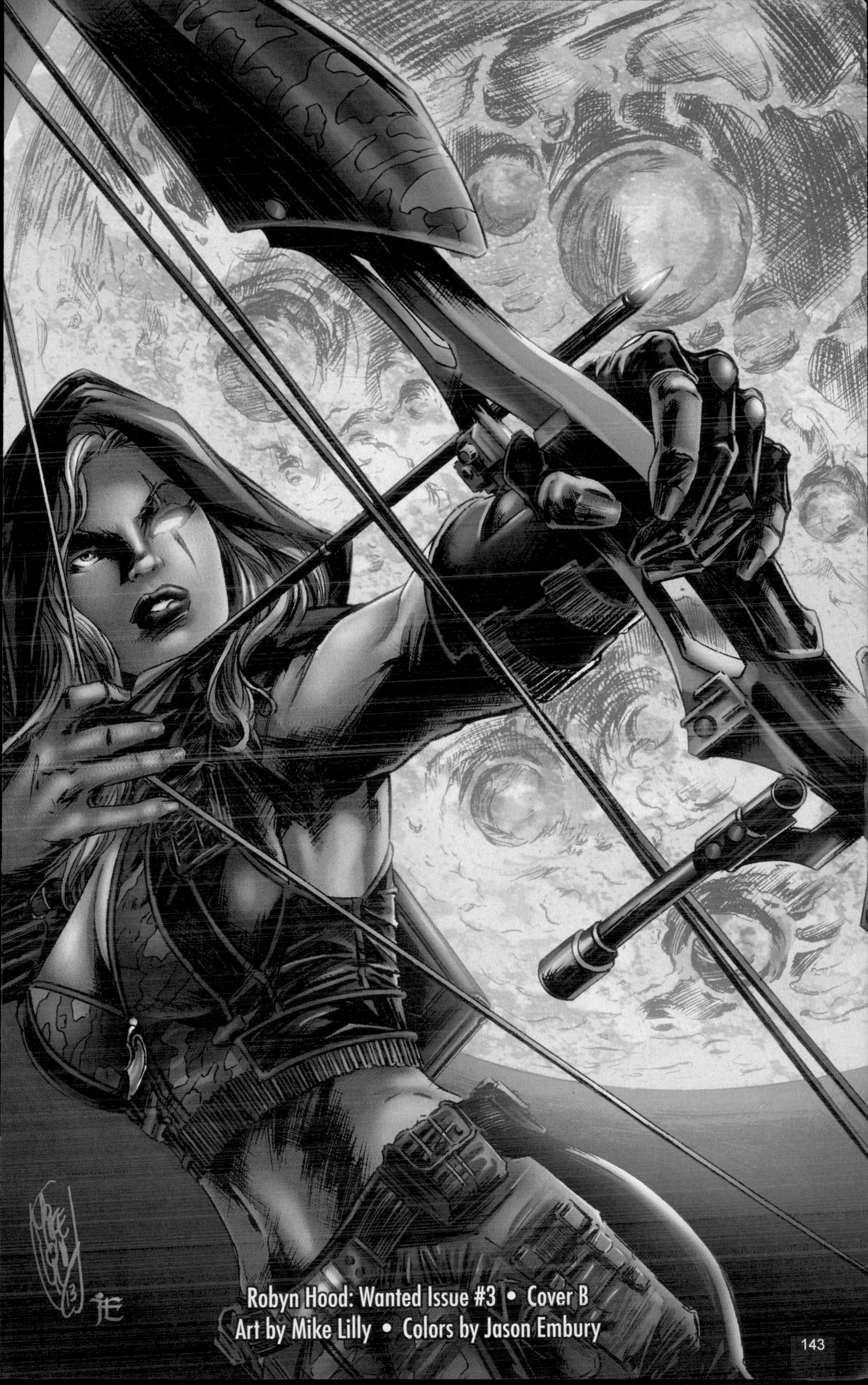

Robyn Hood: Wanted Issue #3 • Cover B
Art by Mike Lilly • Colors by Jason Embury

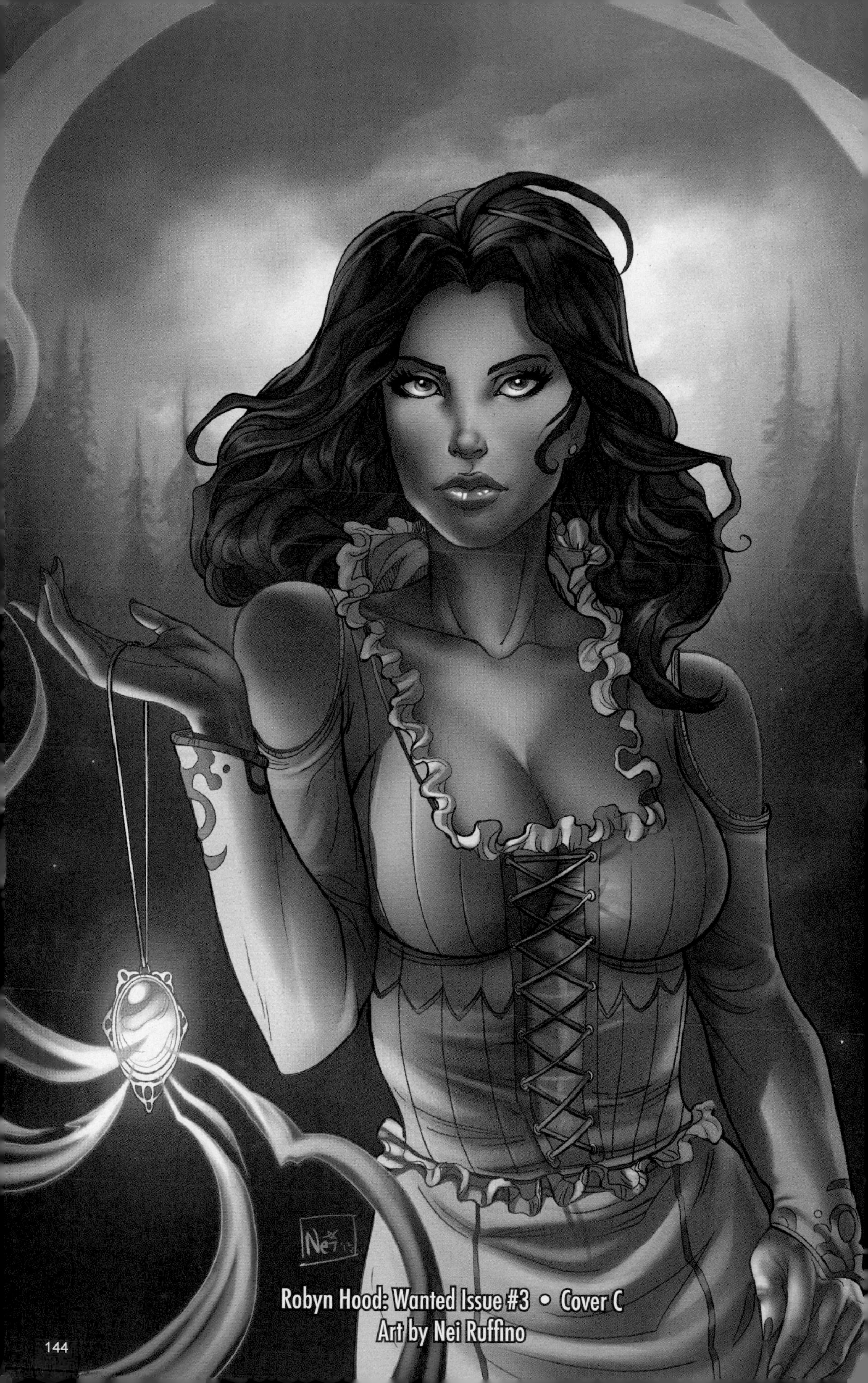
Nei

Robyn Hood: Wanted Issue #3 • Cover C
Art by Nei Ruffino

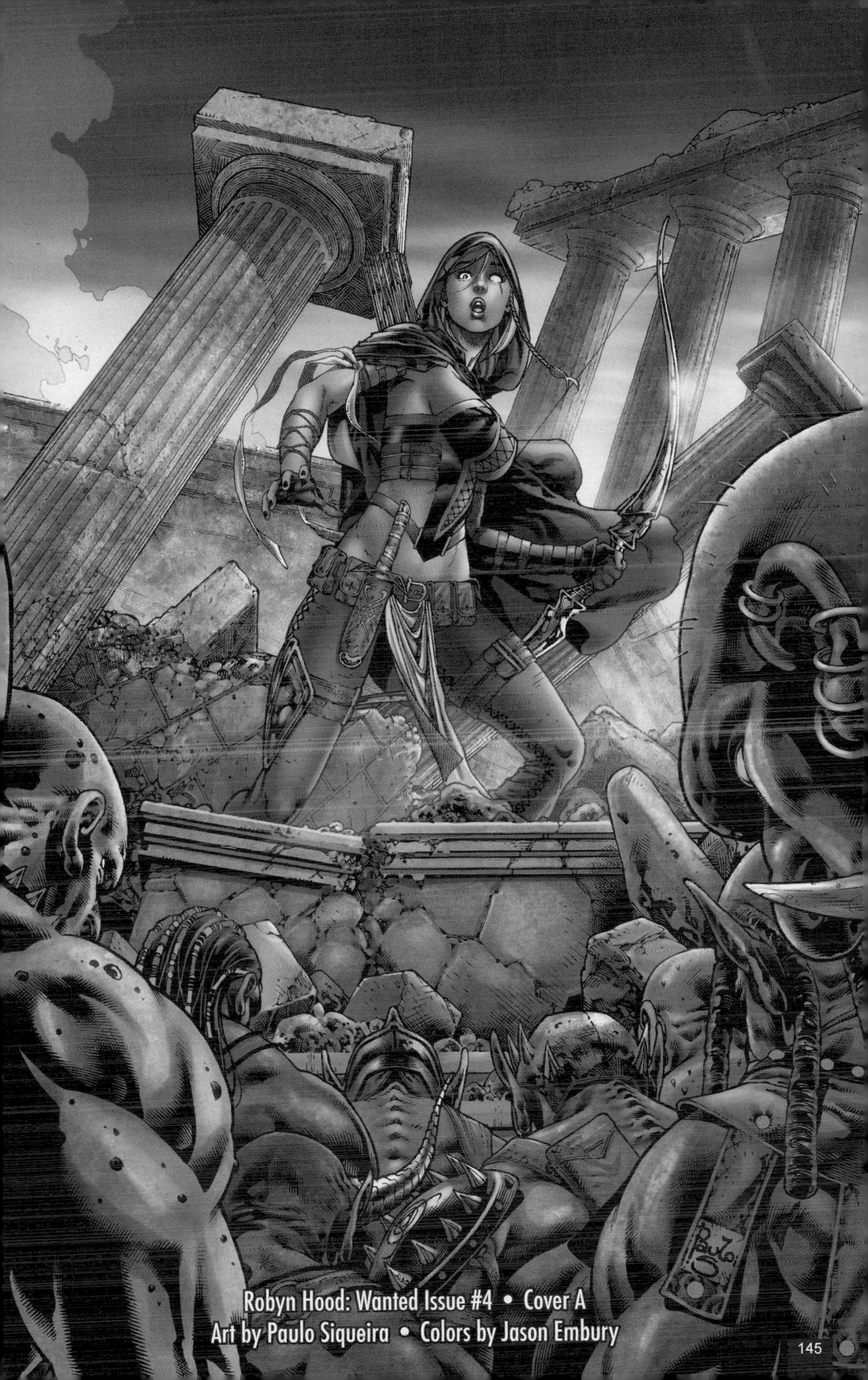

Robyn Hood: Wanted Issue #4 • Cover A
Art by Paulo Siqueira • Colors by Jason Embury

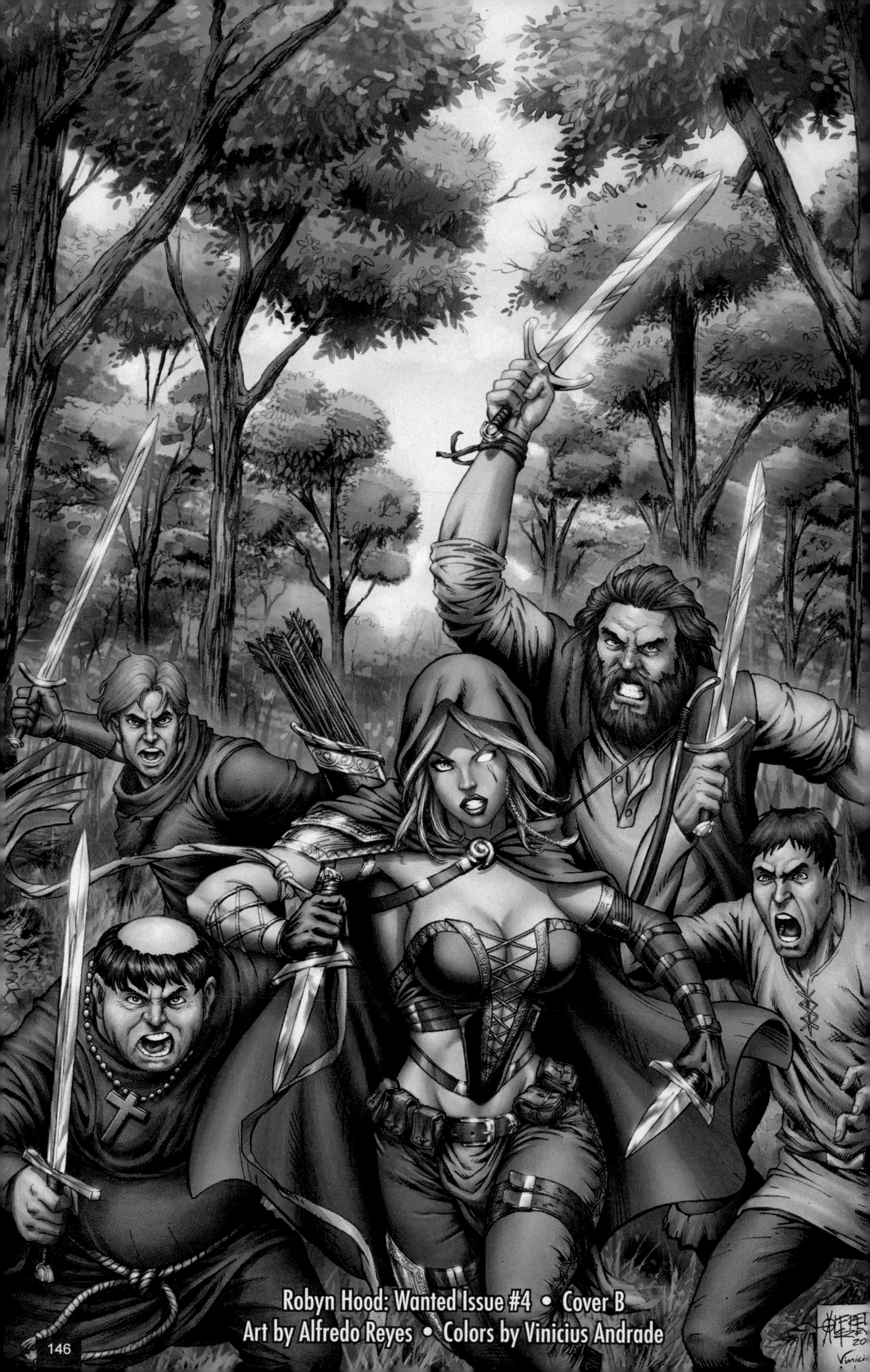

Robyn Hood: Wanted Issue #4 • Cover B
Art by Alfredo Reyes • Colors by Vinicius Andrade

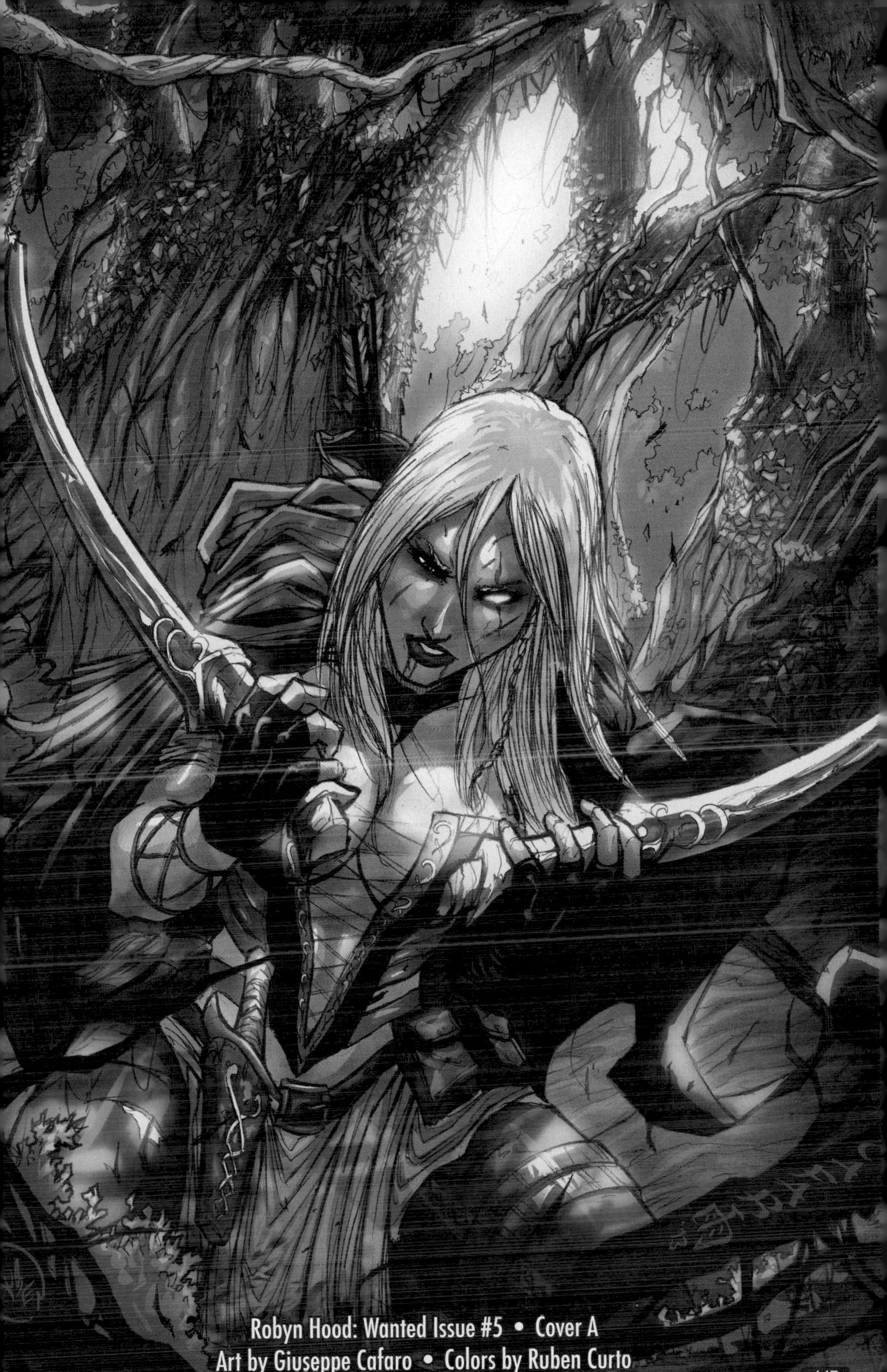

Robyn Hood: Wanted Issue #5 • Cover A
Art by Giuseppe Cafaro • Colors by Ruben Curto

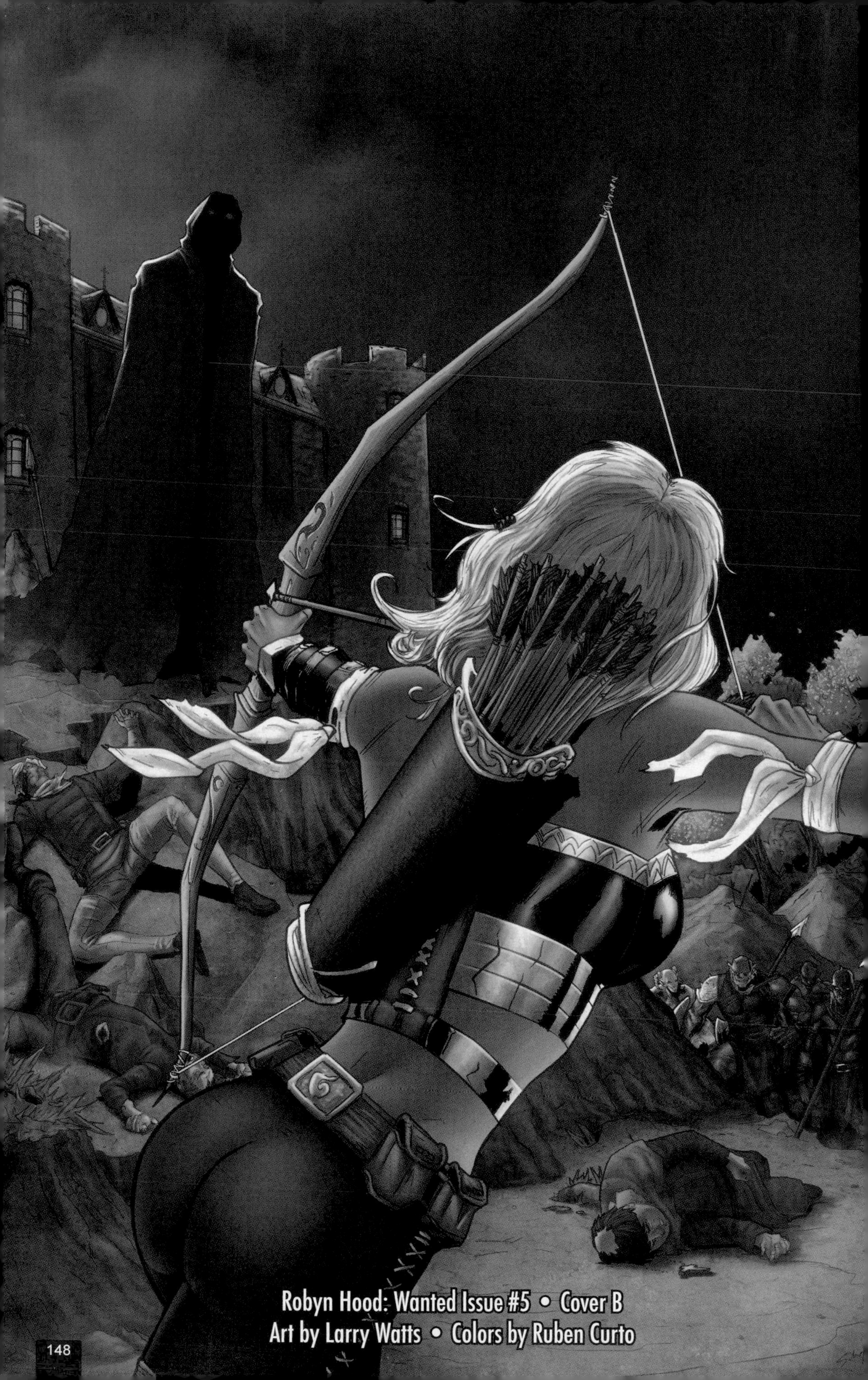

Robyn Hood: Wanted Issue #5 • Cover B
Art by Larry Watts • Colors by Ruben Curto

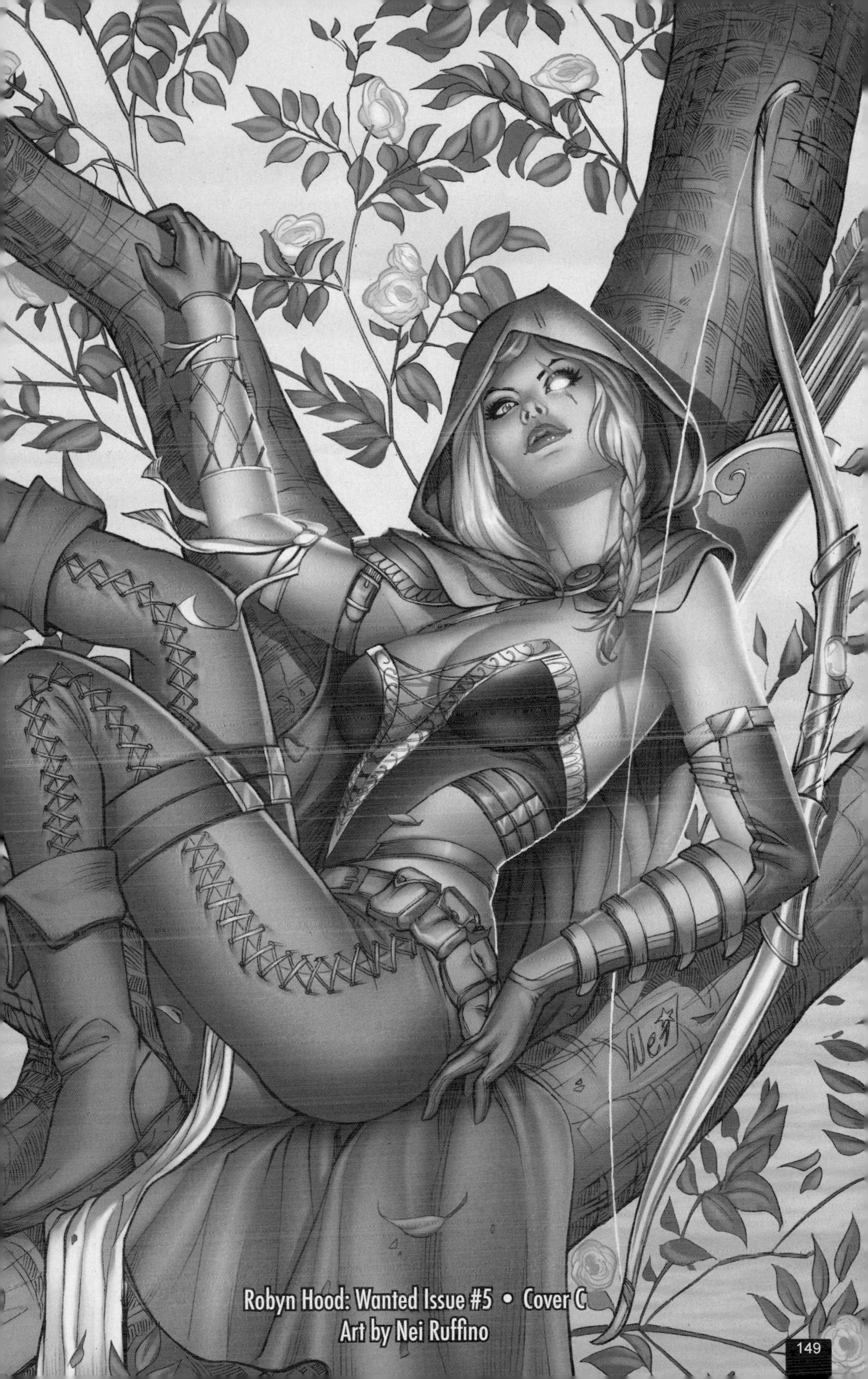

Robyn Hood: Wanted Issue #5 • Cover C
Art by Nei Ruffino

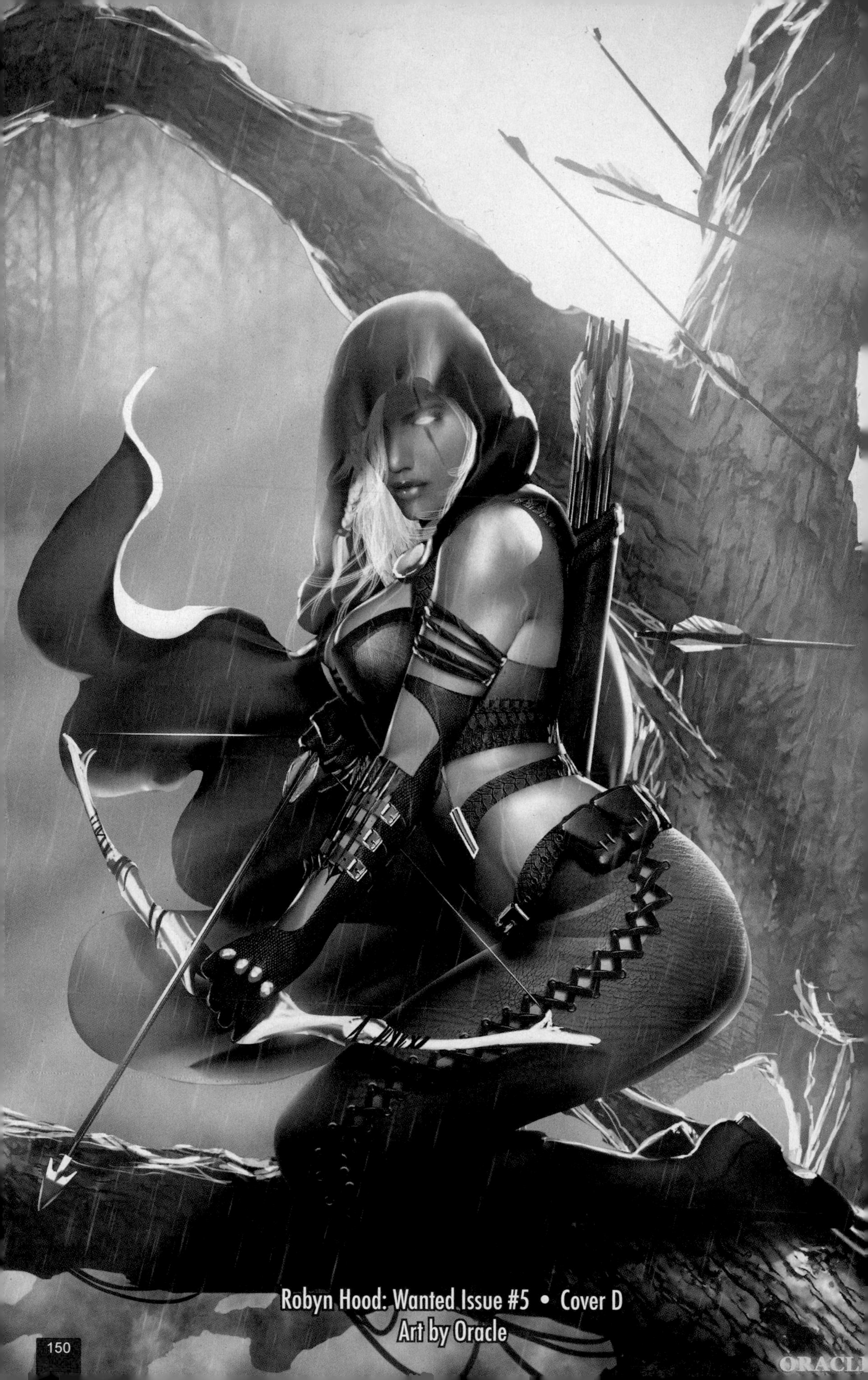

Robyn Hood: Wanted Issue #5 • Cover D
Art by Oracle

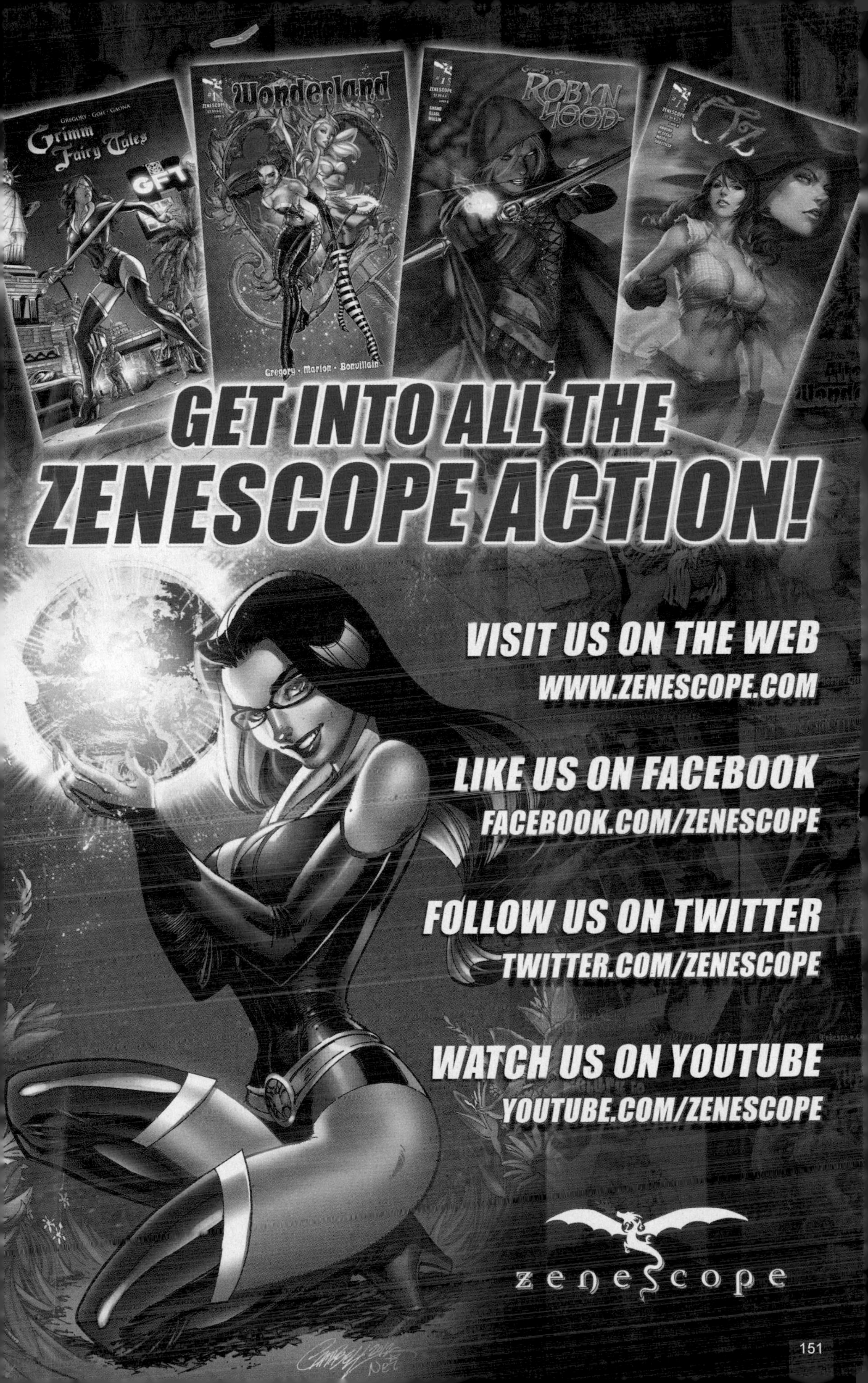
Gregory · Goh · Gaona
Grimm Fairy Tales
Wonderland
Gregory · Marion · Bonvillain
Robyn Hood
Oz
GET INTO ALL THE
ZENESCOPE ACTION!
VISIT US ON THE WEB
WWW.ZENESCOPE.COM
LIKE US ON FACEBOOK
FACEBOOK.COM/ZENESCOPE
FOLLOW US ON TWITTER
TWITTER.COM/ZENESCOPE
WATCH US ON YOUTUBE
YOUTUBE.COM/ZENESCOPE
zenescope

Grimm Fairy Tales presents:

# ROBYN HOOD

## WANTED

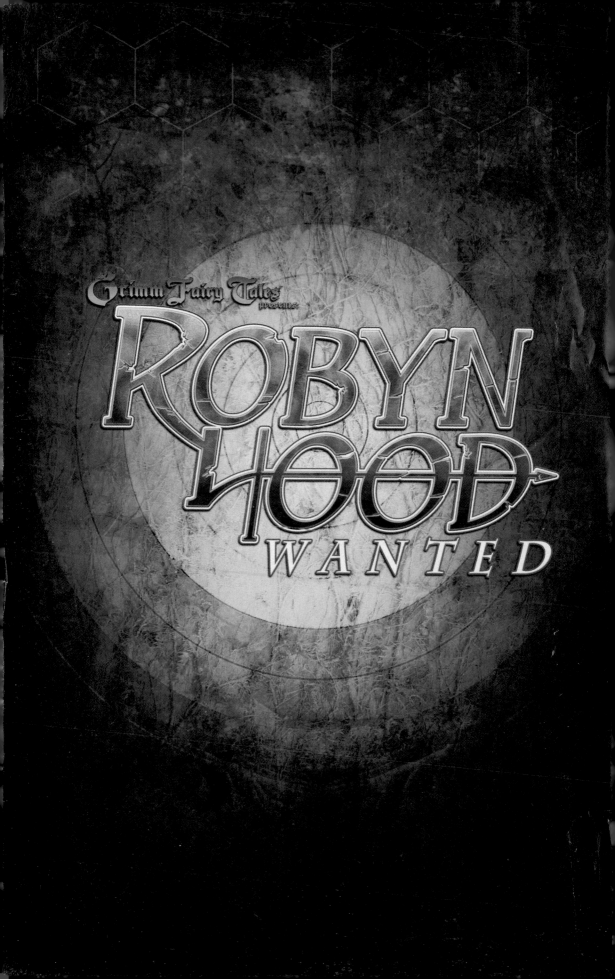